The Edinburgh Horse Tram

ALSO BY ALAN W. BROTCHIE:

Tramways of the Tay Valley, (1965)

Scottish Tramway Fleets, (1968)

Tramways of Fife and the Forth Valley, (Five volumes, 1975–8)

Fife's Trams and Buses, (1990)

Stirling's Trams and Buses, (1991)

Lanarkshire's Trams and Buses, (1993)

The Wemyss Private Railway, (1998)

Falkirk's Trams and Early Buses, (2011)

Rothesay's Trams and Buses, (2014)

WITH HARRY JACK:

Early Railways of West Fife, (2007)

WITH JOHN R. STEVENS:

Pioneers of the Street Railway in the USA,
Street Tramways in the UK ... and elsewhere, (2014)

The Edinburgh Horse Tram

NINETEENTH TO TWENTY-FIRST CENTURY

Alan W. Brotchie

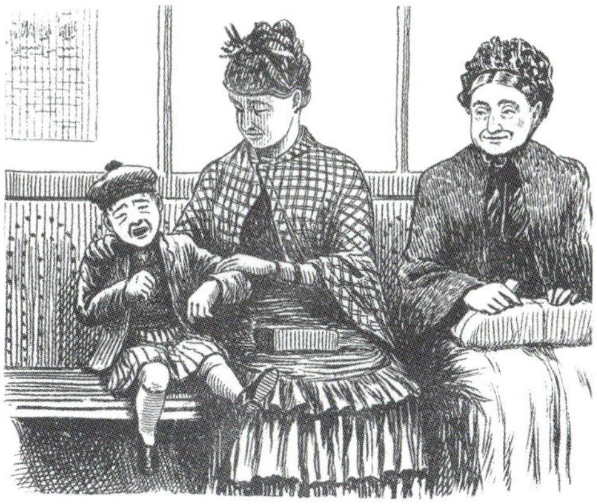

"I WANT TO SEE THE HORSES."

Stenlake Publishing Ltd

First published in 2017 by
Stenlake Publishing Ltd
54–58 Mill Square
Catrine, Ayrshire
Scotland
KA5 6RD
Telephone: 01290 551122
www.stenlake.co.uk

ISBN: 978 1 84033 779 2

British Library Cataloguing-in-Publication Data
A catalogue record for this book is available from the British Library

Designed by Mark Blackadder

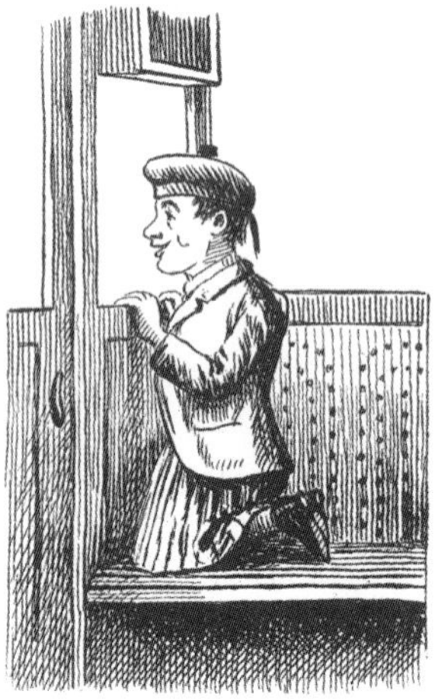

GRATIFIED and GLAD.

Printed in China by Regent Publishing Services Ltd., Hong Kong

Contents

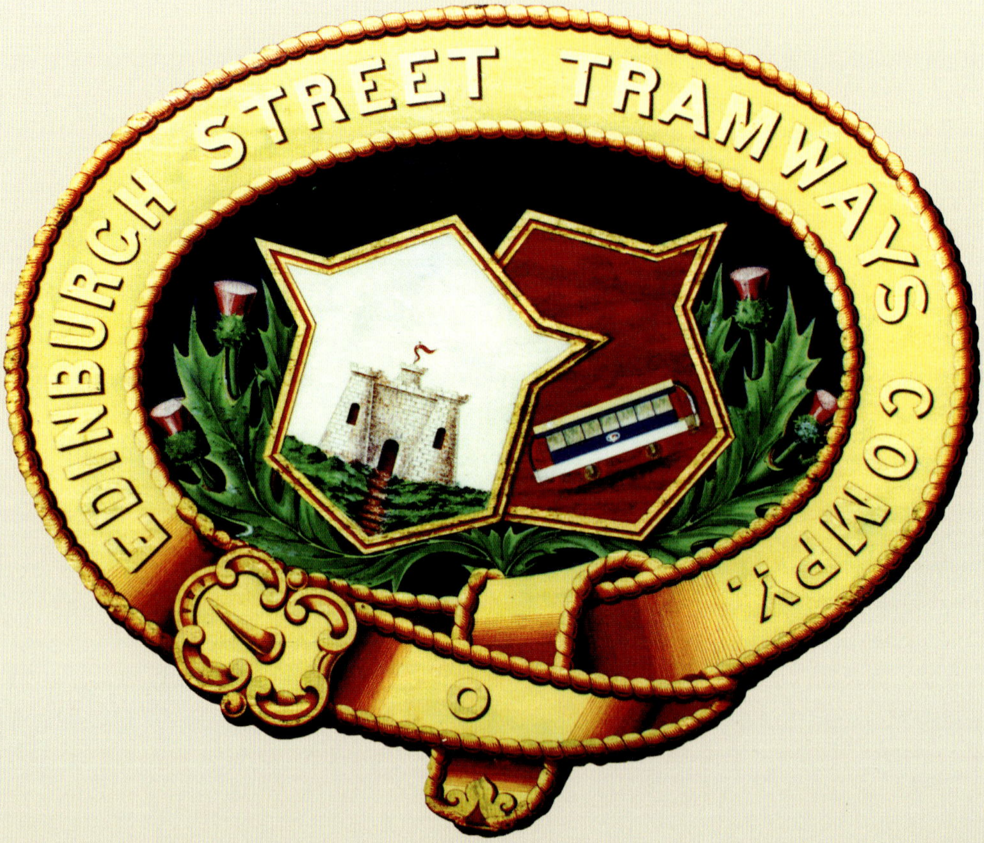

Badge of the Edinburgh Street Tramways Company carried on its tramcars and omnibuses from 1871 until 1904. The garter surround used several different colours. The device bore more than a passing resemblance to that of the North British Railway. (From the collection of G Hartley)

Introduction

Many light rail lines and tramways have been successfully constructed in recent years throughout the world – indeed in this twenty-first century lines have been built in the United States serving such places as Dallas and Tucson. However, Edinburgh's prime place in public transport evolution has been overlooked. The city was the locus for what was probably the first application *in the world* of electricity as motive power on a standard gauge railway. A resourceful Aberdonian inventor, Robert Davidson, with the connivance of the directors of the Edinburgh & Glasgow Railway, ran his carriage, '... at the rate of upwards of four miles an hour, a rate which might be increased by giving greater power to the batteries, and enlarging the diameter of the wheels ... [the] battery which is used for propelling the machine is composed of iron and zinc plates immersed in dilute sulphuric acid ... the weight propelled was about six tons', this quoting from the *Edinburgh Evening Courant* of 24 September 1842. Edinburgh was in the forefront of transport ingenuity, and after its horse tramway had been operational for nine years, one of its tramcars was operated, powered by electricity generated at a distant source; another world first. Having had a major diversion by next operating what was probably the most complex cable powered tramway in the world, Edinburgh electrified its trams – but then threw away this invaluable public asset in a politically driven race to place total dependence upon diesel fuelled buses. Since then the wheel has turned full circle, and after much controversy modern electric trams have returned to the city, in the form of one very costly route. Let us hope this is a foretaste of what might come; a comprehensive electric urban transport system worthy of the city.

Questionable decisions regarding Edinburgh's public transport have been made through the years, not only regarding this new tramway, but also in the past, to persevere with an obsolescent cable powered system in the latter years of the nineteenth century – at a time when electric tramways had been operating successfully for a decade. The desire to avoid despoliation of Edinburgh's architectural and scenic grace with overhead wires was then seen as paramount. Thus in the 1920s, when many British tramways were already approaching the end of their profitable life, the worn-out and increasingly unreliable cable system was replaced by a new electric system. This brought the city up to date – but the entire enterprise was designed to suit the length of vehicle which could be squeezed into buildings constructed for cable traction. The determining factor for all trams for Edinburgh in the 1920s (and thereafter) was the size of the car traverser in Shrubhill works! Fortunately the trend frequently followed elsewhere for trolley-buses as tram replacements was avoided.

At the start of the twenty-first century, another decision was made – now in the name of reduction of congestion and carbon emission – to create on a blank canvas a new modern tramway; but again errors were perpetrated which now form the subject of an inquiry. The new tramway's initial route appears to have been determined as much by expediency as by logic; to serve (even yet un-built) housing planned for Leith and Granton – seen then as the inevitable consequence of anticipated demand – and link also Edinburgh Airport, the new Scottish Office in Leith and the new headquarters of the Royal Bank of Scotland in the green belt at Gogar. Such places as a useful tramway could have benefitted; the new Infirmary complex on the city's perimeter and established high density, low car ownership areas on the city periphery were ignored. Viable plans which could have seen the tramway integrated with the Replacement Forth Road Crossing bridge, serving dormitory areas in South Fife have been unfulfilled. The Scottish Government has now come to the conclusion that modern light rail transit is to be encouraged.

Unless noted otherwise, illustrations are from the author's collection. Thanks must also be recorded to all who have given permission for reproduction of other images. Several drawings come from the 'Thomson' notebook, which was handed in by a Mrs Thomson to the Transport Department office some years ago when it was located at 14 Queen Street. This remarkable jotter has a 'Discription (sic) of all the cars, in Edinburgh' and may possibly have been compiled by a tramway employee (or a remarkably knowledgeable enthusiast) beginning at the division of the system in 1894. It appears to have been maintained until May 1897, the last pencilled date noted being '26. 5. 97'. It also mentions lines in Leith and Portobello as 'worked by the old company' – a situation which changed from 1 July 1898. Without this amateur record, any attempt to unravel the horse tramcar vehicle details would have been much more difficult; indeed, all but impossible. Where particulars can be verified by comparison with contemporary photographs or with the known license records the Thomson book seems to be for the most part accurate. There are however one or two divergences; there are no entries for horse cars 91, 113 and 114 (but the last two were not built until the second half of 1897). Nine drawings are fully coloured to give a remarkably detailed record of the several route liveries; these are reproduced here. Four additional line drawings from this source are also included. The hand written book records details of tramway vehicles in Dundee – again largely correct; it has in addition, two drawings of tramcars from the Glasgow system. Thanks are therefore due to Neil Mackenzie who now has custody of this unique historic record, for permission to reproduce, and to quote from it.

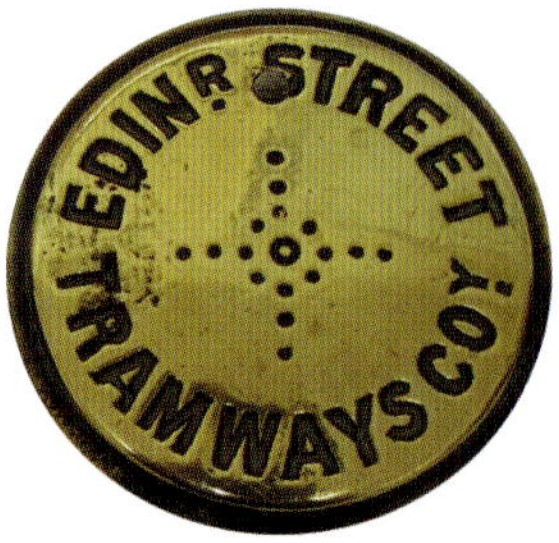

Tramways Company harness decoration.

Preface

This work was planned to place on record the restoration of Edinburgh built horse tramcar number 23 of 1885, to put this in the context of contemporary events, and to put on record historical details and photographs which have only recently come to light. Reference has been made to archival sources not available even ten years ago. Further complementary detail is to be found in the works of the late D L G Hunter, who inspired my interest in recording Edinburgh's transport history. This does not in any way supplant his writing, it has to be read as an addendum to it.

As the story of the restoration might possibly be of interest to a limited number of people, the record has been extended to try to place the vehicle in its social and historical context. There is a deliberate concentration on the actual tramway vehicles; this being an area which has received scant prior investigation. What becomes immediately apparent is that these first generation Edinburgh trams exhibited a remarkable variety of design and appearance, with reconstruction and re-use of suitable parts. This continued through to the days of the first generation of electric trams, with fleet numbers allocated, for the most part, seemingly in a random manner. Even within the so-called standardised 1934 Shrubhill-built design of electric tramcar, David Hunter recorded no less than twenty-one detail differences.

A permanent home in Edinburgh for this unique restored horse tram would be ideal; perhaps it could or should form the nucleus of a transport museum for the city. There is no shortage of potential exhibits, horse bus 83 is temporarily at the Vintage Commercial Vehicle Museum at Leyland, Lancashire; horse tram 23 is currently to be found at Lathalmond Vintage Bus Museum in Fife; electric car 35 languishes at the National Tramway Museum Crich in Derbyshire and many vintage Edinburgh buses are in other collections, including several at Lathalmond. A major gap in the physical historical record will be filled by 1903 cable car 226, at present undergoing restoration in Edinburgh. Let us hope that such a museum can soon come to fruition.

Alan W Brotchie
March 2016

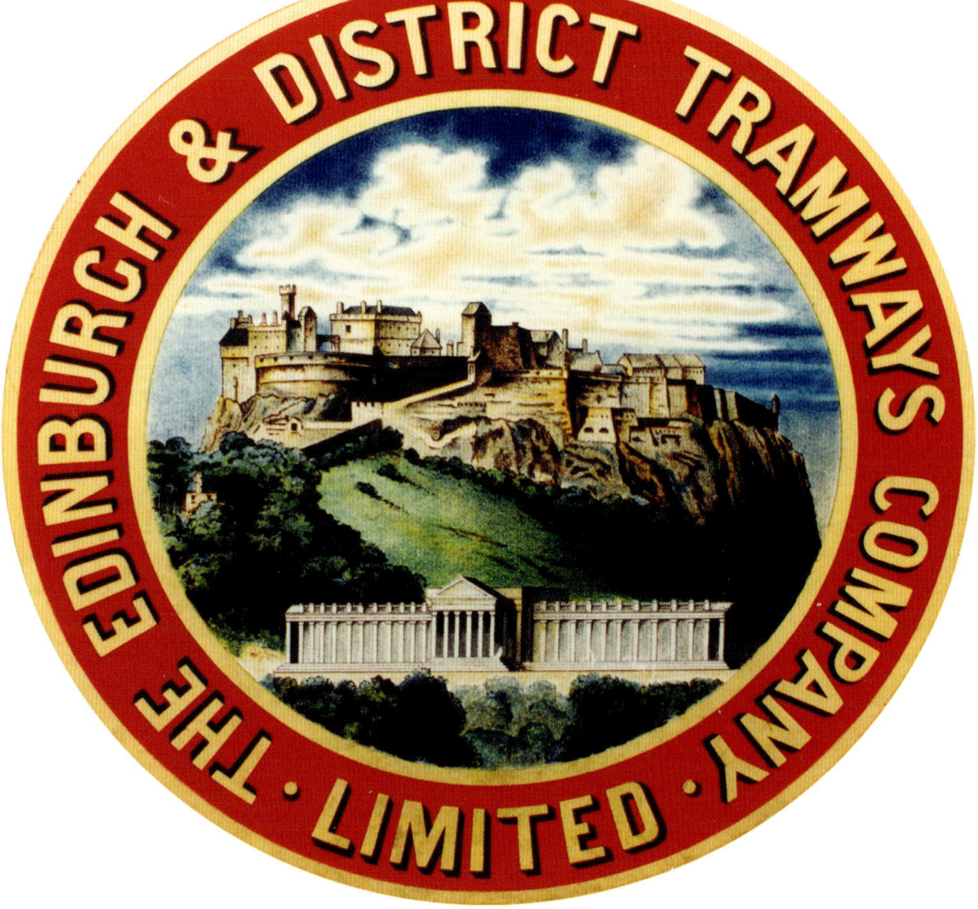

Badge of the Edinburgh & District Tramways Company Limited, introduced on their horse-drawn vehicles after December 1893 and then on cable tramcars until takeover by the Corporation of the cable tram lines in July 1919. (From the collection of G Hartley)

PART ONE

Chronology

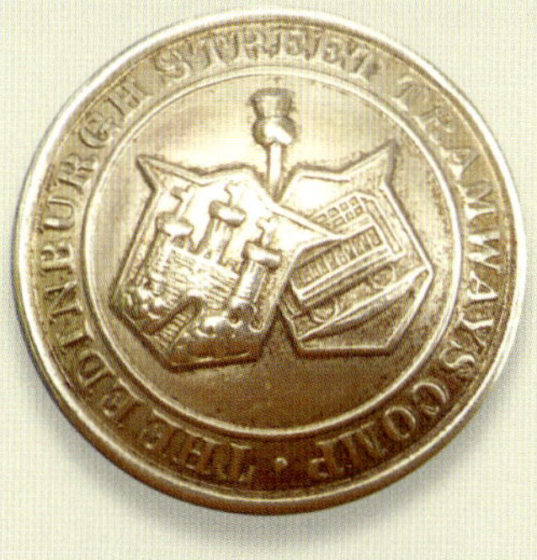

Uniform button of the Edinburgh Street Tramways Company. (From the collection of Ashley Birch)

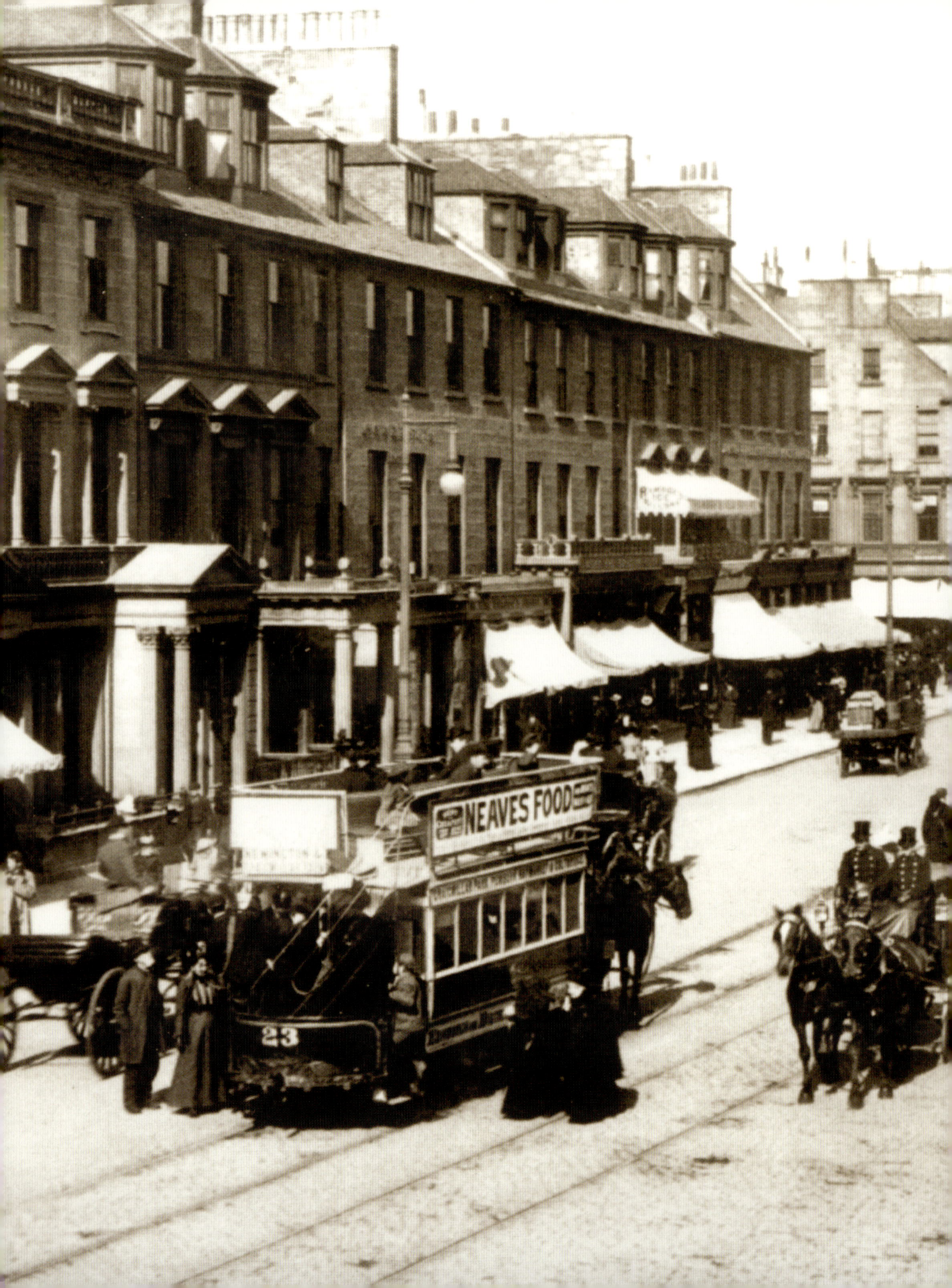
NEAVES FOOD
23

Pre-History

Scotland's capital city, Edinburgh, is known not only as 'Auld Reekie' but also as 'Athens of the North' – built, as is its comparator, on – if not seven – then several hills. When the city expanded, rolling over from its historical situation between the Castle and the Palace down the Royal Mile, to the New Town on the north side of the old Nor' Loch, the need for some form of public communication between its far-flung (and ever further) extremities became increasingly desirable.

The port of Leith on the river Forth was then separated from the capital by two miles of unwelcoming and on occasions distinctly unfriendly lanes; the connection between the Holyrood end of Edinburgh's High Street and Leith was by what became the easter(n) road, after completion of the alternative route by the North Bridge and Leith Street in 1772 and the much improved access by Leith Walk soon thereafter. As early as 1610 the Magistrates granted a 15-year privilege to one Henry Andersen of Stralsund (on the Pomeranian coast of the Baltic) to operate a coach service between Edinburgh and Leith. Coaches, horses and 'servants to run them' were all to be brought from his homeland. A fare of 2d per journey was proposed – a not inconsiderable sum then. It is not known how successful this was, or even if the privilege was exercised. Next recorded was Robert Miller's 1702 application to run four chaises following the same route, then in 1722 another concern was granted permission to run small six-seater coaches. How long each of these enterprises operated goes unrecorded, but there seems to have been significant demand for such a link.[1] Unsurprisingly part of the original planned route of the twenty-first century tramway also traversed the length of Leith Walk. This section has been excluded from the now shortened route, but there is a possibility that it may come in the future.

John Croall in his opposition to the 1871 Parliamentary Bill stated that one-horse 'noddies' for six passengers were in use between Edinburgh and Leith by 1825, but the first reference which has been traced in that century relates to the Seafield Sea Water Baths. A regular public passenger service was inaugurated in July 1833, with two coaches – 'one of them an omnibus on the London plan ...' This reference to an omnibus of 'the London plan' comes a mere four years since the stir occasioned by the appearance of the first 'Omnibus' on the streets of the nation's capital, running between Paddington and the City from Saturday 4 July 1829.[2] George Henderson's buses ran from 2 Princes Street, five times daily, to the Sea Water Baths – within a handsome Georgian building still standing at the corner of Seafield Place and Seafield Road. The fare of 6d effectively placed the bus far beyond the reach of most people, who would be thus denied transport to the swimming pool and seventeen baths 'of varying temperatures'.[3]

The benefits of bus communication were noted by Michael Fox, astute operator of the passenger service along the horse powered Edinburgh and Dalkeith Railway. On Wednesday 6 November 1833 he started a bus feeder link from the Duty House (now Register House) at the east end of Princes Street, leaving 15 minutes before his rail coach was due to depart from St Leonard's; the fare for this bus was 3d.[4] During the following summer the operator of the Union Canal passenger boat followed suit, with a bus from Princes Street to Port Hopetoun from June, also charging 3d.[5] Similar facilities soon linked with steamers operating to Fife from the Chain Pier at Trinity and Newhaven's Stone Pier. Rival operators vied with one another for this traffic, but George Henderson appears to have won the day.[6]

Other than the 'inter-urban' service to Leith, the first pure 'City' service appears to have commenced on 9 October 1837 by James Campbell, from Preston Street, Newington, to India Place, Stockbridge, by way of the Bridges, Hanover Street, Heriot Row and Howe Street, for a fare of 4d.[7] His vehicle was named *Victoria*, but the enterprise did not go unchallenged for long, with a rival starting before the end of the month. Then

Opposite. Car 23, subject of the restoration project, photographed from a first floor window of the Rutland Hotel in the summer of 1897. (Copyright The Francis Frith Collection)

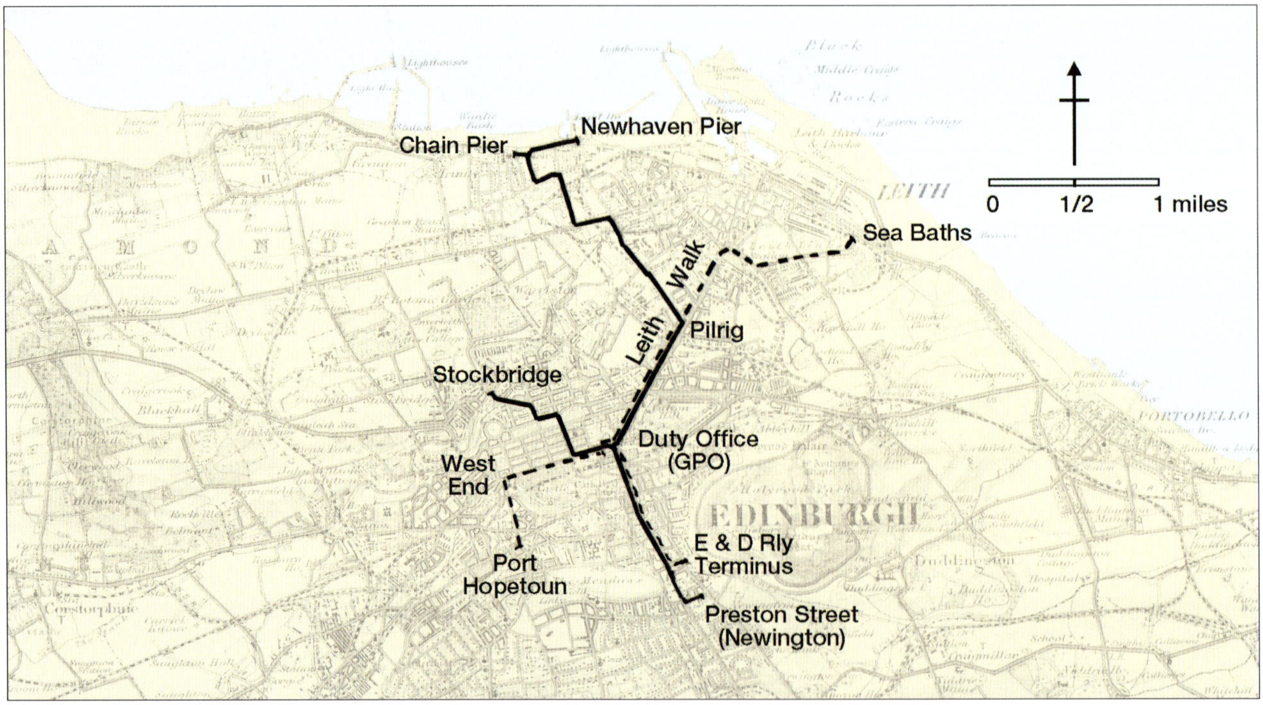

Early horse bus routes

from 12 March 1838 another route was inaugurated between North Frederick Street and Portobello High Street, using the *King Arthur* bus.[8] Campbell also soon ran between Henderson Row and Wright's Houses at Lochrin using the *Sir William*; this operation was then extended to Morningside.[9]

By 1845 it was recorded that Leith Walk was served by twenty omnibuses, carrying about 3600 passengers daily.[10] To bring some semblance of order to the proceedings, the Edinburgh Magistrates issued, on 11 July of that year, their first omnibus regulations. Most, but not all, bus proprietors complied, but Thomson of Swanfield gave up, his vehicles (including three small buses built by Wallace of Perth) quickly sold off by auction.[11] However, ten years later the Magistrates were advised that their powers under the Police Act of 1848 did not include for regulation of coaches or omnibuses.[12] In 1866 further bylaws defining routes, timetables and licensing of vehicles were implemented.[13]

One of the first Scottish coach operators, John Croall, opened a stage route (Stirling to Castlecary) aged just eighteen; he moved to Edinburgh in 1822 and soon was involved, not just with long distance coaches, but also in local transport in the city. His premises at Middlefield beside Shrubhill House, near the boundary between Edinburgh and Leith at Pilrig, became a nucleus for city transport for the next century and a half. He built vehicles there, not only for his own use, but for many other operators; including in 1857 for the 'London French Company' (the General Omnibus Company) founded two years previously in Paris.[14]

An American entrepreneur, George Francis Train arrived in Britain in January 1859, determined to bring American-style street railways to the chief cities of this land. His motives were far from altruistic, he planned his projects to make money for himself and his backers. His prime intention was to see his plans implemented in London, but sensible advice persuaded him to commence in the provinces, where his revolutionary ideas might have better chance of success. He tried initially in Liverpool but having been stymied there, turned his attention to Birkenhead. Here with the blessing of the local authorities he built Britain's first

RAILWAY COAL, REDUCED IN PRICE.

MICHAEL FOX begs leave to intimate to his numerous Friends and the Inhabitants of Edinburgh generally, that he has now completed his winter arrangements for the sale of the Marquis of Lothian's COAL, which he is delivering within the tolls at the following reduced prices, free of any other charge except porterage :—

Best Great Main Jewel Coal, at 10s. 6d. per ton.
Ditto Household ditto, . . at 9s. 6d. "
Ditto Chews ditto, ... at 8s. 6d. "

From the immense sale which this favourite COAL commands in the Edinburgh market, he can assure those favouring him with orders, that they may depend upon it being sent fresh from the pits, as large quantities are daily received in the Railway Depot ; and all the Coal sold by him being delivered by his own horses and carts, with sober and attentive carters, he can with confidence warrant the weight and quality of the coal ordered.

All the other kinds of Coal received by the Railway at the current prices.

N.B.—*As the above prices cannot afford credit, in every case Coals paid on delivery.*

Orders sent to his Office, No. 1, St Leonard's Street, will meet with immediate attention.

TO TRAVELLERS BY THE RAILWAY.

M. F. also takes this opportunity of informing passengers travelling by the Railway, that for their convenience, he commenced on Wednesday last running an OMNIBUS between the Railway Depot and the Duty-House, North Bridge, leaving the Duty-House a quarter of an hour before the starting of the Coaches from St Leonard's, commencing at a quarter before ten A.M., and ceasing at a quarter before six P.M. Fares 3d.

No. 1, St Leonard's Street,
November 8, 1833.
(One concern.)

Scotsman 9 November 1833. The record of Edinburgh's first omnibus?

DOWN WITH MONOPOLY!

OPPOSITION OMNIBUSES BETWEEN EDINBURGH AND NEWHAVEN.

G. HENDERSON begs to announce to the Public, that, having last Summer Season STARTED an OPPOSITION on the ROAD BETWEEN EDINBURGH and NEWHAVEN, reducing the Fares to SIXPENCE in place of *One Shilling*, an overcharge which had been kept up solely *by a system of combination* amongst Coach Proprietors, who thus secured a complete monopoly of the Road, he has, at the request of many Steam-Boat Proprietors and Passengers, been induced to continue that Opposition, on the principle of charging the moderate but remunerating fare of *Sixpence* ; and with that view he has this day commenced running *Omnibuses* between MR WRIGHT'S OFFICE, No. 1, PRINCE'S STREET, and the CHAIN and STONE PIERS, TRINITY and NEWHAVEN, at hours suited to the departure and arrival of the different Steamers.

If the Public would eventually free themselves from a monopoly, which has hitherto been found so grievous, they can only do so by steadily and strenuously supporting G. H.'s Omnibuses ; and G. H. pledges himself that, whilst they continue their support, he will enter into no agreement or coalition with *the Monopolists of the Road*, as has before been done by others, and the fares thus again raised.

G. HENDERSON'S OMNIBUSES.—Fares, Sixpence, —start regularly to meet the departure and arrival of the different Steamers.

Offices, MR WRIGHT'S, 1, PRINCE'S STREET, Edinburgh ; and MR M'WILLIAM'S, NEWHAVEN.
2d June 1837.

Scotsman 3 June 1837. Bus wars!

street railway (tramway), opening to the public on 30 August 1860.[15]

Within a matter of weeks, proposals were being aired that this idea would be suitable for Edinburgh, with Mr Fyfe, Convenor of the Streets and Buildings Committee saying 'such street railways would be a great benefit to Edinburgh'.[16] At the same time, William Miller, an Edinburgh stockbroker and correspondent to *The Scotsman* (who had attended the Birkenhead opening) stated that he had been advised by an eminent engineer 'he did not know of any city better adapted for these railways than our own, and more especially between Edinburgh and Leith. The traffic upon that portion would, no doubt, amply remunerate any company for passengers alone, and, besides, it would be a great boon, by easing the labour of the heavily laden horses on this road'.[17] This writer had, perhaps unwittingly, already identified the difficulty which the proprietors of horse transport in Edinburgh were to be burdened with until mechanisation intervened; the severe toll on horses of the city's hilly streets.

Whether G F Train had intended to include Edinburgh on his 'hit list' or not, he was not long in approaching the city as one of his street railway targets. By mid-November 1860 he was ensconced at the Royal Hotel and engaged in whipping up enthusiasm. Overtures had already been made to the local authority in Glasgow; these two Scottish proposals appearing to pre-date his next assaults, which were upon the various

Extract from the Edinburgh magistrates' Minute Book of October 1860 recording a positive response to the proposals by G F Train for street railways in the city of Edinburgh.

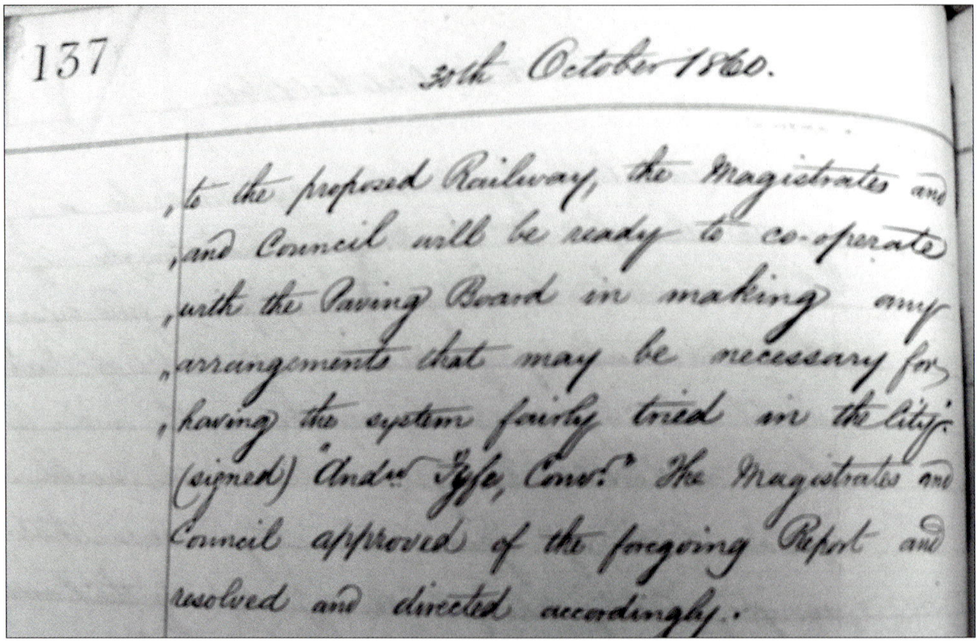

137

30th October 1860.

"to the proposed Railway, the Magistrates and "and Council will be ready to co-operate "with the Paving Board in making any "arrangements that may be necessary for "having the system fairly tried in the City." (signed) Andw Fyfe, Convr." The Magistrates and Council approved of the foregoing Report and resolved and directed accordingly.

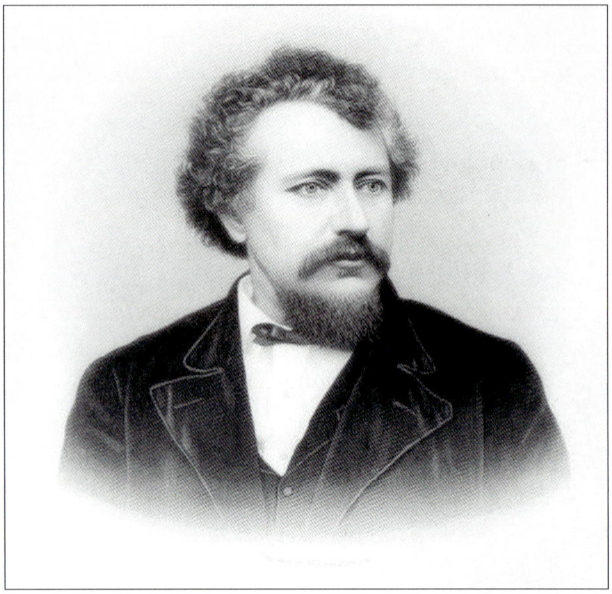

George Francis Train, American tramway entrepreneur.

Vestries of the London Burghs, where he was fully occupied from late November. After much debate three separate short lines were built and opened by Train in London, none of which survived for more than 18 months. Two other lines were promoted by him, in Darlington and the Potteries; the latter – with Birkenhead – being the only two which had any degree of success. Train's failure is generally put down to his use throughout of his patented 'step' design of rail, where the vehicles' flanged wheels ran on an upstand at the edge of a flat rail. This arrangement – which Train claimed as a major benefit for the use of all other wheeled vehicles, also formed an obstruction, and complaints were loud and frequent.

All of these problems lay in the future when Train made his advances to Edinburgh's Council. In early October, his initial letter was passed to the Streets and Buildings Committee, who delayed responding until the Convenor had experienced the Birkenhead line. The subsequent meeting of the Magistrates recorded 'The Committee were … unanimously of the opinion that such a Street Railway … would be a great benefit to the City of Edinburgh if laid in the leading thoroughfares … and that every facility should be afforded by the Council for the formation of such a Railway …'[18] Train's proposals were swiftly crystallised; his line was to run from the west end of Princes Street, then down Leith Walk to terminate at Leith Exchange in Constitution Street; the return route came up by York Place, Queen Street and Castle Street. He demanded a right, should the first line be satisfactory, to build any other lines in the city and its environs within a radius of ten

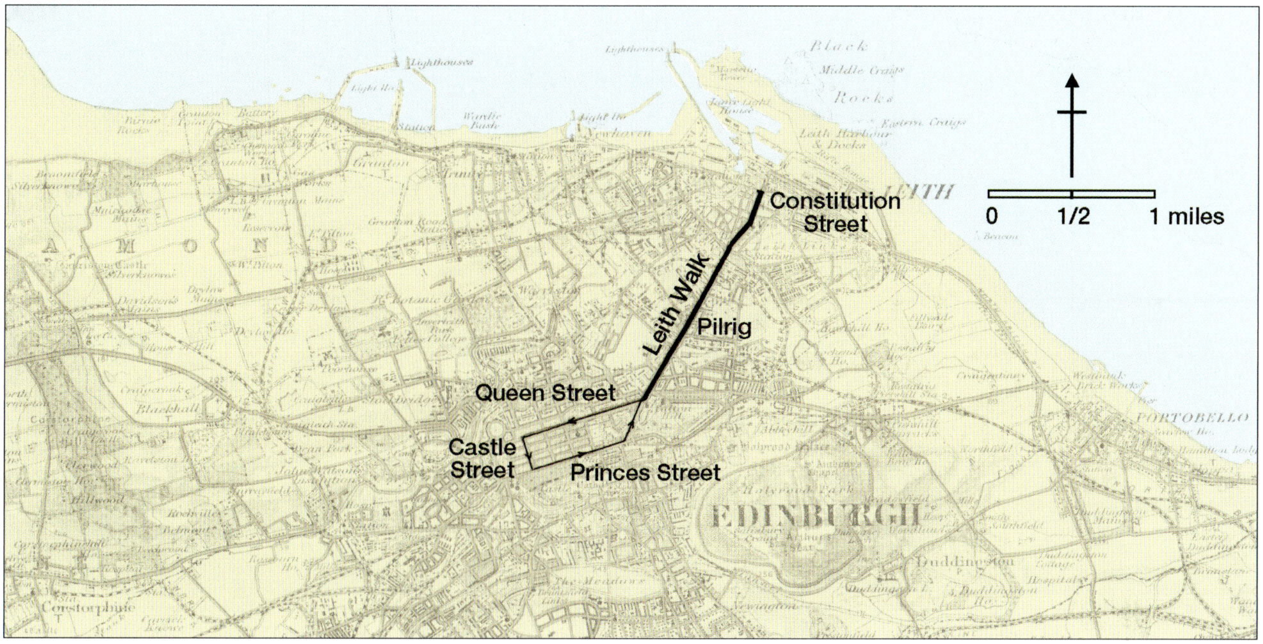

Tramway proposed by GF Train 1860

miles from Sir Walter Scott's monument in Princes Street. Wasting no time he then advertised his intent to obtain a Parliamentary Bill to incorporate a company to construct this line.[19] These matters were discussed at length at a meeting of the City Paving Board on 19 November when, not only Train's scheme, but a rival proposal from a Samuel C Ridley was on the table. Ridley's scheme aped Train's in its route, but [he said] having inspected the line at Birkenhead, could guarantee his would be superior in all respects. Train showed models of the track design, and of a typical car.

Thomas Leburn, chairman of the Board, and other members expressed approval in principle of the proposals, but resolved to contact an Edinburgh exile, James Newlands, Burgh Engineer of Liverpool. His response was emphatic; 'Every day's experience at Birkenhead proves that these railways are great conveniences for the people, the general public, but there is as little doubt that much profane swearing is evoked by them from the upper ten thousand who drive or are driven in their own vehicles ... the Birkenhead Railway is not well constructed ... the opposition evoked arises from the accidents so frequently occurring to carriages crossing these rails ...' Edinburgh's Paving Board thus recommended caution '... let us pause until we see a safe railroad in operation in a large city such as Edinburgh, where there are so many cabs and light carriages ...'[20] Following this half-hearted response, Train exited to London to oversee his street railway activities there.

Notwithstanding this rebuff there appeared in the next edition of the *Caledonian Mercury*, two large adverts pertaining to this same subject. It is not clear if these were from the two parties who had appeared before the Paving Board, but this would appear more than likely. The first was from the Improved Street-Transit Company signalling its intent to apply for Parliamentary powers to lay down iron (or other) rails, plates or trams in the streets of Edinburgh, Glasgow, Manchester, Liverpool, Hull and Birmingham ... and [their] neighbourhoods. This was inserted by Law Agents Dyson & Co of 24 Parliament Street Westminster. The second was prepared by Baxter, Rose & Company of 6 Victoria Street Westminster on behalf of the Street Rail Company (Limited) to form a company to lay down rails upon the streets of the metropolis and any other town in the United Kingdom, and to reserve

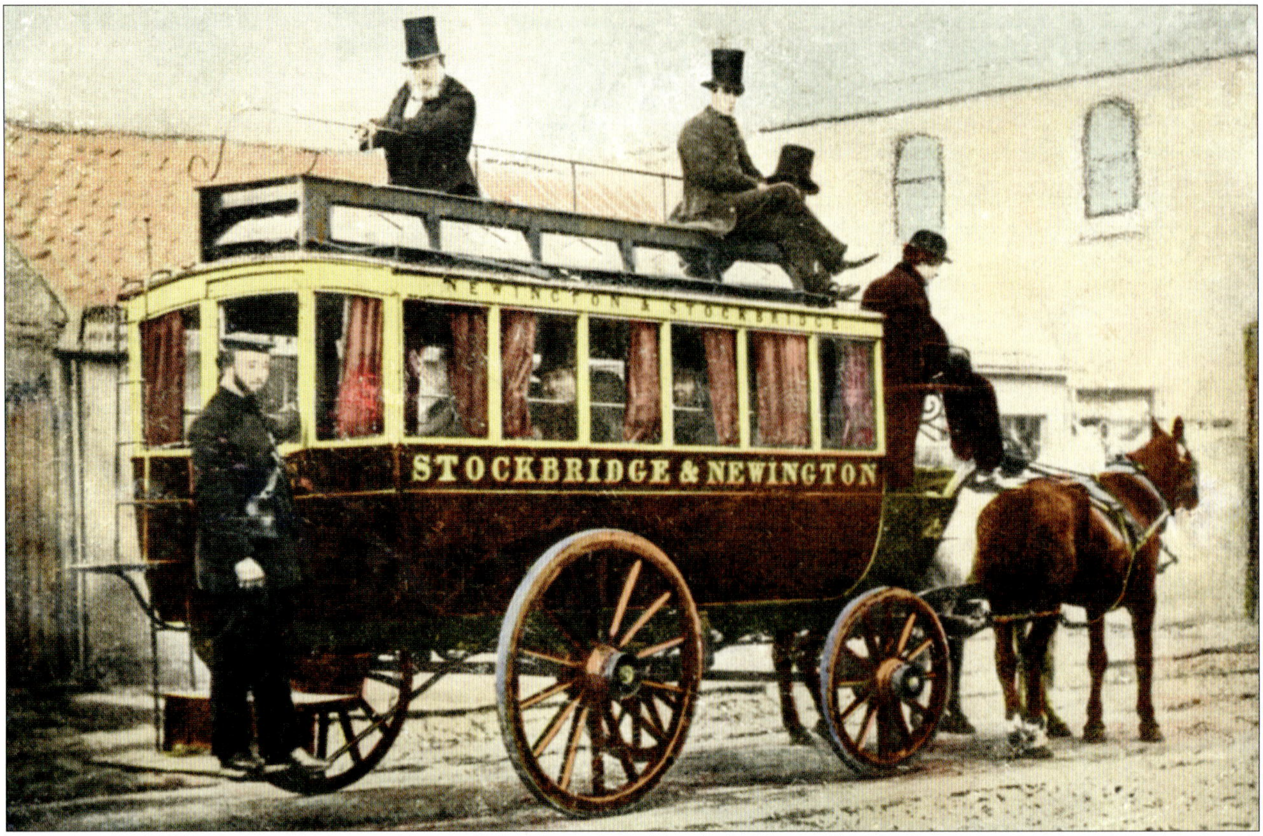

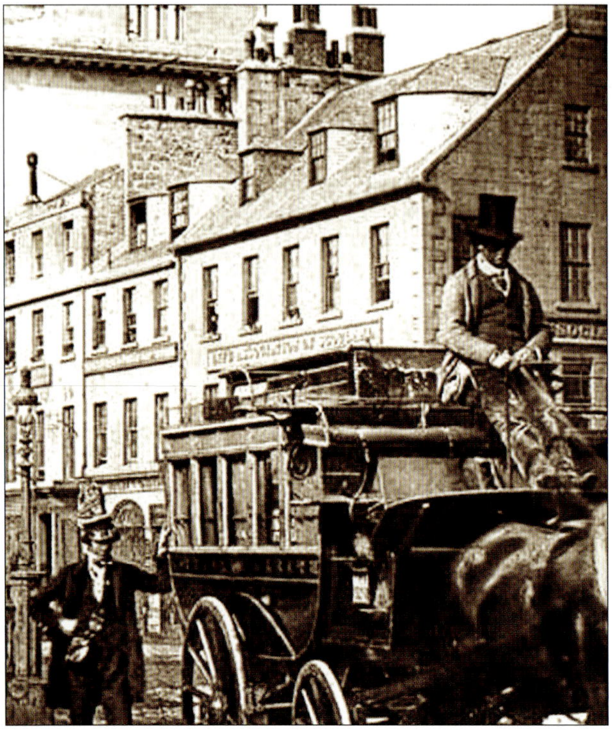

Above. 'The Stockbridge bus of fifty years ago' – a postcard published in the early years of the twentieth century, dating the scene to the late 1850s or early 1860s. It ran from Stockbridge (Kerr Street) to Newington (Minto Street at Duncan Street), o perated by Croall & Atkinson and Adamson.

Left. Mid-Victorian scene with the Leith bus at its stance by the Royal Institution (better known now as the Royal Scottish Academy) opposite the foot of Hanover Street.

Opposite. Viewed from the north side of Princes Street, with a horse bus at the same stance as seen to the left. This view can be dated fairly accurately from the construction under way in North Bank Street at the top of the Mound of the Free Church College, which was completed in 1863. A probable date of the scene would thus be around 1861.

to that company their exclusive use (use of edge rail was stipulated).[21] This not being the problematic rail patented by Train, this particular reference cannot be to his scheme. With nothing further heard of these proposals neither appears to have completed the Parliamentary process. This could have been as a direct consequence of Train's overtures and the problems

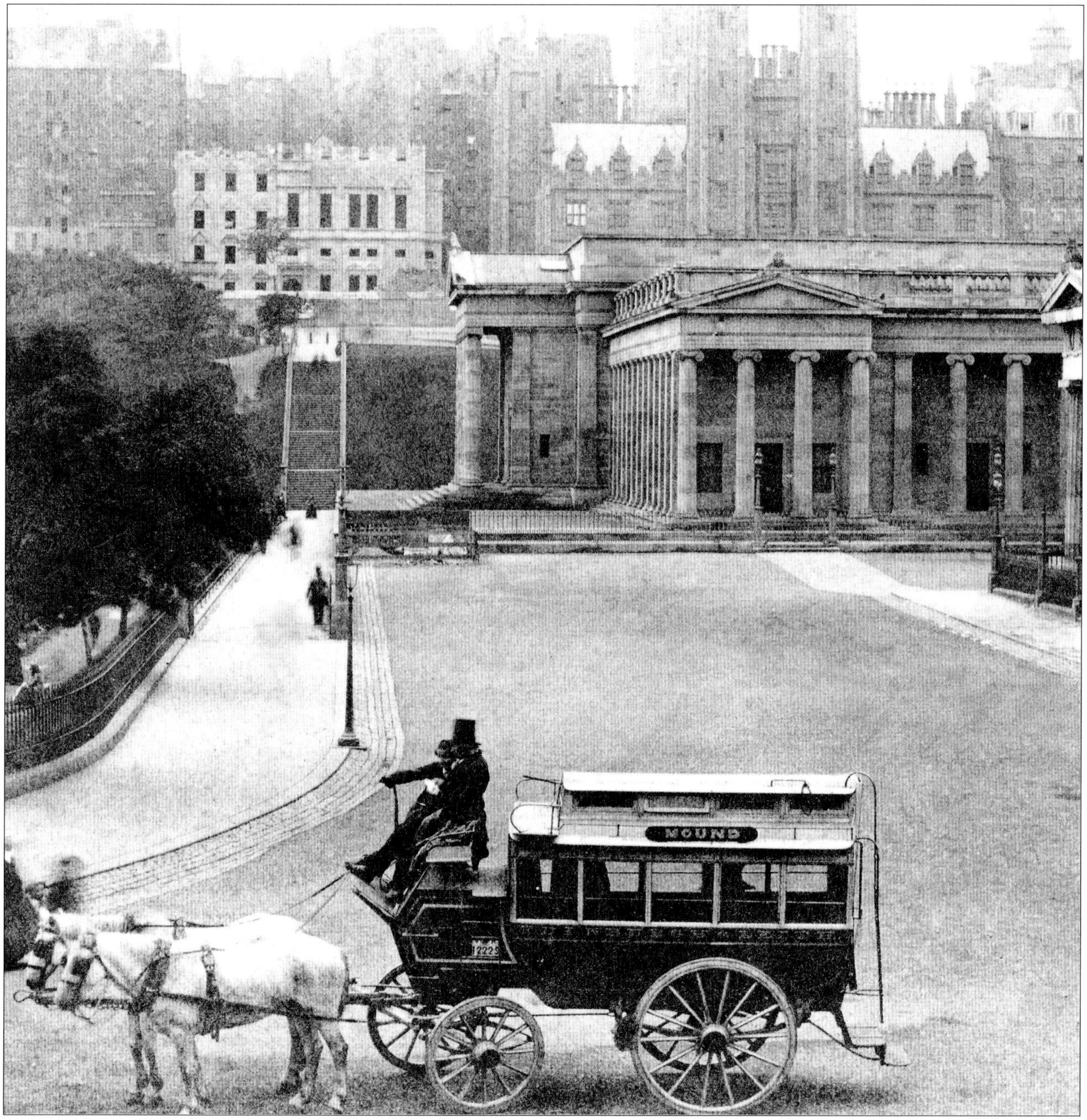

incurred with his ventures in London. Development of street tramways in general in the British Isles may have been delayed by a decade as a consequence of the antagonism he engendered. Ten years later, when serious proposals were again mooted for passenger tramways in Edinburgh, the memory of Train's influence had not been obliterated. 'The notorious George Francis Train managed to disgust the London public with tramways. He laid down a bad rail which hindered the other traffic; and he did the whole thing in such a spirit of bumptious blundering that the very word tramways has had an ugly sound ever since'.[22]

In Edinburgh, the horse bus remained the sole provider of urban transport for further ten years. The

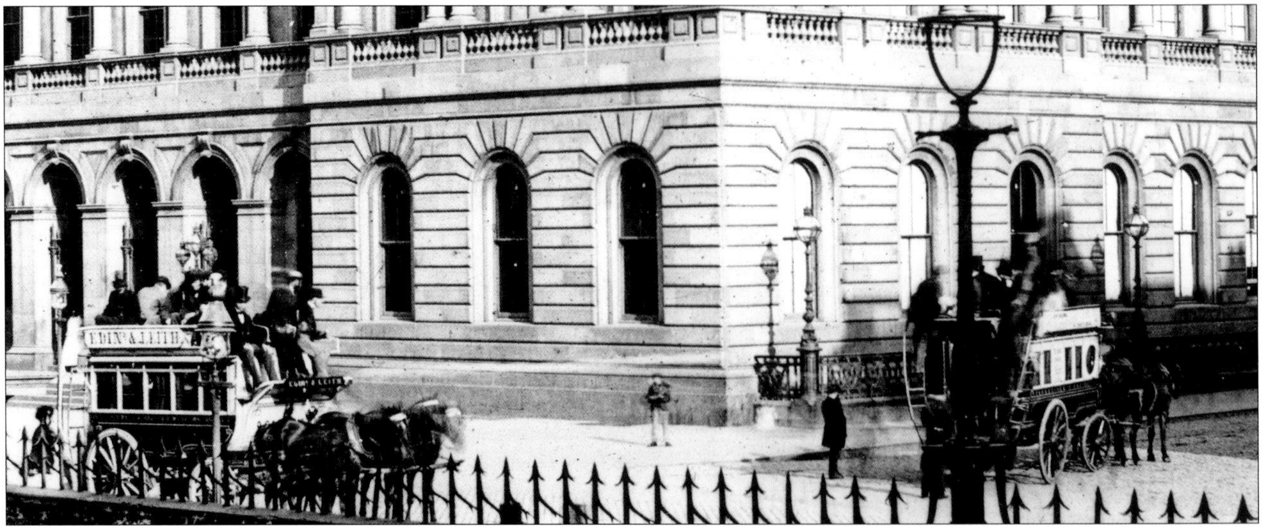

At the GPO before 1871, two buses pause, one on the Leith run, the other heading for Newington. The long exposure has caught several hazy 'ghostly' characters ascending to the top deck seats of the latter, while other passers-by are disembodied blurs.

major demand between Edinburgh and Leith was met by several operators, with Croall, Adamson, Atkinson, and other partnerships licensed. Vehicles running to Leith were painted green, those to Morningside red; Haymarket to Grange were allocated orange as their livery, while Stockbridge to Newington buses were blue. Numbers were issued with the licences – to be painted on the rear of the vehicles in figures 4 inches high and ¾ inch broad and by 1869 thirty-six vehicles had been examined by the Inspector of Hackney Carriages, and issued with licences at a cost of 1/- each.[23]

An inkling that changes were afoot was recorded when the City Road Trustees met in October 1868 with submission by John Buchanan, C E, with plans for a proposed passenger tramway between Edinburgh and Leith. This was allowed to lie on the table, and nothing further was heard. However, at the same meeting an alternative proposal was put forward from one Waldemar Raahauge. This [probably Danish] gentleman, with his brother Sophus, requested authority to '... lay a tramway on the carriageway of Leith Walk ...'[24] Clarification of the intent was made by an advertisement a few days later; 'As some people seem to think that this Railway has only to begin from the Theatre-Royal and end at the foot of Leith Walk, I wish to take this opportunity of informing the public that it is, and always has been, intended to run from the very West-End of Edinburgh (Haymarket) to the very Centre of Leith (Bernard Street) ... I fully informed those gentlemen that I was willing to lay Two Lines of Rails, but, supposing this would take too much room up in the streets, my proposal was for only One Line with the Half-Circle Rails'.[25]

This proposal may have followed from the success of a pioneer horse tramway through Copenhagen opened as early as October 1863, and with which G F Train claimed an association.[26] Although built by an English contractor and probably initially using cars built in Birkenhead, Train's involvement has not been confirmed.[27] However, after five years successful operation the Copenhagen tramways were an established and profitable venture, so it is perhaps not surprising that two enterprising Danes attempted to bring the benefits to Edinburgh. Their efforts also must have fallen on deaf ears as nothing further was heard from, or of, them. What is intended by the 'Half-Circle Rails' can only be guessed at.

Steam Buses

It may have seemed like a good idea at the time, but Edinburgh's next venture into public transport provision was to prove to be a cul-de-sac. Tennant and Company, based at Bowershall Works in Leith, manufactured light steam powered traction engines to the patent of their Manager Andrew Nairn, and thoughts turned to the application of these 'tractors' to passenger haulage as well as goods. They had already constructed similar machines to the design of Mr R W Thomson, who had agreed to supply such a vehicle to 'one of the largest towns of England'; this machine being tested on the streets of Edinburgh on 19 August 1869. With an omnibus attached, the 'road-steamer with its omnibus started from Constitution Street , and ran at best omnibus speed up Leith Walk and Leith Street, making no account whatever of their steepness. The dexterity with which it picked its way between strings of cart-horses, omnibuses, and cabs, and the docility with which it stopped or turned whenever it was required, were marvellous. It ran from one end of Princes' Street to the other without stopping, then turned down south Charlotte Street to Forres Street, where, at the steepest point, where the descent looked really dangerous, it was brought to a sudden stand-still, to show how completely it was under command, and how entirely it could dispense with any kind of brake. This was its final display, and it then went quietly and rapidly back to Leith ... those who saw it will perhaps be glad to remember that they witnessed the journey of the first steam engine built for omnibus traffic in towns'.[28] Much was made of the absence of damage to the road surface, the consequence of the driving wheels being ribbed with india-rubber, supplied by the North British Rubber Works in Fountainbridge. The steam tractor was in Paris in November, hauling a fifty-seat Versailles omnibus without difficulty.

In October of that year (1869), permission was sought by John Ritchie for a steam bus to operate for

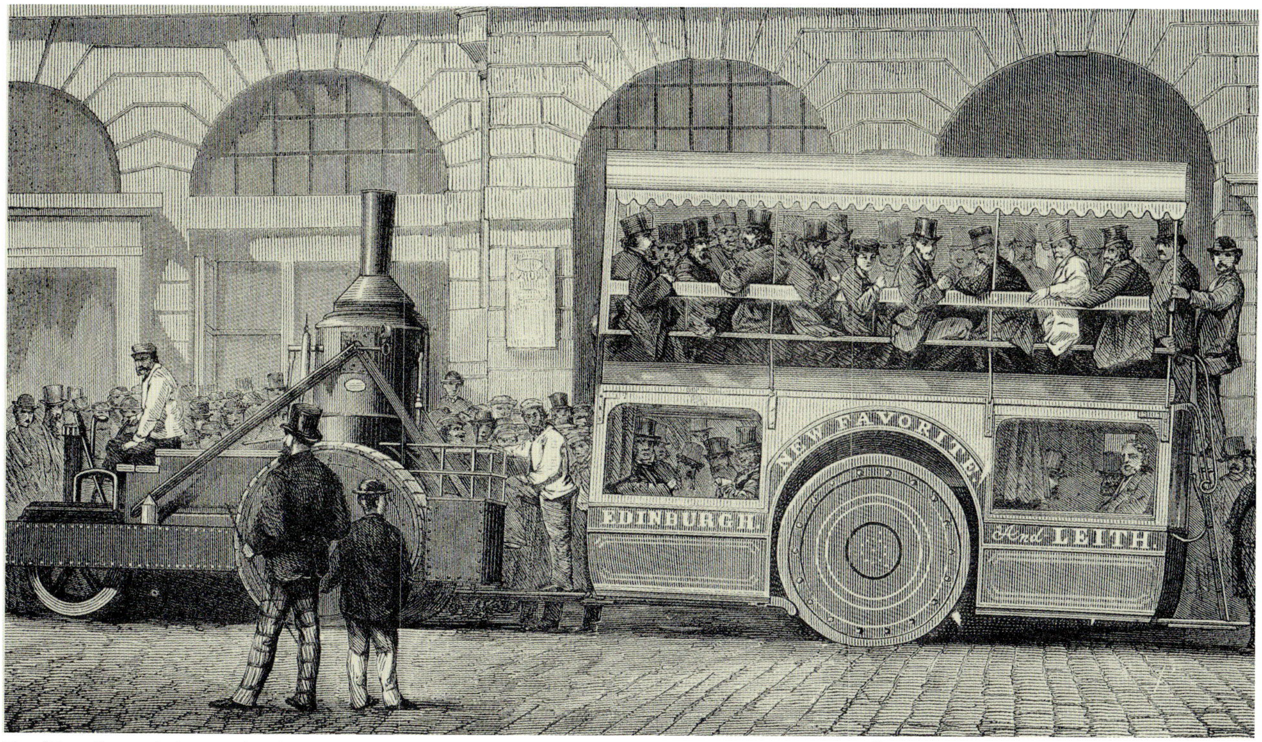

The *'New Favourite'* steam hauled bus on a demonstration run, pictured in the High Street at the Royal Exchange, better known now as the home of Edinburgh's City Chambers. The passenger carrying coach element (built by Drew & Burnett of Fountainbridge, who went on to build some trams) was then exported to India.

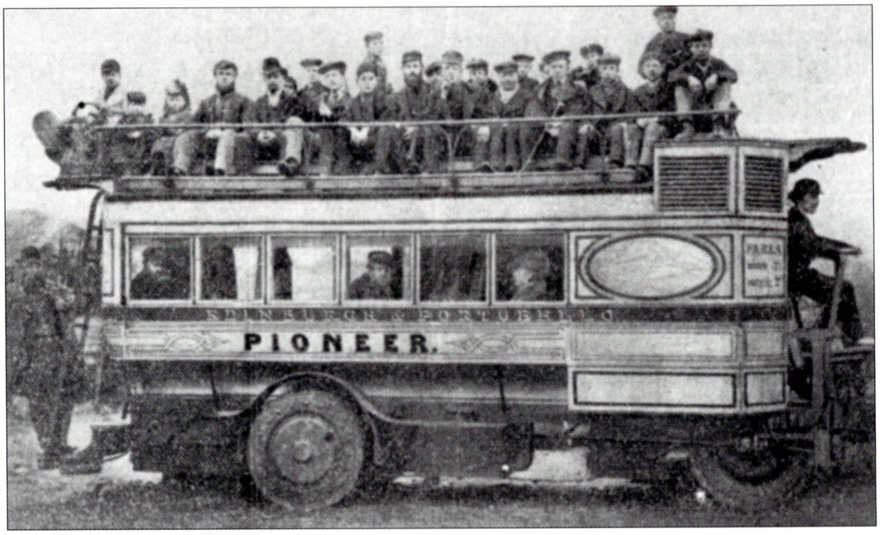

Nairn's '*Pioneer*' steam bus was of self-contained design and in mid 1871 ran for a short time to Portobello. Without any mechanical assistance , the driver would soon develop strong arms.

passengers between West End and Leith. This was not approved, and it was not until 2 June 1870 that Andrew Ritchie was authorised to use it from Waterloo Place to Portobello; it made six return trips on that day.[29] The following year a Mr David Charles of Bonnington Road wrote to explain that he was the proprietor of Nairn's patent Steam Omnibus, and he had let it on hire originally to Andrew Ritchie, then to Thomas Johnstone who also used it on the Portobello run.[30] The 'tractor' part of the assemblage was one of Tennant's 6 horse power steam engines, while the large omnibus trailer (named '*New Favourite*') had been built by Drew and Burnett of Fountainbridge. Balanced on a single axle, it had seats for twenty-one inside and further forty-four outside.[31] The road-steamer idea was seen as having great potential for military use and particularly in un-developed colonies. However the principle was possibly too far ahead of the practicalities of operation, particularly in rough or arduous conditions. Of six machines delivered to British Columbia, four were returned to the manufacturer as unsuitable for the purpose for which they had been sold. It had been discovered, in most dramatic fashion, that on very steep hills the boiler water (unsurprisingly) flowed to the lower end with the boilers consequently exploding.[32] Two steamers were exported to Labuan (Malaysia), with sixteen wagons for transport of coal to the harbour.[33] Several operated reasonably successfully, including one, the '*Don*' in Aberdeen, which was noted as having hauled an excursion party, complete with their musician accompaniment on a train of five wagons.[34] The road-steamers were, however, not a practical success for public transport. Their novelty value provided short-term attraction, but despite claims of minimal road damage, this was found in practice to be a major problem in sustained operation. A Court of Session hearing throws some light on events. R W Thomson obtained patent rights on his design for India-rubber shod wheels specifically for road-steamers, and granted Tennant sole manufacturing rights for three years, stipulating that if demand could not be met (given six weeks to build each machine), the said agreement would be void. Orders for eleven steamers were referred to, including no less than eight which Tennant had refused to accept on various grounds; Thomson then stated that Tennant had broken the agreement, the matter eventually settled out of court.[35]

Practical Tramway Proposals

Early in September 1870 Edinburgh Magistrates were faced with another application to build tramways in the city. This came from Messrs H & A Inglis W S, who had acted for tramways already operating in London and Liverpool. They proposed formation of a company

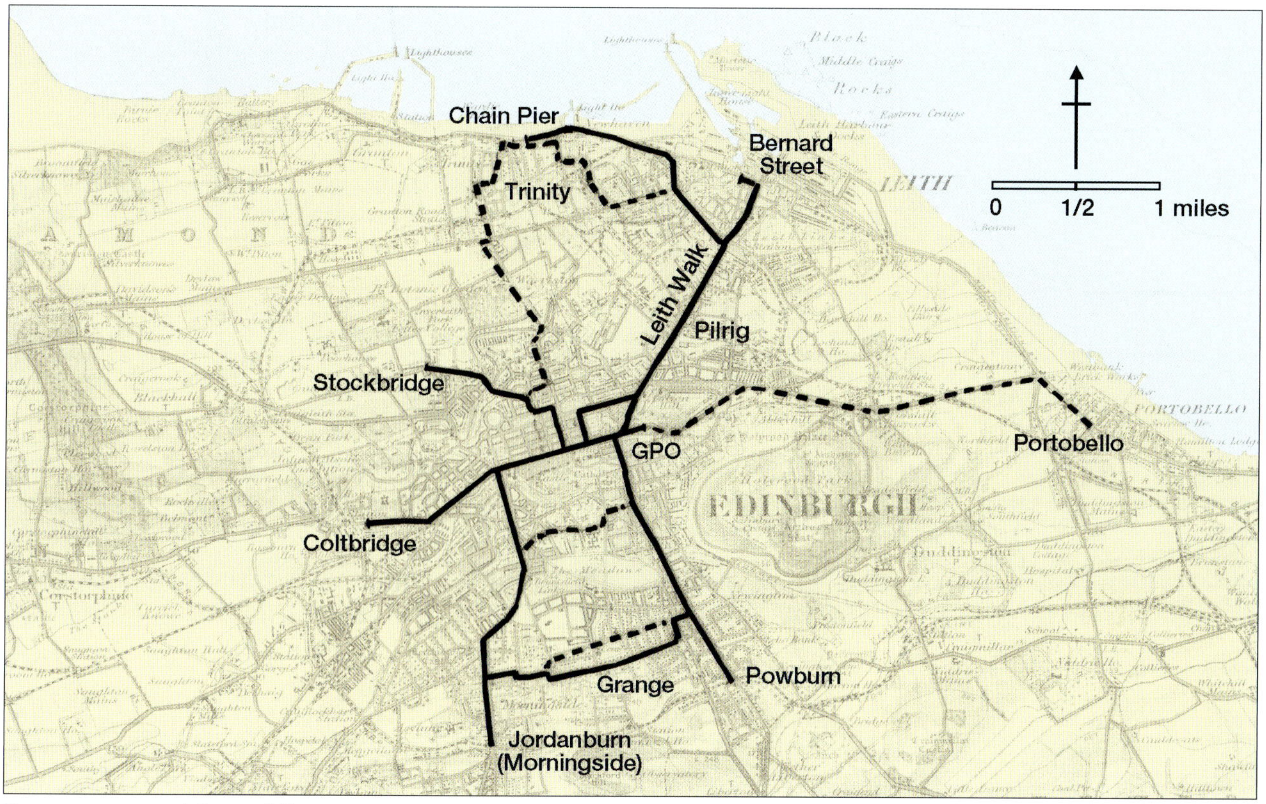

Tramways proposed 1870 and 1871

to lay the following standard gauge lines; North Bridge to Minto Street via Clerk Street; Princes Street to Murrayfield via Haymarket; West End to Morningside via Tollcross; Newington to Morningside via Grange Road, Lauder Road, Grange Loan and Church Lane (or such other suitable route); Waterloo Place to Portobello via Regent Road. It was added that a line to Leith had been originally included, but as this was also planned by others, it had been omitted from their proposals. The company wanted exclusive use of the rails for their carriages, but acknowledged that the Corporation should have power to license other parties also using flanged wheel vehicles. These suggestions were now looked upon with great suspicion by the Road Trustees, who stipulated that the tramway should not be built across the (then very narrow) North Bridge unless the new company paid for it to be widened; this the company confessed it was unable to finance. The Lord Provost (William Law) stated 'They could by no means consent to have their streets tampered with by a company composed of one or two engineers and two or three lawyers … they could not allow streets like Princes Street and Leith Walk to be tampered with by any flying jackanapes, unless they were quite sure that they had regular men to deal with. If their speculation paid, the promoters would go on with their scheme; if they did not pay, they would go to wreck, and leave the streets in such a state that they would all have to be lifted and repaired … Edinburgh was not a town for tramways at all … the streets of Edinburgh were very sacred, and he did not think that they should allow them to be tampered with, except by first-rate people, or by themselves …' With this totally unbiased opinion, the matter was passed to the Works Committee.[36]

By mid-November, the promoters, undeterred by the chilly reception, had reconsidered their thoughts about leaving the Leith tramways to others, and put forward their proposals for a Bill [as the Edinburgh and Leith Tramways Company] to the next session of Parliament. This Bill included the lines above mentioned plus Princes Street to Bernard Street (Leith) via Leith Walk and Constitution Street; Junction Street to Trinity (Chain Pier) via Newhaven; St Andrew Street to Leith Walk via York Place; Hanover Street to Comely Bank via Heriot Row and Stockbridge.

Only then did the other contenders [now named as the Edinburgh Street Tramways Company], represented by Lindsay, Paterson & Hall, W S, and with Thomas Bouch as their engineer, put their cards on the table, with a generally similar set of proposals, but routing their Newington to Morningside link by way of Grange Road and Clinton Road. They also had differing routes in the north of the city. Capital for this scheme was to be £30,000 in £10 shares; the other proposal had capitalisation of just £20,000.

In the nineteenth – as even in the twenty-first centuries – tramways had their supporters and 'A Civil Engineer' wrote in the *Scotsman* '… It strikes me that [the Lord Provost, William Law] is showing himself, if not quite ignorant of the merits of, at least very antagonistic to what promises to be one of the greatest boons conferred on Edinburgh for many years. I refer, of course, to the proposed system of tramways, and it seems to me that what his Lordship objects to most of all is the speculative character of the parties (engineers and lawyers) who are taking all the preliminary risk and expense which must be incurred before tramways can be laid down … I feel sure that, if he had seen how they work, and used them, as I and many others have in Paris, Brussels, Berlin, Vienna, &c., he would no longer say that they had no ground to go on. Travelling on the streets of these towns is made equal in comfort to travelling by rail on our best railways – that is, you have roomy, comfortable cars, heated in winter by stoves, and there is really no comparison in the comfort afforded with that which we have in our omnibuses at present …'[37] Law considered it necessary to respond '… what I do most earnestly object to is to allow a handful of mere speculative strangers, who have no interest in Edinburgh, and for whom Edinburgh cares nothing, to come here, to invade our streets, and to attempt to force upon us, by means of an Act of Parliament, a benefit which we are not asking, of which we are not convinced, and which, if we were convinced, we could obtain very much easier and better without their assistance. I object, in the second place, to the constitution of these so-called companies of nobodies, who are prosecuting the two rival schemes. An engineer or two and a few parliamentary agents could float any number of miles … and as soon as it was fairly on the way to construction, the engineers and agents, with their pay in their pockets, float quietly out of all responsibility and liability too – very much in the same style as our present urgent benefactors did in the case of Glasgow'.[38] Law had a reasonably astute point here, as it was later shown that promoters of the contemporary and similar Glasgow scheme individually feathered their nests to the extent of tens of thousands of pounds.

To be fair to Law, he then visited (at his own cost), the tramways then operating in London, Liverpool and Birkenhead. What he found did not alter his opinions, but he now felt that, should passenger tramways in the streets be such a fine idea, they should be retained in the hands of the Corporation. Nobody can have by then advised him that the relevant legislation, the Tramways Act of 1870 at Clause 19, expressly prohibited local authorities from operating just such enterprises ['… nothing in this Act contained shall authorise any local authority to place or run carriages upon such tramway …'] – but not from constructing them and then leasing them out. This restriction on operation was removed some years later.

The Road Trust commissioned a report on tramways which was presented at the end of December 1870. It included details of construction and operation of the three tramways mentioned above, and was particularly critical of the worn-out condition of the Birkenhead line, where the track was already in very poor condition. It went into some detail regarding the vehicles used: 'The tramway carriages, or cars, especially those in London, externally and internally of a handsome construction, and are much longer and wider than the best of our street omnibuses … The cars used in

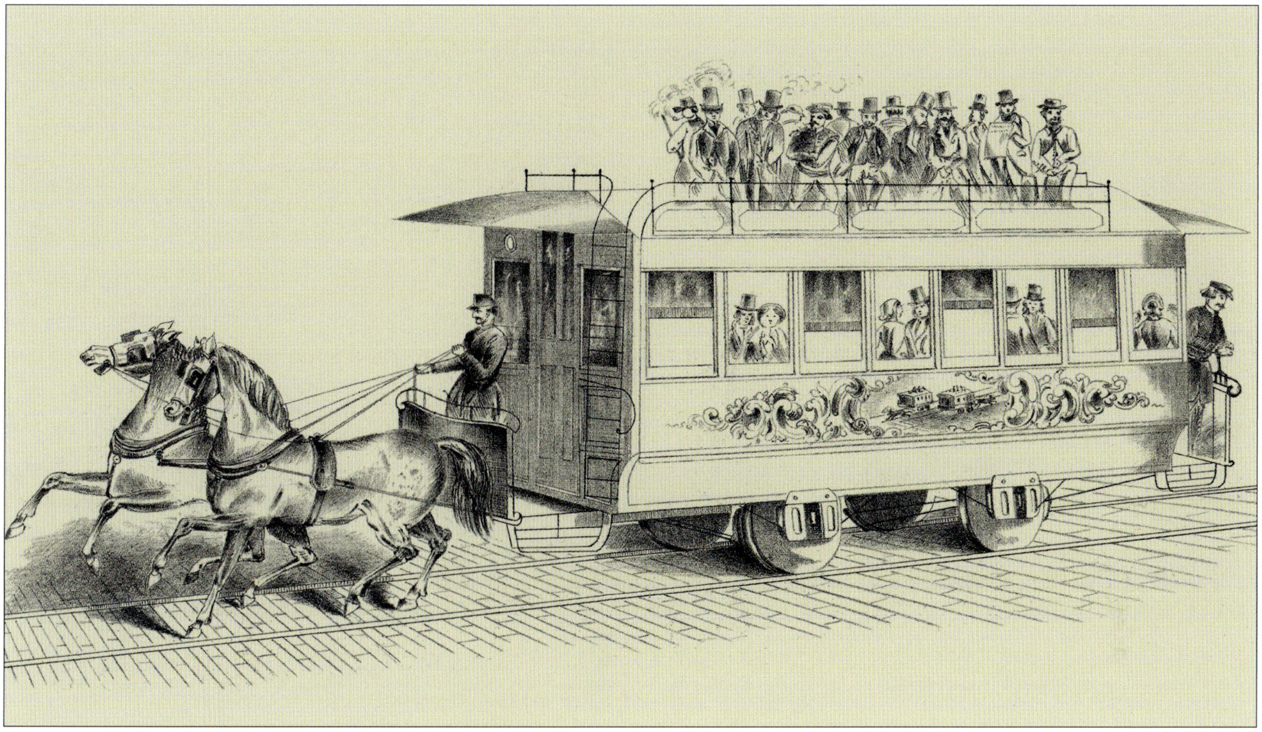

The *Report on Tramways* by the Edinburgh Road Trust of December 1870 included this engraving of a horse tram, to indicate just what was intended. Where the engraver got his inspiration from is not known.

Liverpool are smaller and lighter than those in London [as] the streets are much steeper , and the curves much sharper, than in London ... The Liverpool cars are constructed to carry sixteen passengers inside and eighteen outside, and the London cars to carry twenty-two inside and twenty-four outside. The average cost of each London car is about L200. The cars are constructed at various places, some at Birkenhead, others at New York, and others at Copenhagen. The Copenhagen cars in use on the Tramway from Lambeth to Brixton are of an elegant construction ...' The report also referred to the situation in Glasgow, where the Corporation intended to construct the lines themselves. With two Edinburgh schemes under consideration the prospect arose, if both were authorised, there could be four lines of rails in some streets – a quite unacceptable outcome. The eventual recommendation was, basically, to wait and see what happened in Glasgow.[39]

To enable 'proper' consideration of the report, eight council members were taken to London at the expense of Lindsay Paterson & Hall. Needless to say Mr Law was scathing in his comments (he was not included in the party). 'It is a mode they take to "thirl" the Council, if they can. The system they first adopted was to give splendid dinners, and to ask members of the Council to attend, and talk over the bills. I would not call that bribery; but it is a pleasant way of trying to overcome a man's objections ... I rather gather the agitating men in the Council mean to support Lindsay & Paterson's company'. When put to the vote, the Provost's motion to have the Works and Law Committees examine both Bills and report back was carried – but by only a single vote.[40] Soon the unnecessary duplication of two competing Bills was accepted, and in early January it was announced that the rival promoters had agreed to proceed with one application, based upon Lindsay Paterson & Hall's version – this being said to have greater local approval. With some haste, the Bill was lodged with the Examiner for Standing Orders on 24 January 1871.

However all was not quite as had been represented, and several years later when the Street Tramways Company's accounts relating to its formation costs were being examined, it was discovered that large sums had been paid to H & A Inglis, and their London partners, who were actually Messrs Fisher & Parrish, tramway contractors with American antecedents. The other party was the 'professional' tramway promoters, Ashurst, Morris & Co. This long established London legal practice – in particular partners and brothers John and William Morris – saw, and grasped assiduously, the considerable financial benefits to be gained from promotion then selling on of tramways. Generally speaking their ploy appears to have consisted of setting up a company, promoting and steering the Bill through Parliament, then selling on the powers to a newly constituted locally based organisation at a highly beneficial rate for themselves. A number of individual tramway schemes were floated by them, then in May 1871 the brothers registered the British and Foreign Tramways Company, which in its prospectus proclaimed unashamedly 'The intention of the Company is generally to invest its own capital in the construction and development of the Tramways selected by it, and to dispose of the same from time to time when tested by the experience of actual working, in which way the public will be protected against unsound and merely speculative projects'.[41] Between them, Ashurst & Morris and the British & Foreign Tramways Co had significant involvement in a multitude of tramway promotional schemes, including at Glasgow, Aberdeen, Dundee, and Stirling in Scotland, Cardiff, Plymouth and others in England, several including Brussels, Madrid and Barcelona on the continent as well as Bombay, Calcutta and Buenos Aires further afield. The basis of the British and Foreign Tramways Company was succinctly described, 'It was, in a way, a kind of investment trust in tramways ...' the prospectus went on to say that the directors were to be paid a fixed sum of £150 each year plus 5 per cent of the profits in excess of 10 per cent.[42]

The preliminary sums paid by the fledgling Edinburgh Street Tramways Company, when they were available for scrutiny, raised much concern, and the suggestion was aired that certain bailies and councillors had been 'manipulated'. In an unusual, for the period, piece of investigative journalism, the *Scotsman* was highly critical. 'One lesson taught by the whole affair ... is the utter rottenness of the system of deputations. They are sometimes necessary, and when men go honestly to serve the interests of the City, the City ought to pay them. But men often go in other circumstances. Sums are drawn from the City Chamberlain occasionally by men who practically appoint themselves on deputations, and whose object in London is not the business of the city, but to be present at festivities, or to look after their own affairs. A shockingly loose sense of morality prevails in this and other respects, and there ought to be a change for the better'.[43]

A total amount of £18,418 18s 7d was expended on the 'preliminaries' of which Lindsay & Paterson claimed £2,783 13s 2d; Mr Paterson personally, £5,105 3s 11d; Messrs Ashurst & Morris £2000 and John Morris £3000. These latter two amounts were the price of Ashurst & Morris theoretically (but not practically) dropping out of the running. [Earnings equivalent of £1000 in 1871 is approximately £500,000 at time of writing] Paterson was friendly with several members of the Council, and much emphasis was given to the 'revelation' that Mr Duncan, Clerk to the Road Trust, had after his London trip (paid for by the promoters) revised his opposing stance, perhaps because the promoters were now going to contribute £2,500 towards widening the North Bridge. The necessary change had been achieved, so when the matter was discussed by the Lord Provost's Committee, the tramway proposal was adopted by 31 votes to 3. This was not achieved without barbed comments regarding the 'unfortunate' expedition by elected members to London – however Bailie Miller stated 'before going to London, [I] had rather strong prejudices against tramways – but the moment I saw them in operation, and had experience of driving in them, my prejudices were scattered. I am satisfied that a greater benefit could not be conferred on the community than to introduce tramways to Edinburgh ...'[44]

John Croall and Sons, the long-established coach operators, were vociferous in their opposition. As providers of many local omnibus services, they not surprisingly saw their trade threatened. Their petition against the Bill listed their operations; nine buses running Edinburgh to Leith, three from Register House to Morningside and one from Stockbridge to Newington. Croall's opposition was however overcome by agreement of a beneficial guaranteed contract for the supply of the necessary 'horse power' to the tramway. The council now petitioned in favour of the Bill, having extracted a final agreement that cars would not operate on Sundays. A request was made by Andrew Ritchie, who was then running the *New Favourite* steam bus to Portobello, to be allowed to operate two cars on the tramways, but nothing further was heard from him.[45] The Bill appeared to be having an easy passage, but at the last moment the Caledonian Railway threw a spanner in the works by indicating that they intended to oppose, and demand that the gauge be changed to allow them to connect to the tramway and run their wagons along it. The Roads Trust, in giving approval had stipulated against use of the lines for this purpose, hence this was strenuously opposed by the promoters and by the North British Railway. The Caledonian threat was dismissed, the Bill receiving Royal Assent on 29 June 1871.[46]

The directors of the new Edinburgh Tramways Company met on 3 July, when Robert Hutchison of Carlowrie (chairman also of the Edinburgh & Bathgate Railway Company) was appointed chairman. No time was wasted, with a detailed prospectus appearing in the *Scotsman* just two days later. Other directors were pillars of Edinburgh society, adding an immediate air of local involvement and security; however it was also now apparent that, far from having passed their scheme to a local undertaking, Ashurst & Morris were still very much involved, only now with Lindsay & Paterson as their local agents in lieu of H & J Inglis. Thomas Bouch came as Engineer but he was then heavily involved in the design of his Tay viaduct (which opened at the end of May 1878, only to fail in the most spectacular and disastrous fashion just eighteen months later). Other directors were Daniel Ainslie, Thomas Hill, and James Taylor, all directors of the Caledonian Railway, Charles Cowan and John Crabbie, directors of the London and Edinburgh Steam Shipping Coy, John Dickson, banker, Lt-Col Ryley and Alex Wood M.D.[47] The last named proved to be a most astute inclusion. Wood was a highly respected physician and philanthropist who was credited in 1853 with the first ever practical application of the hypodermic syringe (modelled by him on the bee sting). Despite his multitude of other responsibilities and involvement in good causes, he devoted henceforth a large part of his time and energy to Edinburgh's tramways.

In offering for subscription £150,000 worth of £10 shares (half the total authorised), the prospectus emphasised the benefits of tramways to Edinburgh, drawing on Ashurst, Morris's prior experience. Within a few weeks, this initial share issue was over-subscribed by a factor of six. The prospectus advised that there would be no need to create a stud of horses, since agreement had been reached with Croall, who in return for withdrawal of his competing bus routes, would provide the necessary horse flesh for the tramcars. This was soon found to satisfy John Croall very well, but cost the company dearly. It was also noted '... it has been found that one horse on the tramway will do the work of more than three horses on an ordinary street ... the [carriages] are lower hung, so that the timid and infirm can get in and out of them without difficulty, the central passage gives ample room for passengers to pass from one end to the other, and they are as lofty as a first-class railway carriage.'

Construction and opening

By the end of July the tender of James Gowans for construction of the track between Haymarket and Bernard Street (including the line by St Andrews Square and York Place) was accepted and work commenced on Monday 7 August 1871, with a required completion date of end November. For every week beyond that date Gowans was liable to a penalty of £200, for every week in advance he was to receive a like bonus. 'Before the denizens of the locality were well awake, half the street between Coates Crescent and Maitland Street was torn up, and tons of iron and granite blocks laid down. Operations will be commenced at once from the Leith end, as also at some half-dozen places along the route; so that there is every prospect of the undertaking being finished by November'.[48] Gowans was a quarry master and railway contractor who later (in 1885) became Edinburgh's Lord Dean of Guild and was then knighted. [The Dean of Guild Court at that time fulfilled in the city essentially as today's Planning and Building Control Departments.] At an early stage the company appears to have fallen out with Bouch, as no reference is made to him after July 1871. From then John Macrae (who had worked under Bouch) acted as engineer to the company.

Construction of the 3½ miles of track was swift and basic. The existing road formation was excavated 10 inches deep to a width of 16 ft 6 inches. Into this was laid concrete 4 inches deep. Longitudinal sleepers of red fir were laid on top of the concrete on which iron rails were screwed, level with the road surface. Tie bars between the sleepers maintained the gauge. By the 1870 Tramways Act, the company had to maintain the width of street occupied by the tramway, plus 18 inches beyond on each side. The rails intended were to be 60 lb/yard, but due to supply difficulties, most were actually only 52 lb/yard. The Road Trust's engineer was very critical of this rail fixing method, saying that the vertical screwed bolts through the thinnest part of the rail would simply direct rain-water into the timber and cause rot. He was soon proved to be only too correct.

With track construction almost complete, a practical experiment was conducted in the Caledonian Railway goods yard, off Lothian Road. To demonstrate the carrying capacity of the rail, a section of track was laid at the end of one of the sidings. On to this several railway wagons, of up to 8 tons weight, were shunted with no ill-effect. It was found however that the wagon wheels flanges could not fit into the narrow groove of the tram rail.[49] It was also found that where the wheels did run in the rail grooves, these had moved closer by ¾ inch. This was a precursor to a similar test in Glasgow where the same process proved that, should it be intended to run railway wagons on the tramway, the rails had to allow the wagon wheel flanges to run on the base of the groove. Tramway rails throughout the west of Scotland were hence laid to 4 ft 7¾ ins gauge to permit this possibility. As the first section of track in Glasgow's Great Western Road was already at the wider gauge, it had to be lifted and relaid.[50]

To work the Edinburgh lines an order was placed with the Tramway Car and Works Company of Greenwich for twenty cars, the first of which was delivered on 20 October to the Caley goods yard off Lothian Road. It was placed on the new Princes Street track and pulled to Croall's stables at Middlefield (Shrubhill) where a track was laid to new car sheds . With the rails cleaned out to permit this, Gowans considered he had met the contract terms and claimed his bonus of five weeks at £200 per week and it was proposed that the line would open on 1 November.[51] As each batch of new cars arrived, passers-by took the chance of a free ride on the new vehicles, all aware of an immediate great improvement over the old buses. On 27 October the inspection prior to public use was undertaken by Colonel Yolland of the Board of Trade. He walked the route, inspecting it minutely, and had a car in attendance which was taken up and down Leith Street several times – without mishap. The next few days were occupied accustoming horses and drivers to their new tasks.

There were already, however, criticisms being voiced relating to the standard of the materials and workmanship of the permanent way. An independent engineer, Hugh C Bell, was employed by the council to examine the work, of which he was highly critical. He found many shortcomings; the paving, concrete, sleepers, the quality of the timber, tie rods, the rail fixings – practically nothing, according to him conformed to specification. All had been sacrificed for speed to complete and claim the bonus. In particular he condemned the concrete foundations, said to be of inferior materials (mud or dirty sand) which would fail. The curve between York Place and North St Andrew Street was 'a most reprehensible piece of work … and has destroyed the street. Hurried work is never good work …'. The only satisfactory items were the castings for points and crossings.

These matters were put to the Company, who responded that Bell had exceeded his duties, that his knowledge of tramway construction was superficial and his statements inaccurate while his report displayed his *animus* against the company.[52] Their engineer, John Macrae, disagreed with virtually every element raised by Bell; on the matter of the concrete base, however, he had to accept that there was justification for some criticism, since on more than one occasion he had required the contractor to replace unsatisfactory work. At York Place corner, the outer rail had been raised 2 inches to give superelevation; this he considered had improved the roadway at this point. Macrae ended '[Bell's] objections to the details of construction were often of the most frivolous description, and clearly showed what he himself admits, that his education in tramway construction began with his appointment, and was not very far advanced when he drew up this report …'. It is remarkable that such exchanges were so quickly made public, when in today's climate, commercial confidentiality would be used as an excuse for 'no comment', or recourse would be made to the Freedom of Information Act to uncover any (probably heavily redacted) exchanges.

It was only when sufficient cars had been received that a timetable was put to the Magistrates, the first day of operation being Monday 6 November 1871. The cars appeared on the streets, operating to the timetable sanctioned, without fanfare or ceremony.[53] The York Place line was not in use, but the number of passengers, some 12,000 – many no doubt merely along to experience the new mode of transport – 'exceeded the most sanguine expectations of the promoters … two or three times the cars ran off the rails, but they were drawn on to the track again without the cars stopping …'. Track was double throughout, with just a short

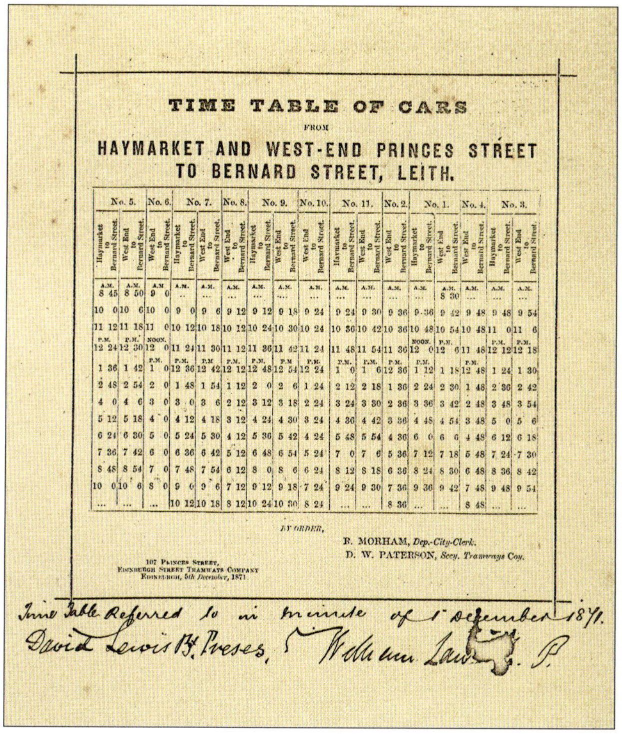
TIME TABLE OF CARS
FROM
HAYMARKET AND WEST-END PRINCES STREET
TO BERNARD STREET, LEITH.

No. 5. Haymarket to Bernard Street.	No. 5. West End to Bernard Street.	No. 6. West End to Bernard Street.	No. 7. Haymarket to Bernard Street.	No. 7. West End to Bernard Street.	No. 8. West End to Bernard Street.	No. 9. Haymarket to Bernard Street.	No. 9. West End to Bernard Street.	No. 10. West End to Bernard Street.	No. 11. Haymarket to Bernard Street.	No. 11. West End to Bernard Street.	No. 2. West End to Bernard Street.	No. 1. Haymarket to Bernard Street.	No. 1. West End to Bernard Street.	No. 4. West End to Bernard Street.	No. 3. Haymarket to Bernard Street.	No. 3. West End to Bernard Street.
A.M. 8 45	A.M. 8 50	A.M. 9 0	A.M. ...	A.M. ...	A.M. ...	A.M. ...	A.M. ...	A.M. ...	A.M. ...	A.M. ...	A.M. ...	A.M. ...	A.M. 8 30	A.M. ...	A.M. ...	A.M. ...
10 0	10 6	10 0	9 0	9 6	9 12	9 12	9 18	9 24	9 24	9 30	9 36	9 36	9 42	9 48	9 48	9 54
11 12	11 18	11 0	10 12	10 18	10 12	10 24	10 30	10 24	10 36	10 42	10 36	10 48	10 54	10 48	11 0	11 6
P.M. 12 24	P.M. 12 30	NOON. 12 0	11 24	11 30	11 12	11 36	11 42	11 24	11 48	11 54	11 36	NOON. 12 0	P.M. 12 6	11 48	P.M. 12 12	P.M. 12 18
1 36	1 42	P.M. 1 0	P.M. 12 36	P.M. 12 42	P.M. 12 12	P.M. 12 48	P.M. 12 54	P.M. 12 24	P.M. 1 0	P.M. 1 6	P.M. 12 36	P.M. 1 12	1 18	P.M. 12 48	1 24	1 30
2 48	2 54	2 0	1 48	1 54	1 12	2 0	2 6	1 24	2 12	2 18	1 36	2 24	2 30	1 48	2 36	2 42
4 0	4 6	3 0	3 0	3 6	2 12	3 12	3 18	2 24	3 24	3 30	2 36	3 36	3 42	2 48	3 48	3 54
5 12	5 18	4 0	4 12	4 18	3 12	4 24	4 30	3 24	4 36	4 42	3 36	4 48	4 54	3 48	5 0	5 6
6 24	6 30	5 0	5 24	5 30	4 12	5 36	5 42	4 24	5 48	5 54	4 36	6 0	6 6	4 48	6 12	6 18
7 36	7 42	6 0	6 36	6 42	5 12	6 48	6 54	5 24	7 0	7 6	5 36	7 12	7 18	5 48	7 24	7 30
8 48	8 54	7 0	7 48	7 54	6 12	8 0	8 6	6 24	8 12	8 18	6 36	8 24	8 30	6 48	8 36	8 42
10 0	10 6	8 0	9 0	9 6	7 12	9 12	9 18	7 24	9 24	9 30	7 36	9 36	9 42	7 48	9 48	9 54
...	...	...	10 12	10 18	8 12	10 24	10 30	8 24	...	...	8 36	...	...	8 48	...	...

BY ORDER,
R. MORHAM, *Dep.-City-Clerk.*
D. W. PATERSON, *Secy. Tramways Coy.*

107 PRINCES STREET,
EDINBURGH STREET TRAMWAYS COMPANY
EDINBURGH, *5th December*, 1871

Time Table Referred to in minute of 1st December 1871.
David Lewis Bt. Preses, William Law J.P.

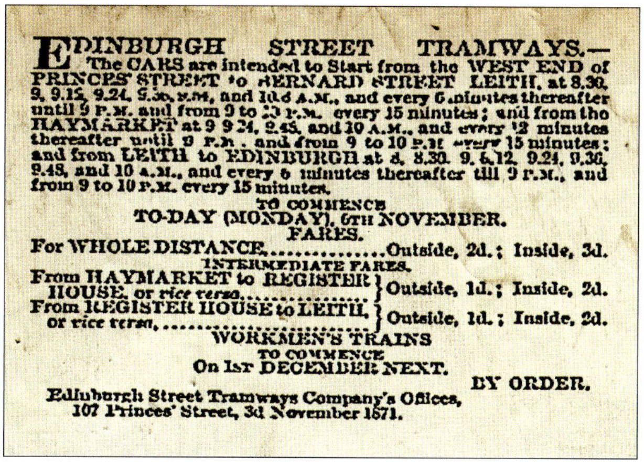
EDINBURGH STREET TRAMWAYS.—The CARS are intended to Start from the WEST END of PRINCES' STREET to BERNARD STREET LEITH, at 8.30, 9, 9.15, 9.24, 9.30, [illegible], and 10 A.M., and every 6 minutes thereafter until 9 P.M. and from 9 to 10 P.M. every 15 minutes; and from the HAYMARKET at 9 9.24, 9.45, and 10 A.M., and every 12 minutes thereafter until 9 P.M. and from 9 to 10 P.M. every 15 minutes; and from LEITH to EDINBURGH at 8, 8.30, 9, 9.12, 9.24, 9.36, 9.48, and 10 A.M., and every 6 minutes thereafter till 9 P.M., and from 9 to 10 P.M. every 15 minutes.
TO COMMENCE
TO-DAY (MONDAY), 6TH NOVEMBER.
FARES.
For WHOLE DISTANCE.................Outside, 2d.; Inside, 3d.
INTERMEDIATE FARES.
From HAYMARKET to REGISTER HOUSE, or *vice versa*.................. } Outside, 1d.; Inside, 2d.
From REGISTER HOUSE to LEITH, or *vice versa*,.......................... } Outside, 1d.; Inside, 2d.
WORKMEN'S TRAINS
TO COMMENCE
On 1ST DECEMBER NEXT.
BY ORDER.
Edinburgh Street Tramways Company's Offices,
107 Princes' Street, 3d November 1871.

Above. *Scotsman* 6 November 1871. First timetable advertisement for trams.

Left. The first timetable, authorised on 1 December 1871, is very detailed, and indicates each journey by each car. A six-minute frequency service was provided for most of the day from West End, with every second car continuing to Haymarket. This timetable perpetuated the Magistrates' habit (their practice for existing omnibus timetables) of defining each journey by vehicle number. This led to operators using transferrable number plates on their cars and buses.

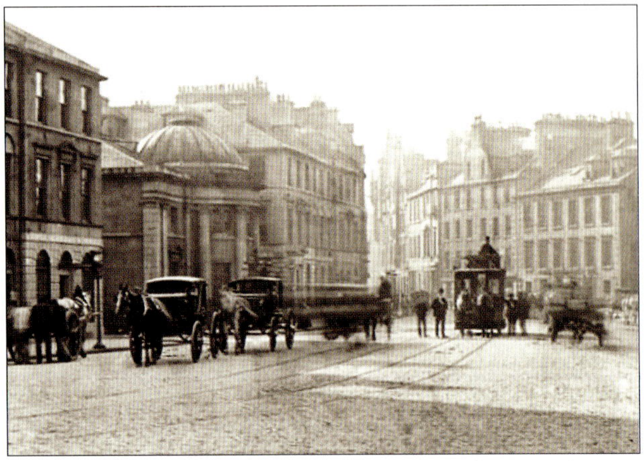

A very early scene at Bernard Street terminus of the initial route. The street appearance and architecture have not changed perceptibly over the century and (almost) half since this photograph was taken. The tramcar is one of the very earliest designs, with light spiral ladders for access to the upper deck seats.

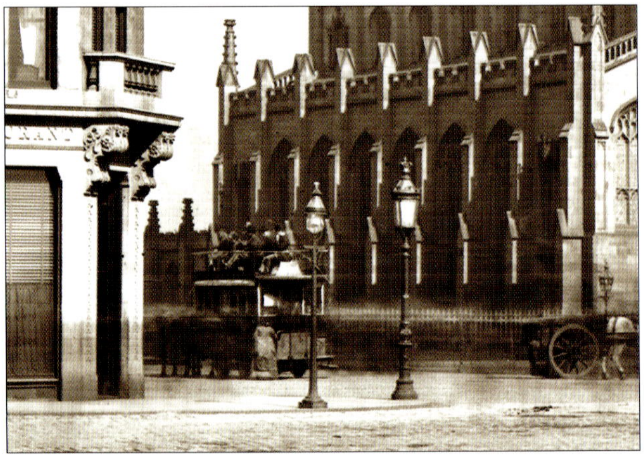

The West End and St John's Episcopal Church from Hope Street. These first cars appear to have soon had a sloping board fixed over the ventilators, perhaps to prevent ingress of rain-water.

single length in Constitution Street. The rails continued for 100 yards up Waterloo Place, which was later used as a terminus for cars via York Place. At the time of construction, points and crossings were laid for planned extensions, including at the foot of Frederick and Hanover Streets, but these were removed within a year. Paper tickets were issued with advance purchases offered at a discount. The new cars, intended to weigh less than two tons, were found to be so heavy that on the steepest stretch of Leith Street four horses were required to pull heavily laden vehicles. By the first week, any cars not delivered were cancelled, and a fleet of lighter cars ordered.[54] This major problem was to dog the fortunes of Edinburgh's horse tramways for their entire existence.

The first shareholders' meeting was held at the Company's offices at 107 Princes Street on 27 December, when Dr Wood was appointed deputy-chairman and from the first days he took an active part in management of the undertaking. John Macrae gave a report on the achievements of the previous six months, and noted that Gowans had started to build the next line, along Great Junction Street, on the same terms and conditions as before. Despite a promising start, it was considered premature to contemplate a dividend.

Expansion from the initial single route was necessary, and this was in now process. [Resonating with the situation regarding Edinburgh's new tram] It appears that the Great Junction Street line opened (without Board of Trade inspection) during the last week of March

EDINBURGH STREET TRAMWAYS.

CARS ON EDINBURGH AND LEITH SECTION.

HAYMARKET TO LEITH—
8.20, 8.40, and 9 a.m., and every eight minutes thereafter till 9.32 p.m., after which at 9.48 and 9.56 p.m.

EAST END OF PRINCES' STREET TO LEITH—
8.36, 8.56, 9.16, 9.24, 9.32, 9.40, 9.48, 9.56, and 10 a.m.; and every four minutes thereafter till 9.52 p.m.; after which at 10.4, 10.8, 10.12, 10.16 p.m.

LEITH TO EDINBURGH—
(From Bermard Street to the East End of Princes' Street, by way of York Place.)
9.36 and 10 a.m., and every eight minutes thereafter till 10.16 p.m.
(To Haymarket, by way of Leith Street)—
8, 8.30, and 9 a.m., and every sixteen minutes thereafter till 9.32 p.m
(From the Junction Bridge)—
8.40 and 9.8 a.m., and every sixteen minutes thereafter till 9.8 p.m., after which at 9.40 p.m.

N.B.—All the CARS between BERNARD STREET and the EAST END of PRINCES' STREET go to Edinburgh by YORK PLACE and return to Leith by LEITH STREET. Those between LEITH and HAYMARKET go and return by LEITH STREET

Tickets of the value of 10s. and upwards, can be obtained at the Office at a discount of 10 per cent.; also School Tickets, price 2d. and 1½d. each when bought in lots of the value of 10s.

Complaints to be made to the Secretary in writing, specifying the number of the Conductor, and the hour at which the matter complained of occurred.

Time Tables of the Hours may be obtained at the Company's Office.

BY ORDER.

EDINBURGH STREET TRAMWAYS COMPANY'S OFFICE,
107 Princes' Street, 21st March 1872.

Scotsman 30 March 1872. Tram timetable

1872 (probably on the 25th). Cars now ran from Haymarket to Bernard Street Leith with every fourth one running to Junction Bridge; an additional service ran from Bernard Street to the east end of Princes Street coming up by York Place and returning by Leith Street.

Edinburgh's Magistrates rapidly realised that, while they had bye laws for omnibus traffic, they had nothing dealing with tramways, so proceeded to remedy this matter.[55] By the end of March they laid down their requirements, including, *inter alia*:

> Every car ... to be examined by the Inspector of Hackney Carriages
>
> Every car, before commencing to ply, to have a number issued, which, with owners or contractors name, painted legibly in letters 2 ins long outside … the number of passengers the car is built to carry, inside and outside, with fares, shall also be painted inside in letters 1 inch long.
>
> Every car to have a mat for the floor, no straw or hay to be used except in wet weather
>
> Every car to have ventilators kept in good order; side and door glasses and rods inside to be arranged not to rattle and annoy passengers. A one-stroke bell to be fitted
>
> Every car to have strong iron steps where roof is seated, at each end, also strong fence rails
>
> Every car to have its route painted on outside of car, or on boards fitted to
>
> Car conductors shall wear on their belt, the number of the car of which he is in charge
>
> All cars leaving the Register for Leith to be regulated by the Police so as to give an interval of at least 2 minutes between cars
>
> All cars leaving Pilrig to be regulated to give minimum of 2 minutes between cars
>
> No person to stand between seats when all are full
>
> No car to carry a greater number of passengers than constructed for, allowing every separate seat 18 inch inside and 16 inch outside. [Could this be related to the space necessary to accommodate women's fashions – when that sex were not expected to use the narrow spiral stair to the top deck – generally a male, and smokers preserve?]

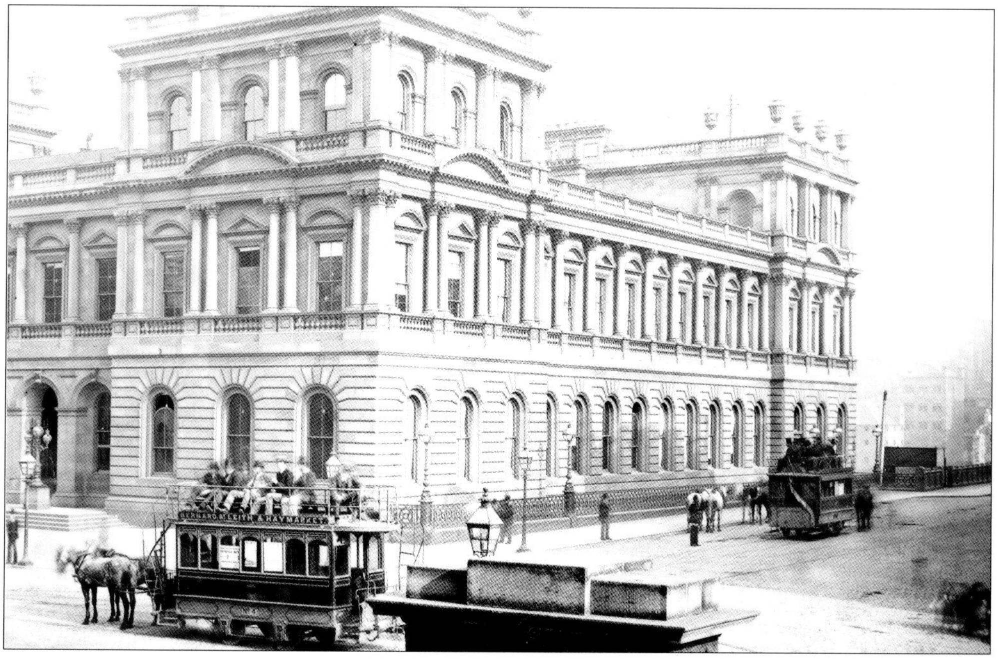

The number plate of car 'No 4' is clearly seen in this view at the General Post Office. This car is quite different in design from the very earliest supplied, but retains some basic features. The stair is of the primitive light spiral design and the suspension is also of an early style; this is probably one of the lighter cars purchased in 1872. One of the window posters refers to the Portobello route, opened in May 1875. A Newington car sits at the end of the North Bridge, one of the original heavy design. (G W Wilson collection, Aberdeen University Library)

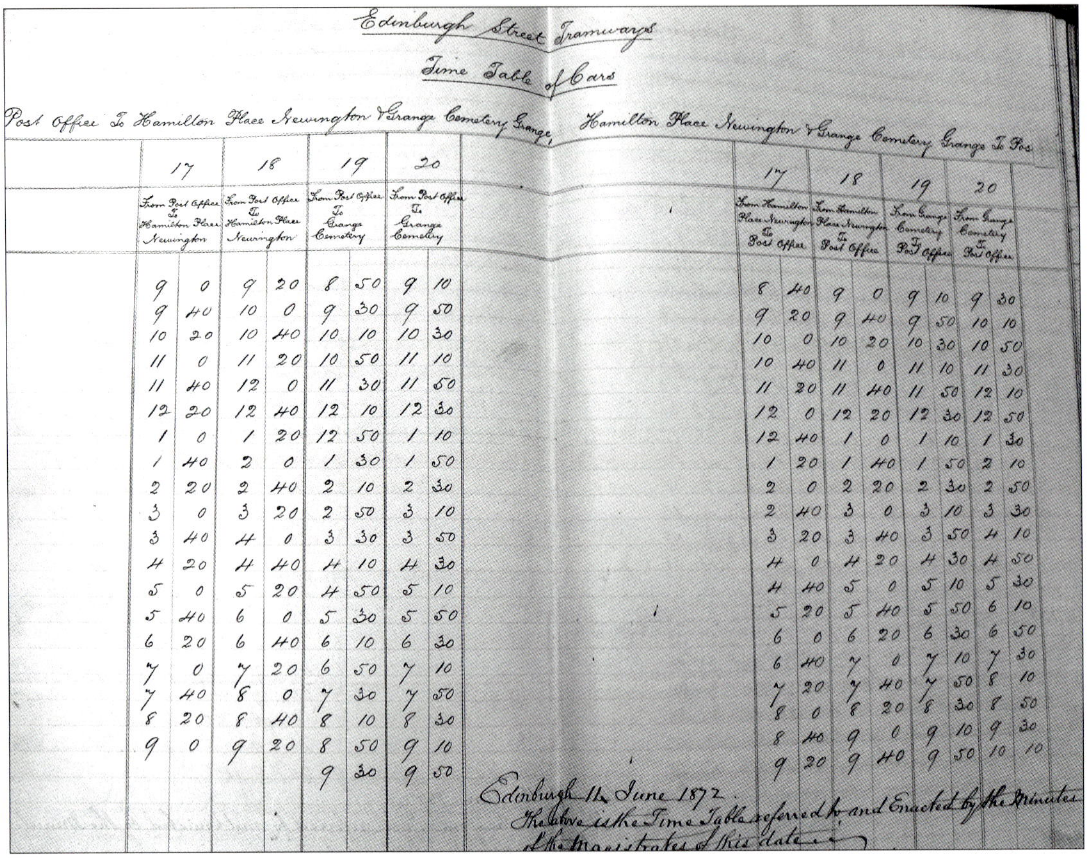

Edinburgh Street Tramways
Time Table of Cars

Post Office To Hamilton Place Newington & Grange Cemetery Grange

17 From Post Office To Hamilton Place Newington		18 From Post Office To Hamilton Place Newington		19 From Post Office To Grange Cemetery		20 From Post Office To Grange Cemetery	
9	0	9	20	8	50	9	10
9	40	10	0	9	30	9	50
10	20	10	40	10	10	10	30
11	0	11	20	10	50	11	10
11	40	12	0	11	30	11	50
12	20	12	40	12	10	12	30
1	0	1	20	12	50	1	10
1	40	2	0	1	30	1	50
2	20	2	40	2	10	2	30
3	0	3	20	2	50	3	10
3	40	4	0	3	30	3	50
4	20	4	40	4	10	4	30
5	0	5	20	4	50	5	10
5	40	6	0	5	30	5	50
6	20	6	40	6	10	6	30
7	0	7	20	6	50	7	10
7	40	8	0	7	30	7	50
8	20	8	40	8	10	8	30
9	0	9	20	8	50	9	10
				9	30	9	50

Hamilton Place Newington & Grange Cemetery Grange To Post Office

17 From Hamilton Place Newington To Post Office		18 From Hamilton Place Newington To Post Office		19 From Grange Cemetery To Post Office		20 From Grange Cemetery To Post Office	
8	40	9	0	9	10	9	30
9	20	9	40	9	50	10	10
10	0	10	20	10	30	10	50
10	40	11	0	11	10	11	30
11	20	11	40	11	50	12	10
12	0	12	20	12	30	12	50
12	40	1	0	1	10	1	30
1	20	1	40	1	50	2	10
2	0	2	20	2	30	2	50
2	40	3	0	3	10	3	30
3	20	3	40	3	50	4	10
4	0	4	20	4	30	4	50
4	40	5	0	5	10	5	30
5	20	5	40	5	50	6	10
6	0	6	20	6	30	6	50
6	40	7	0	7	10	7	30
7	20	7	40	7	50	8	10
8	0	8	20	8	30	8	50
8	40	9	0	9	10	9	30
9	20	9	40	9	50	10	10

Edinburgh 11th June 1872.
The above is the Time Table referred to and Enacted by the Minutes of the Magistrates of this date.

Timetable of June 1872 for Post Office to Newington (Hamilton Place) or Grange Cemetery. Generally a 20-minute service was given, with alternate cars to either terminus. The four cars used, given numbers 17–20, possibly tends to confirm that the first heavy cars numbered sixteen in total.

From 1 May use of the York Place line ceased temporarily and the basic service reverted to Haymarket to Bernard Street, with only limited operation on Junction Street. Gowans, having constructed these initial lines, was now instructed to continue with those on the south side of the city. First tackled was from Register House to Minto Street, which involved laying rails across the North Bridge and up North Bridge Street. It was the council's intention to widen the Bridge and its approach, and they had extracted from the Company, as part of the deal struck when giving their consents, a substantial contribution towards this. Much municipal hot air was generated relating to the question of double track against single track on these streets, but when the line opened on 29 May 1872, double track was laid throughout.

Gowans then pressed on with the line from Princes Street West End, via Tollcross and Grange to meet the recent extension at Salisbury Place. Again many of these streets were narrow, but double track was laid where possible, using numerous cross-over lines to allow cars to operate past any obstruction as required. This new work opened in two sections, Salisbury to Grange Cemetery on 6 July, the remainder on 11 November, the second part delayed by several months by strikes in the contractor's labour force.[56] On this route, four sharp right-angled bends were encountered, all laid as single track. To assist the wheels passing round these curves, the outer rail at each bend was laid upside-down, with its flat un-grooved surface level with the road surface. Gowans had amended the design of track construction, using a rail shape which he later patented, of as it was then called, the champagne-glass shape.[57] This removed the requirement for wooden sleepers, the rail now being laid directly on the concrete foundation.[58] Three services were operated; Bernard Street to Haymarket (showing a red light at night), Bernard Street or Junction Bridge to Newington or Powburn (red and green lights), and the circular route Post Office to Morningside, both clockwise and anti-clockwise (green light).

A rather self-congratulatory tone was evident at the second shareholders' meeting, with a dividend of 8% declared for the half-year – and this before the new work was completed. Six months later, at the third meeting, shareholders heard that they would receive a reduced dividend (6%) on that period's operations, the result of poor weather. Until this time, continuous construction had been undertaken of the authorised lines and the chairman advised that, but for the high cost of labour and iron, construction would have continued on the lines to Roseburn and along Ferry Road (iron had risen from £8.2.6d per ton in 1871 to £16.10s per ton in mid-1873). However as the allowed period for constructing the other lines was coming to an end, they intended to ask Parliament for an Act to

STAGE COACHES.

OFFICE, 4 PRINCES STREET.

EDINBURGH TO		LEAVES.
Bilston,	9.30 a.m. and 4.15 p.m.,	9 and 5.
Blackshiels,	3.30 p.m. Thursdays at 2.30,	8.30 a.m.
Corstorphine,	11. 1.30, 4.15. 8. Saturday, 3 p.m.,	9.20, 12. 3. 8.45.
Dalkeith,	10.30, 4.30, 8,	9. 2. 6.30. Thurs. 2.30.
Dunfermline,	8. 12. 4.	7.40, 11.45, 3.45.
Greenlaw,	9.30 a.m., 4.15 p.m.,	8.50 and 4.40.
*Inverkeithing,	8. 12. 4.	8. 12. 4.
Lasswade,	10. 1. 4, 8,	8.30, 12. 2.30, 6.15.
Lauder,	3.30 p.m. Thursdays at 2.30,	7 a.m.
Loanhead,	10. 1, 4, 8,	8.45, 12.15, 2.45, 6.30.
Musselburgh,	11. 2, 6, 8.30,	8.45, 12.40, 4.15, 7.15.
Pathhead,	3.30 p.m. Thursdays at 2.30,	8.45 a.m.
Penicuik,	9.30 a.m. and 4.15 p.m.,	8.45 and 4.30.
Portobello,	11. 11.30, 12, 1, 2, 3, 4, 5, 6, 7, 8, 8.30, 9.45,	9.10, 10, 11 a.m.; 12; 1, 2, 3, 4, 4.35, 6, 7, 7.35, 9 p.m.
Ratho,	4.15, and on Saturdays 3 p.m.,	8.30 a.m.
Roslin,	11 a.m., summer months only,	3.45 p.m.
South Queensferry,	8, 12, 4,	8.45, 12.45, 4.45.

* Passengers to and from Inverkeithing and Edinburgh pay 6d. each at Queensferry.

CITY OMNIBUSES.

EDINBURGH AND LEITH, HAYMARKET AND REGISTER OFFICE.

The Omnibuses and Tramway Cars on this route run so frequently as to pass the REGISTER OFFICE every few minutes during the day. The Tramway Cars run between Bernard Street, Junction Bridge, Haymarket, *via* Register Office. The Omnibuses run between Bernard Street and High Street only. Fares between Leith, Register Office, and High Street, Inside 2d., Outside 1d. To Haymarket from Leith, Inside 3d., Outside 2d. From Register Office, Inside 2d., Outside 1d.

NEWHAVEN AND MOUND, *VIA* INVERLEITH ROW.

From Mound at 9 a.m., and every hour thereafter till 7, and at 8.30 p.m.
„ Newhaven at 9.30 a.m., and every hour thereafter till 7.30, and at 9 p.m. Fares 3d. and 2d.

MORNINGSIDE AND REGISTER OFFICE.

From Morningside to Register Office, *via* Newington, at 8.35 a.m., and every 20 minutes until 9.15 p.m., returning *via* Lothian Road at 9.5 a.m., and every 20 minutes until 8.15 p.m.
„ Morningside to Register Office, *via* Lothian Road, at 8.45 a.m., and every 20 minutes until 9.25 p.m., returning *via* Newington at 9.15 a.m., and every 20 minutes until 8.55 p.m. Thus giving a service to Morningside every 10 minutes. Fares, Inside 3d., Outside 2d.

STOCKBRIDGE AND NEWINGTON.

From Stockbridge at 9.10 a.m., and every twenty minutes till 8.50 p.m. Last 'Bus, 9.45 p.m.
„ Newington at 9.20 a.m., and every twenty minutes till 9 p.m. Fares, Inside 3d., Outside 2d.

REGISTER OFFICE TO NEWINGTON.

From Register to Newington, and *vice versa*, by Tramway Car or Omnibus every five minutes during the day. Fares, Inside 2d., Outside 1d.

From Register Office, by the Bridges, to Grange and Morningside, returning by Lothian Road and Princes Street.

17	19	28	26	21	24
A.M. 7 55	A.M. 8 15	A.M. 10 45	A.M. 10 25	A.M. 8 35	A.M. 10 5
8 55	9 15	11 45	11 25	9 35	11 5
9 55	10 15	P.M. 12 45	P.M. 12 25	10 35	P.M. 12 5
10 55	11 15	1 45	1 25	11 35	1 5
11 55	P.M. 12 15	2 45	2 25	P.M. 12 35	2 5
P.M. 12 55	1 15	3 45	3 25	1 35	3 5
1 55	2 15	4 45	4 25	2 35	4 5
2 55	3 15	5 45	5 25	3 35	5 5
3 55	4 15	6 45	6 25	4 35	6 5
4 55	5 15	7 45	7 25	5 35	7 5
5 55	6 15	8 45	8 25	6 35	8 5
6 55	7 15	9 45	9 25	7 35	9 5

From Register Office, by Princes Street and Lothian Road, to Morningside and Grange, returning by the Bridges.

18	20	22	27	23	25
A.M. 8 0	A.M. 8 30	A.M. 9 10	A.M. 10 40	A.M. 9 50	A.M. 10 20
8 50	9 30	10 10	11 40	10 50	11 20
10 0	10 30	11 10	P.M. 12 40	11 50	P.M. 12 20
11 0	11 30	P.M. 12 10	1 40	P.M. 12 50	1 20
NOON. 12 0	P.M. 12 30	1 10	2 40	1 50	2 20
P.M. 1 0	1 30	2 10	3 40	2 50	3 20
2 0	2 30	3 10	4 40	3 50	4 20
3 0	3 30	4 10	5 40	4 50	5 20
4 0	4 30	5 10	6 40	5 50	6 20
5 0	5 30	6 10	7 40	6 50	7 20
6 0	6 30	7 10	8 40	7 50	8 20
7 0	7 30	8 10	9 40	8 50	9 20

COLTBRIDGE AND POWBURN.

30	31	29	30	31	29
Coltbridge to Powburn.	Coltbridge to Powburn.	Coltbridge. to Powburn.	Powburn to Coltbridge.	Powburn to Coltbridge.	Powburn to Coltbridge.
A.M. 9 15	A.M. 10 15	A.M. 8 15	A.M. 8 30	A.M. 11 0	A.M. 9 0
10 45	11 45	9 45	10 0	P.M. 12 30	10 30
P.M. 12 15	P.M. 1 15	11 15	11 30	2 0	NOON. 12 0
1 45	2 45	P.M. 12 45	P.M. 1 0	3 30	P.M. 1 30
3 15	4 15	2 15	2 30	5 0	3 0
4 45	5 45	3 45	4 0	6 30	4 30
6 15	7 15	5 15	5 30	8 0	6 0
7 45	8 45	6 45	7 0	9 30	7 30
...	...	8 15	8 30	...	...

Edinburgh 9th January 1874
Referred to and Enacted by
Minute of the Magistrates
of this date. —
Lord Provost.

Above. *The Edinburgh and Leith Post Office Directory* for 1872–3 gives a comprehensive summary of country coaches, omnibuses and tramcars then being operated.

Left. Timetables of 9 January 1874 for the Morningside Circle and Coltbridge to Powburn routes. The former used six cars on the outer or clockwise circle and a like number for the inner anti-clockwise direction, this remaining the pattern for many years. The highest number of tramcar licence number now used was 31.

extend this time. He also alluded to the cost of the horsing contract, suggesting that the directors would be looking at alternative motive power, and that powers for this should be sought at the same time.

When put to Parliament however, the Bill was completely emasculated, with all contentious elements deleted. Dropped were clauses to lay tramways in to the passenger areas of the railway stations at Haymarket and Princes Street, to construct crossovers and passing places, to carry small parcels, and – most importantly, to use mechanical rather than horse power to pull the cars. This last followed the bad experience of trying to operate with the original heavy vehicles up Edinburgh's hills, plus the punitive contract for horsing which had been naively entered into with Croall. The directors rapidly became aware that they had fallen into a very poor agreement in their initial anxiety to placate Croall and remove his competition. The most suitable type of mechanical power for street tramways was a subject which taxed the ingenuity of many a Victorian mind. Such was the degree of interest in the quest, that the Society of Arts in 1872 created a medal for the best engine to replace horse power on tramways; this must surely have engaged the Edinburgh Company's directors. Despite the now limited scope of the Bill it was nevertheless strenuously opposed by the City and its only achievement was a one year extension of time for unbuilt lines.

It was therefore no surprise when the Company announced that it would return to Parliament a year later with a more comprehensive Bill. This was to remove the obligation to build all lines north of Princes Street and also that from Tollcross to Chambers Street. It had been proved by bitter experience that the gradients of the existing lines severely taxed the horses, and with the gradients of the northern lines even steeper, it was decided that it was quite impractical to work conventional horse tramways. Instead powers were requested for small omnibuses to serve these areas. A new enterprise, the Edinburgh and Leith General Omnibus Company had a short life competing with the trams, but when they went out of business the Company purchased their five vehicles and leased their

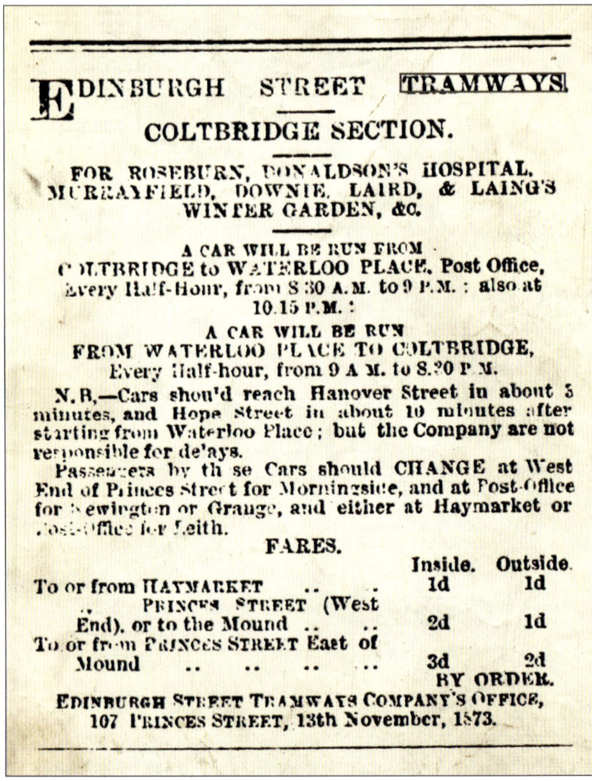
EDINBURGH STREET TRAMWAYS

COLTBRIDGE SECTION.

FOR ROSEBURN, DONALDSON'S HOSPITAL, MURRAYFIELD, DOWNIE, LAIRD, & LAING'S WINTER GARDEN, &c.

A CAR WILL BE RUN FROM COLTBRIDGE to WATERLOO PLACE, Post Office, Every Half-Hour, from 8.30 A.M. to 9 P.M.: also at 10.15 P.M.:

A CAR WILL BE RUN FROM WATERLOO PLACE TO COLTBRIDGE, Every Half-hour, from 9 A.M. to 8.30 P.M.

N.B.—Cars should reach Hanover Street in about 5 minutes, and Hope Street in about 10 minutes after starting from Waterloo Place; but the Company are not responsible for delays.

Passengers by these Cars should CHANGE at West End of Princes Street for Morningside, and at Post-Office for Newington or Grange, and either at Haymarket or Post-Office for Leith.

FARES.

	Inside.	Outside.
To or from HAYMARKET	1d	1d
" PRINCES STREET (West End), or to the Mound	2d	1d
To or from PRINCES STREET East of Mound	3d	2d

BY ORDER.

EDINBURGH STREET TRAMWAYS COMPANY'S OFFICE, 107 PRINCES STREET, 13th November, 1873.

Edinburgh Evening News 15 November 1873

stables to end this new undertaking. The Bill included an extension of time to build the Portobello route – the only other part of the original scheme then not built. As the North Bridge widening (started in November 1873) was not completed within the allowed time – although the Tramways Company had paid their £2500 – an extension of time for this work was also included.

Operating difficulties

However the Tramways Company was now coming under fire from a new direction. The Scottish Society for the Prevention of Cruelty to Animals (SSPCA) was most vociferous regarding what was perceived as cruelty to, and abuse of, the tram horses. The Society obtained a report from two veterinary experts who

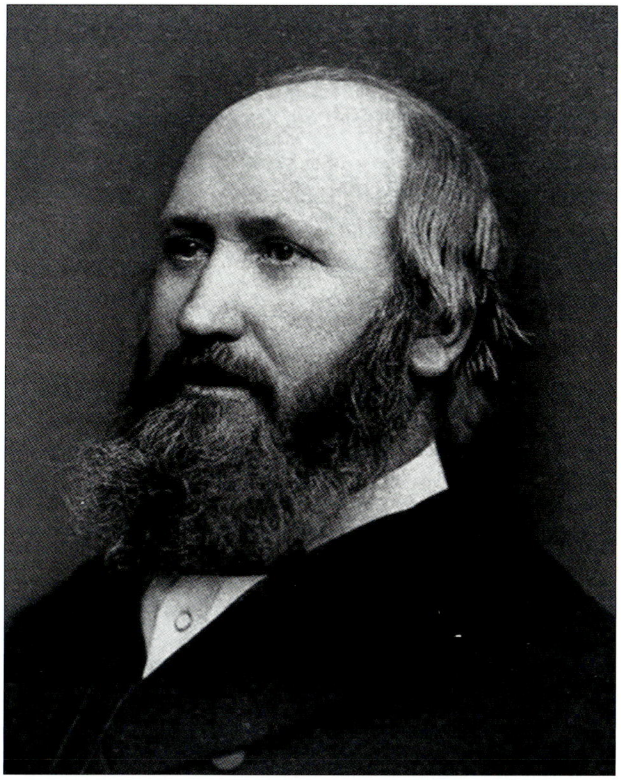

Portrait of Dr Alexander Wood, 1817 – 1884, physician (and inventor of the first true hypodermic syringe) and tramway manager extraordinary.

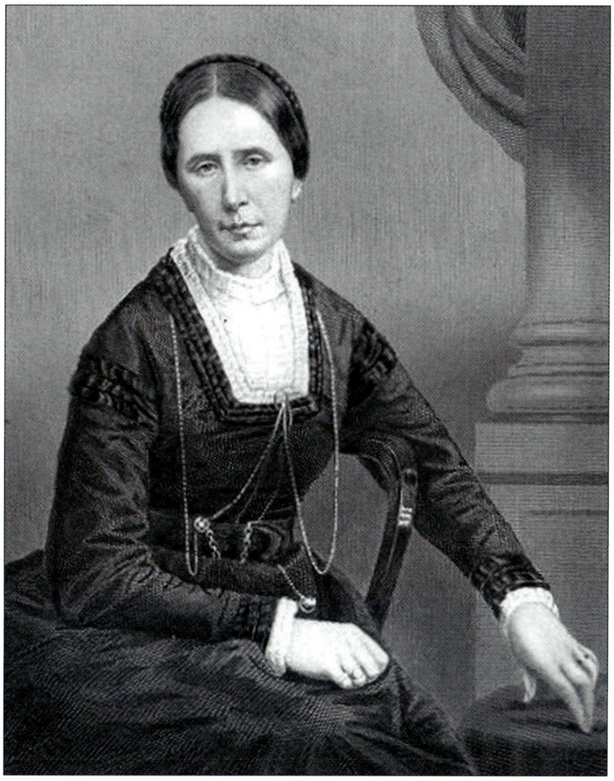

Angela Burdett-Coutts, 1814 – 1906, richest woman in Britain, philanthropist, first woman Baroness in her own right, first woman Burgess of Edinburgh, and possibly bane of Wood's life.

recorded their concerns in a *Report on the General Condition of the Horses Used in the Tramway Cars in Edinburgh*. Some 25% to 33% of the stud was considered unfit, with the best animals kept for the prestigious but less demanding Morningside and Newington routes. The poorest, smallest, animals were mostly to be found on the Leith routes, and comment was made that the small cars should be used here, rather than the heaviest. It was noted that horses had great difficulty in hot weather, when the granite setts became polished, in heavy rain, in snow – and indeed the only suitable conditions were when there was light rain and a thin layer of mud on the road! A box for sand was hung from the front dash of the car, and from this the driver had to throw handfuls under the horses' hooves whenever required. This, considered the SSPCA vets, was a highly dangerous practice.

These concerns were articulated by no less a person than the redoubtable Baroness Angela Burdett-Coutts, who (rather pointedly) at the SSPCA meeting presented medals to drivers of the country buses in appreciation of 'care and kindness to horses under their charge'. A silver medal was presented to William Elliot, driver for 30 years of the Musselburgh coach.[59] The formidable spinster took a special interest in the tram horses' welfare, and put her strong feelings directly to the Lord Provost and to Dr Wood. She was a force to be reckoned with throughout the land; the richest woman, a philanthropist of note (having inherited a fortune via the Coutts' banking group) and the first Baroness created in her own right by Queen Victoria. She raised many eyebrows when (as probably the most eligible woman in Britain) at the age of 67 she married her 38 years younger secretary! The tramway officials responded 'when the North Bridge was widened only a single line of rails would be used for the tramway

Tram and bus information from the *Edinburgh & Leith Post Office Directory* of 1873–4

TRAMWAY CARS.

FROM LEITH (Bernard Street and Junction Bridge) TO COLTBRIDGE AND NEWINGTON as follows:—

Note.—Those marked * run from Junction Bridge to Coltbridge and Bernard Street to Newington. All others run from Bernard Street to Coltbridge.

A.M.	A.M.	A.M.	A.M.	NOON.	P.M.	P.M.	P.M.	P.M.	P.M.	P.M.	P.M.	P.M.	P.M.	P.M.
...	9.0	*10.0	11.0	12.0	1.0	2.0	*3.0	*4.0	5.0	6.0	7.0	8.0	*9.0	...
...	9.5	10.5	*11.5	12.5	1.5	2.5	3.5	4.5	*5.5	6.5	7.5	8.5	9.5	...
...	9.10	10.10	11.10	*12.10	*1.10	2.10	3.10	4.10	5.10	*6.10	7.10	8.10	9.10	10.10
...	9.15	10.15	11.15	12.15	1.15	*2.15	3.15	4.15	5.15	6.15	*7.15	*8.15	9.15	...
*...	*9.20	*10.20	11.20	12.20	1.20	2.20	*3.20	4.20	5.20	6.20	7.20	8.20	*9.20	...
8.25	9.25	10.25	*11.25	12.25	1.25	2.25	3.25	*4.25	*5.25	6.25	7.25	8.25	9.25	...
...	9.30	10.30	11.30	*12.30	1.30	2.30	3.30	4.30	5.30	*6.30	7.30	8.30	9.30	...
8.35	9.35	10.35	11.35	12.35	*1.35	*2.35	3.35	4.35	5.35	6.35	*7.35	8.35	9.35	...
...	*9.40	10.40	11.40	12.40	1.40	2.40	*3.40	4.40	5.40	6.40	7.40	*8.40	*9.40	...
...	9.45	*10.45	*11.45	12.45	1.45	2.45	3.45	*4.45	5.45	6.45	7.45	8.45	9.45	...
8.50	9.50	10.50	11.50	*12.50	1.50	2.50	3.50	4.50	*5.50	*6.50	*7.50	8.50	...	...
8.55	9.55	10.55	11.55	12.55	*1.55	2.55	3.55	4.55	5.55	6.55	7.55	8.55	9.55	...

FROM COLTBRIDGE AND NEWINGTON TO LEITH.

Note.—Those marked * run from Coltbridge to Junction Bridge and Newington to Bernard Street. All others run from Coltbridge to Bernard Street.

A.M.	A.M.	A.M.	A.M.	NOON.	P.M.	P.M.	P.M.	P.M.	P.M.	P.M.	P.M.	P.M.	P.M.	P.M.
...	*9.0	10.0	11.0	12.0	1.0	2.0	*3.0	4.0	5.0	6.0	7.0	*8.0	*9.0	10.0
...	9.5	*10.5	*11.5	12.5	1.5	2.5	3.5	*4.5	5.5	6.5	7.5	8.5	9.5	10.5
...	9.10	10.10	11.10	*12.10	1.10	2.10	3.10	4.10	*5.10	*6.10	7.10	8.10	9.10	10.10
...	9.15	10.15	11.15	12.15	*1.15	2.15	3.15	4.15	5.15	6.15	*7.15	8.15	9.15	...
...	*9.20	10.20	11.20	12.20	1.20	*2.20	*3.20	4.20	5.20	6.20	7.20	*8.20	9.20	...
8.25	9.25	*10.25	11.25	12.25	1.25	2.25	3.25	*4.25	5.25	6.25	7.25	8.25	*9.25	...
...	9.30	10.30	*11.30	*12.30	1.30	2.30	3.30	4.30	*5.30	6.30	7.30	8.30	9.30	...
...	9.35	10.35	11.35	12.35	*1.35	2.35	3.35	4.35	5.35	*6.35	*7.35	8.35	...	...
8.40	*9.40	10.40	11.40	12.40	1.40	*2.40	3.40	4.40	5.40	6.40	7.40	*8.40	9.40	...
8.45	9.45	*10.45	11.45	12.45	1.45	2.45	*3.45	*4.45	5.45	6.45	7.45	8.45	*9.45	...
...	9.50	10.50	*11.50	12.50	1.50	2.50	3.50	4.50	*5.50	6.50	7.50	8.50	9.50	...
...	9.55	10.55	11.55	*12.55	*1.55	2.55	3.55	4.55	5.55	*6.55	7.55	8.55	...	...

REGISTER OFFICE TO MORNINGSIDE *via* LOTHIAN ROAD AND NEWINGTON.

ROUTES.	A.M.	A.M.	A.M.	A.M.			P.M.	P.M.	P.M.	P.M.
Lothian Road .	...	8.0	9.0	10.0	and every hour thereafter till		7.0	...	...	...
Newington .	7.55	...	9.6	10.6	,,	,,	7.6	...	...	...
Lothian Road .	...	8.12	9.12	10.12	,,	,,	7.12	...	...	...
Newington .	...	8.18	9.18	10.18	,,	,,	7.18	...	...	...
Lothian Road .	...	8.30	9.24	10.24	,,	,,	7.24	8.24	...	...
Newington .	...	...	...	10.30	,,	,,	7.30	8.30	9.30	...
Lothian Road .	...	...	9.36	10.36	,,	,,	7.36	...	...	...
Newington .	...	8.40	9.42	10.42	,,	,,	7.42	...	...	...
Lothian Road .	...	...	...	10.48	,,	,,	7.48	8.48	9.40	...
Newington .	...	...	...	10.54	,,	,,	7.54	8.54	9.50	...

MORNINGSIDE TO REGISTER OFFICE *via* LOTHIAN ROAD AND NEWINGTON.

ROUTES.	A.M.	A.M.	A.M.	A.M.			P.M.	P.M.	P.M.	P.M.
Lothian Road .	...	...	...	11.5	and every hour thereafter till		7.5	8.5	9.5	10.5
Newington .	...	9.0	10.6	11.6	,,	,,	7.6	8.6	...	10.10
Lothian Road .	...	9.15	10.17	11.17	,,	,,	7.17	8.17	...	...
Newington .	...	...	...	11.18	,,	,,	7.18	8.18	9.18	...
Lothian Road .	8.30	...	...	11.29	,,	,,	7.29	8.29	9.29	10.25
Newington .	8.30	9.30	10.30	11.30	,,	,,	7.30	...	...	...
Lothian Road .	...	9.41	10.41	11.41	,,	,,	7.41	...	...	...
Newington .	8.42	9.42	10.42	11.42	,,	,,	7.42	...	...	...
Lothian Road .	8.53	9.53	10.53	11.53	,,	,,	7.53	...	...	...
Newington .	...	9.54	10.54	11.54	,,	,,	7.54	8.54	...	...

traffic, thus the speed in going up the incline at the south end of the bridge may be increased, and the horse draught very much lightened …'[60] As the existing tracks were double there, it is difficult to follow this logic. Lighter cars were to be substituted, and she opined that trace-boys and drivers should be licensed and issued with badges. This Wood objected to 'I am sorry to say that among the drivers and stable-men drunkenness is very prevalent, leading to constant changes which licensing would render very troublesome …'[61]

An extension from Haymarket to Coltbridge [now

July 1875 timetables for trams plying between West End of Princes Street and Newhaven (Stanley Road). These added workings for vehicles numbered up to 39.

EDINBURGH STREET TRAMWAYS.

TIME TABLE OF CARS.

Commencing on 10th July 1875.

WEST END OF PRINCES STREET AND STANLEY ROAD.

From WEST END of PRINCES STREET to STANLEY ROAD.				From STANLEY ROAD to WEST END of PRINCES STREET.			
3	8	38	39	3	8	38	39
A. M. 9 10	A. M. 9 30	A. M. 8 50	A. M. *9 50	A. M. 8 30	A. M. 8 50	A. M. 9 30	A. M. *9 10
10 30	10 50	10 10	11 10	9 50	10 10	10 50	10 30
11 50	P. M. 12 10	11 30	P. M. 12 30	11 10	11 30	P. M. 12 10	11 50
P. M. 1 10	1 30	P. M. 12 50	1 50	P. M. 12 30	P. M. 12 50	1 30	P. M. 1 10
2 30	2 50	2 10	3 10	1 50	2 10	2 50	2 30
3 50	4 10	3 30	*4 30	3 10	3 30	4 10	*3 50
5 10	5 30	4 50	5 50	4 30	4 50	5 30	5 10
6 30	6 50	6 10	7 10	5 50	6 10	6 50	6 30
7 50	8 10	7 30	8 30	7 10	7 30	8 10	7 50
9 10	9 30	8 50	9 50	8 30	8 50	9 30	9 10
...	...	...	...	...	†10 10	...	...

* These Cars go by York Place.

* These Cars go by York Place.
† This Car goes to Register Office only.

Edinburgh 25 September Referred to the Minute of the Magistrates of this date Geo Cowan B

Winter timetable for the Portobello Route of October 1875, using cars of licence numbers 33 to 36. The line opened in May of that year, this representing the pattern for operation during the first winter with a 20 minute frequency achieved by four vehicles. Summer operation was restricted by the track being built as single line with passing places, but had managed a 15 minute frequency with cars numbered 32 to 37.

TIME TABLE OF CARS.

PORTOBELLO SECTION.

OCTOBER 1875.

FROM WATERLOO PLACE.				FROM PORTOBELLO.			
33	34	35	36	33	34	35	36
A.M. 9 10	A.M. 9 30	A.M. 8 50	A.M. 9 50	A.M. 8 30	A.M. 8 50	A.M. 9 30	A.M. 9 10
10 30	10 50	10 10	11 10	9 50	10 10	10 50	10 30
11 50	P.M. 12 10	11 30	P.M. 12 30	11 10	11 30	P.M. 12 10	11 50
P.M. 1 10	1 30	P.M. 12 50	1 50	P.M. 12 30	P.M. 12 50	1 30	P.M. 1 10
2 30	2 50	2 10	3 10	1 50	2 10	2 50	2 30
3 50	4 10	3 30	4 30	3 10	3 30	4 10	3 50
5 10	5 30	4 50	5 50	4 30	4 50	5 30	5 10
6 30	6 50	6 10	7 10	5 50	6 10	6 50	6 30
7 50	8 10	7 30	8 30	7 10	7 30	8 10	7 50
9 10	9 30	8 50	10 0	8 30	8 50	9 30	9 10
...	...	...	...	...	...	...	...

Edinburgh 25 September Referred to the Minute of the Magistrates of this date Geo Cowan B

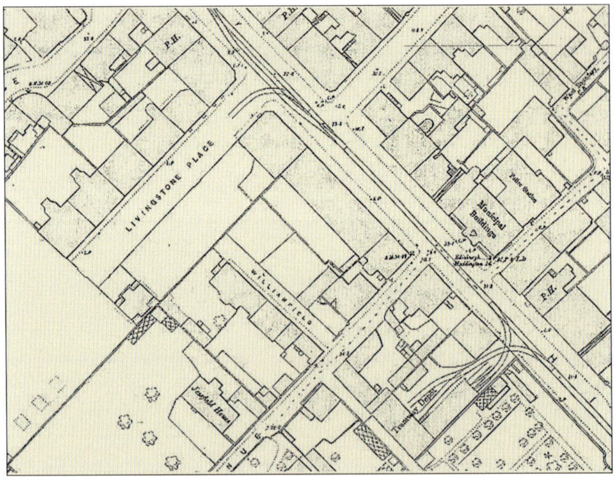

Portobello Depot detail from OS plan surveyed 1894

Roseburn] was opened on 2 June 1873, and in Leith, the new line from Junction Bridge by Ferry Road to Newhaven (Stanley Road) followed on 17 January. This just left the Portobello route, construction of which was heavily pushed for by their council and provost, still to be undertaken. Having by their 1874 Act been permitted to build this as single track with passing loops, work eventually started in October. The new Act also required that buses be run where the northern tramways from the 1871 Act had been abandoned, so from 16 November 1874 the company became bus operators, on routes from Waterloo Place to Stockbridge, and Princes Street (Foot of Mound) to Trinity.[62]

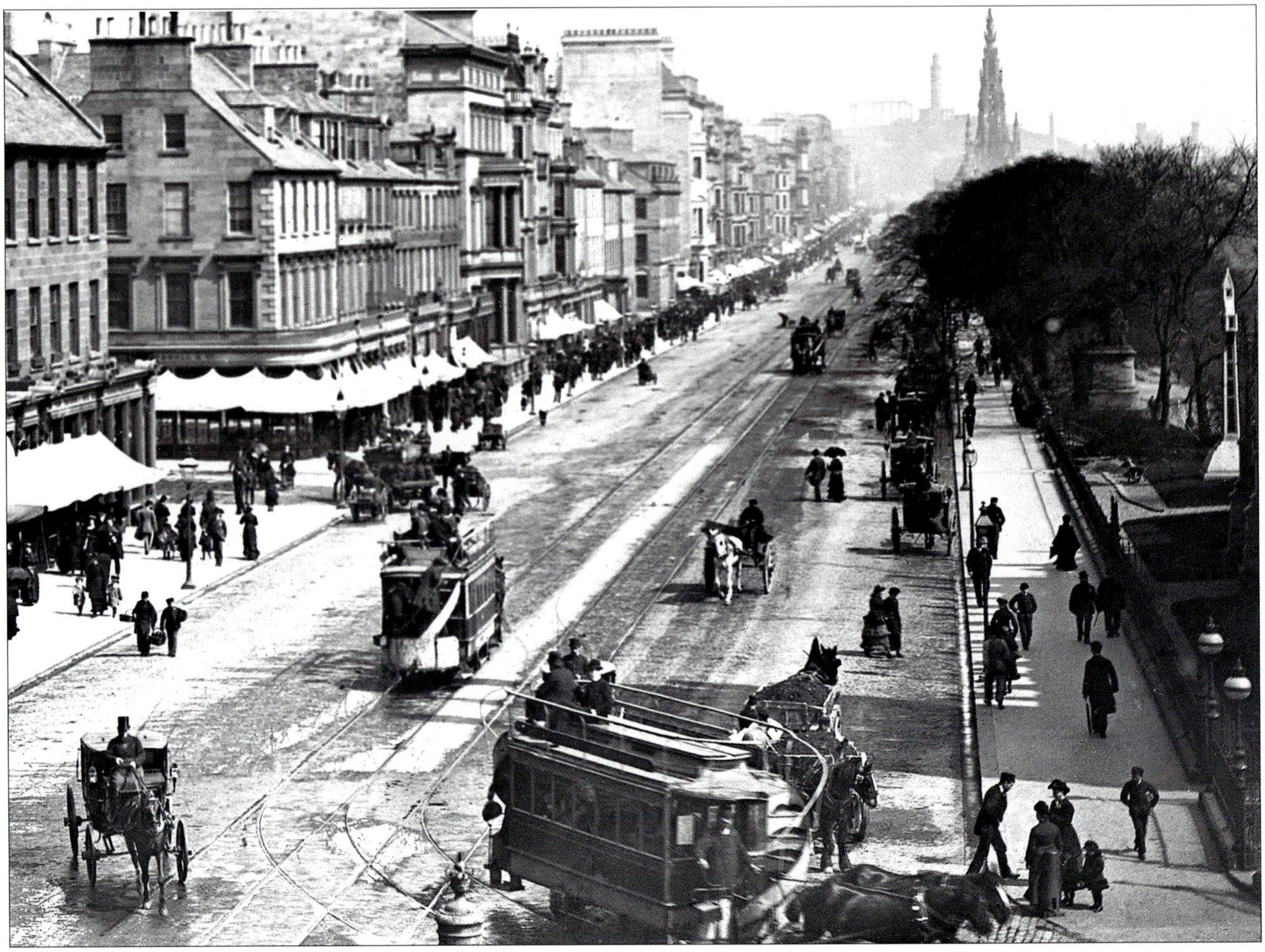
Probably from the late 1870s, this view looking east along Princes Street, again from the first floor window of the Rutland Hotel, shows later developments in tram design. On the nearer vehicle the perilous stair has been replaced by a design which seems to have been unique to Edinburgh. More substantial, it protruded through the dash and obscured the drivers' vision. Note the cut-out in the canopy, necessary to give clearance to the tall 'lum' hats worn by many male passengers.

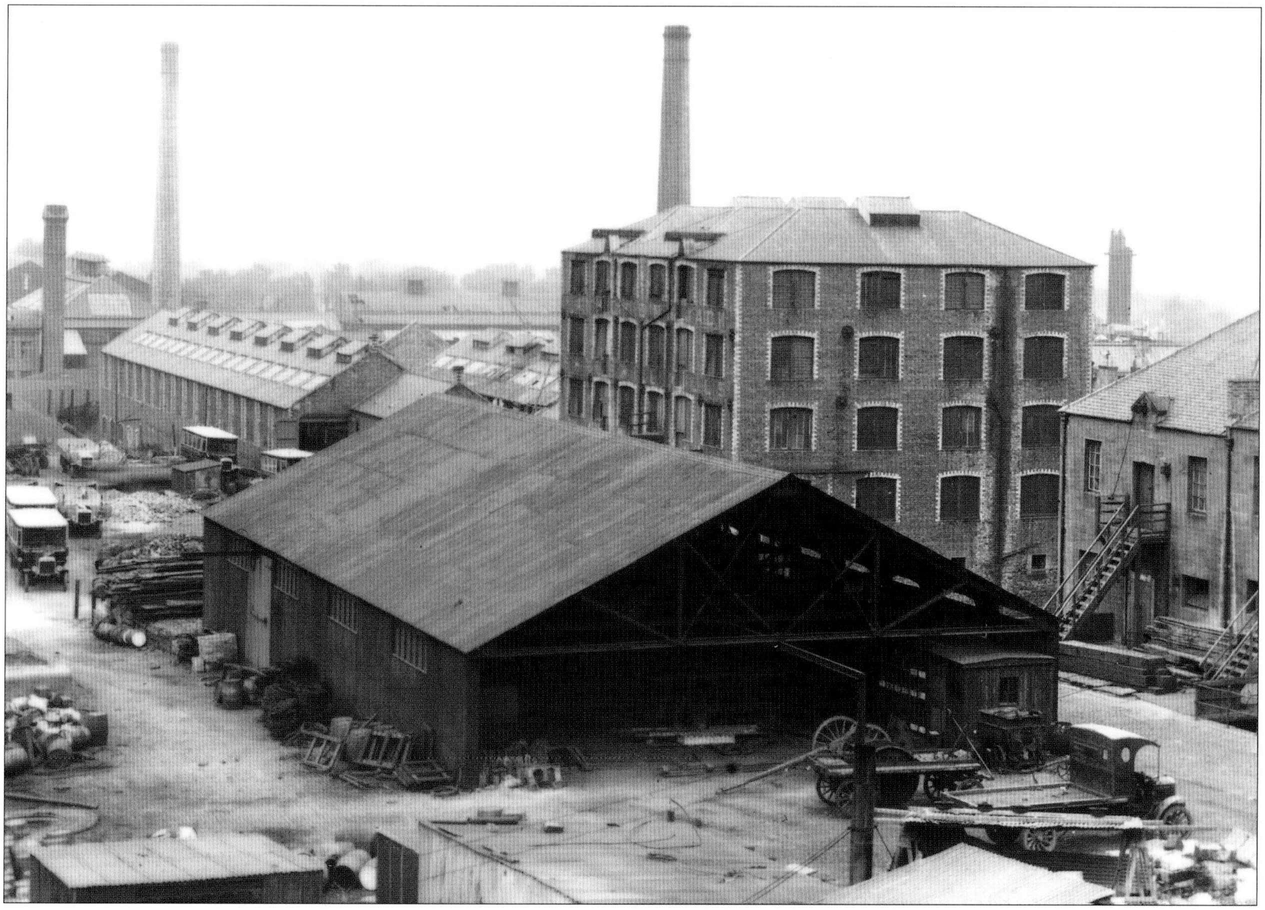

The buildings at the north end of Shrubhill Works in many cases dated back to horse car days. The major expansion of 1881–2 produced , from the right, stables, the granary, then the vehicle building and repair shops. The pitched roof building in the centre, latterly used by the permanent way department, had tracks for horse car storage, with the structural frame made from reused worn-out rails. (E O Catford)

Croall's horsing contract was terminated at Whitsunday 1874, with the Company purchasing their sheds and stables at Middlefield (Shrubhill) for £15,000 plus 350 horses at £28 each. Most of these were soon replaced by heavier Irish horses, the change bringing immediate benefit. Croall's contract had paid them 10¾d per mile for horsing the cars; the Company now found their actual cost was just 7½d per mile. Shareholders' next dividend doubled from 3% to 6%.

Following completion of the 3½ mile long Portobello line and its official inspection, it was opened on 12 May 1875 with a 15 minute frequency. This brought the length of line to over 13 miles. To operate this new service, a small depot was built off Portobello High Street holding 20 horses and a few cars. Unusually for a large undertaking, the Tramways Company concentrated their stables at a single location, at Shrubhill. To minimise potential for spread of infection it was usual practice to have several smaller stables. To service suburban buses such stables were later provided at Corstorphine and Dalkeith, while in 1878 Mavisbank Farm at Loanhead was purchased, also to be used for horse rest and recovery. Development of the Shrubhill site was soon extended by feuing 4½ acres land to the north from Heriot's Governors, where a large granary, stables, car making and repair shops were built (seen above).

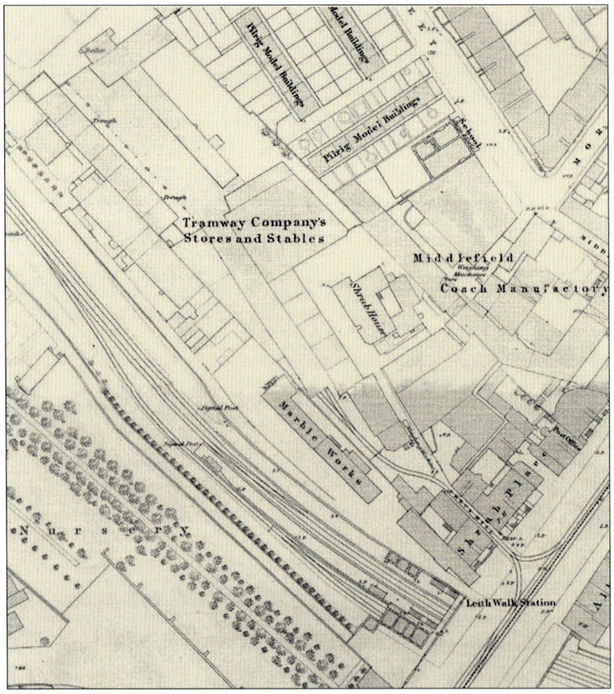

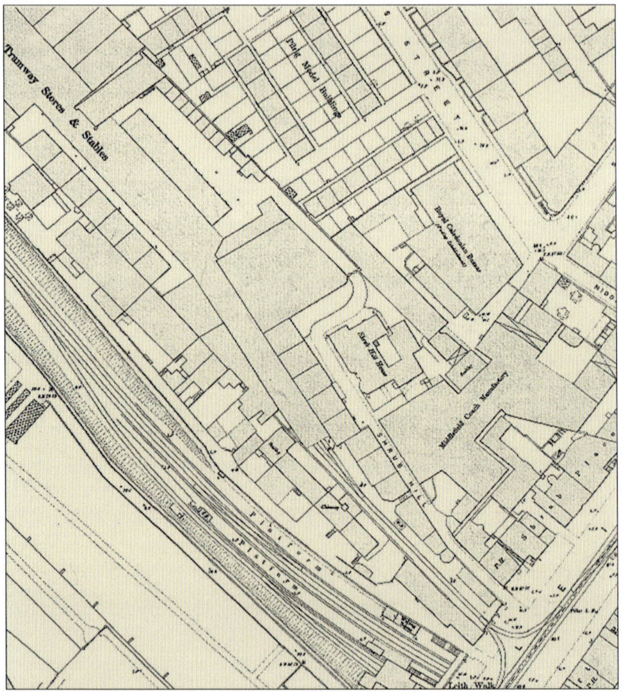

Above left. Shrubhill Depot showing original entrance, from OS plan surveyed 1877

Above right. Shrubhill Depot with new entrance, from OS plan revised 1894.

Right. 1881–2 extensions behind Shrubhill Depot, from OS plan revised 1894

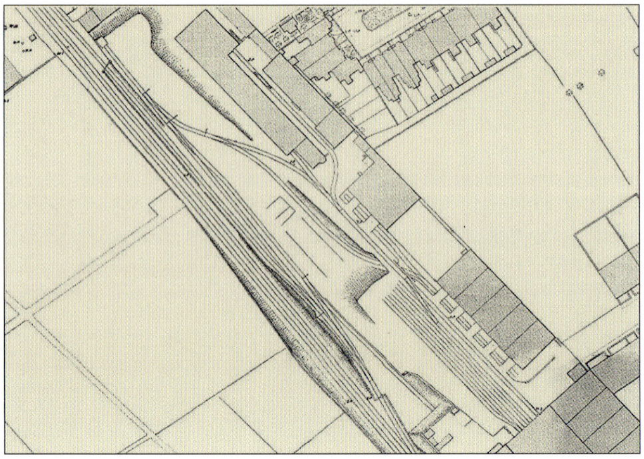

Trace boy experiences and staff conditions

Dr Wood was considerate of staff welfare, and in 1875 a canteen was provided at Shrubhill, followed shortly after by a dormitory for trace boys. Difficulty had been found in attracting the 'right sort of boy' and in an effort to overcome this, a number of lads from the Western Isles were recruited and lodged at Shrubhill.[63] 'Through the kindness of a lady known for her exertions on behalf of the Western Islanders, they brought from the Island of Harris sixteen boys, and others are expected soon. They are boarded and lodged in the premises under the charge of the Home Inspector'.[64] Unfortunately this social experiment proved a disaster – the island boys away from home proving very unruly (and very possibly their propensity to speak Gaelic to each other did not help them integrate with their peers). Wood soon had to report 'Unfortunately, none of the company's officials had gone to select the boys, and the general character of those sent might be guessed when he told them that one was an idiot, that many were so ill fed as to be totally unfit for labour,

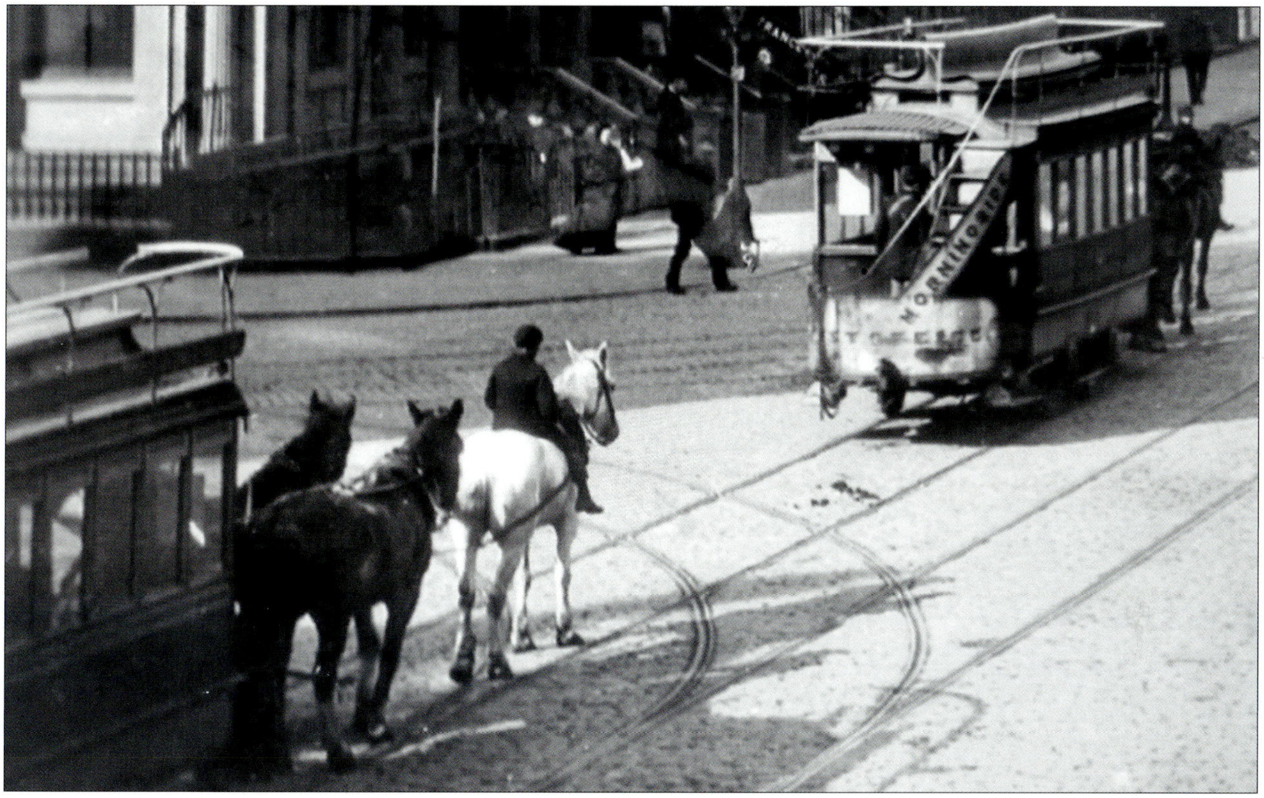

Above. Two unladen cars at the GPO junction, just having arrived by Leith Walk and Leith Street, both with trace boys riding their charges bare-back. To avoid congestion at the busy junction, trace horses were not detached until Waverley Steps. Heavily-laden cars were given two trace horses for this climb, probably the most arduous on the city's tramways. (G W Wilson collection, Aberdeen University Library).

Right. Busy scene at the top of Waverley Steps, with the trace boy, having loosed his two charges from the car, watching them following their routine walk to their accustomed stand at the kerb-side. In the left foreground is one of the pink granite 'street-fountains' or drinking wells, several of which formerly adorned Edinburgh's central streets. These also provided a low-level bowl for dogs. Beyond are several three-in-hand wagonettes, bound for Roslin or the Forth Bridge.

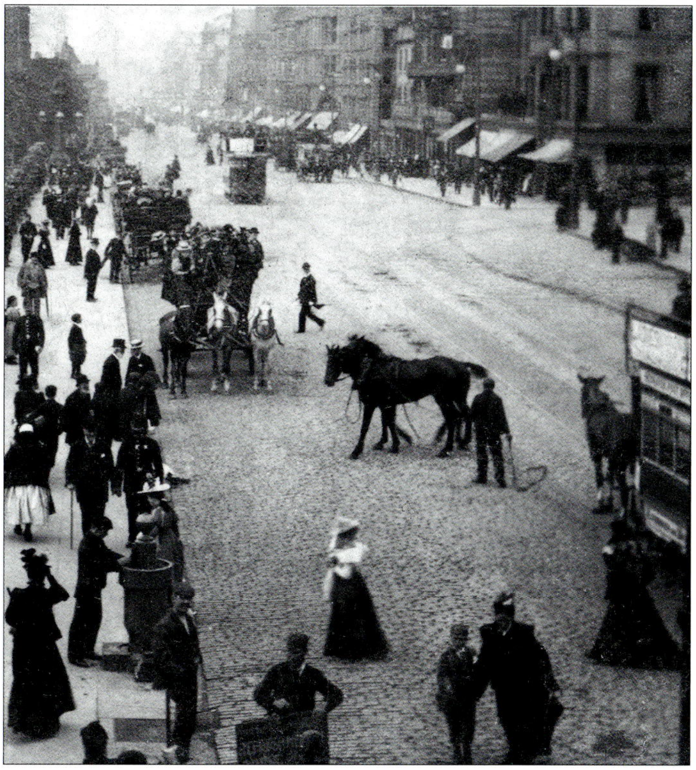

and that nearly the whole of the others were greatly disinclined for anything like hard work. After various trials the directors had thought it better to send the lot back to ornament their native island'.[65] Edinburgh trace boys thought themselves a cut above their contemporaries; their bare-back riding exploits and the gallop down Leith Walk at the end of the day's shift were a source of considerable comment, and frequent reprimand.

Eighty years ago one of these lads – John Munro – recalled his experiences;

> 'On a Monday morning I arrived at Shrubhill yard just as the cars were going out. I approached the gaffer, an elderly man of the name of David Munro, no relation to me. He asked me if I could ride and I said yes. I was sent down to the stables for a horse. In those days there used to be morning horses which would take a car from the gate to Register House. Perhaps you did one journey, perhaps you did two; you received three-pence for each journey. You were only on the spare list. The regular trace boys came in about seven-thirty in the morning till about twelve midnight, with an hour off for dinner and one night off a week.
>
> I was not long in getting a constant job, and it was on Portobello Road. I had two good horses, White Jock and Nellie. We used to trace the cars from Meadowbank opposite the show-ground up to the gate of Calton Jail, the journey taking half-an-hour, quarter of an hour each way. In the summer time as the car drew up at Meadowbank to get traced up the horses got their meal and water. At times the meal used to go missing, probably for porridge.
>
> In the summer time open cars used to be very popular with the public, and many a good tip we used to get from them. But in the winter – and it was real hard winters then, with rain and snow – we had to sit bareback for twelve hours at least and thought nothing of it. You had to be healthy and active or you did not remain long. We could be seen standing on the horses' backs going down Portobello Road at a good canter, it being soft ground, setts only being laid where the rails were. There were seven pairs of horses on the Portobello route. We used to be up to all sorts of dodges when the gaffer was not on the scene.
>
> Sometimes we would wait till the last car and then gallop home four abreast. The road we took was down Regent Road, along London Road, and down the Walk. One night when it was raining very hard and we all waited for one another so as to have a good canter home to the stables. We were tearing along for all we were worth when to our amazement who was standing in the middle of the road with his arms outstretched but the Chief-Inspector, who was going to take our names for furious driving. But he thought better of it and ran to the side. We never knew what might have happened. We felt sure he would be at our heels to catch us coming out at Shrubhill, but he was too late. In a trice we had unbridled our horses and chased them down the yard to their stables, every horse knowing its own stall.
>
> There was an eating-house inside the depot kept by a woman, Mrs Freer, who would let you have something to eat on showing your badge, which was a brass armlet with a number. The boys not working used to obtain food by borrowing a badge from another man, and on pay-day the cook was at the office to receive what you owed her. At that time I was getting ten shillings a week.
>
> I also was tracing on the North Bridge from Lipton's shop to Newsome's Circus, where the Empire is now. There was a competition open to trace boys in Newsome's Circus, the first prize being a ham and the second a roll of sausages, to any boy who could remain on a bronco pony belonging to the circus for

two minutes. There were about twenty of us who entered, I for one had a pair of clogs on, and you would have laughed to see us getting flung all over the shop; in fact one boy landed among the spectators. However, after a good struggle, I managed to win second place. I think we ate the sausages before we left the circus. Mr Newsome, the proprietor, approached some of us to join the circus to do some trick riding. Mr Pitcairn the late Tramway Manager, was in the audience.

We had our horses trained to do almost anything. We had to be kind to them, and we were. I remember while tracing on the High Street, that was from Hyam's shop to Melbourne Place, it was a single horse and it knew its work all right. You just had to hook on your draw chain and let it go, and it came back without anyone looking after it. The driver of the car had to see to its traces being put right.

We had all sorts of dodges to get our horses a rest. Some used to break the reins so as to get down to the saddler's at Shrubhill; others would loose their shoes so as to get down to the blacksmith's shop to have a nail put in. One trace boy named Kane had his horse so well trained that it used to limp as if it were lame. Of course, down to Shrubhill to see the vet. He came once too often.

The horses had a good pull from Pilrig to the Register and soon got knocked up, the hard setts going for their feet. Every month a number of them were sent to the 'grass' at Loanhead and Corstorphine, and they used to come back as fresh as two-year-olds.

When the horses became old and unfit for further service they were sold by auction at Croall's in Castle Terrace. Quite a good lot of them got a good home. On sale day the trace boys would get hold of a decent farmer and tell him the (tale) pedigree of a few horses. On one occasion I took a horse to a farm at Midcalder. I rode it all the way, and poor Billy was ready for a feed and so was I when we got there. I felt quite down in the mouth at parting with one of our old pals, but I knew it would be well looked after.[66]

A missionary to attend the moral and spiritual welfare of the tramway employees was appointed; it is to be hoped that the outcome benefited the morals of the staff. As a social reformer of note, it should not be considered surprising that Dr Wood took such an active interest in the wellbeing of all employees. He well understood that there were costs involved in training staff, hence retention of these trained men was to the benefit of the company '... the more they promoted the comfort of the men in their establishment, and the more they did to withdraw them from those temptations to which in their situation they were peculiarly exposed, the better it would be ... even though they should thereby incur a little expense ... they should have a staff of men who would stay with them, in whom they would have more confidence, and in whose character they could place more reliance. A drunken driver might in a single moment involve them in great expense by causing a single accident ... it was a matter of congratulation that they had done a great deal to elevate the character of the class of men who before were a by-word and a reproach in Edinburgh'.[67] The Isle of Harris experiment had not been a success. The chairman reported 'After a trial of several months, it was thought expedient, both in the interests of the company and of the boys themselves, to allow them to return home. It is still in contemplation to carry out the idea of having trace-boys indentured and boarded at Shrubhill'.[68] He added 'The directors had been much grieved and annoyed at the character of the trace boys [and] thought it better to import an entirely new lot ...they would endeavour to procure boys of their own selection from somewhere nearer home than the Western Islands'.[69]

The canteen or dining room became a much used and well-appreciated facility; '... a kitchen and dining room for the men [is provided] where cheap and well-

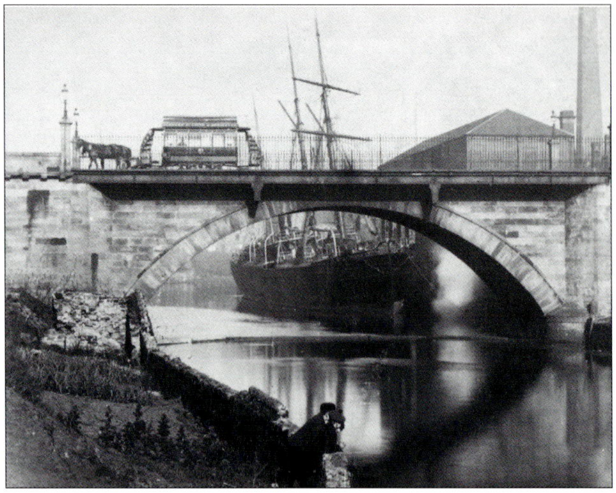

Junction Bridge scene looking north c1880 showing the 1818 bridge which was widened in 1909. An attractive scene, but in reality the Water of Leith was an open sewer – fortunately flushed twice daily by the tide. The sailing vessel is lying by the yard of Hawthorn & Company, long-established marine engineers who also built railway locomotives. The site has been replaced by modern flats of Sheriff Park and the area has returned to a sylvan appearance as a tree-lined length of the Water of Leith Walkway.

cooked food can be obtained at trifling cost. The company provide rooms, coals, and gas, and a female cooks the food, who carries it on as a speculation on her own behalf – of course under the supervision of the Company. The principal charges are: bowl of soup, 1d.; cup of tea or coffee, 1d.; plate of bread and butter, 1d.; plate of meat, 2d. or 3d.; and other articles proportionately cheap. The dining-room, where tables and forms are provided, with a good fire – is largely taken advantage of during the relief journeys, and the whole thing is most admirable, both morally and physically. The benefit of having a warm and comfortable place to sit in, after cold, wet, and weary journeys, and of being able to get something warm to eat, cannot be over-estimated'.[70]

Steam power experiments

Wood was earnest in his endeavours to replace horse flesh by a practical form of mechanical traction, and whenever any such became available, he saw it as his duty to bring it to Edinburgh to persuade the authorities to relax their restrictions. We will digress slightly to follow these events chronologically. According to D K Clark, the credit for first application of steam power to street tramways belongs (like many innovative ideas) to a Scot, Leonard Jennett Todd. He wrote 'L J Todd, of Leith, it appears, was the first steam-locomotist who, in 1871, designed an engine for tramways, specially adapted for passing through common roads and streets, avoiding noise, smoke, and steam, and possessing great facilities for starting and for stopping quickly'.[71] Todd's locomotive was used on the Tramvia de Santander in northern Spain (where it was named – perhaps with feeling – *Prima Donna*). The engine weighed 5 tons, with wooden driving wheels of 5ft 6ins diameter and a leading bogie truck. It does not appear to have survived long; the large driving wheels would be damaging to light-weight horse tramway track.[72]

Although built in Leith, and while the *Prima Donna* has claim to be probably the first successful application of steam to tramways, there seems no suggestion that it was used on Edinburgh's new tramway. A later patent for Todd's *New Pony* engine was couched in language implying that it was built, but this is unproven. Described as with 'ample pulling and stopping powers, the capability of running in either direction, in turning the sharpest curves, noiseless, smokeless, steamless, free of glare by night, can be worked by a single attendant, not complicated, and of sightly appearance'.[73] With all these attributes it is amazing that tramway owners did not beat a path to Todd's door. Regrettably, it all seems to have been too good to be true.

Leith at this time was a hotbed of steam traction innovation, and following his *Prima Donna*, Todd built a steam bus, the *Edinburgh*, which ran for a short time between the West End and Bernard Street. With seats for 20 inside, it had no fewer than 70 seats outside. But two other Leith engineers had already beaten him to the draw. R W Thomson's patented 6-horse power *New Favourite,* operated by a Mr Ritchie, was licensed to run from the GPO to Portobello from 2 June 1870. A month earlier the Magistrates inspected the vehicle,

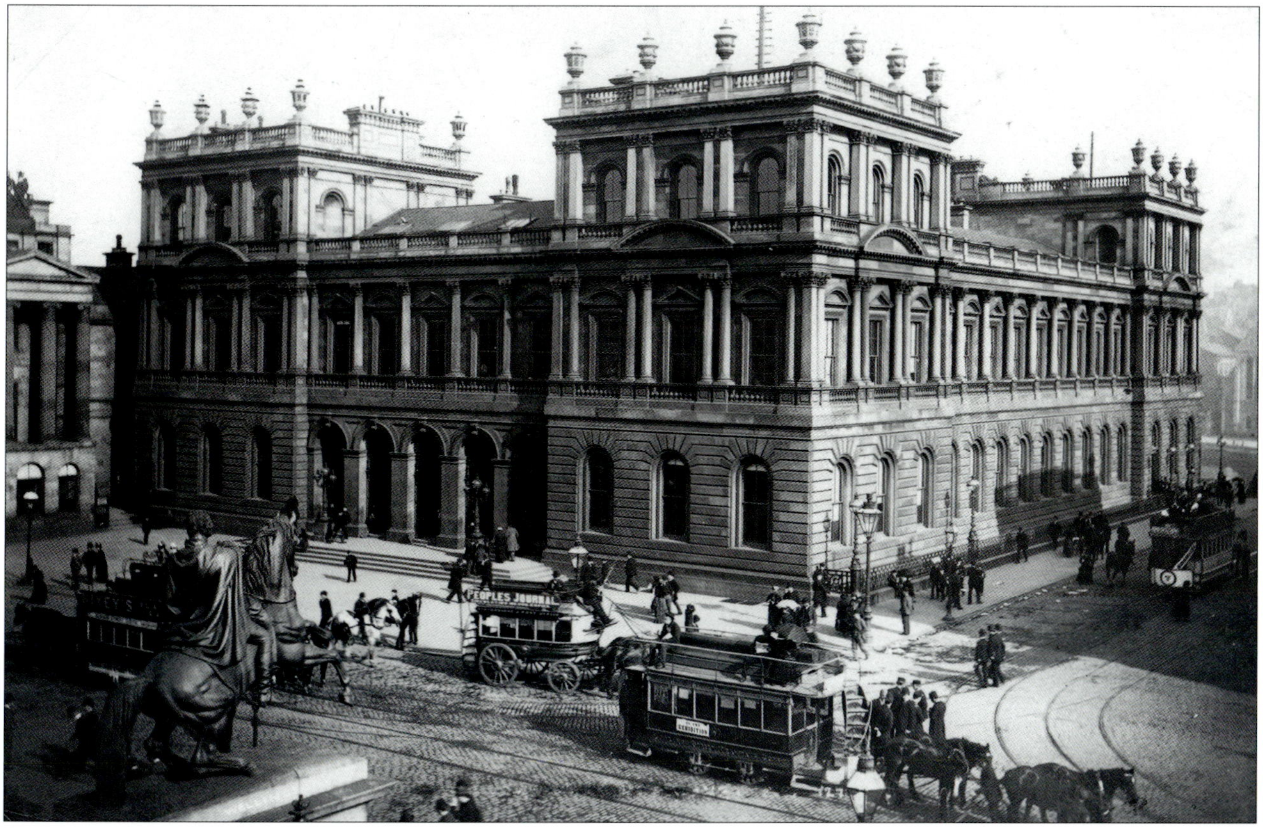

For once, this scene can be reliably dated as having been recorded in July 1886. From General Register House looking to the GPO almost all road traffic is public transport. Nearest to the camera is an old 6-window tram with a poster 'To the Exhibition'. Behind is the Tramways Company Stockbridge bus, while on North Bridge is car 7 of the Morningside Circle. On extreme left , partly hidden by Wellington's equestrian statue, is another 6-window car heading down Leith Street for Bernard Street.

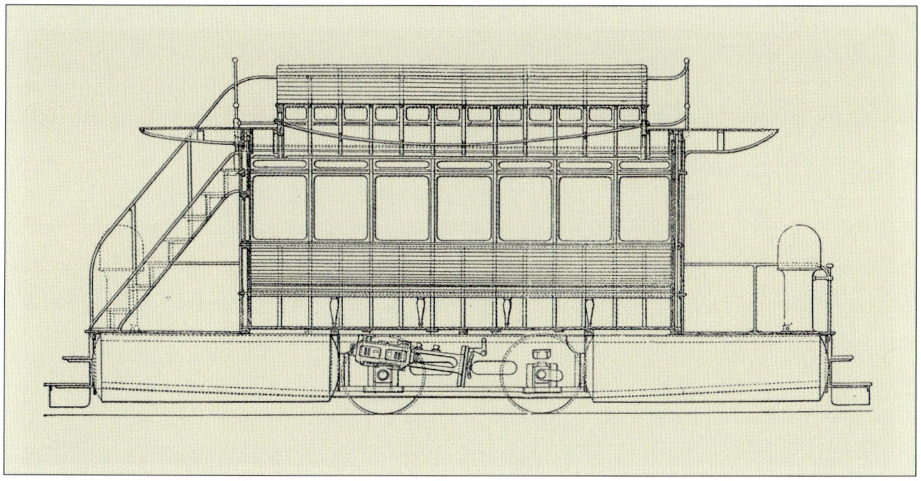

So keen were the directors of the Street Tramways Company to advance the use of mechanical power that in 1875 they allowed inventor W D Scott-Moncrieff the use of one of their horse cars to sit on his compressed-air engine unit. This drawing may be a fair representation of the detail of their first, heaviest, cars (being the type most readily parted with). It would be more likely, however, that the top deck knifeboard seat would be the same length as the saloon.

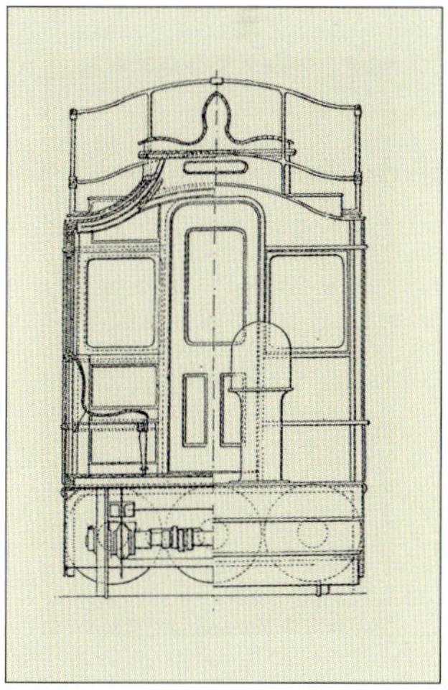

Cross section of Scott-Moncrieff's car showing the air cylinders (three under each end) and the flat construction of the saloon sides.

EDINBURGH STREET TRAMWAYS.

NEWHAVEN AND MORNINGSIDE ROUTES.

On and after SATURDAY, the 10th July, the Car now running between POST-OFFICE and BARCLAY CHURCH will be Discontinued.

NEWHAVEN ROUTE.

Omnibuses are now running between the Mound and Newhaven every 20 minutes.
From the Mound to Newhaven every 20 minutes from 8.50 A.M. to 8.30 P.M.
And from Newhaven to the Mound every 20 minutes from 9 A.M. to 8.40 P.M.

CARS BY JUNCTION BRIDGE.

Two additional Cars will be put on from Newhaven to West End of Princes Street. The service will then be—
From West End of Princes Street to Newhaven every 20 minutes from 8.50 A.M. to 9.50 P.M.
From Newhaven to West End of Princes Street every 20 minutes from 8.30 A.M. to 9.30 P.M.; and from Newhaven to the Register Office at 10.10 P.M.

Note.—The Cars leaving Newhaven at 9.10 A.M. and 3.30 P.M., and West End of Princes Street at 9.50 A.M. and 4.30 P.M., go by York Place.

BY ORDER.

Edinburgh Street Tramways Office,
107 Princes Street, 7th July, 1875.

Above. *Edinburgh Evening News* 9 July 1875

Right. Tram and bus details from *Murray's Pocket Timetable* of December 1875

EDINBURGH TRAMWAY CARS.

Secretary, D. W. Paterson, 107 Princes Street, Edinburgh.

COLTBRIDGE TO LEITH—9-40 am. and 10-15 pm.
COLTBRIDGE TO POWBURN—8-40, 9-10, 10-10 a.m., and ev half-hour till 8-40; then 9-40 p.m.
HAYMARKET TO LEITH—8-35, 8-55, 9-10 a.m, and every few minutes till 10-20 p.m.
LEITH TO COLTBRIDGE—9 am. and 9-25 pm.
LEITH (Bernard St.) TO HAYMARKET—8-0, 8-30, 9-0, and every few minutes till 10-15 p.m.
LEITH (Bernard St) TO NEWINGTON—8-45, 9-20 a.m, & every 15 min. till 9-5, then 9 35 p m.
MORNINGSIDE TO POST OFFICE (via Grange and Bridges)—8-20, 9-0, 9-20, 9-40, 10-0, 10 20 a.m, and every 10 minutes till 9-10, 9-30, 9-45. 10-10 p.m.
MORNINGSIDE TO POST OFFICE (via Lothian Road)—8-30, 8-50, 9-10, 9-30, 9-50, 10-10, 10-30 a.m, and every 10 minutes till 9-20, 9-40, 10-0, 10-20 p.m.
NEWHAVEN TO PRINCES STREET (West End)—8-30 a.m., and every 20 min. till 9-30 p.m.
NEWINGTON TO LEITH—8-45, 9-15, 9-25, 9-35, 10-0 am., and every 15 min. till 9-0, then 9-30 pm.
PORTOBELLO TO WATERLOO PLACE—8-30 a m. and every 20 min. till 9-30 p.m.
POST OFFICE TO MORNINGSIDE (via Lothian Road)—7-50, 8 30, 8-50, 9-10, 9-30, 9-50 a.m., and every 10 minutes till 8-40, 9-0, 9-15, 9-40 p m.
POST OFFICE TO MORNINGSIDE (via Bridges and Grange)—7-55, 8-15, 8-35, 8-55, 9-15, 9-35, 9-55 a.m., and every 10 minutes till 8-45, 9-5, 9-25, 9-45 p.m.
POWBURN TO COLTBRIDGE—8-25, 9-25 a.m., and every half-hour till 8-55 p.m.
POWBURN TO LEITH—8-40 and 9-10 a.m., 10-25 p.m.
PRINCES STREET (West End) TO NEWHAVEN—8-50 a.m, and every 20 min. till 9-50 p.m.
WATERLOO PLACE TO PORTOBELLO—8-50 a.m, and every 20 min. till 9-30, then 10-0 p.m

EDINBURGH CITY BUSES:

MOUND TO NEWHAVEN, via Trinity—9-0 a.m., and every half-hour till 8½ p.m.
NEWHAVEN TO MOUND, via Trinity—9 a.m., and every half-hour till 8½ p.m.
STOCKBRIDGE TO WATERLOO PLACE—every 15 minutes from 9 a.m. to 8¾ p.m.
WATERLOO PLACE TO STOCKBRIDGE—every 15 minutes from 9 a.m. to 8¾ p.m.

EDINBURGH COUNTRY BUSES.—From 4 Princes Street.

Blackshields,—3-30 pm Thur. 2-30. From Blackshields—8-30 am Fares—2s 6d, 2s, 1s 8d.
Carfrae Mill,—3-30 p.m. Thur. 2-30. From Carfrae Mill—7-30 a.m. Fare, 4s, 3s, 2s 6d.
Corstorphine,—8-30, 11, 1½, 4-15, 8. From Corstorphine—9-15, 12, 3, 5, 8-45. Fares—6d, 4d.
Crighton Dean,—3-30 Thur. 2-30. From Crighton—8-45 a.m. Fares—2s 4d, 1s 10d, 1s 6d.
Dalkeith,—10-30 a.m., 4-0, 8 p.m. From Dalkeith—8-15 a.m, 2-15, 6-30 p.m. Fares—8d, 7d.
Dunfermline,—8, 12, 4-20. From Dunfermline—7-40, 11-45 3-45. Fares—3s 6d, 3s, 2s 6d.
Inverkeithing,—8, 12, 4-20. From Inverkeithing—8, 12 n'n, 4. Fares—2s 6d, 2s, 1s 6d.
Lasswade,—10 a.m., 1, 4, 8 p.m. From Lasswade—8-30, 12-0, 2-30, 6-15. Fares—1s, 9d, 7d.
Lauder,—3-30 p.m. On Thursdays, 2-30 p.m. From Lauder—7-0 a.m. Fares—4s, 3s, 2s 6d.
Loanhead,—10-0, 1-0, 4-0, 8-0. From Loanhead—8-45, 12-15, 2-45, 6-30. Fares—10d, 8d, 6d.
Musselburgh,—11, 2, 4, 6, 8½. From Musselburgh—8-35, 12½, 4½, 6½, 7½. Fares—9d, 8d, 6d.
Pathhead,—3-30 p.m. Thur., 2-30. From Pathhead—8-45 a.m. Fares—2s., 1s. 6d., 1s. 3d.
Portobello,—11-0 a.m., 2-0, 4-0, 6-0, 8-30 p.m. Fares—4d, 3d,
From Portobello—9-0 a.m, 1-0, 4-35, 6-0, 7-35 p.m. Fares—4d, 3d.
South Queensferry,—8-0 a.m., 12-0 noon, 4-20 p.m.
From Queensferry—8-45 a.m., 12-45 p.m., 4-45 p.m. Fares—1s 9d, 1s 6d, 1s 3d.

Passengers to and from Inverkeithing, pay 6d each at Queensferry.

but refused permission on a route from Princes Street to Strathearn Road. Another, 'Nairn's Patent Steam Omnibus', the *Pioneer*, belonging to David Charles of Bonnington Road, and operated by Thomas Johnstone, ran briefly from June 1871 between Waterloo Place and Portobello. Despite considerable press attention to the introduction of these innovating vehicles, virtually nothing is recorded of their operation, then subsequent rapid disappearance.[74]

Mid 1875 saw trials of William Dundas Scott-Moncrieff's pneumatic (compressed air) tramcar. For this he was given use of an Edinburgh horse tram (presumably one of the original heavy design) and had Neilson of Hyde Park Works, Glasgow, build an independent under-carriage with air receivers and cylinders, on which the tram body sat. This machine was first tried on the (standard gauge) Govan branch of the Caledonian and Glasgow & South Western Railways Joint line, then with equal success on the 4 ft 7¾ ins gauge Vale of Clyde track. For two weeks in January 1876 it ran there in public service. Scott-Moncrieff turned down a contract to run his car at 6d per mile, as conditions imposed were too onerous. His vehicle weighed eight tons empty, plus further two tons if a full load of passengers was carried. Dr Wood decided that this would be too damaging on track designed for two-ton horse cars (four tons fully laden). Scott-Moncrieff later stated that this car was never used subsequently.

Edinburgh's tramways directors were always anxious to pursue the benefits of mechanical traction, having seriously underestimated the horsing costs needed to overcome the steep gradients of several Edinburgh streets. The formidable animal champion, Baroness Burdett-Coutts was becoming ever more vociferous in her complaints regarding perceived cruelty to the tram horses. At the January 1876 company meeting, in reply to a question from the floor asking if '... anything was being done to promote the use of power other than horse in the working of the cars ...' Dr Wood advised that several schemes were being investigated; the Scott-Moncrieff car was dismissed as under powered – although still in use in Glasgow. 'With the agreement of the Magistrates I will show it to the citizens of the Capital ...', but this never happened. Another scheme involved a spring wound up by steam power, but this along with others disappeared without trace.[75]

Wood soon reported 'a number of persons interested in the question of applying other than animal power to tramways had initiated experiments in Leicester and had seen a car drawn up a gradient of 1:20. Finding the Tramways Company could not afford to invest in such an engine a number of gentlemen has joined together and got an engine made and have been able to add several improvements ... within two weeks he would be able to show the engine in Edinburgh. This enterprise was not conducted by the Tramways Company but by a number of private gentlemen [but] some persons are already making preparations to oppose ...'[76] This machine, built by Henry Hughes in Leicester, was taken to Portobello stables, then tried on 9 September 1876. With a single car attached it ran tolerably well, reaching Waterloo Place with difficulty. From there it was returned to Portobello, pulled ignominiously by a team of horses.[77]

In his testimony to the Commons Select Committee on Tramways (Use of Mechanical Power), D W Paterson, Secretary of the Street Tramways Company was explicit about his Company's awareness of all manner of mechanical traction – but he also pointed out the total lack of co-operation from the city authorities. He reiterated his anxiety to find an alternative to horse power, listing schemes under review '... Perkins' high pressure engine; ... then we tried Mr Grantham's engine; ... Messrs Merryweather's engine is not sufficiently powerful for our traffic; ... Mr Scott-Moncrieff's pneumatic car we thought at first would succeed, but it also is not sufficiently powerful for our traffic; ... a high pressure pneumatic engine at Woolwich Arsenal; ... and an engine being built for a Gentleman at Leeds ... by Messrs Greenwood & Batley ...'. Paterson tried to clarify the number of Hughes engines; '... I and the Chairman ... saw the second one, I think, that was made by Mr Hughes, and we were so well satisfied with it that a number of gentlemen (not as a company, for the company have no power to acquire engines) gave Mr Hughes an order for an engine which he said would fulfil all the conditions required in working the traffic between Edinburgh and Portobello ... we tried it continuously for a whole week, beginning between 4 and 5 o'clock in the morning, and running till about 9 o'clock, and then occasionally during the day; but latterly, when we put it on the regular traffic, we found that it was not suitable for some of the gradients ... I saw that engine after it had run several weeks at Govan, and it appeared even then to be quite as free from objection as at first ...'[78]

Further experiments were made in Edinburgh using this engine – on 13 September, with Colonel Hutchinson of the Board of Trade present, it made several journeys to and from the GPO and on 20 and 29 September it ran to the North Bridge. Thereafter it was sent to the Vale of Clyde line, 'to compete with one built by Messrs Merryweather.' Henry Hughes said, with regard to the Edinburgh trials, 'although we took full loads up the steepest gradients it [the engine] was not heavy enough for constant use ... we ran past a troop of soldiers on horseback, and the commander was kind enough to let us run backwards and forwards by them to see how many [horses] did shy ... they were not frightened, they just moved in their places ... might I say that the horses are not frightened at this engine. We proved that very much, where at the same time we ran a car down without an engine to it, they were quite as frightened at the car without an engine as they were with an engine and car.'

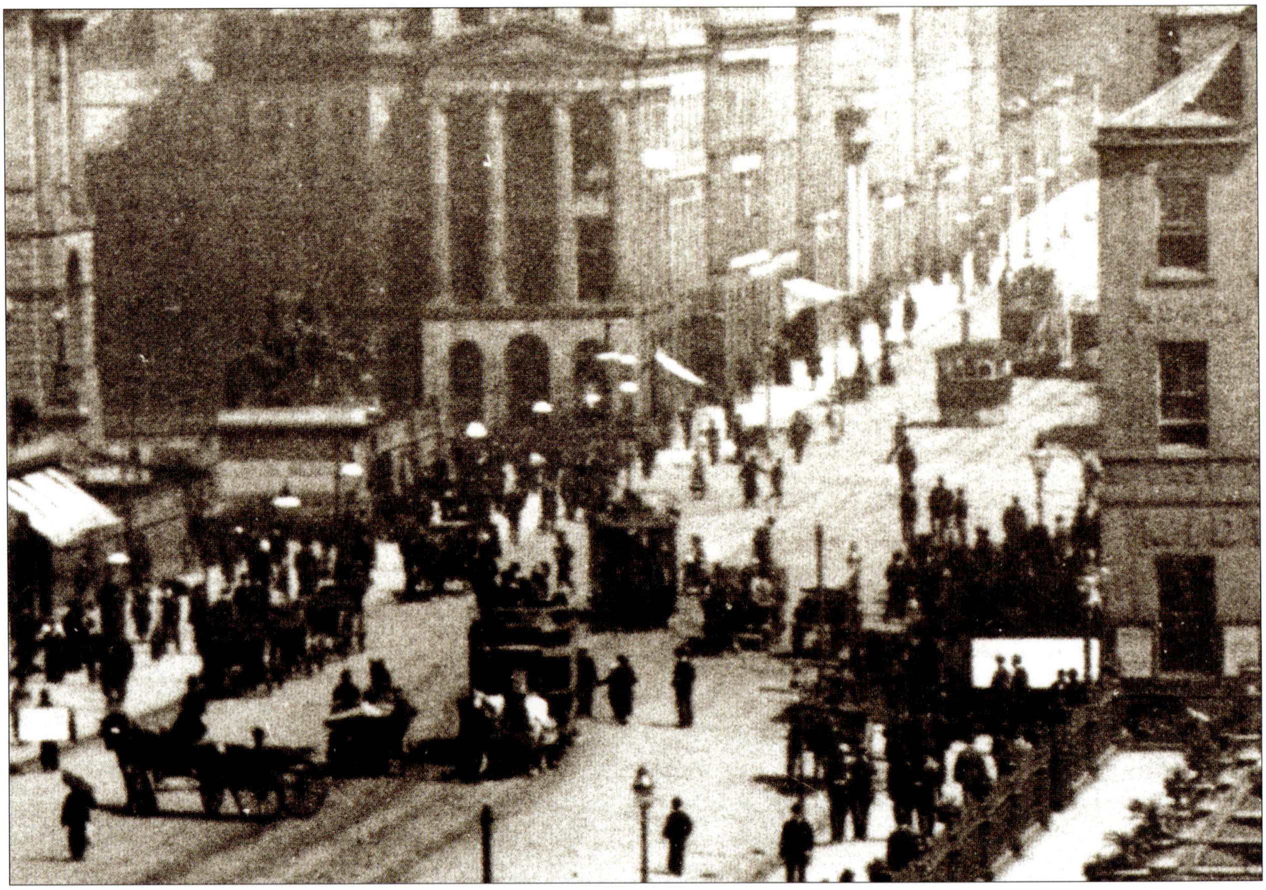

Despite this being a gross enlargement of a view of Calton Hill from the Scott Monument, it is full of interest. The photographer has caught, in Waterloo Place, one of the Kitson steam tram engines which were used between April 1881 and October 1882 on the Portobello route; this being the only known record of their use. A single ended or reversible tram is approaching.

The unhelpful attitude of Edinburgh authorities was exemplified in the testimony of Lord Provost Falshaw to the Commons' Select Committee. An established civil engineer, he turned down every invitation from the Tramways Company to witness each experiment to alleviate the labour – and cost – of the tram horses. His Lord Provost's Committee considered that he should not attend in an official capacity and when asked privately he responded 'I could not have divested the private visit from my official position, and I thought it better to stay away ... they are under obligation to us not to work the tramways by other than animal power. However '... we [later] despatched our burgh engineer and the engineer of the road trust to Glasgow to see the engine which was said to be working on the Vale of Clyde Tramway, which was found to be put aside in a shed and not to have been used for a length of time; they proceeded to Leicester, and there the engine had been shunted and laid aside in a shed, for a length of time; and the tramways both in Leicester and Glasgow were being worked by animal power ...'. Each opportunity to see trials being made on their doorstep was deliberately ignored.

One exchange is worthy of record:

Mr Floyer MP – '... you would prefer that those experiments should be made rather out of the streets than in?' Sir James – *'Yes, certainly'*.

'In short, you wish to satisfy yourself of the practicability of steam power before you

> introduce it into your crowded thoroughfares?' – *'Undoubtedly'*.
>
> 'I suppose the popular voice is tolerably represented in the Corporation of Edinburgh, is it not?' – *'Yes, tolerably'*.
>
> 'And there is no indisposition to attend to the wants of the working-classes, with regard to locomotion and other matters?' – *'None whatever. We give every possible encouragement to the working-classes in every way consistent with keeping within the law.'*

Sir James proposed that, to prove the efficacy of any steam tram engine, prior to it being permitted to run in Edinburgh, a track with similar gradients should be constructed – he suggested part way up Arthur's Seat! Sir James Falshaw may not have been altogether altruistic in his opposition – he had spent most of his career on promotion and construction of railways (and was on the boards of several, including the NBR) and probably foresaw the successful application of mechanical operation to tramways as a threat to short distance railway passenger traffic.[79]

By 18 April 1877 another Hughes engine was working from Portobello, '... specially made for steep gradients. One of the same class was tried some months ago and found of insufficient power ...' This new machine had 7in by 13in cylinders and 24 inch diameter steel wheels. It ran again on 23, 27 April, then 2 and 3 May, '... more adverse reaction and fright was caused to passing horses by the red flag carried 100 yards ahead of the tram under the requirements of the Locomotive Act, than by the tram locomotive itself'. A *recherché* lunch was provided at the Royal Hotel, Portobello.[80] This engine was then taken to Govan, with much interest taken in Edinburgh of the experiments there.

In December a 'combined' steam tram was tried in Greenock. Constructed to the patented design of Robertson & Henderson of Kent Road Glasgow, its body was formed from one of the Glasgow Tramway Company's old cars.[81] On 13 December, guests – including a deputation from Edinburgh – travelled on it before it arrived in Leith by way of the Forth & Clyde Canal. Its initial trial in Edinburgh was on 28 December 1877, when it (just) made it from Shrubhill to the GPO, including the climb up Leith Street, but needed to pause before the final ascent to allow steam pressure to recover.[82] Dr Wood advised the next Company meeting that they intended to purchase it for the Portobello route and by the middle of March it was undergoing further trials. Passengers were carried, and as fares could not be charged, it was exceedingly popular. On 29 March, with the Board of Trade's Hutchinson aboard, it made a foray from Shrubhill along Princes Street, up Lothian Road, round the Morningside Circle, to the GPO then to Portobello and back. Hutchinson commented favourably '... many of the streets that we went through were much crowded with a superior description of horses, drawing carriages. It was in the middle of the afternoon, from three to four o'clock, when the fashionable people in Edinburgh were out. I never saw so little effect produced on carriage horses as by this particular engine and car combined. I do not remember noticing one horse of superior description frightened. But the strange thing was that the tramway horses were those that were the most frightened. We passed a number of tramcars, and the drivers had apparently great difficulty in keeping their horses on the road at all. They were close to the engine. No doubt it was from the unusual fact of seeing a tramcar passing near them without any apparent means of being moved. Otherwise the ordinary traffic horses were very little frightened. The cab-horses on the cabstands next the tramway cars were the next most frightened. They showed signs of restiveness as the steam tramcar passed them'.[83] It ran again in Edinburgh only once, and was sent thereafter to Stirling, where its use was again stymied by local authority intransigence.

In mid-1880 yet another machine was in Edinburgh, this one patented by Duncan, Wilson & Co of Liverpool. A contemporary description reads 'The machinery is enclosed in a framework of wood and glass similar in construction to the body of an ordinary car, except that the outside seats and top rail are wanting ...'. On 2 July tests were conducted on the

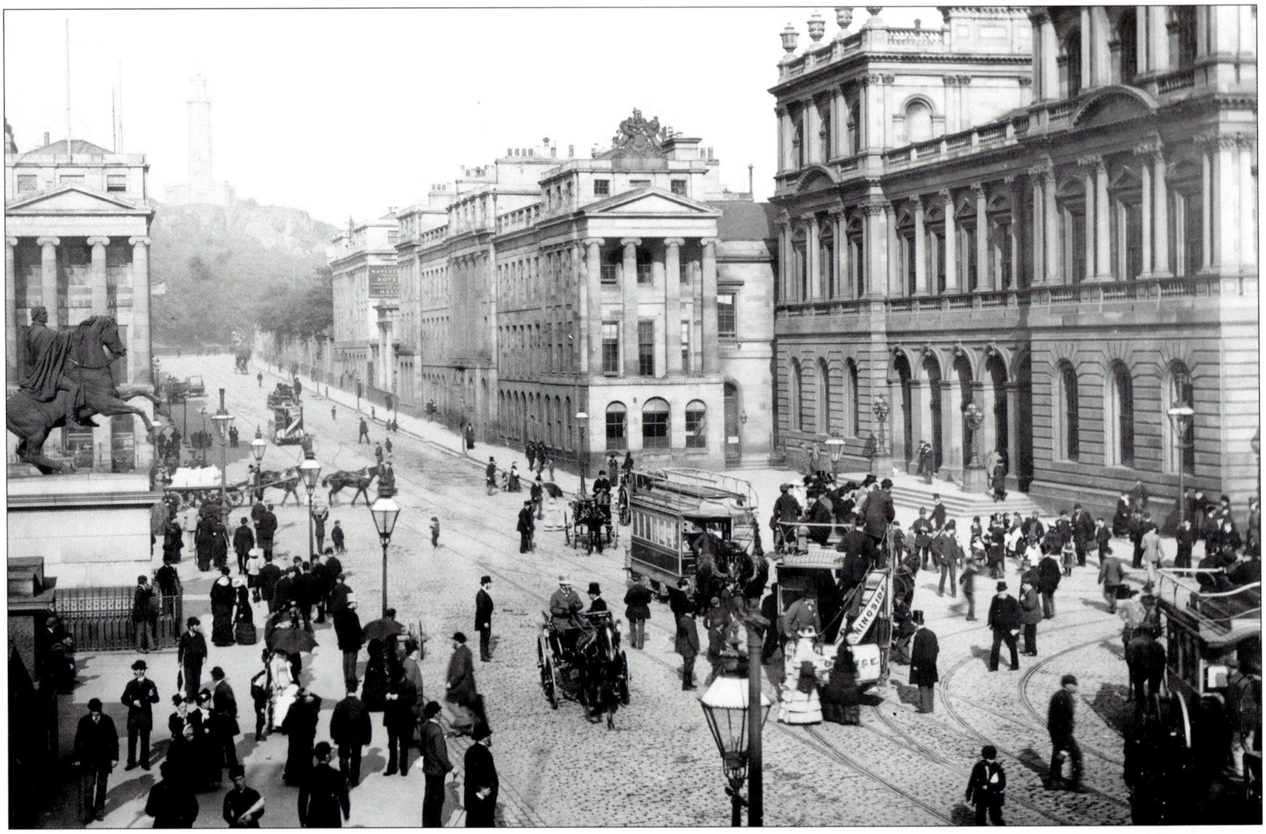

A favourite vantage point for Victorian photographers was a first floor window of the Crown Temperance Hotel (the site later occupied at the East End of Princes Street by Woolworth's store). The busy scene has much of interest, not merely from the transport point of view. The car on the right has at least one pair of wheels off the track and re-railing will not be aided by the large number of passengers aboard, none of whom seem inclined to lend assistance. On extreme right is the Loanhead bus, while an older 'Liverpool' style car 'No 45' on the North Merchiston route waits for the way to be cleared.

Portobello line, with an open 'toastrack' horse car attached.[84] It was said to be almost noiseless, and emitted no smoke, but no further reference has been found to its use in the capital. It had previously been used in Liverpool, whence it returned in November. At the next meeting, Edinburgh shareholders were advised that all experiments conducted had been at the entire cost of the engines' owners, and that all had proved deficient in one way or another.[85]

Early in 1881 Kitson of Leeds supplied two tram locomotives, one to Edinburgh, the other to the Vale of Clyde, and on 12 April Hutchinson inspected both. The first had arrived in Portobello on 2 February and was seen as a great improvement on all its predecessors. It had additional condensers and overcame Leith Street '... with a heavy car attached, filled with stones ... The guests, including Portobello Magistrates and Councillors from the City, then successfully travelled from Waterloo Place to Portobello and back ... the rails were slippery due to rain, but the steepest gradients were taken with no apparent difficulty'. Hutchinson passed the line for steam use. '... The Company intends to arrange to work the route as soon as it receives sanction, but it will be several months before Kitson can supply the machines'.[86]

Practical, in service, operation of this engine started on Saturday 23 April 1881, running ten journeys, each taking 25 minutes – five minutes less than with horses. The following day an open workmen's car was attached to the ordinary one and 'both made a pleasant journey to Portobello'.[87] Despite Board of Trade approval, Portobello Council complained that they had not given permission – and did not do so until October – but this did not stop use of the engine.[88] The July company meeting was advised that the engine had missed only two days work, caused by a broken piston rod.[89] A second engine was despatched by Kitson on 22 February 1882, entering service on 14 March.[90]

The Edinburgh Street Tramways (Mechanical Powers) Bill was enacted in July 1882 but did not resolve licensing, which was left with the local authorities. Permission for steam operation now became a political football, with the councils of Edinburgh and Portobello each withholding consent until concessions were wrung from the unfortunate Tramways Company. Portobello was 'bought off' by the Company agreeing to lay setts over most of their High Street. Then on 12 September Edinburgh refused to renew permission, so the steam tram only ran to Jock's Lodge: but the Company then resumed until expiry of their permit on 27 October.[91] Perhaps as a result of worsening relations, the Company abandoned any further attempt to prolong these reluctantly given permissions. The engines would be re-used elsewhere, certainly one was in Dundee for a time. In April 1883 when another attempt to promote use of steam was refused, the Company had reluctantly to accept that their chances of success were nil; they could not overcome the obstacles put in their way.

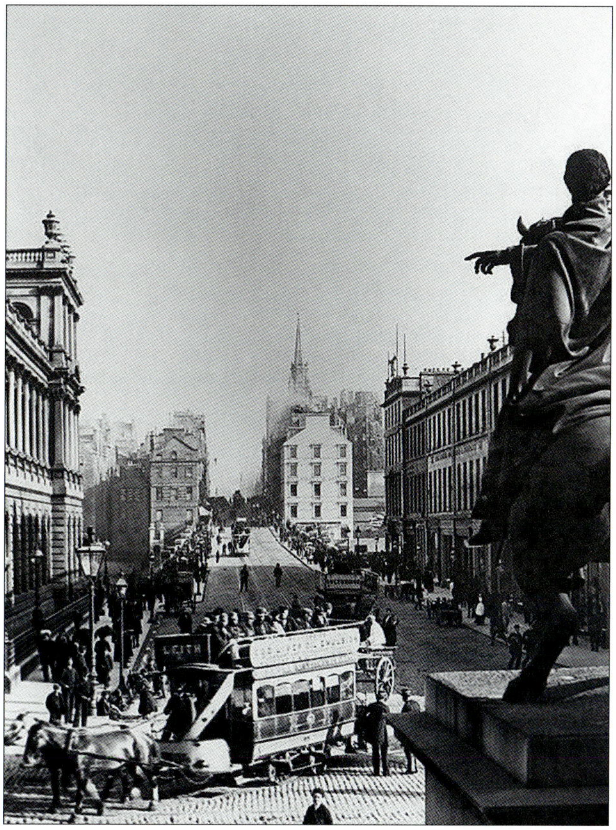

Early 1880s view from General Register House looking beyond the Duke of Wellington equestrian statue to the North Bridge. The well-laden car is of a smaller design with a six -window saloon seating 16 passengers inside.

Progress and consolidation

Returning to the chronological record, the success of the Portobello line required additional passing places to allow an improved ten-minute service. On 13 September 1876 these were inspected by Colonel Hutchinson when he re-examined the Hughes engine.[92] These steam experiments attracted the attention of other operators faced with similar needs. In Scotland however, only at Dundee and Govan did they find favour, giving satisfactory service in the former place from 1885 until 1902.

Company finances continued in a satisfactory manner, but in August 1876 that half-year's dividend was reduced to 4%. This resulted from the litigation costs from two accidents. However, shareholders were reassured by being advised that the Edinburgh Company's earnings amounted to 1s 5½d per mile, 1½d more than achieved in Glasgow, while the latter city ran trams on seven days per week, the capital operating only on six days. Within a year dividends rose to 8%, then increased to 8½% shortly thereafter. Heavy expenditure was incurred in the re-laying of the original tracks which had not lasted as expected. Princes Street reconstruction was undertaken during the second half of 1878, and as the street had recently been widened on the gardens side, the opportunity was taken to re-locate the track more centrally. New rails were laid south of the southerly (west-going) track, which then became the new east track, with the original east-going line lifted. The cost of this was £6565 – a not inconsiderable unforeseen outlay. In North Bridge Street the original double track was removed from the narrow thoroughfare and replaced by a single line. This was considerably less convenient for the operation of the tramway, but allowed carriages to stand outside the various shops. Track over North Bridge itself remained double.

The obvious benefits brought by the tramway were more and more appreciated and the directors were put under pressure for extensions; to the Merchiston area to the south-west of the city centre, to Corstorphine and to Musselburgh. Their Bill to Parliament in 1876 had proposed to extended the Portobello line to Joppa and on to Pinkie Dykes at the east end of Musselburgh High Street, but this failed to receive support from the County Road Trustees and was dismissed by failing to comply with Parliamentary Standing Orders. Perhaps surprisingly, no immediate attempt was made to revive this proposal.

The good reason why many operators with large numbers of horses did not centralise stables and associated departments was graphically illustrated when a major fire broke out at the Shrubhill feed store on 23 February 1879. At 3 am on the Sunday morning the night-watchman saw smoke and alerted Richard Goodyer, the superintendent, who released a large number of horses from the stables, probably saving them. About 200 animals set off in all directions, but were rounded up from as far afield as Granton and Portobello the following day. The cost of damage, fortunately covered by insurance, was estimated at over £2000[93]. Goodyer came to the Tramways Company in 1875 from his former employer, John Croall & Sons, but left Edinburgh to be manager of the new Rothesay Tramway in 1882. From there he soon moved south to further his transport career as manager of the Road Car Company in London. After this experience he spent time on tramways in Paris, his final position being as the manager of Cardiff tramways, from January 1890.

Further expansion

The Company coaching or bus department was expanding, with routes running to Loanhead, Corstorphine and Tynecastle. The Loanhead coach, which was conveniently used for breaking in of fresh horse stock, suffered an unfortunate serious accident in September 1879 when it overturned after striking a boulder at the side of the road. During the following year it was replaced by a new vehicle, designed by Harry Booth and built at Shrubhill coach works. This had seating for 13 inside and 18 outside (the previous vehicle had seats for 14 in and 18 out and had been built some ten years earlier by John Brabner of Bellevue for Adamson's route between Haymarket and Newington) and was eight inches lower, by using cranked axles. The new vehicle was also wider by 2½ inches and nearly three feet longer[94].

From 2 February 1880 the Company commenced or perhaps re-commenced issue of tickets to passengers, of various denominations, torn from a roll. Each ticket carried – as a security measure – the number of the car on which it was issued. Unsurprisingly receipts increased, but costs also increased as inspectors were needed to monitor the operation and clerks to administer details. There had been earlier ticketing schemes allowing a discount for advance purchase in quantity. In the December prior to introduction of the 1880 scheme, it was announced 'The Tramway Company have discontinued the sale of tickets to the public in advance of the new system from 15 January next of checking money taken ...'[95]. Losers under the new arrangements appear to have been children; to this time those up to ten years of age travelled for half fare. This now became restricted to those under five years[96]. The Chairman was eventually forced to admit '... it might be that the loss that had been prevented was not equal to the cost of prevention, but it must be remembered that regularity of system and efficiency of superintendence was valuable in many other respects than merely checking the returns of the conductors'[97].

The question of tramways to serve Merchiston was not to be resolved easily. The initative for a tramway to

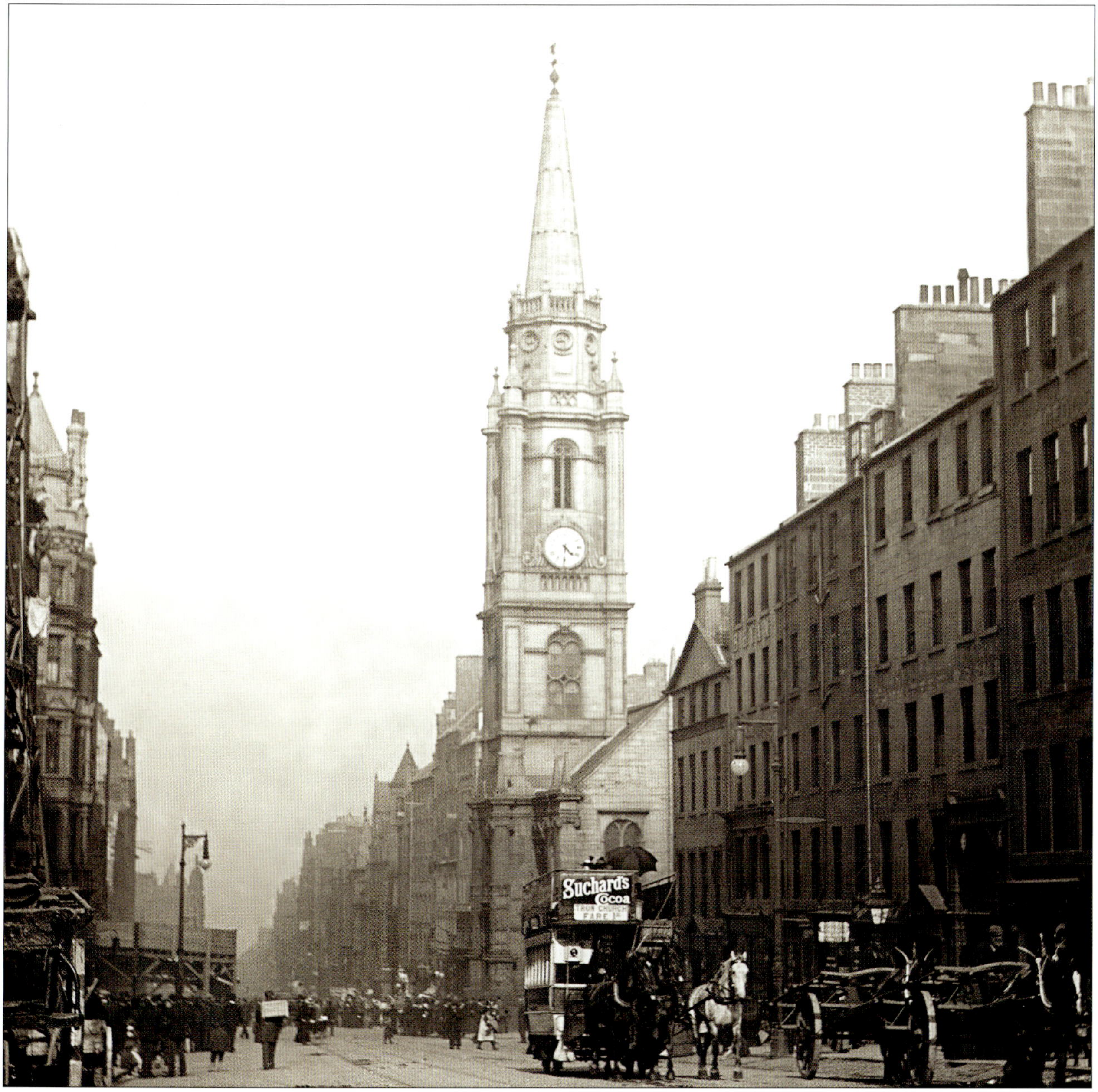

Most of the extensions authorised in 1881 opened for traffic during the following year, including that between Tron Church and Tollcross. This view shows a tram proceeding up High Street, with a trace horse providing assistance to the Lawnmarket. Latterly this line operated as a shuttle, fare 1d and using – at peak times – five cars.

serve this virtually undeveloped area, most of which was still to be feued by Edinburgh's Merchant Company, was completely speculative, well ahead of actual construction and needless to say shareholders were not convinced of its justification or of the profitability of any such tramway. However in September 1880 the Dalry and Merchiston proposals resurfaced[98]. Dalry was to be served by a line from Haymarket to the foot of Ardmillan Terrace by Dalry Cemetery; Merchiston by a line from Bruntsfield down Spylaw Road, from where there was potential for extension as far as Colinton, and also the link north towards Dalry.

With regard to Colinton, the foresight of the Tramway's directors saw them entering negotiations with several of the area's landed proprietors to have them provide land for a new turnpike road which would have provision for a tramway, the existing road being considered totally impractical. Much traffic was anticipated to be generated by the Craiglockhart Hydropathic establishment, opened that very year.

A line was now intended to link Tollcross and the South Bridge by Forrest Road and Chambers Street. This had been one of the original 1871 proposals, but had been dropped since Chambers Street had not been completed. Also included in this radical major extension plan was from Powburn in Newington to Mayfield. Doubling of the Portobello line was proposed, as was its extension to Joppa and potentially as far as Musselburgh and Levenhall. To the west, the directors proposed to build from Coltbridge 2 miles out to Corstorphine, and to this end land had been feued at the west end of the village for stables and car shed. This opened – for a bus service to Coltbridge – in the first half of 1881. In Leith a line extended from Junction Bridge down North Junction Street as far as Commercial Street.

Opposition was orchestrated by Councillor Clark of Leith who suggested that the decisions of the directors particularly with regard to the extensions were being led by '... the Council, the Merchant Company ring, and Mr James Gowans, merchant, contractor, and builder of villas which would neither sell nor let, and who was not the holder of any of the company's stock. Mr Gowans had the contracts for construction of the company's lines, and they saw how badly they had been executed, as they had to be constructed over again. Mr Gowans sucked the orange and left them with the skin'[99]. He considered that the extensions in the Merchiston area would undoubtedly lead to the bankruptcy of the company. His suspicions may have been fuelled by the knowledge that the rails now being specified for renewal work were of a design patented by the same James Gowans. For the relaying of part of the route from Lothian Road to Tollcross, another of Mr Gowans' ideas was experimented with; this track was relaid using railway-style 'bullhead' rail, with the groove formed alongside by specially shaped chilled iron blocks.

Immediately following the first half-yearly meeting of 1881 notice was received from Mr D W Paterson, the Company secretary, that he wished to leave his

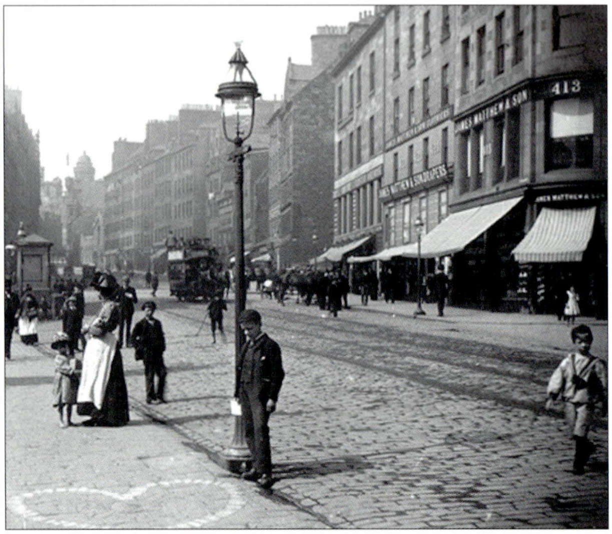

At Lawnmarket the line turned south along George IV Bridge. In this atmospheric scene by John Patrick, the lad in the foreground is looking, wistfully perhaps at the heart-shaped design on the footway, the permanent memorial 'The Heart of Midlothian' marking the site of the City's Old Tolbooth.

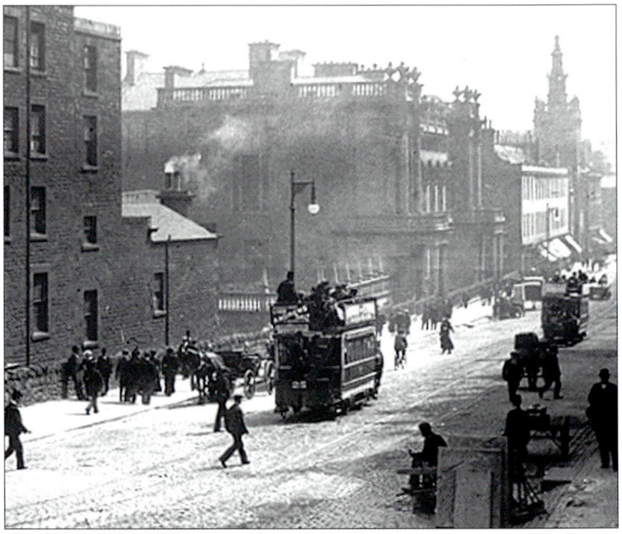

Horse tram scene on George IV Bridge looking south from the Melbourne Place and Lawnmarket junction. To the left is the rear of the former Midlothian County Building; the front, on the other side facing Parliament Square can be seen on the left hand side of the previous photograph.

employment with the Company. He was persuaded to remain in post until the Bill had passed through Parliament, this accomplished on 11 August. Doctor Wood now relinquished his role as chairman and took an even more hands-on position as Secretary and General Manager, in addition to his multitudinous other responsibilities.

After much heated debate regarding which routes were to be included, this contentious Bill was enacted on 11 August 1881, giving authority to most of the proposals. In one form or another most were eventually built, but not those to either Corstorphine or Colinton. The Merchiston proposal was fine tuned to run, instead of by Spylaw Road, to go by Gilmore Place as far as Colinton Road, and the Tollcross to South Bridge proposal went by High Street instead of Chambers Street. The contentious link between the Polwarth and Dalry lines was included. This ran across an undeveloped area on a line which later became Harrison Road through Harrison Park, with a continuous climb to cross the Union Canal. The Musselburgh extension disappeared, yet again, but instead came a short branch in Leith east from Foot of Leith Walk to Restalrig Road. The doubling of the Portobello line was now undertaken with alacrity, Major General Hutchinson inspecting it on 21 December 1881 'in a new car drawn by four horses'[100]. The short Restalrig Road branch became the first of the additions to be built, opening on 1 May 1882 with a service to Waterloo Place via York Place. On the same day the Tramways Company commenced a bus from the Portobello tram terminus to Musselburgh and Levenhall; this was seen as but a precursor to introduction of a tramway[101].

When work commenced on the new line from Granville Terrace (Polwarth) and on to the High Street, the contract was – yet again – let to James Gowans, this being remarked on by several disgruntled shareholders. When the following contract was let, for the North Junction Street branch, it went to Andrew Waddell, who henceforth shared most of the Company's work with Gowans. With one exception these new lines were completed and inspected by Hutchinson on 11 July 1882, but not until 1 August were they brought into regular use. There was at this date no sign of the link line between Dalry and Polwarth. The new road (Harrison Road) was in course of construction, paid for by the Merchant Company to give access to their feus. With no immediate dwellings occupied (or potential passengers) it was not a difficult decision to allow the road formation to consolidate for a reasonable period prior to tramway construction.

In the meantime, and possibly not unconnected with the resignation of D W Paterson as secretary to the Tramways Company, the *Scotsman* newspaper devoted a considerable number of column inches to what might be described today as 'investigative journalism'[102]. With regard to the initial promotion of tramways to serve the capital city, it got hold of figures (referred earlier) relating to '... the dealings of the Tramway adventurers with Bailies and Town Councillors ... [but] ... it is felt that there is much more that ought to be known before a full understanding of all the evil-doing can be arrived at.' The Company's books to which the newspaper had access showed the preliminary expenses amounted to £18,418.18.7d [equivalent to £2 million at time of writing]. The two competing

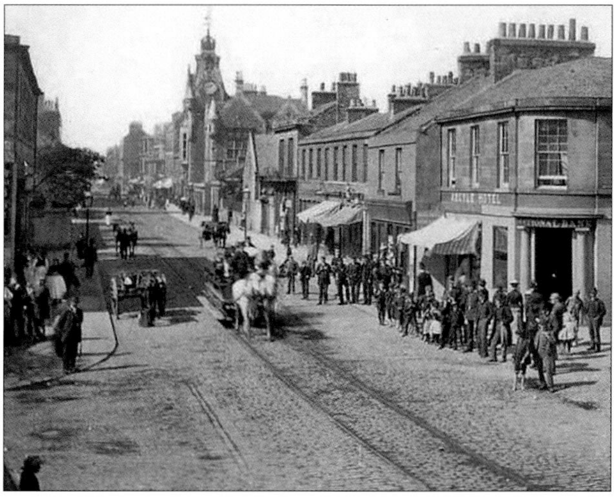

Portobello High Street at the top of Bath Street, with a large number of local children to hand. The view shows one of the open cars first in service in 1876 and very popular in the summer. They were also used for workmen's and football specials at all times of the year – not always so much appreciated. The small Portobello Depot was located on the south side of the thoroughfare, almost opposite the imposing and still extant Town Hall (the building with the clock).

1871 London based entrepreneurial solicitors did very well from their (brief) Edinburgh involvement. £2000 went to Fisher & Parrish as compensation for withdrawal of their competitive scheme, while £3000 went to John Morris as commission of 1% on capital for taking 'risk'. More than ten years after the events the revelations provoked little, if any, reaction. All then was water under the bridge. The *Scotsman* was careful to apportion no blame: 'It will thus be seen that the kindly gentlemen who undertook to provide a Tramway Bill for Edinburgh were not badly paid. There is not a word to be said against the payments to them. They entered into a speculation, and they conducted it to a successful conclusion.' The sting was in the tail: '... Mr Paterson, who enabled them to be successful, did so with the assistance of men who ought to have been most careful to have nothing to do with speculators in such a case'.

The new lines opened for traffic on 1 August 1882, with operation from Polwarth to Post Office alternately by Lothian Road and Lauriston and Dalry to Powburn via Princes Street. Seafield cars were extended to Haymarket and those from the North Junction Street branch ran to West End; a new service was introduced between Haymarket and Grange Cemetery. Unfortunately the expenditure on rail renewals plus the extensions, additional horses, cars and staff, resulted in a dividend reduced to 5%. A separate Act of Parliament obtained in July 1882 authorised a one-mile branch south from Churchhill as far as Morningside Drive. The first half of this, as far as the foot of the hill (beside what was to become Morningside Road Station) came into use during November, the remaining length following on 26 May. Special small single deck cars were built at Shrubhill to serve this steeply graded extension[103].

The winter of 1882-3 was severe, with heavy snowfall in the city from early December. Combined with temperatures as low as 6°F and dense fog, tram services were much disrupted, then totally abandoned, with snow approaching 15 inches deep. Agreement with the Roads Dept had tramway employees clear from Leith Walk to the West End, while they concentrated efforts elsewhere. Tram services had to be totally abandoned from 7 December, the Company calculating their cost as £200 for every day lost. Their snowplough was in action, hauled by no less than twelve horses. Unfortunately packed snow frozen into the rail grooves rendered the efforts futile and an alternative device was more successful. This was the 'spring scraper' – fitted in front of the front wheels of a tram, which cleared the rail groove fairly successfully[104]. Harry Booth claimed several patents for such devices. Disruption followed for the best part of two weeks, affecting income considerably.

The J C Robinson (brief) interlude

Early in March 1883 the Tramways Company astutely appointed – from forty applicants – a relatively young man (then just 35 years of age) as Manager and Secretary in place of Dr Wood who resigned due to ill health. This was J Clifton Robinson who served under the American who brought the philosophy of street railways (tramways) from America to Britain – George Francis Train. Robinson already claimed to have accumulated his tramway experience from Birkenhead, New York, Liverpool, London, Dublin, Cork and Bristol[105]. His appointment was contentious, as it became known that in addition to his salary, he was to receive a bonus of £50 for every ½% of dividend above 5%. However, he continued on his peripatetic career, stopping in Edinburgh for only 11 months, but even in that short time managed to exert his influence in several significant areas. Wood died just a year after his retiral, on 26 February 1884.

One of Robinson's first actions was to hold a 'familiarisation' meeting with his outdoor staff. They were not reticent in airing their grievances and took the opportunity to voice their dissatisfaction regarding lengths of shifts, and the short times allowed for meal breaks. An average day consisted of fourteen hours, and on Saturdays this was fifteen hours – on an open platform, completely devoid of shelter, in all weathers. It was also stated that trace boys were 'roughly used'. Robinson attempted to introduce betterment in conditions with a general revision of routes imple-

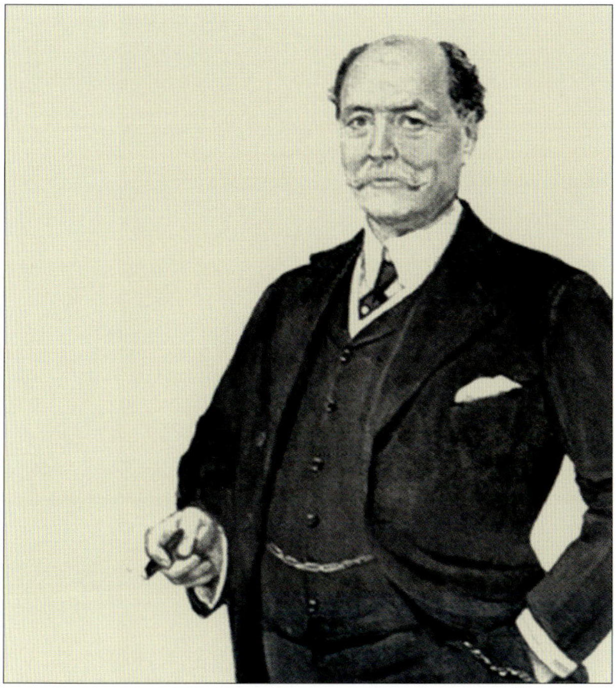

Above. James Clifton Robinson spent just a short time (March 1883 to February 1884) as Edinburgh's tramway manager, but managed to exert significant influence during that period. This is a later portrait; he became well known as 'The Tramway King' and was knighted in 1905.

Right. *Scotsman* 27 April 1883

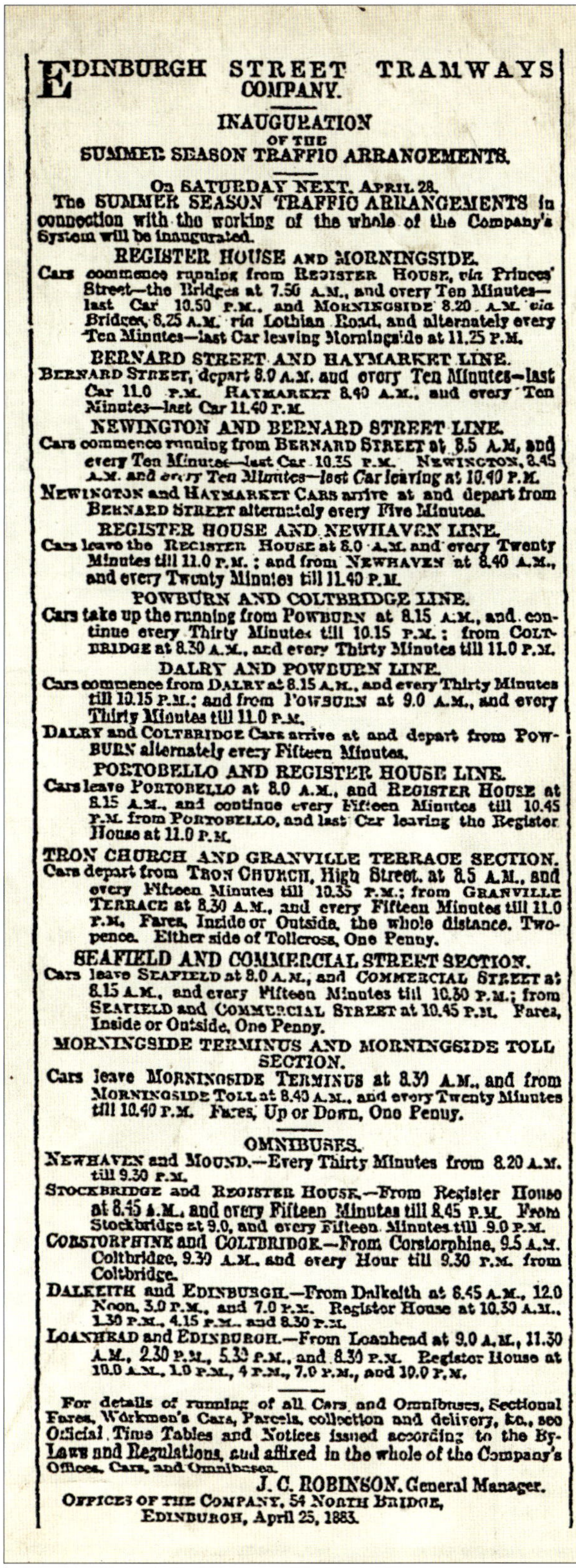

EDINBURGH STREET TRAMWAYS COMPANY.

INAUGURATION OF THE SUMMER SEASON TRAFFIC ARRANGEMENTS.

On SATURDAY NEXT, APRIL 28,

The SUMMER SEASON TRAFFIC ARRANGEMENTS in connection with the working of the whole of the Company's System will be inaugurated.

REGISTER HOUSE AND MORNINGSIDE.

Cars commence running from REGISTER HOUSE, *via* Princes' Street—the Bridges at 7.50 A.M., and every Ten Minutes—last Car 10.50 P.M., and MORNINGSIDE 8.20 A.M. *via* Bridges, 8.25 A.M. *via* Lothian Road, and alternately every Ten Minutes—last Car leaving Morningside at 11.25 P.M.

BERNARD STREET AND HAYMARKET LINE.

BERNARD STREET, depart 8.0 A.M. and every Ten Minutes—last Car 11.0 P.M. HAYMARKET 8.40 A.M., and every Ten Minutes—last Car 11.40 P.M.

NEWINGTON AND BERNARD STREET LINE.

Cars commence running from BERNARD STREET at 8.5 A.M, and every Ten Minutes—last Car 10.35 P.M. NEWINGTON, 8.45 A.M. and every Ten Minutes—last Car leaving at 10.40 P.M.

NEWINGTON and HAYMARKET CARS arrive at and depart from BERNARD STREET alternately every Five Minutes.

REGISTER HOUSE AND NEWHAVEN LINE.

Cars leave the REGISTER HOUSE at 8.0 A.M. and every Twenty Minutes till 11.0 P.M. ; and from NEWHAVEN at 8.40 A.M., and every Twenty Minutes till 11.40 P.M.

POWBURN AND COLTBRIDGE LINE.

Cars take up the running from POWBURN at 8.15 A.M., and continue every Thirty Minutes till 10.15 P.M. ; from COLTBRIDGE at 8.30 A.M., and every Thirty Minutes till 11.0 P.M.

DALRY AND POWBURN LINE.

Cars commence from DALRY at 8.15 A.M., and every Thirty Minutes till 10.15 P.M.; and from POWBURN at 9.0 A.M., and every Thirty Minutes till 11.0 P.M.

DALRY and COLTBRIDGE Cars arrive at and depart from POWBURN alternately every Fifteen Minutes.

PORTOBELLO AND REGISTER HOUSE LINE.

Cars leave PORTOBELLO at 8.0 A.M., and REGISTER HOUSE at 8.15 A.M., and continue every Fifteen Minutes till 10.45 P.M. from PORTOBELLO, and last Car leaving the Register House at 11.0 P.M.

TRON CHURCH AND GRANVILLE TERRACE SECTION.

Cars depart from TRON CHURCH, High Street, at 8.5 A.M., and every Fifteen Minutes till 10.35 P.M.; from GRANVILLE TERRACE at 8.30 A.M., and every Fifteen Minutes till 11.0 P.M. Fares, Inside or Outside, the whole distance, Twopence. Either side of Tollcross, One Penny.

SEAFIELD AND COMMERCIAL STREET SECTION.

Cars leave SEAFIELD at 8.0 A.M., and COMMERCIAL STREET at 8.15 A.M., and every Fifteen Minutes till 10.30 P.M.; from SEAFIELD and COMMERCIAL STREET at 10.45 P.M. Fares, Inside or Outside, One Penny.

MORNINGSIDE TERMINUS AND MORNINGSIDE TOLL SECTION.

Cars leave MORNINGSIDE TERMINUS at 8.30 A.M., and from MORNINGSIDE TOLL at 8.40 A.M., and every Twenty Minutes till 10.40 P.M. Fares, Up or Down, One Penny.

OMNIBUSES.

NEWHAVEN and MOUND.—Every Thirty Minutes from 8.20 A.M. till 9.30 P.M.

STOCKBRIDGE and REGISTER HOUSE.—From Register House at 8.45 A.M., and every Fifteen Minutes till 8.45 P.M. From Stockbridge at 9.0, and every Fifteen Minutes till 9.0 P.M.

CORSTORPHINE and COLTBRIDGE.—From Corstorphine, 9.5 A.M. Coltbridge, 9.30 A.M., and every Hour till 9.30 P.M. from Coltbridge.

DALKEITH and EDINBURGH.—From Dalkeith at 8.45 A.M., 12.0 Noon, 3.0 P.M., and 7.0 P.M. Register House at 10.30 A.M., 1.30 P.M., 4.15 P.M., and 8.30 P.M.

LOANHEAD and EDINBURGH.—From Loanhead at 9.0 A.M., 11.30 A.M., 2.30 P.M., 5.30 P.M., and 8.30 P.M. Register House at 10.0 A.M., 1.0 P.M., 4 P.M., 7.0 P.M., and 10.0 P.M.

For details of running of all Cars and Omnibuses, Sectional Fares, Workmen's Cars, Parcels, collection and delivery, &c., see Official Time Tables and Notices issued according to the By-Laws and Regulations, and affixed in the whole of the Company's Offices, Cars, and Omnibuses.

J. C. ROBINSON, General Manager.

OFFICES OF THE COMPANY, 54 NORTH BRIDGE,
EDINBURGH, April 25, 1883.

mented on 28 April. This endeavoured to give a minimum five minute frequency on all main streets and is reproduced in full as it was advertised at the time[106]. This also attempted to reduce the working hours of the platform staff.

A highly visible change now introduced was painting of cars according to the route they ran on, with the 'prestige' Morningside Circle route becoming white and gold. The practice eventually extended to at least nine different route liveries until this feature was lost with the coming of the cable tram some 20 years later. The white Morningside cars became a well recognised feature of the late Victorian Edinburgh street scene, with the other cars, yellow, green , blue, red, etc adding splashes of colour. The colours aided identification by illiterate potential passengers. The 'timetable' car number plate system appears to have been given up at this time with cars now conventionally numbered

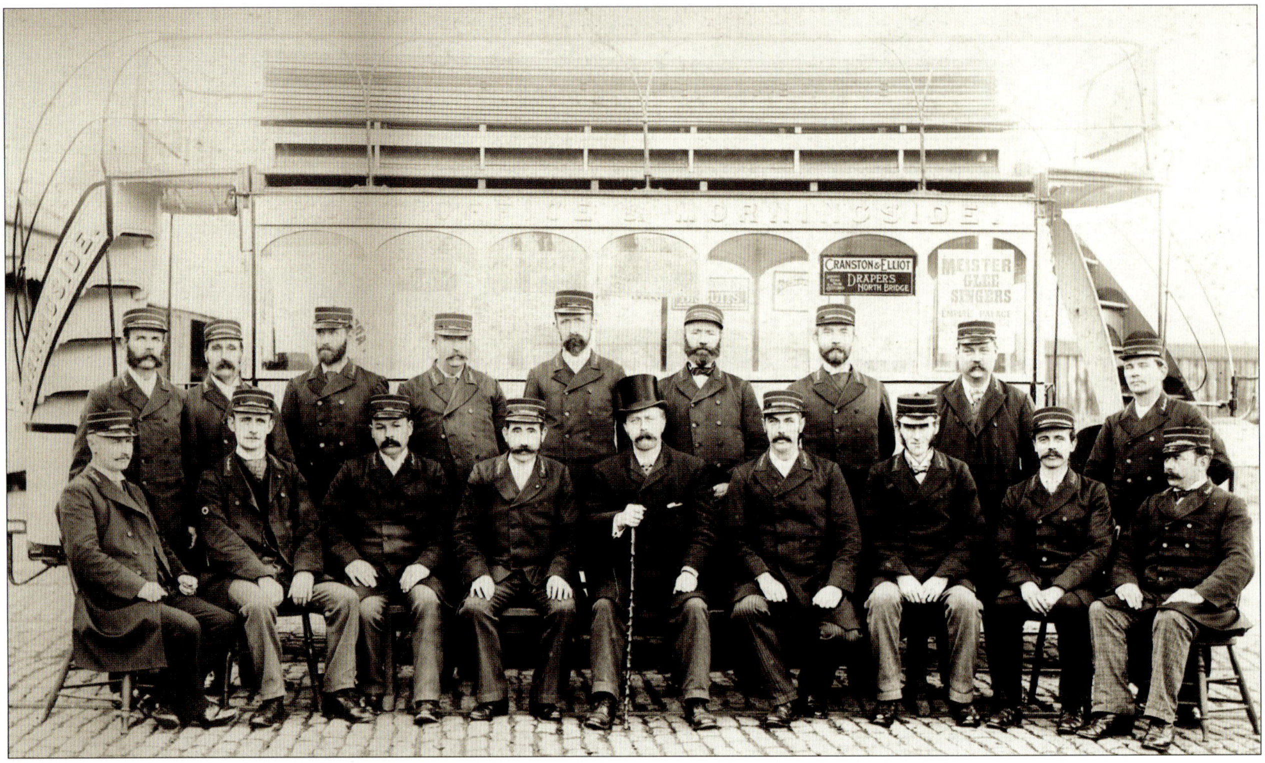

Inspectors with manager John Pitcairn, photographed behind Shrubhill stables. The car is in the white livery of the prestige Morningside Circular service, illustrating the route colours introduced in April 1883. Pitcairn assumed his position in June 1884.

consecutively from 1 (although spare cars and the open summer or workmen's cars appear to have been renumbered as required to maintain their place at the end of the series). By starting the Polwarth car from Tron Church the traffic volume using the single track of North Bridge Street was considerably reduced. On three of these new routes (Morningside Toll, Polwarth and Seafield to Commercial St) ticket issue was discontinued, fares being recorded by boy conductors on a waybill at the same time ringing a bell. Seats were provided for drivers and saddles for trace boys – neither of these two 'luxuries' lasting long. A bonus scheme for conductors who exhibited 'best returns' was also proposed.

These variations appear to have done little to placate the workforce and another deputation went to see Robinson, concentrating on the excessive hours which still prevailed under the new arrangements; for example, on number 15 car on Bernard St to Haymarket the shift started at 7.50 am, through to 12.05 the following morning, with a 45 minute lunch break; and number 29 car on Register House to Newhaven the shift was from 7.30 am until 11.40 pm. Striking was mentioned, but on 6 May Robinson met the men at Shrubhill with a more conciliatory outcome. It was agreed to give the new working arrangements a fair trial, and in the meantime drivers and conductors were to receive a 2 shilling per week wage increase; the drivers scale started at 23s. 0d and rose to 26s. 0d; conductors now started at 21s. 0d, rising to 25s. 0d after two years unblemished service[107].

As an aside, at this time Robinson also had to deal with the matter of the manure contract. To give an idea of the scale of the 'output' from just one of the many establishments employing large numbers of horses in every city, the anticipated stable manure from Shrubhill amounted to 300 tons per month, plus 15 tons from the Loanhead farm, 12 tons from Portobello and 6 tons from Corstorphine. When this is multiplied by all the other horses on the streets, the scale of the problem becomes apparent. Shrubhill was now well provided for, as in the extension of the stabling to the north, the opportunity was taken to put in a railway siding alongside the building, assisting disposal. This railway siding was also physically connected to the tramway lines here. Robinson suffered a nasty accident at the end of May when, during a night-time fire at the hay shed in Shrubhill he fell into the pit between the rails used to gain access to the underside of the trams; he was shaken, but not badly injured.

During June 1883 work laying the lines in Harrison Road and west from Granville Terrace as far as Colinton Road commenced, the time allowed for their execution expiring on 11 August. In this instance flat-bottom railway rails were used, with the groove formed by the cast iron blocks of the type which had recently been trialled on Lothian Road. These were completed and inspected by Major Marindin of the Board of Trade on 11 October, but not brought into use immediately. Early in November the existing route from Powburn to Dalry Cemetery was extended up Harrison Road, while the Tron Church to Granville Terrace route was extended along Polwarth Terrace to its junction with Colinton Road.

Robinson's hopes of major remuneration benefits must have seemed unattainable when with the Company half-yearly report of June 1883 the dividend was declared as just 3%, and at the next period had increased to 5%, the bench mark from which his performance related pay kicked in. The reductions were blamed on the winter costs, track renewals and the cost of unprofitable extensions, but may have focussed his mind on a move. In what became an annual event after 1878, the staff Festival of 1884 was held on a Sunday evening at the start of January. Much disquiet was expressed by the local chapter of the Lord's Day Observance Society when on that occasion the Company used the Sabbath for events of this nature; there was of course no Sunday tram operation, hence having such meetings on that day did not interfere with normal operation – previously held on a week-night, staff were released in relays. The coach building workshop was decorated with evergreens and flags and the large number in attendance were served a dinner and tea, accompanied by sacred music. Uplifting for the souls of their workers in the best spirit of Victorian philanthropy, 400 staff attended, plus 150 wives and daughters, all seated according to status and position in the Company hierarchy. One table was reserved for 75 drivers, another for 75 conductors. 100 stablemen and 100 trace and stable boys had two tables each, while the female guests were seated apart from the men. Senior management, directors, invited guests – and Robinson of course – sat at a table on a dais[108].

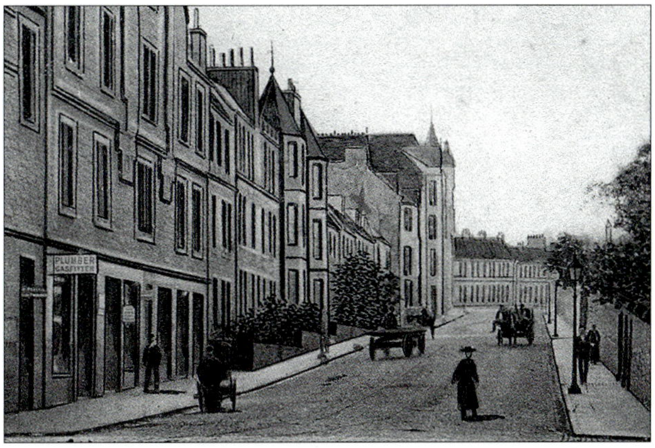

The 1881 extension lines included a speculative link from the previous Gorgie terminus, up Ardmillan Terrace and Harrison Road to cross the Union Canal before joining Polwarth Terrace. The climb from Gorgie was long and steep, as can be seen from this view of Ardmillan Terrace in horse car days. When first constructed there were few dwellings built and the whole exercise was considered a drain on resources.

These events were thoroughly enjoyed by all present, perhaps even more so by Robinson, who just a few weeks later handed his resignation to the chairman. There had been already talk of a new form of tramway, operated by moving cables below street level serving the northern side of Edinburgh from which the horse tramway was excluded by virtue of the severe gradients of the streets, the first of this nature in

Europe, ascending Highgate Hill in London was just about to open. A salary of £1000 per annum, and the chance to be in at the beginnings of this new form of transport (which had been operational in the USA for ten years) was more than enough to tempt him south. That company eventually went bankrupt, but this was no impediment to JCR's career. He went on to manage the highly successful London United Tramways Company and in 1905 received a knighthood for his efforts.

Enter John E Pitcairn

Robinson's successor was John E Pitcairn, formerly the Chief Clerk in the General Manager's office of the North British Railway – a seemingly unlikely choice, but obviously an astute one, as the tramway prospered under his guardianship and he served the Company for more than 20 years. As in most years, services were reduced over the winter period; at the beginning of November 1883 in addition to the normal reductions, several route changes were made, as referred to by the advertisement shown on page 56[109].

A system of cable tramways to serve the northern side of Edinburgh appears to have been first mooted late in November 1883. To this the directors of the Street Tramways Co decided to respond by promoting a competing Bill '... to preserve the interests of their shareholders in view of the opposition with which they had been threatened'[110]. Their plans projected cable lines on the Hallidie system from Princes Street to Goldenacre and to Stockbridge. The opposition's intent was to use Low & Grim's system with, in addition to

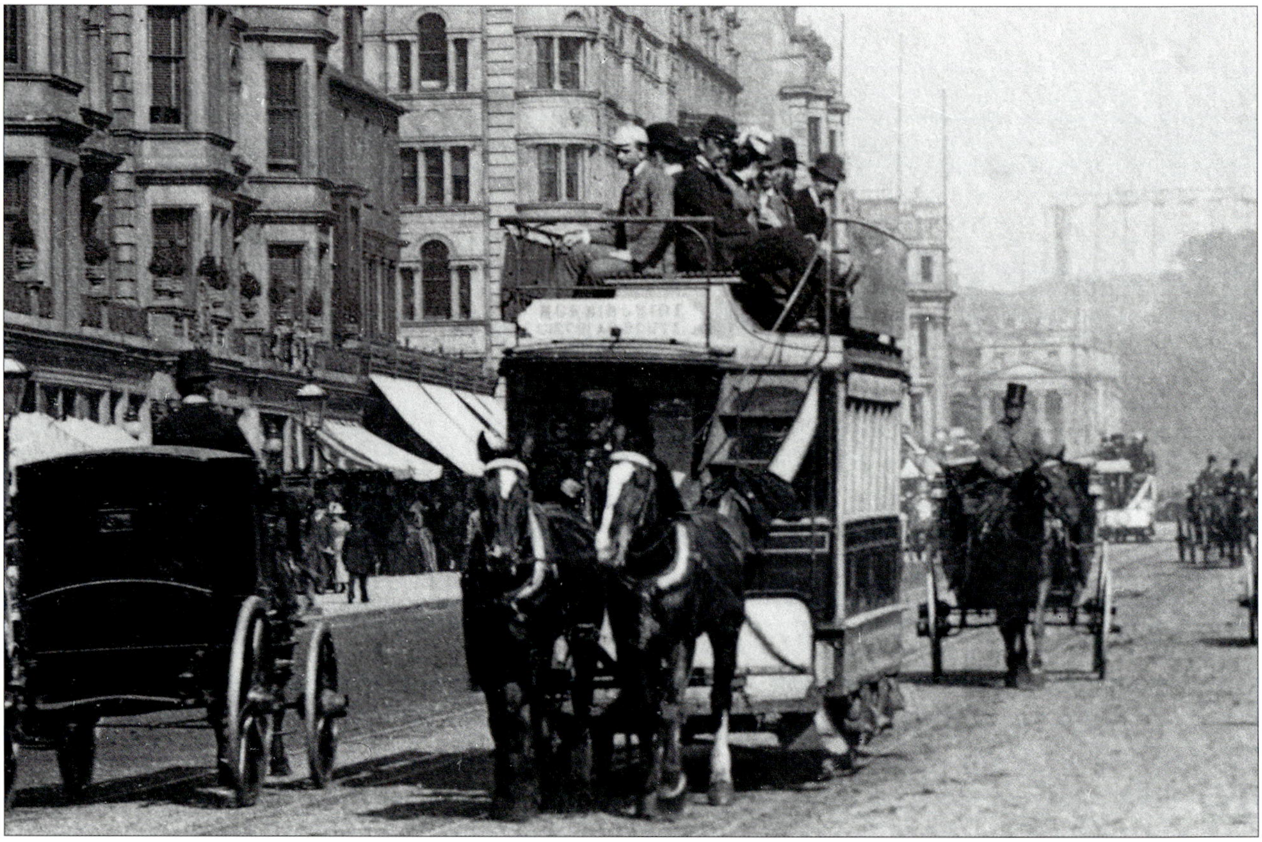

Proceeding in a westerly direction along Princes Street is one of the cars with the 'Liverpool' style of waist panel. It may be running as an extra, as although displaying 'Morningside Circular Route' on the destination board, it is not in the white livery. In the distance can be seen a car heading in the opposite direction on the 'Outer' circle which is painted appropriately.

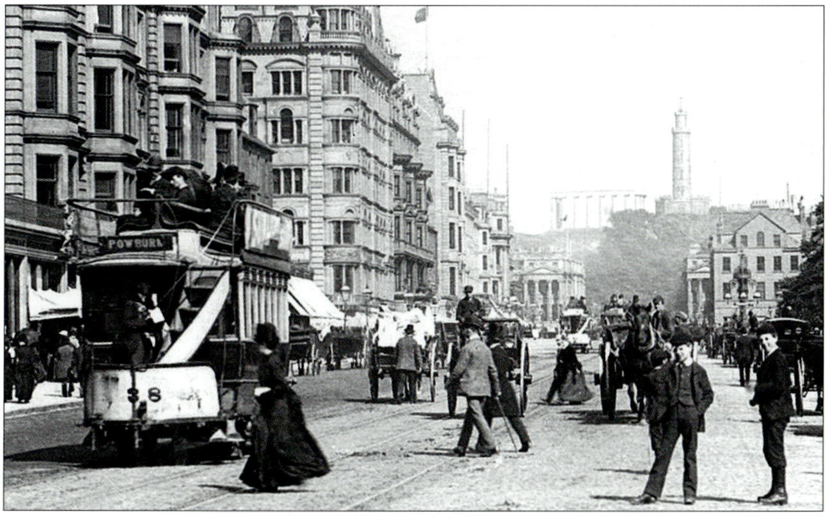

Photographed at the same location opposite the Scott Monument, car 38 is heading in the opposite direction on the Coltbridge to Powburn route and would be painted chocolate brown with buff rocker panels. These destinations are perhaps unfamiliar to present day travellers, but Roseburn to Newington would present little difficulty.

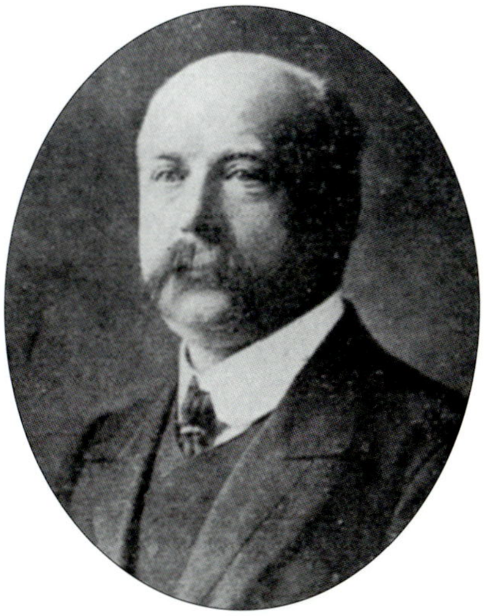

John E Pitcairn, Tramway Manager, 1884–1906.

these lines mentioned, to extend to Trinity and then by Newhaven to Leith Custom House in Commercial Street. However several shareholders raised objections about the Tramways Company's proposals, so at the next half-year meeting in the following January it was advised that the cable bill had been dropped for the time being, although the directors would reserve their views regarding the prospect of converting some of their more steeply graded lines in the future. Dividends were depressed but maintained at 5%, the change in fortunes being laid at the unprofitable newly constructed lines, this despite operating costs being at a new low, in fact they were claimed to be (at 64%) the lowest percentage of any British company. It was said that the 1881 extension lines formed an 'incubus' (amongst several meanings, this could be interpreted as a nightmare!). The length of tramways operated had increased now to 18 miles 15 chains, nearly 5 miles having been added by the lines authorised in the 1881 Act. Passenger numbers before the extensions reached an annual maximum of 10½ million (in year ending 30 June 1877) but failed to reach this level again until after the 1884 Exhibition[111].

The newly formed Edinburgh Northern Tramways Company (cable tramways) put forward a Bill which was unsuccessful, but when re-submitted, with the Leith lines deleted, and the gauge altered from 3 ft 6 ins to standard 4 ft 8½ ins, it was accepted. The Street Tramway Co had extracted an agreement that the new company would not endeavour to force through-running onto their lines. Details of the Northern Company's travails do not form part of this account; suffice to say that their first section eventually opened for passengers at the end of January 1888[112].

Searching for an acceptable form of mechanical traction was never out of the thoughts of the directors and during 1884 they had a request from Colonel Beaumont for permission to operate his compressed air tram engine between the West End and Coltbridge during the Forestry Exhibition to be held that year in the grounds of Donaldson's Hospital. The machine had seen some use in Stratford, East London, but Edinburgh's douce civic leaders considered that letting it loose amongst the throngs heading for the exhibition could be dangerous, so refused permission (although they seemed unsure if they actually had powers to so act in this manner). The machine seems to have subsequently been used briefly in Liverpool[113].

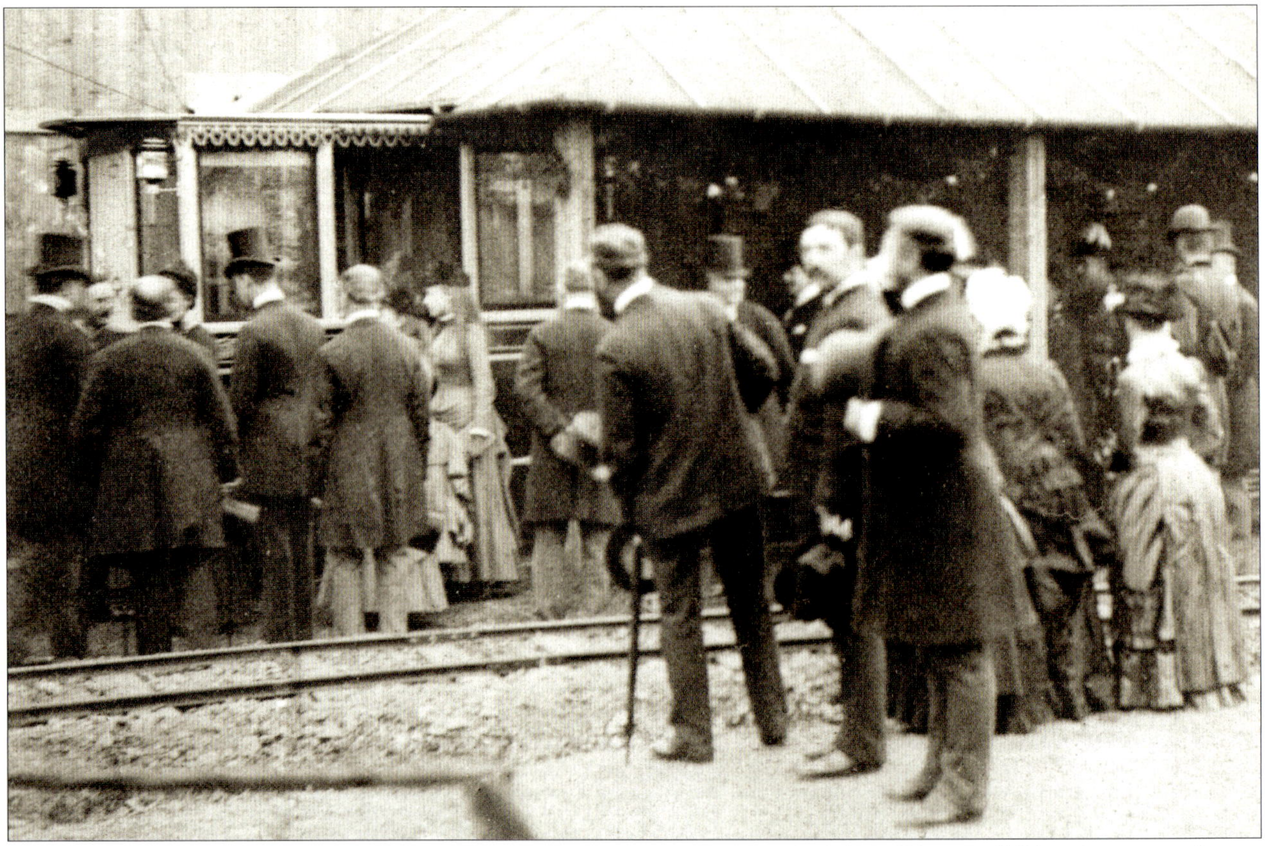

The royal inspection on 22 August 1884 of Henry Bock Binko's electric railway which was demonstrated at the Forestry Exhibition held in the grounds of Donaldson's Hospital, West Coates. Extreme left is the Prince of Wales, then Binko is just visible, with on his left the Princess of Wales; the next gentleman with the tall hat is the Duke of Clarence. It can be seen that the shed was built slightly too low for the *Alexandra* coach so a piece had to be cut from the edge of the roof.

Binko's electric experiment

One of the highlights of the Exhibition was the electric railway of Henry Bock Binko. This Austrian inventor had operated his pioneer electric railway at Crystal Palace in London then brought it to Edinburgh for the Forestry Exhibition. Bad weather delayed track laying hence this attraction did not open until 17 July 1884. Soon after, on 22 August, the line was graced by the patronage of the Prince and Princess of Wales and their family, for which occasion an ornate little carriage named *Alexandra* was built by John Hislop of Antigua Street (the Prince had to be convinced of the safety of the operation, but calmed his nerves by having a quick cigarette). The little car was used a week later when Prime Minister William Gladstone visited the Exhibition. When at Crystal Palace Binko used for motive power a small electric locomotive named *Volta*, but on the ½ mile long Edinburgh line had another, the more utilitarian *Ohm*. During the exhibition a conversation between the new tramway manager, John Pitcairn and Binko debated the possibility of applying these avant-garde principles to tramways, and to the near-by line in particular. Perhaps surprisingly, on 8 October permission was given for a trial run to take place[114].

It had been hoped to run the car from the exhibition to Register House, but this was curtailed to Haymarket Station. A row of heavy timbers was laid between the tram rails, with two copper strips (separated by a thin wooden strip) fixed on top. Power was

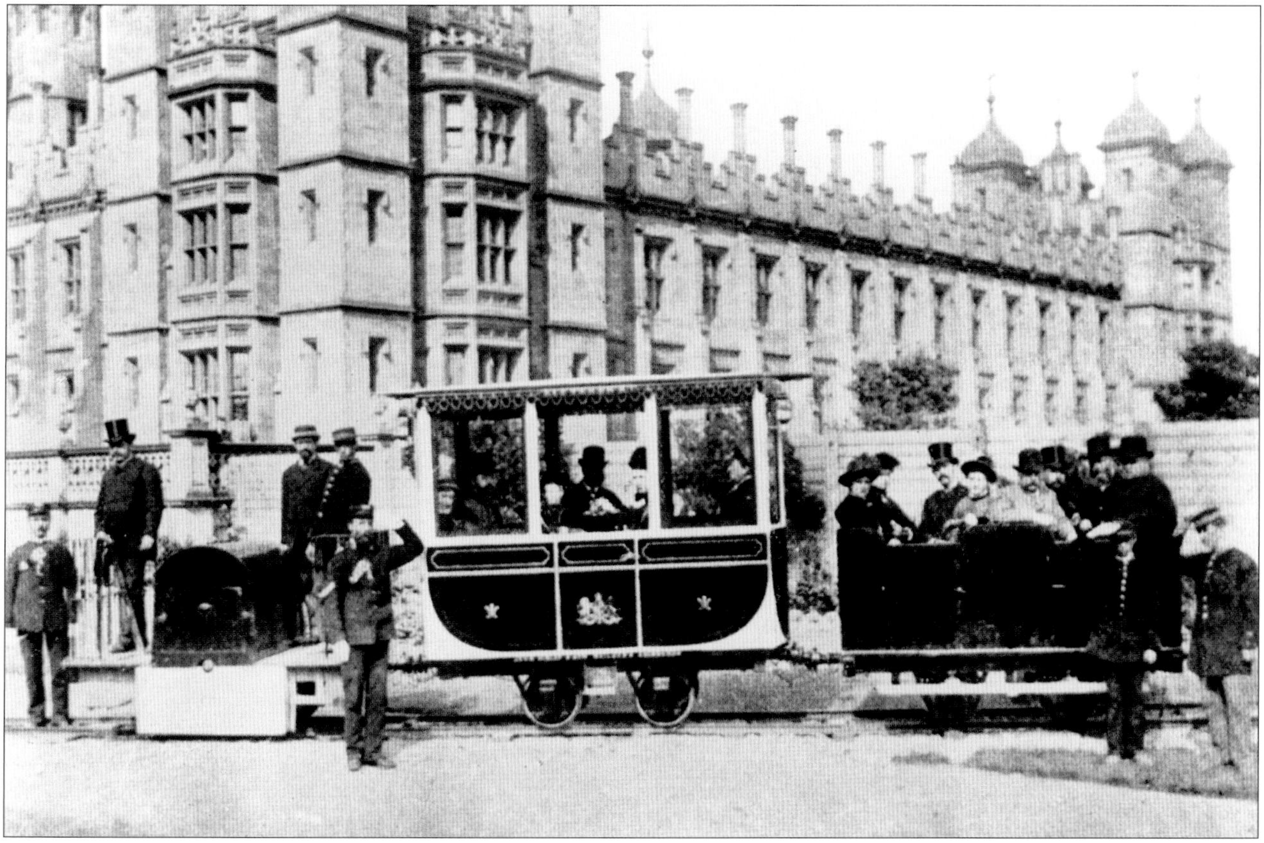

A suitable pose in front of the imposing Hospital building, with, perhaps surprisingly, no sign whatsoever of anything else relative to the Exhibition. With the royal party safely aboard the *Alexandra* and with his staff at the 'salute', Binko has taken his place on the electric locomotive.

Designed by William Playfair and completed in 1851, the benefaction by newspaper editor James Donaldson was for many years a specialised school for deaf children. The A-listed structure is to be converted to flats after the school moved to purpose-built premises in Linlithgow.

supplied from the generator in the exhibition grounds and relayed to a small wheeled trolley running on the timbers. The motor from *Ohm* (actually a dynamo acting as a motor) was mounted in the centre of one of the ordinary tramcars with the armature rotation transmitted to the car's axle by belting. Starting at 2 am several satisfactory trips were made, with this trial gaining a special place in transport history as the first electric street tramway in the United Kingdom using power generated from a distant source of supply. Binko used his plant and railway in Great Yarmouth the following year, but his financial acumen was not as well developed as his inventive talent and he was declared bankrupt. Edinburgh gained nothing from its prime historical position; it lay to the Burgh of Blackpool to agree, just three weeks later, to give approval for the first successful electric street tramway in the UK which opened on 29 September 1885[115].

Returning to Edinburgh matters, the finances of the Company benefitted from the increased patronage brought by the Forestry Exhibition and the dividend relating to the second half of 1884 was increased to 6½%; the converse effect was recorded in the next statement, with the dividend reduced to 5%. The explanation for this, as given by the Chairman at the half-yearly meeting, was mostly the result of compensation paid following a bus accident, extension to the bus routes, and the cost of joining into the tour business. A tourist coach was inaugurated running excursions to the Forth Rail Bridge, already two years into its

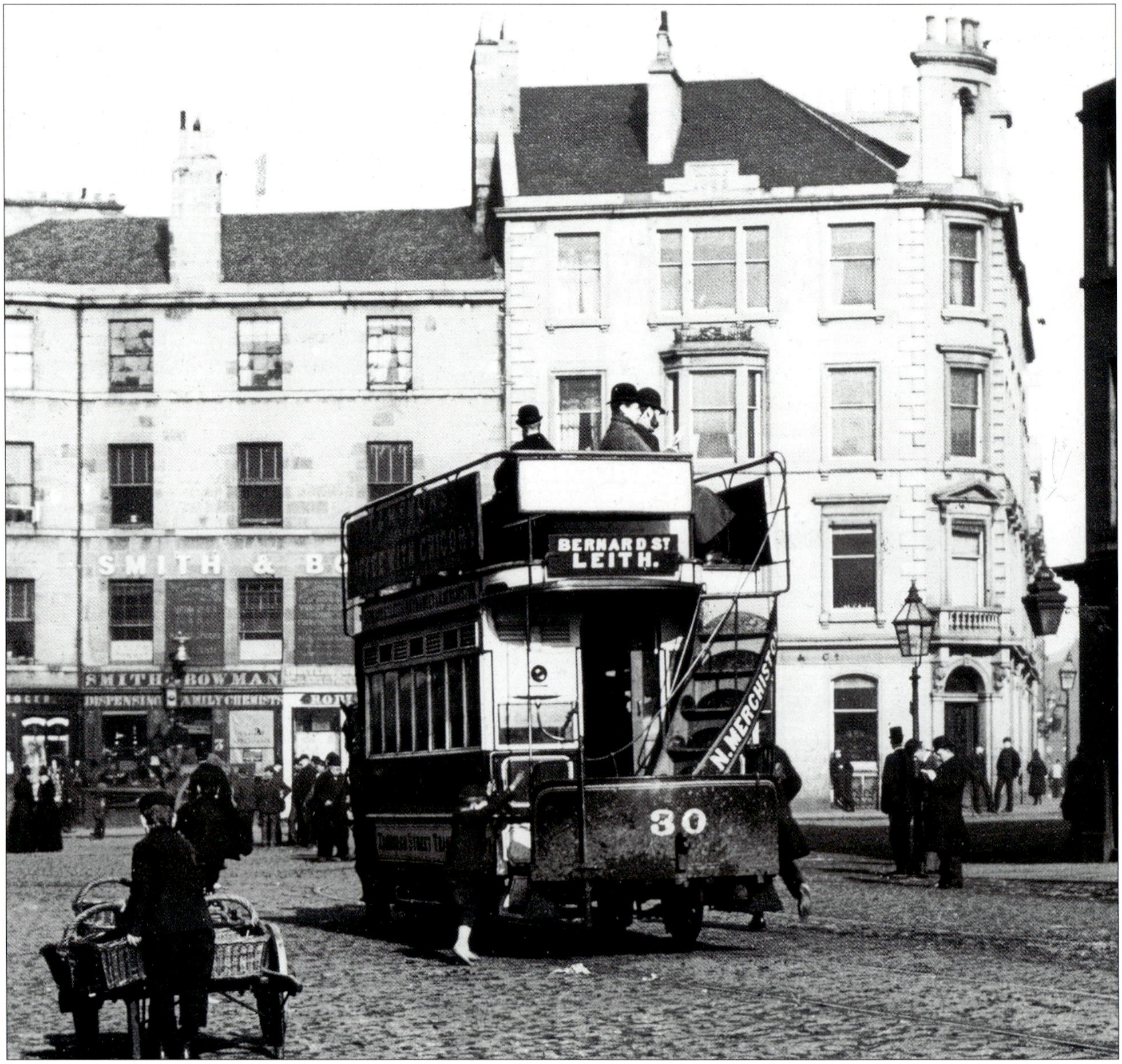

Red car 30 at the 'Fit o' th' Walk' (Foot of Leith Walk) with a bare footed lad sneaking a fly ride while the conductor's attention is elsewhere. The car is of the 'Exhibition' style, built at Shrubhill, the first of which was awarded a gold medal at the International Exhibition held on the Meadows in 1886. More than 40 cars were then built to this design, most with reversible 'garden' seats on top, this increasing outside capacity from 18 to 26 passengers. Ten cars were used on this route.

construction, and a spectacular sight which became more and more breathtaking with each passing month[116]. Even after completion in 1890 the bridge remained a magnet for tourists.

The late Victorian era spawned many such exhibitions in Britain and abroad, the medals presented adding prestige to those so awarded and featuring largely on letterheads and advertising. The next in Edinburgh, for 'Industry, Science and Art', came in 1886 and was held on the western end of the Meadows. Several of the tram routes were extended to give extra access to the site, plus eight cars 'which previously had been the property

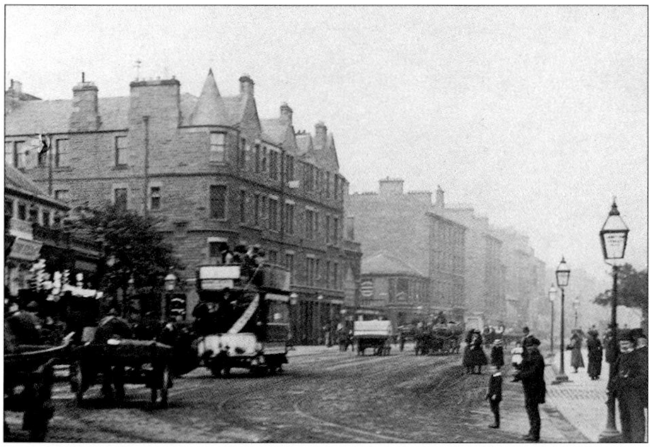

Looking up Leith Walk in 1891, prior to construction of Leith Central Station which replaced the buildings to the extreme left of the image. The tram, number 41 on route from Newhaven (Stanley Road) to Morningside Drive, has stopped to allow passengers to board. Male passengers were expected to jump on without the car stopping, also cars were not expected to be stopped at all on severe gradients. (City of Edinburgh Council – Edinburgh Libraries www.capitalcollections.org.uk)

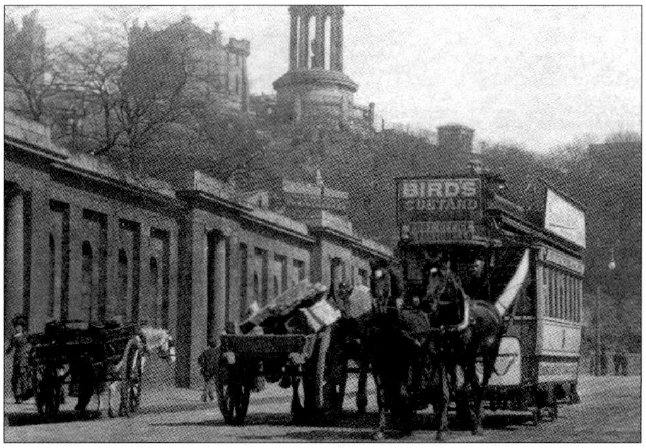

A disadvantage of the route colour identification of the vehicles was the confusion created when they were transferred to another route. Here we have a white Morningside car on the Portobello service, normally the preserve of yellow cars. Yellow does not display well on the orthochromatic photographic plates of the time, rendering as a fairly dark grey, and red appearing almost black. The scene is at the top of Waterloo Place with the City Observatory and Dugald Stewart's Monument.

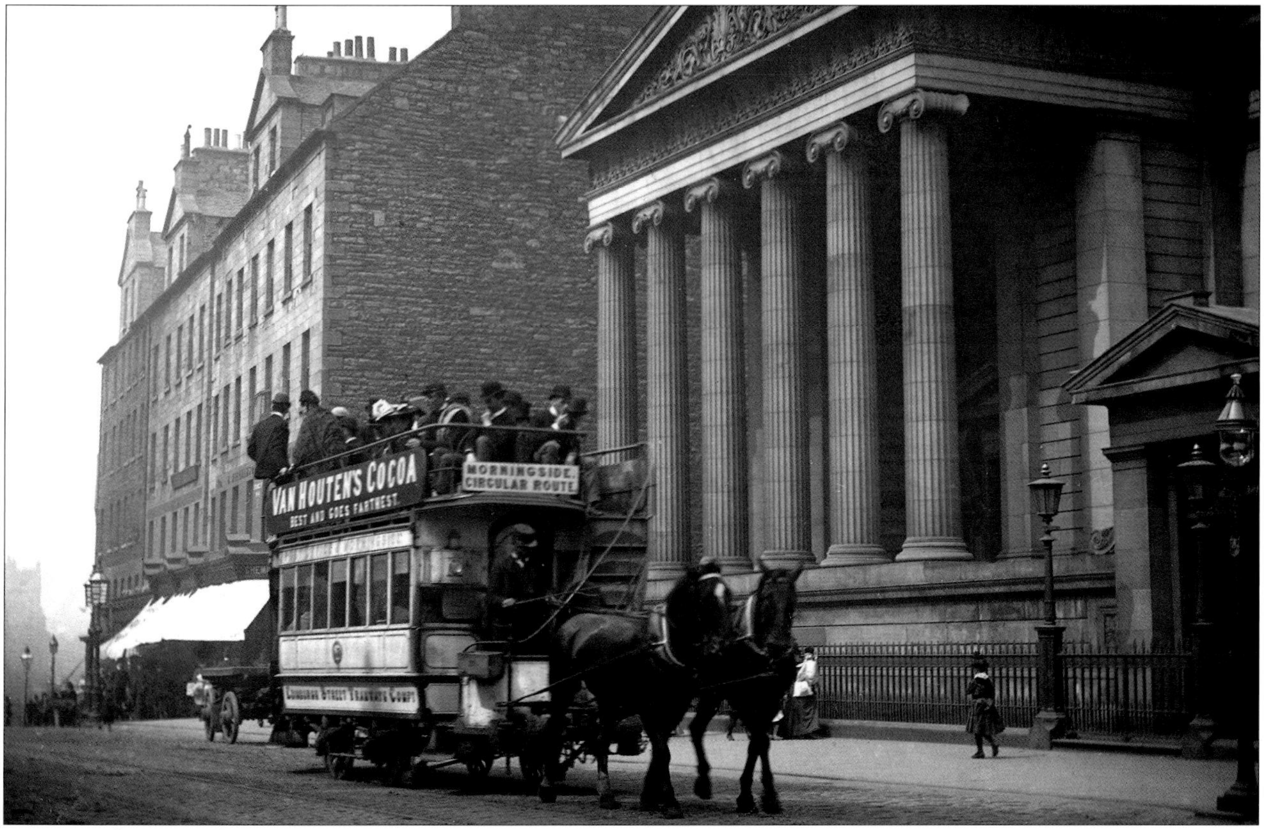

A white car (number 10) on its correct Circle route, on Nicolson Street passing the Surgeon's Hall (another Playfair building from the 1830s). The 36 seat car – or more accurately its conductor – is breaking several bye-laws relating to overcrowding and standing passengers on the top deck. Very surprisingly, with such a load, it has no assisting trace horse.

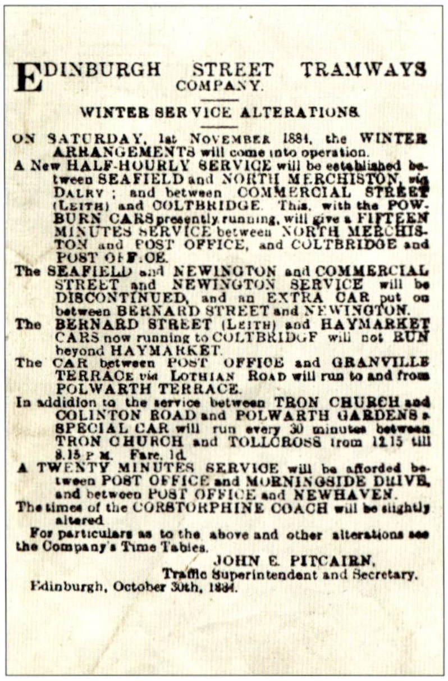

EDINBURGH STREET TRAMWAYS COMPANY.

WINTER SERVICE ALTERATIONS.

ON SATURDAY, 1st NOVEMBER 1884, the WINTER ARRANGEMENTS will come into operation.

A New HALF-HOURLY SERVICE will be established between SEAFIELD and NORTH MERCHISTON, via DALRY; and between COMMERCIAL STREET (LEITH) and COLTBRIDGE. This, with the POWBURN CARS presently running, will give a FIFTEEN MINUTES SERVICE between NORTH MERCHISTON and POST OFFICE, and COLTBRIDGE and POST OFFICE.

The SEAFIELD and NEWINGTON and COMMERCIAL STREET and NEWINGTON SERVICE will be DISCONTINUED, and an EXTRA CAR put on between BERNARD STREET and NEWINGTON.

The BERNARD STREET (LEITH) and HAYMARKET CARS now running to COLTBRIDGE will not RUN beyond HAYMARKET.

The CAR between POST OFFICE and GRANVILLE TERRACE via LOTHIAN ROAD will run to and from POLWARTH TERRACE.

In addidion to the service between TRON CHURCH and COLINTON ROAD and POLWARTH GARDENS a SPECIAL CAR will run every 30 minutes between TRON CHURCH and TOLLCROSS from 12.15 till 8.15 P.M. Fare, 1d.

A TWENTY MINUTES SERVICE will be afforded between POST OFFICE and MORNINGSIDE DRIVE, and between POST OFFICE and NEWHAVEN.

The times of the CORSTORPHINE COACH will be slightly altered.

For particulars as to the above and other alterations see the Company's Time Tables.

JOHN E. PITCAIRN,
Traffic Superintendent and Secretary.

Edinburgh, October 30th, 1884.

Above. *Scotsman* 1 November 1884

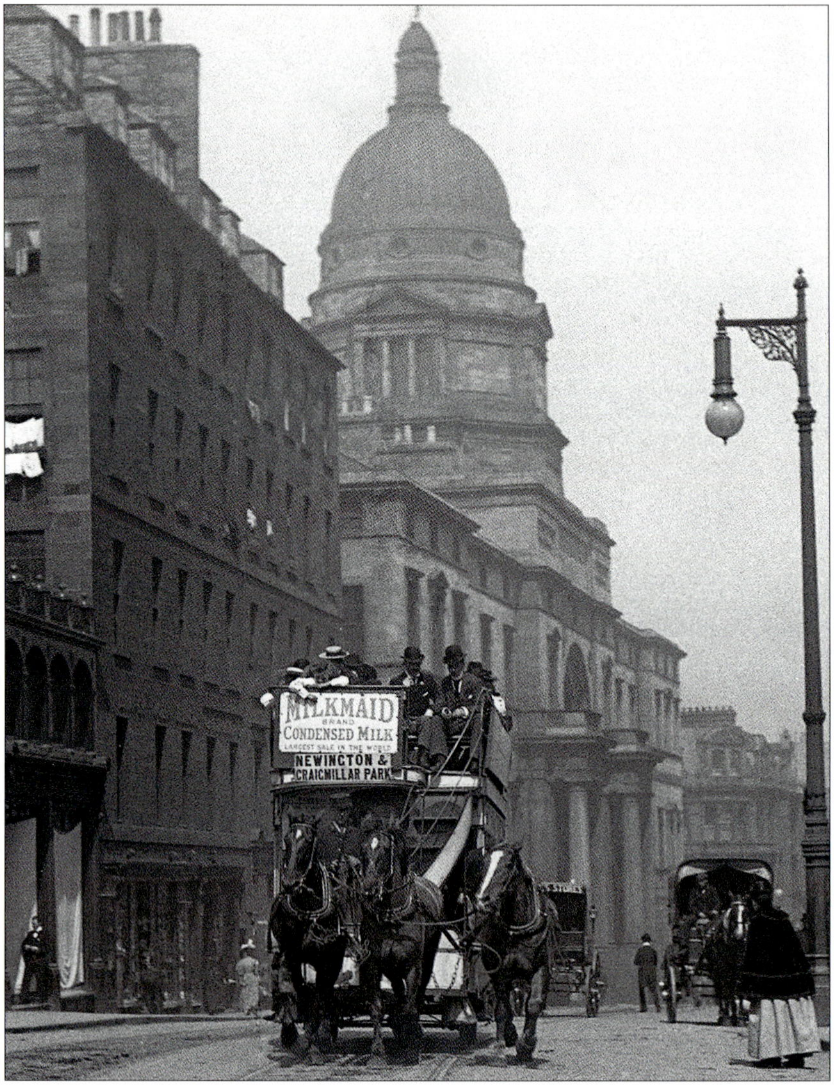

Right. Looking to the South Bridge (no bridge can actually be seen – it is entirely below this street level) from Nicolson Street. This car does have a trace horse to assist on the rise up to Nicolson Square. Behind is the stolid Old College building of the University of Edinburgh now with the dome finally added in 1879 to the Adam designed building. Most Edinburgh buildings' fine pale golden Craigleith sandstone had absorbed a grey pallor from the constant coal-fire 'reek' which gave rise to the nick-name 'Auld Reekie'. The six columns at the entrance to the Old Quad are each from a single 22 foot long piece of this fine grained stone.

of the company but had not been in use' were used to increase the regular complement. The Company exhibited its latest tramcar constructed at Shrubhill, which gained for the builders a silver medal. It incorporated upholstered seats in the saloon – a feature of the very first cars which had been dropped on health grounds – also its (normally brass) fittings were electro-plated.

This exhibition also featured an electric railway laid parallel to the north side of the site, linking the western entrance at Brougham Place, then south of North Meadow Walk, to the east entrance half a mile distant. For the line two cars were supplied free of charge by the North Metropolitan Tramways Company of London. Described as 'handsome and substantial', one was double deck seating 20 in the saloon and 26 on top, the other was open, seating 25[117]. It is probable that the former was the first 'garden seat' car seen in Edinburgh, as the Street Tramways Company introduced this style of seating from the following year since it allowed more passengers to be carried, and in greater comfort. Rails were supplied – also gratis – by the Barrow Steel Company with power generated by a 7 horse power engine from Marshall & Co of Gainsborough; this was located mid-way between the termini.

Between the rails was a 'third rail' consisting of a copper strip fixed to wooden baulks. The car had a fifth wheel which ran along this strip, held in place by a spring. The dynamo was connected by two cables, one to the rails, the other to the copper conductor rail. The electrical work was supervised by Messrs King, Brown & Co of Rosebank, their efforts earning them a silver medal. Fares of 2d adult and 1d child were charged, and during the six months of the exhibition the cars successfully carried more than 85,000 passengers, with over 3000 carried one particularly busy day[118]. The fate of the two vehicles following closure of the exhibition at the end of October is not known; it seems probable they were returned to their supplier in London.

A period of consolidation

Corstorphine residents were still keen to have a tram connection to their village, and in November 1886 sent a deputation in an endeavour to persuade the Tramways Company to oblige. Their plan was to obtain a Provisional Order for a two mile single track tram line, it being noted that the existing bus made a profit of over £300 per annum. The deputation were authorised to under-write any loss to the level of £500 per annum for five years. However, following disagreements regarding the propriety of the 1881 extensions (to which many shareholders had objected), the directors had agreed to refer any such extension proposal to their

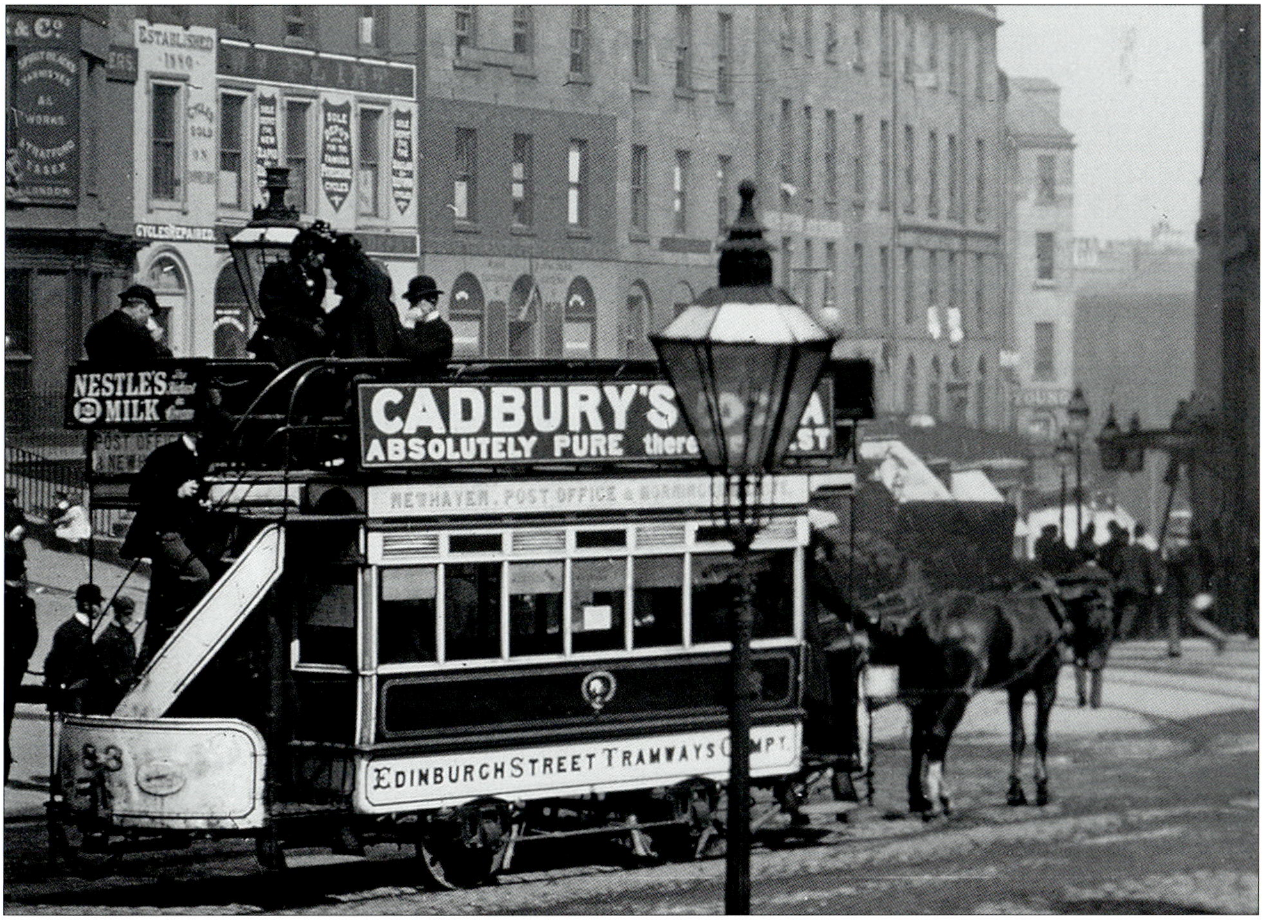

Car 83 waits at the top of Leith Street about to start down one of the steepest grades on the system. Almost the entire two mile length of Leith Street and Leith Walk was lined on both sides by a succession of tenements and small shops, with the Tramways Company's stables just on the Edinburgh side of the Leith boundary at Pilrig. Car 83 was obviously well maintained as after it passed to Leith Corporation in 1903, it was sold to the Stirling & Bridge of Allan tramway where it ran until 1920.

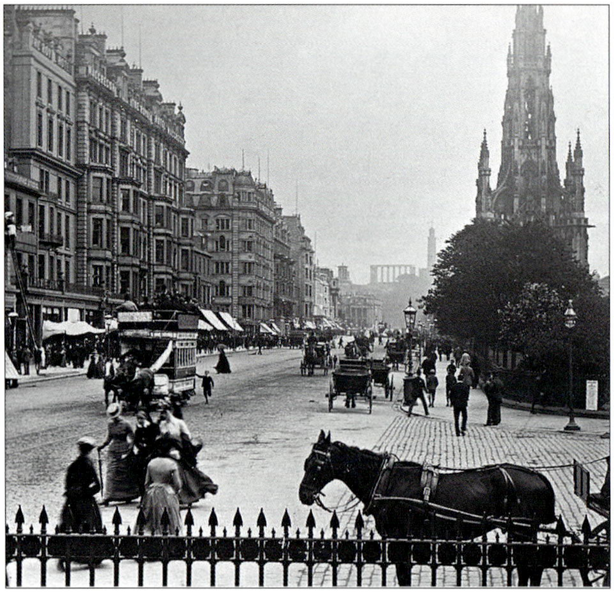

From the Royal Institution at the foot of the Mound, looking east to the Scott Monument and Calton Hill. Young lads running after and jumping on and off trams in motion lead to not infrequent accidents. Princes Street was widened in 1877-8, with the south footpath moved several yards into the garden area. The line of the existing footpath at the (now) Royal Scottish Academy shows the former width, the 'pinch point' here still creating an impediment to twenty-first century traffic.

shareholders. The chairman had 1920 votes for, and 1457 against, but these were said not to be on a proper proxy basis. When the matter was put to such shareholders actually present at the meeting on 21 November, just 17 votes were cast for, 26 against – consequently the suggestion had to be dropped forthwith. Thoughts of a tram line to Corstorphine rumbled on for a while, and there was talk of a separate company being set up, but noting materialised[119].

Increased patronage benefitted the Company's shareholders with the first dividend declared after the Exhibition being 5%, plus a special bonus of 2½%. The directors were now increasingly more aware of the looming date of expiry of their original lease – 29 June 1892 – but hoped to enter into negotiations with the Council for an extension. Earnings remained fairly constant with dividends regularly around 5%, but over every decision hung the certainty of the termination of the lease.

Yet another fire at Shrubhill stables in July 1889 highlighted the dire conditions of some of the Company's employees. A shed used for storage of peat moss for horse bedding was burned to the ground and it was soon realised that two trace boys (15 and 16 years old) and a 22 year-old strapper had been sleeping there – all three being 'of no fixed abode'. They escaped harm, but were suspected of being the cause of the conflagration. Some 20 horses had to be evacuated and workmen's cars stored nearby were promptly moved out of danger. In another court case, the Company was sued by A & J Munro of Broughton Market for £150 – the price of a groove cleaning car made to the Company's order – but unfortunately they were unable to prove that specific clear instruction had in fact been given[120].

The 1890 Exhibition and its electric tram

A third major International Exhibition was arranged in the city for 1890, and once again an electric railway was to be a major attraction. This time the locus was at Meggetland, on a site bounded by the Union Canal on the south, the Caledonian Railway to the north, but bisected by the NBR Suburban line. A temporary terminal loop was added to the tramway in Polwarth Terrace bringing cars close to the entrance, and a number of additional passing places were built between the entrance and Gilmore Place. Various short-term extensions were made to tram services and a temporary horse bus route was run down Colinton Road from Churchhill[121].

For this event the electric railway was not just intended as a curiosity – it had to serve the practical purpose of taking visitors from entrances to the exhibits area. Before making their decision, on 27 December 1889 the Committee visited Carstairs in Lanarkshire to examine the private electric railway of Mr Joseph Monteith which ran from Carstairs House to Carstairs Junction village[122]. This 1¼ mile long line was the first such *permanent* electrically operated line in Scotland, and was the brainchild of the estate's proprietor. Power was generated at Cleghorn Falls on

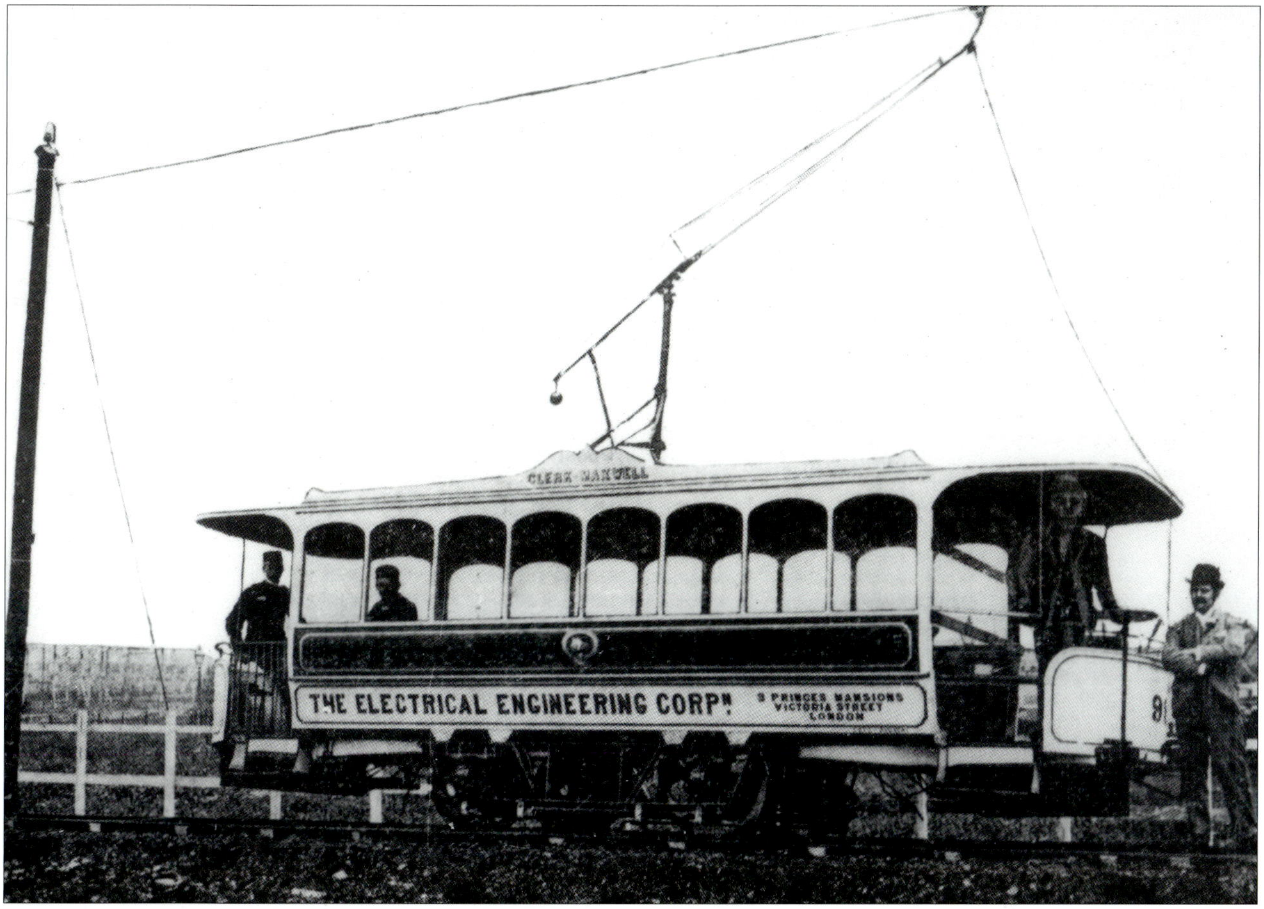

The Tramways Company supplied two tramcars of this 'canopy' design for the electric line at the 1890 International Exhibition at Meggetland. Operational for only three months, the cars (named *Clerk Maxwell* and *Faraday*) with the electric equipment removed, were taken into the Company rolling stock after closure of the unsuccessful event.

the Mouse Water some three miles away. It is said that Mr Monteith had been inspired by the electric line at the 1888 Edinburgh Exhibition, and that some (undefined) equipment from that exhibition ended up at Carstairs. The committee members must have been sufficiently impressed however, as they decided to build a half mile long electric tramway from the Polwarth entrance to the temporary Exhibition Station on the Caledonian Railway's line to West Calder and Carstairs. The line was constructed by the Electrical Engineering Corporation (Ltd), but although the exhibition opened on 1st May, the two vehicles (which were built at Shrubhill) did not arrive until the end of June. Even then trials rapidly established that the track was unsatisfactory in several places; accordingly the line was not opened until 25 July. The two single deck cars were named *Clerk Maxwell* and *Faraday* and were given numbers 98 and 99. When the exhibition closed on 1st November these two, with their electrical equipment removed, were taken into the Tramways Company stock. The Company benefitted from increased patronage to the extent of an extra 1½ million passengers during the period, but the exhibition itself was a financial failure. Takings at the 1886 event amounted to over £68,000, at this 1890 event to just £39,000. This was blamed on poor weather and the remote location of the site. The latter of course had helped the Tramways Company's coffers, but while use of the lines had increased, so had the expense incurred in providing these augmented services.

EDINBURGH STREET TRAMWAYS COMPANY.

'BUS SERVICE

BETWEEN

MERCHISTON TERRACE

(East End) AND

EXHIBITION.

12th MAY 1890,

and until further notice.

Tickets, including Admission to the Exhibition, will be issued by the 'Bus for the sum of **1s.** each.

JOHN E. PITCAIRN,
Traffic Supt. and Secretary.

54 North Bridge,
12th May 1890.

Merchiston Ter. to Exhibition.

a.m.	p.m.	p.m.	p.m.	
11 10	1 50	4 50	7 50	...
11 30	2 10	5 10	8 10	...
11 50	2 30	5 30	8 30	...
p.m.	2 50	5 50	8 50	...
12 10	3 10	6 10	9 10	...
12 30	3 30	6 30	9 30	...
12 50	3 50	6 50	9 50	...
1 10	4 10	7 10	10 10	...
1 30	4 30	7 30	10*30	...

* To Stables.

Exhibition to Merchiston Ter.

a.m.	p.m.	p.m.	p.m.	p.m.
11 20	1 20	4 0	6 40	9 20
11 40	1 40	4 20	7 0	9 40
noon.	2 0	4 40	7 20	10 0
12 0	2 20	5 0	7 40	10 20
p.m.	2 40	5 20	8 0	...
12 20	3 0	5 40	8 20	...
12 40	3 20	6 0	8 40	...
1 0	3 40	6 20	9 0	...

FARES (either way)

Inside 2d., Outside 1d.

Timetable 12 May 1890 for the bus service to the 1890 Exhibition.

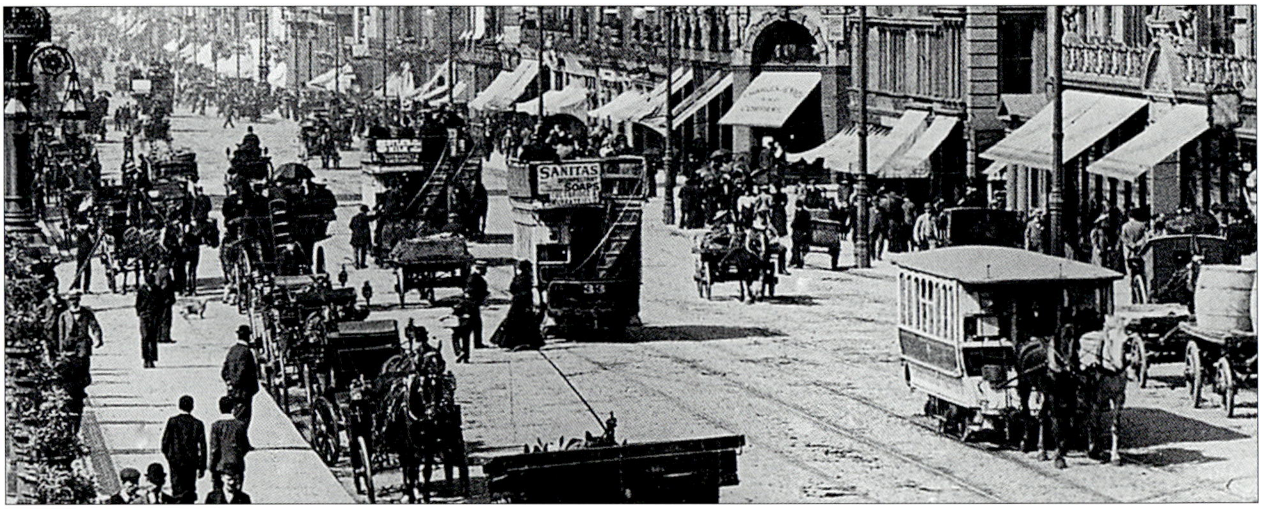

Canopy cars were initially just open toastracks with light canopies of canvas or wood, but the term was extended to refer to all single deck cars other than the totally open toastracks. There were several differing designs, but most had three outside seats on each platform to cater for smokers. This example is on Princes Street approaching South St Andrew Street.

End of the lease looms

At this stage the minds of all those involved began to concentrate on the imminent expiry (on 29 June 1892) of the Company's lease. Edinburgh Council's Tramways Sub-Committee met with their equivalents from Glasgow Corporation at the end of July 1890, but there were major differences in the way in which each city had originally dealt with their first tramways. In Glasgow all lines had been promoted, constructed, and were consequently owned by the local authority; this did not apply in Edinburgh, where these elements had all been undertaken speculatively by the Tramway

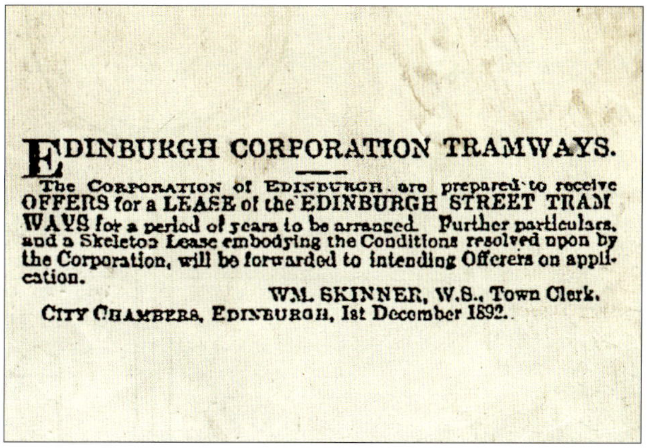

EDINBURGH CORPORATION TRAMWAYS.

The Corporation of Edinburgh are prepared to receive OFFERS for a LEASE of the EDINBURGH STREET TRAMWAYS for a period of years to be arranged. Further particulars, and a Skeleton Lease embodying the Conditions resolved upon by the Corporation, will be forwarded to intending Offerers on application.

WM. SKINNER, W.S., Town Clerk.

City Chambers, Edinburgh, 1st December 1892.

Scotsman 2 December 1892 advert seeking lessees for Edinburgh's tramways.

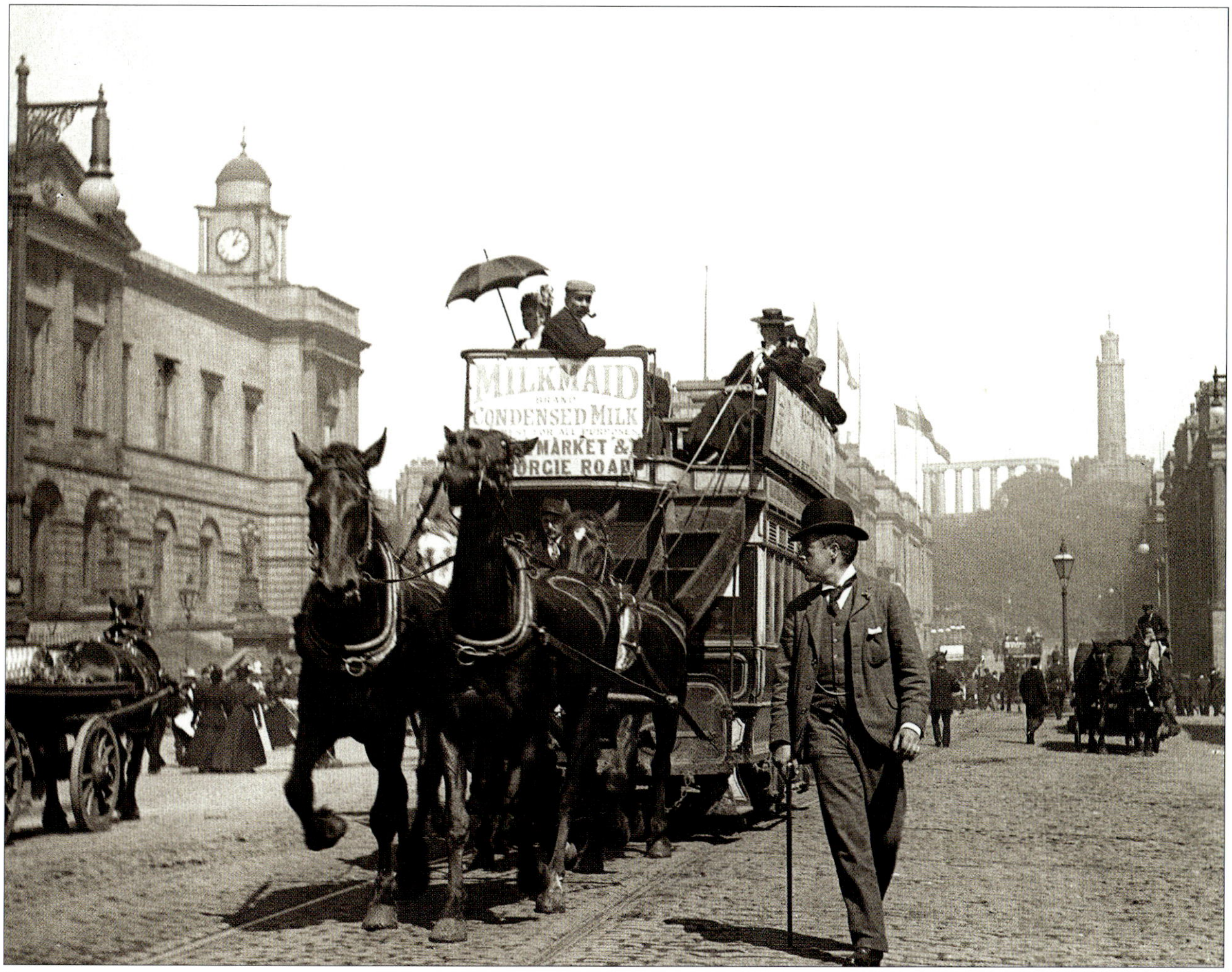

'Jay walking' on Princes Street was fraught with danger. This dapper gent appears surprised by the tram appearing behind him as he makes to cross the road. The car has its full complement of motive power, the two trace horses will be discharged at Waverley Steps. A sunny afternoon, to judge by the lady with parasol on the top deck – at just after 2 pm by the Register House clock.

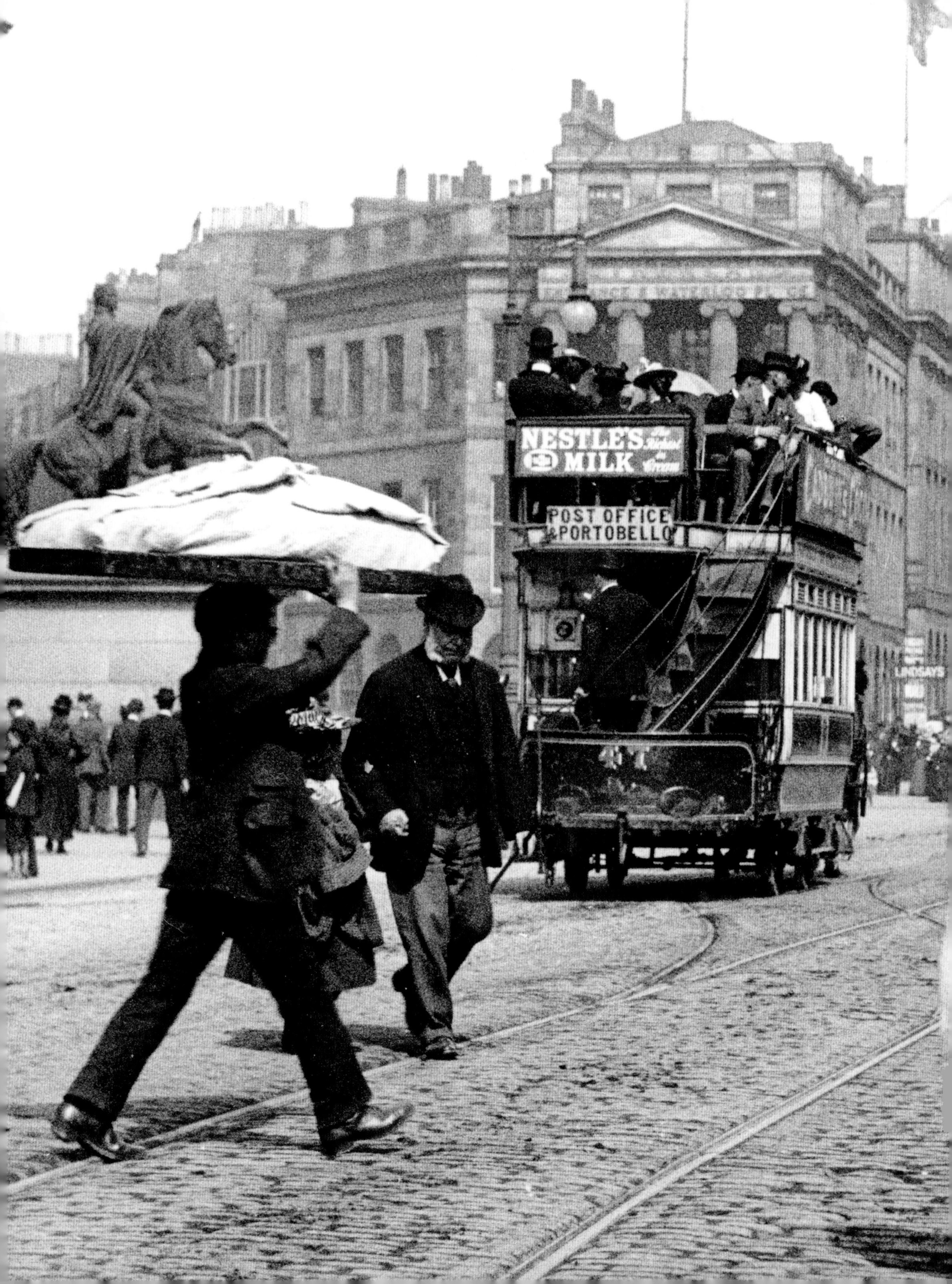
NESTLE'S MILK
POST OFFICE & PORTOBELLO
LINDSAYS

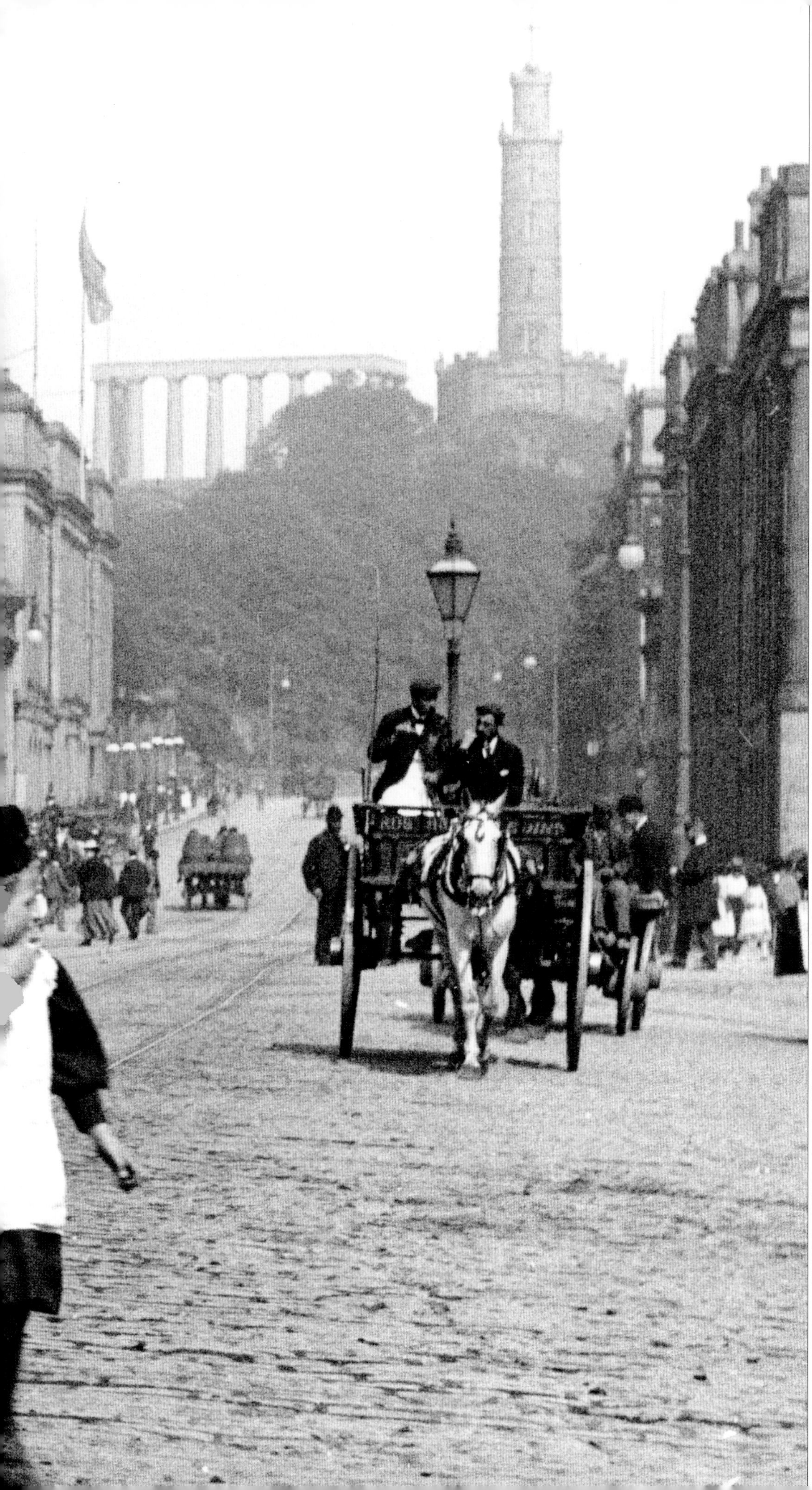

An animated scene at the same spot – possibly on the same occasion – the same flags appear to be in evidence. The scene is focused on the bakers' boy on the left carrying, in time honoured traditional manner, his tray of bread or rolls on his head. Tram 47 behind appears in more Edinburgh photographs than any other individual horse tram.

Company. Matters were also complicated in Edinburgh's case by the involvement of the Councils of Leith and Portobello – then separate entities – plus the piece-meal opening at differing dates of the local lines under separate Acts. Portobello was joined to its larger neighbour in 1896, but it was not until 1920 that Leith and Edinburgh amalgamated – very much against the wishes of most Leithers. [Two plebiscites undertaken both gave six times as many votes against, as votes for.]

In August 1890 Edinburgh Council adopted the report recommending that the tram system should be acquired by the Corporation and then leased to an approved operating company (preferably the existing company). It strongly rejected any suggestion that the Corporation should operate trams themselves. A major issue was the firm belief that there should be but a single operating company for all the city tramways. The Company drew to the attention of its shareholders the significant point that this decision had been made without any consultation with the two other local authorities, with the chairman indicating that Leith Council was inclined to extend the lease for those lines lying within their burgh. The Company subsequently met both authorities, making their case effectively and filling any vacuum created by Edinburgh's inaction. Thus were the seeds sown for long and difficult negotiations, leading ultimately to an impractical and disruptive outcome.

On 4 June 1891 Thomas Landale, now the Tramways Company chairman, took the initiative by writing to the Corporation laying out terms for continued operation of the city's tramways. This, and its reply were promptly 'leaked' to the Press[123]. Landale firstly pointed out that his Company, under its existing powers, was prohibited from leasing the tramways if they were to be purchased by the local authorities; the company had been established to create and work the lines detailed by the various Acts of Parliament. He suggested, however, that a new company could be formed to overcome this, to examine suitable forms of mechanical traction, and to study possible extensions to the lines. Of course, some sort of guarantee would be required to allow this; a new 21 year lease was suggested. Landale was able to assure his shareholders 'Conferences of a friendly nature have been held ... and the directors have submitted proposals for an amicable settlement.' The feeling then was that, although the Corporation had decided to buy the lines, they were nevertheless '... most anxious that the Company should continue to work them on fair terms ...'.

The decision regarding any change of power source was left unresolved; it appears Edinburgh was reluctant to embrace the new technology of electric traction – despite several British systems having operated successfully for a number of years. The necessity to expand the tramway system to embrace new suburbs was pressing more and more urgently and the Company indicated their willingness to expand – should agreement be reached – to Corstorphine, Liberton Dams, south from Morningside, and also build a new central line up the Mound and across the Meadows to Warrender Park Road, to serve the new developments under construction there. This latter was to be cable operated; until the traction question was resolved other lines were to remain horse operated.

Leith Council were increasingly irritated by what they saw as Edinburgh's high-handed attitude, and on 16 November they decided against joining the dialogue. A joint approach (on anything) was seen by them as the thin end of an amalgamation wedge and so had to be resisted. Edinburgh is usually seen as the intransigent party in these negotiations and the originator of the subsequent 'Pilrig Muddle', but at this stage, Leith's representatives appear equally inflexible. Edinburgh followed their initial convictions, and on 1 December 1891 ratified the decision to purchase all tracks within the city, with no agreed approach achieved relative to those lines lying beyond the City boundary, in Leith, Portobello or Midlothian. Of the total mileage operated by the Company (18 miles 14 chains) some 13 miles 24 chains lay within the City, 3 miles 3 chains were in Leith, 54 chains lay in Portobello and the remaining 1 mile 13 chains were in Midlothian. [In pre-metricated British lineal measurement, 80 chains constituted one mile.]

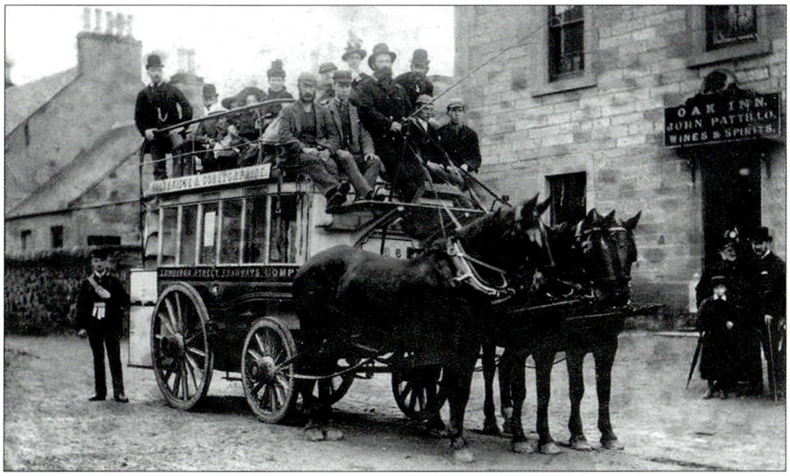

Left. Outside the Oak Inn, Corstorphine, is the Street Company's bus for Coltbridge, where it met trams for Newington. The Tramways Company had good intentions to extend their line as far west as Mayfield Place in the village and even built a small depot there. (Courtesy Corstorphine Trust)

Below. Another of the Street Tramways Company's suburban horse bus routes ran from Haymarket to the Grange and Blackford Hill, terminating at West Savile Terrace. The bus in seen on Blackford Avenue at Mortonhall Road c1900 (Photograph by H B Kirk, courtesy Rev W L Kirk).

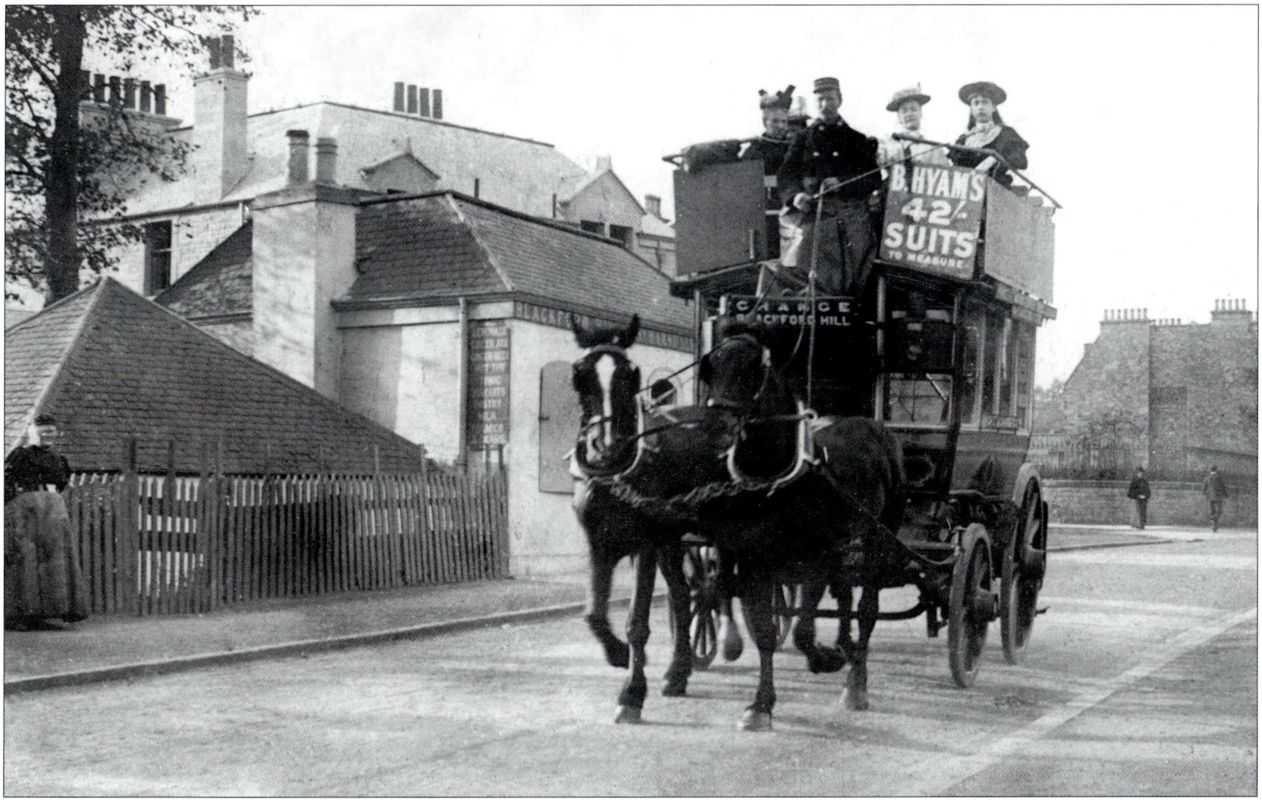

Through this unsettling time the Company continued, and perhaps with an eye on the future, commenced to expand the omnibus side of the undertaking. New routes were opened, on 31 October, from West End to Ravelston Park via Queensferry Road and Angle Park Terrace to Hope Park Terrace via Fountainbridge and Melville Drive (this extended to Cameron Toll from the beginning of November). The Coltbridge to Corstorphine bus remained, plus the 'country' services to Dalkeith and Loanhead.

Now that Edinburgh Council had declared their intention, although practical difficulties remained, any feeling of uncertainty was removed and the Company moved to regularise its position in the light of these changing circumstances. A Bill was presented to Parliament which was enacted with opposition only from Edinburgh, whose objections to every clause were not accepted by the Parliamentary Committee. This – the Edinburgh Street Tramways Act 1892 – now permitted the Company to enter into leasing arrangements and confirmed the agreement which had been reached with Leith Corporation. This latter covered several extensions in Leith (authorised by a separate Act the following year), an undertaking to continue through services over the boundary into Edinburgh, fares and wayleave payments (£500 per annum) were defined and the Company agreed to introduce mechanical power on Leith Walk if and when the lines from the south to Pilrig were converted. In return Leith undertook not to implement their right to purchase for fourteen years, or twenty-one years if the change had been made to (undefined) mechanical traction.

The Company valued their undertaking at £383,675 17s 3d (equivalent at time of writing to about £44 million) of which they considered 75% represented the worth of the portion the Council wished to acquire[124]. Within this figure it is noteworthy that the value of horses was more than twice that of the vehicles they hauled. Included were properties owned, not just at Shrubhill (stables, depot and workshops etc plus a house for the Superintendent and two additional dwellings) but also offices on North Bridge, Mavisbank at Loanhead, stables at Corstorphine and Portobello, and further property in Portobello at Jessfield and Livingston Place. The value of the Company was then adjusted down to £305,000 based on rental and construction value.

In early December 1892 Edinburgh Council advertised for tenders to lease the lines and before the end of the month the Street Tramways Company had theirs lodged. Plant and other tangible assets were to be repurchased at the figure which the Corporation had purchased them (from the same Street Tramway Coy) who in return for a twenty-one year lease would pay £10,500 per annum. This was not accepted. The Press was vituperative in commenting on the manner in which the Council was undertaking negotiations '... their decision yesterday means that they have been playing at business, and it confirms in the simplest manner the suspicion ... that they are not capable of negotiating successfully with well directed bodies. It is impossible to speak too severely of the course that has been taken. All pretence of seeking to protect the city's interest by stipulations in the terms of the lease must be regarded either as hypocrisy or as imbecility. If it be thought that this characterisation is too severe, let any one look at the discussions that have taken place and the decision yesterday ...'[125].

Consideration of mechanical power for their newly acquired lines was also high on the agenda of the council. Electric operation was considered unproven (and they would probably have opted for conduit supply, if the proposals had crystallised) while cable traction was proven, economical (to run, but not to build) and was already present in the city in the shape of the Edinburgh Northern Tramways Company. After much deliberation a further Act of Parliament was obtained in June 1893 which included the sanction to construct, with approval from the Board of Trade, cable powered tramways to be operated under lease from the Corporation; the terms of the lease were also subject to the Board's approval. In light of the lack of progress in achieving a tram link to Corstorphine, in July a proposal for an electric line from Coltbridge to the village was floated by the Caledonian Electric Supply Co Ltd. This was turned down, and this short lived company's attempts to obtain generating powers for several other Scottish communities including Stirling Galashiels and Ayr also came to naught so it was soon dissolved.

In the meantime the Corporation and the Company had failed to agree the value for assets to be transferred, and the matter was passed to an arbiter appointed by the Board of Trade, Mr Henry Tennant, recently retired General Manager of the North Eastern Railway Company. With all discussions held in camera, commencing in January 1893, his decision following detailed evidence from all involved, was eventually handed down some nine months later. This amounted

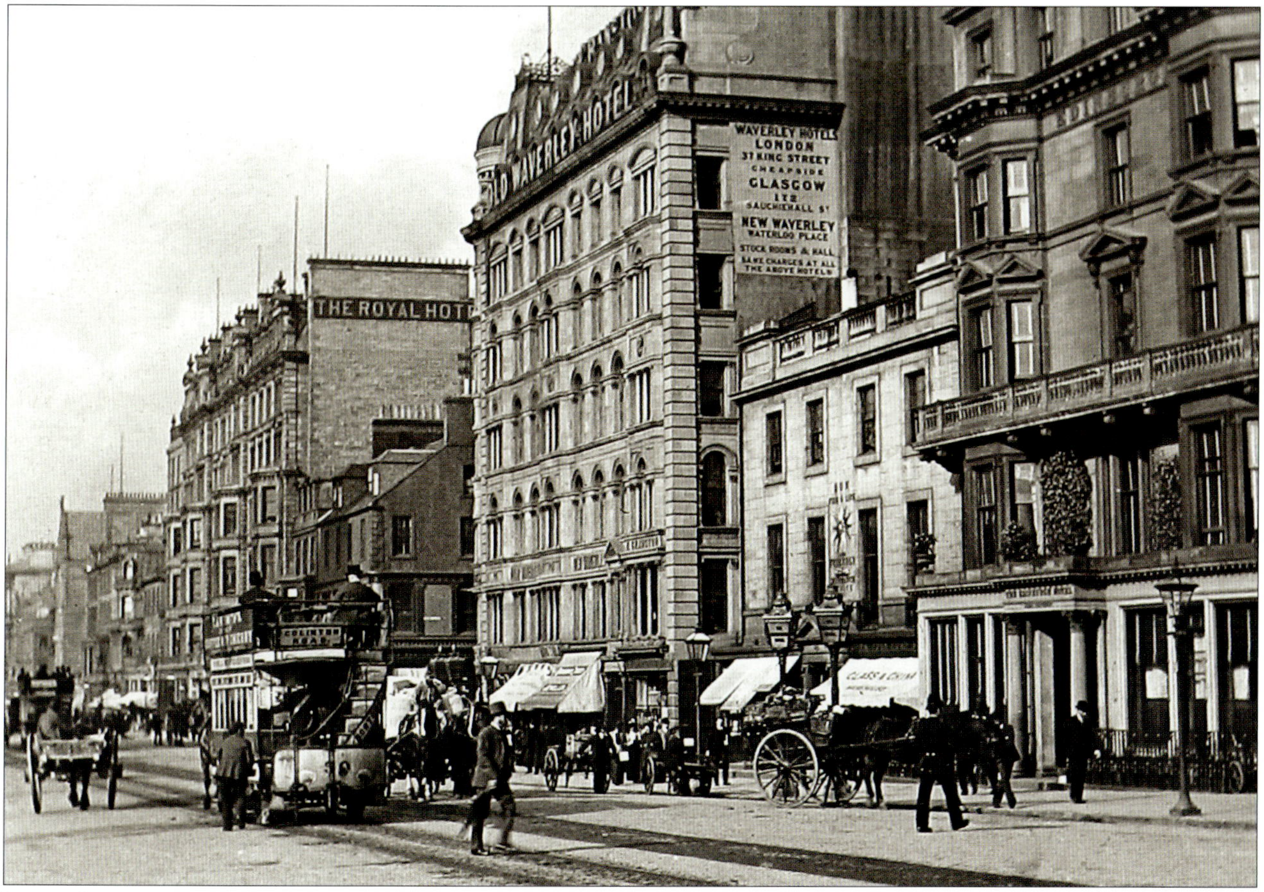

Princes Street's architecture changed rapidly during the Victorian period, the result being the hotchpotch which entirely fails – even to this day – to do justice to the unique setting of Edinburgh's principal thoroughfare. Car 50 is one of the yellow cars on the Portobello to Colinton Road service and is of the most numerous 'Exhibition' design.

to £212,979 7s 6d and was considerably lower than the Company had valued that part of their undertaking serving the city, at £287,756.

The new regime

On 7 October 1893 the Tramways Committee met to consider appointing the new lessee. Three offers were on the table; firstly from the existing Company, one from the Edinburgh Northern Tramways Company and a third, perhaps surprisingly, from the Glasgow Tramway & Omnibus Co. The Glasgow offer was quickly dismissed, it being understood that that Company's articles precluded it operating outwith that city. Next the Street Tramways offer was also rapidly disposed of. Despite the council reportedly being anxious to have continuity of operation, it was dismissed for having too many qualifications; perhaps the Company were all too aware of the reality of the situation. The final offer was in effect from the major (90%) shareholder in the Northern Tramways Company, Dick, Kerr Ltd of Kilmarnock. All subsequent dealings were thereafter done under the name of Dick, Kerr. One of the conditions contained in the new lease was imposition on the lessee of a reduction in working hours for the tram platform staff. This was in future not to exceed 54 hours per week or 12 hours in any one day – but soon seen as an interference in practical working of the undertaking by an authority

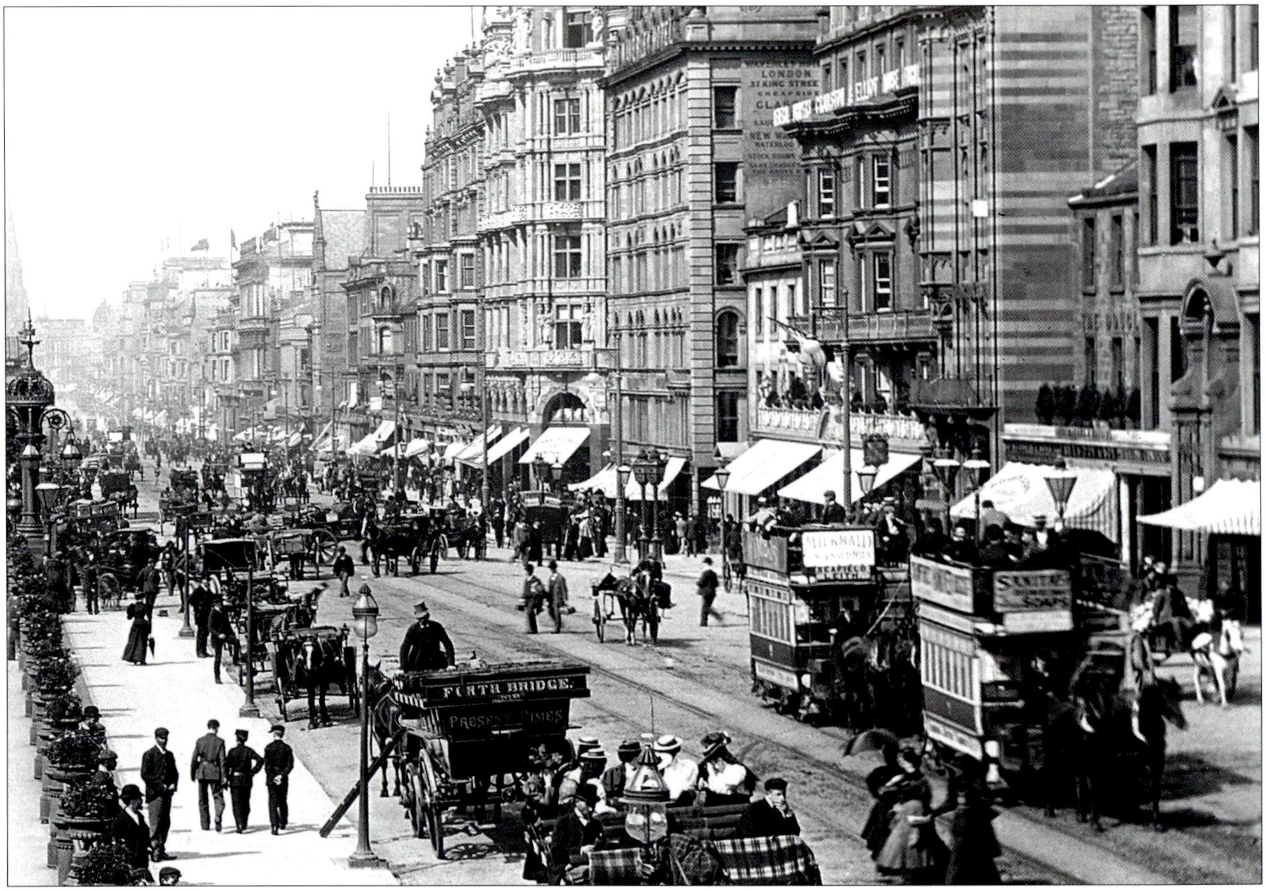

The south side of Princes Street alongside the roof gardens of Waverley Market was the recognised starting point for coaches to Loanhead and Roslin and for charabanc excursions to the Forth Bridge. The ladder access to the high seats was a treacherous ascent for most ladies. In the busy scene are three Post Office telegraph messenger boys with their distinctive pill-box caps.

which did not have to operate the lines. Dick, Kerr's offer was on the basis 'that the present arrangement of sixty hours per week suits the service'. As operation was still confined to six days, with no operation whatsoever on the Sabbath, this imposed an average working day of ten hours.

This decision was immediately referred to the Board of Trade by the incumbent Company who expressed astonishment at this turn of events. An important issue raised was that Dick, Kerr's articles of association did not include for them to lease tramways, hence they would only be able to operate in Edinburgh by tolerance, with no legal rights, consequently none of the obligations of the lease would be enforceable. Also listed in the submission to the Board were thirteen paragraphs detailing reasons why this lease should be refused; not least among which was that splitting of operations at Pilrig was illogical and of severe inconvenience to the travelling public. Over 9000 passengers crossed the boundary daily, and of the ten services operated only three lay entirely within the city. The tramway had been developed as a unit and it made absolutely no sense to create an artificial barrier at Pilrig – or anywhere else.

As the date approached for the new lease to take effect (18 November) so pressure was applied by the Street Tramways Company; Tennant's award of £212,979 7s 6d had been given on 14 November but was immediately contested. The difference of some £80,000 was fundamentally the value of the element

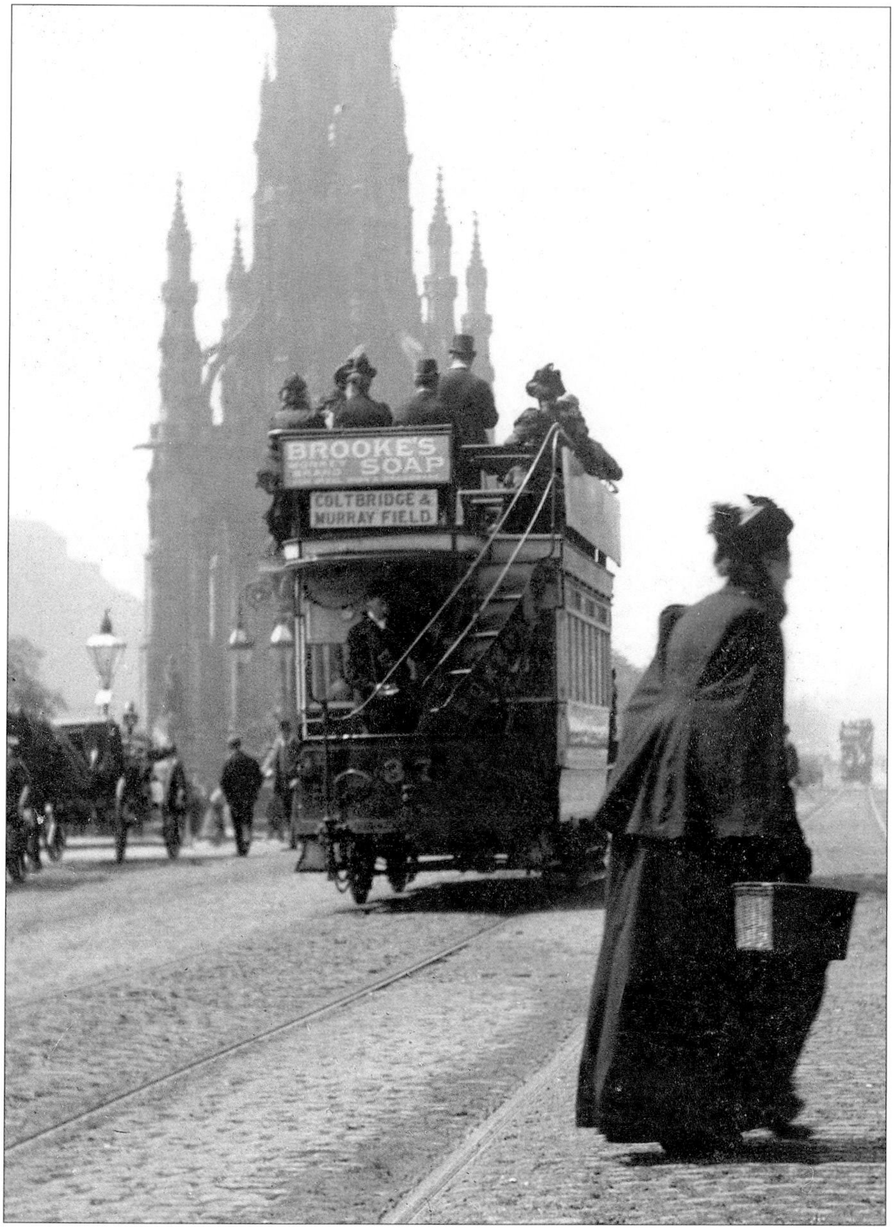

Another Victorian Princes Street scene of similar vintage; one can't help but wonder just what is being carried carefully in the basket . . .

which Tennant had considered to be excluded from the valuation under the terms of the 1870 Tramways Act – this being the perceived 'value' of the rental or goodwill – which the Company obviously considered vital. This had not been resolved satisfactorily, but was of great significance (Edinburgh's was the first instance where this was tested – and many other tramway operators in a similar position were watching developments carefully). Edinburgh Council lodged the due amount in a bank account, but the Company applied for interdict on the basis that until the Board of Trade had approved the lease, in reality it did not exist. It was proposed that a judicial factor should be appointed to run the tramways after the 18th, but in the event, the existing arrangement was allowed to continue until agreement was achieved. The Board of Trade sent representatives hot-foot to Edinburgh and a new clause, relating specifically to through running, was agreed following

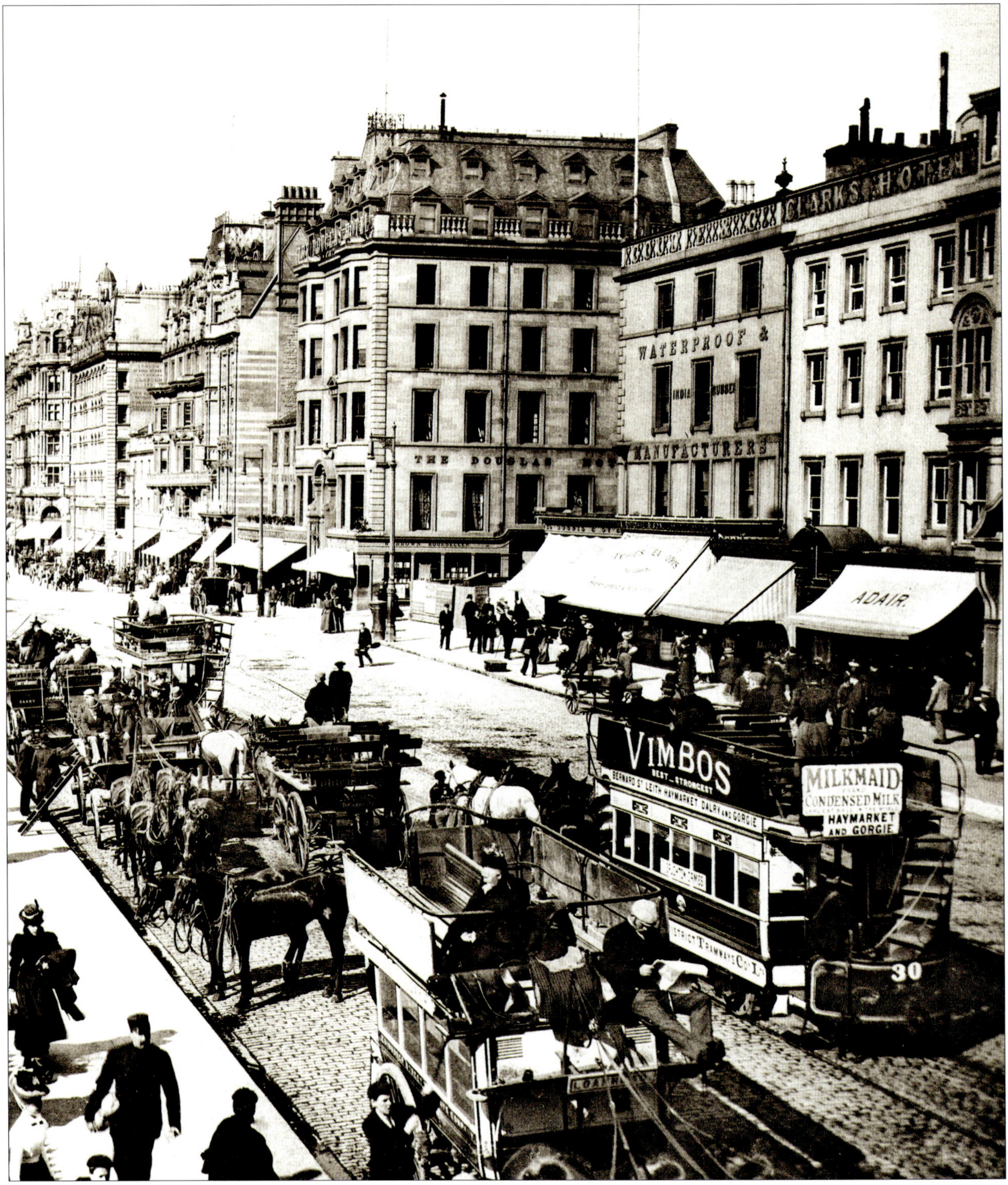

Favourite vantage point at the top of Waverley Steps. The busy scene includes much of transport interest. The Street Tramways Company bus in the foreground is of an old knifeboard seat style, for Loanhead; the more distant bus is one owned by the Glasgow Tramway and Omnibus Co, running to Lasswade and Roslin and appears of a much heavier design. Between is a char-a-banc for the Forth Bridge. Alongside the kerb are several trace horses patiently waiting the call to return to Leith Walk.

meetings on the 22nd and 23rd. The new lease was agreed and signed on 24 November; yet further delay having been incurred because the Board would not allow the new clause to be appended to the old lease – the whole document had to be revised to ensure that the new clause was in its appropriate place.

The date and time for the transfer to take place was agreed as 12 midnight on Saturday 9 December 1893 – and as there was no operation on Sunday, the new regime's first operation was on Monday morning. The Company sold what they were required to to the Corporation who immediately resold everything necessary to the new undertaking. In the public eye, nothing changed, apart from introduction of some new 1d fares which had been stipulated in the lease. All employees retained their positions and Mr Pitcairn presided over both enterprises. No ceremony marked the change; the new company became operator of some 11 miles and 1541 yards of tramway with 680 horses and 70 cars, plus the Shrubhill property and stables at Loanhead. The old company were given six months to reorganise their activities and to remove themselves from Shrubhill. Initially all operational matters were shared, with receipts on joint routes split on a 3:1 basis. The sum paid to the Street Company was, after deduction of mortgages etc, distributed to shareholders by an initial payment of £5 per share, the share capital of £300,000 in £10 shares was thus reduced in value to £150,000.

In the midst of all this turmoil Dick, Kerr wrote to Edinburgh Council to ask permission to sub-let the tramways – without intimating that the Street Tramways Company had expressed an interest in being that sub-tenant. However, the Corporation promptly replied that the conditions of the lease were quite clear – there was to be no such sub letting. Consequently the suggestion was rather quickly withdrawn[126]. A shadow company, the Edinburgh Tramways Company Limited had been registered on 8 November 1893, but it was never activated and was dissolved some eighteen months later. With regard to the valuation of rental, at the Street Company meeting at the end of January 1894 it was noted that in the similar situation of the London Street Tramways Company the decision had been the opposite to that of Mr Tennant, and that their disagreement with his award would be appealed. This ultimately went all the way to the House of Lords. On 30 July this, the highest authority in the land, made the decision that the Tramways Company – and all other similar tramway companies in the same situation – did not want to hear; that the decision of the arbiter was upheld.

The Street Tramways Co temporarily occupied space in Shrubhill (for which they had to pay rent) until in May 1894 gave notice that they were moving to new premises at Morton Place Leith Walk, built at a cost of £20,000. This now became the centre of their operations, then in 1905 was used as the site for Leith Corporation Tramways new electric tram depot. From 18 July John Pitcairn confined his managerial duties to the new District Company, the like role for the Street Tramways was filled by John S Adam, long serving treasurer of that Company. The Street Tramways Company also still ran the tramways in Portobello and retained their omnibus routes in the city.

The new District Tramways Company

This new Company was incorporated on 6 March 1894, and before long intimated that the joint through working agreement of 9 December 1893 was to be terminated on 21 August 1894; this later extended to 1 September, probably being the date when the Street Tramways Co assets were physically removed to its new premises at Morton Place. From 3 September the long route from Portobello to Colinton Road was split, with no running through beyond Waterloo Place. More Leith bound cars were now routed by York Place, considered an inconvenience by many travellers. The gradients of North St Andrew Street were difficult for horse cars, this probably the reason for most routes using the busy – but also steep – artery of Leith Street in preference. The companies suggested that from this date both should confine their operations to their own areas and that all through running should cease.

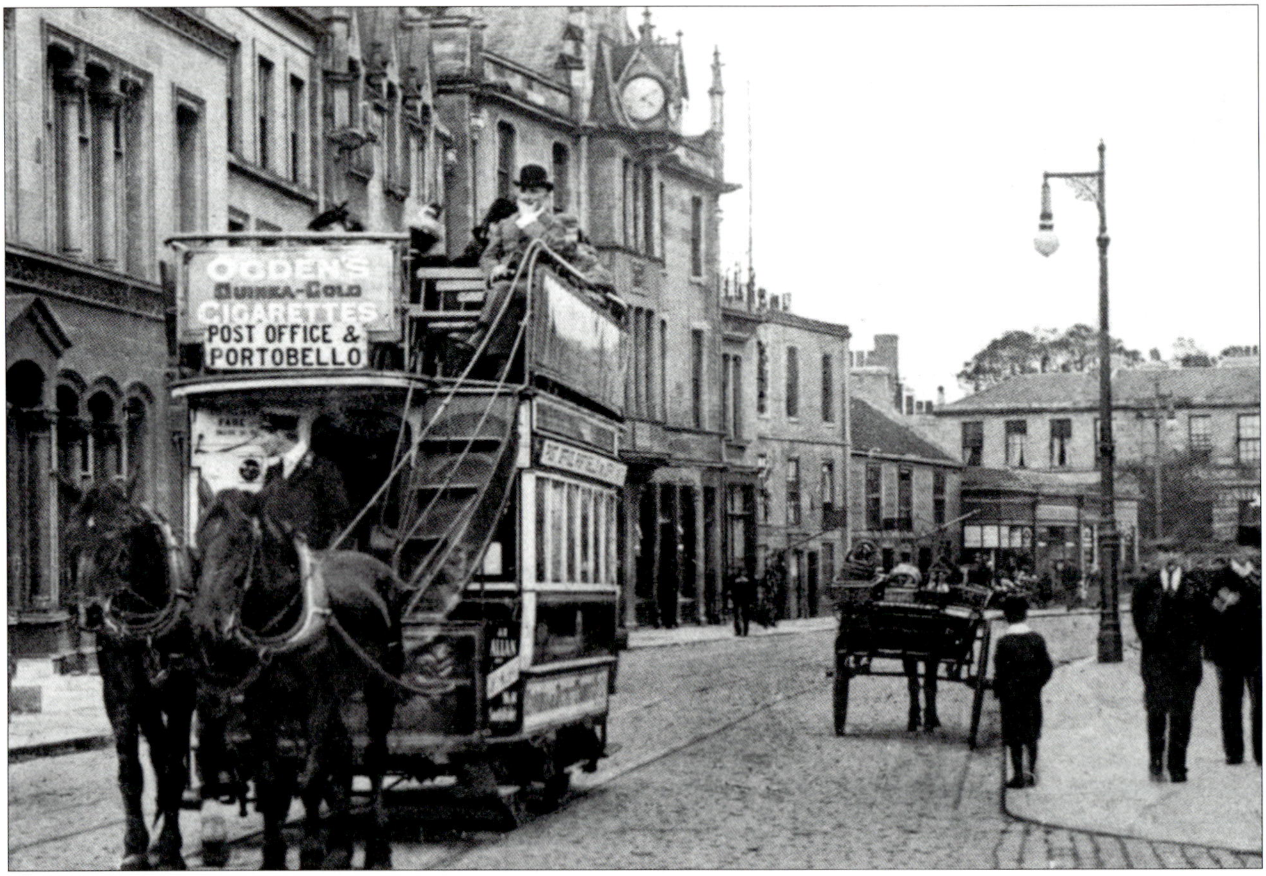

High Street Portobello at the top of Regent Street in the final days of the nineteenth century. The horse car is one of the final design used on the local tramways. The prominent clock is no longer there to count the passing hours.

However, the recently signed lease specifically referred to ensuring continuation of through traffic. The District Company interpreted this that only the cars themselves need provide the cross-border continuity, and that horses and staff should be confined to their respective areas. Again this was referred to the arbiter, who at the start of December issued his findings, fundamentally confirming what had been originally proposed.

On Monday 24 December the new arrangements commenced, as described in detail in the advertisement from the local press on page 76. While the Portobello to Colinton Road through line was reinstated, horses and crews had to be changed at Waterloo Place. This was not a major inconvenience with a 15 minute frequency service being run, but the story at Pilrig was quite the opposite. With six different routes crossing the boundary here cars were frequent, thus the potential for confusion considerable, so such concerns were entirely justified. Problems were anticipated and both operating companies had spare men and horses standing by, with extra staff on hand to deal expeditiously with the unyoking and yoking up of the sets of horses. A new crossover was laid in on the Edinburgh side of the boundary, but even with these precautions some initial confusion was only to be expected; Messrs Pitcairn and Adam were both available to monitor events. The general ambience, with the centre of Leith Walk at Pilrig resembling a horse market was not appreciated by many, nor were delays, however brief or on occasions, not so brief. Ticketing arrangements caused misunderstandings, with new 2d through fare

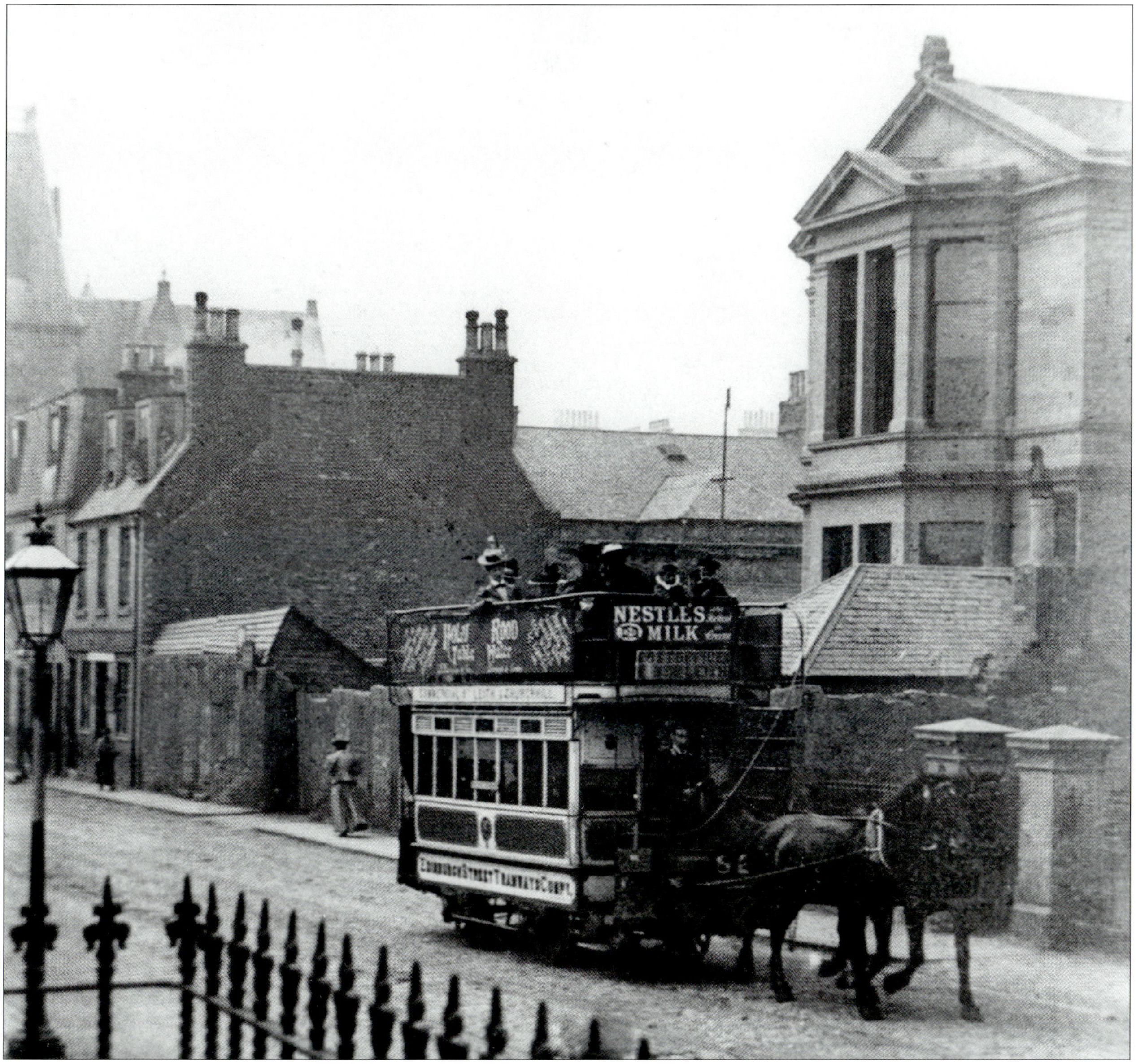

Salisbury Place with car 82 on the jointly operated route from Churchhill to Commercial Street Leith. This ran for a short time after cable tracks were laid in Strathearn Place and prior to cessation of through running at Pilrig. Behind is Longmore Hospital, built for 'Incurables'. This car remained with the Street Company and ended its days operated by Leith Corporation.

tickets which had to be exchanged at the boundary for a ticket valid on the other system. After two weeks a 3d through fare was introduced from Newhaven, passengers being given a 1d local ticket plus a 2d through ticket[127].

At the end of 1894 both companies managed to return a 5% dividend to their respective shareholders despite the Pilrig disruption. The Street Tramways Company was far from downbeat, but the situation was so inconvenient to the travelling public that both Leith Council and the Street Company approached the Board of Trade to request that the situation revert to the previous arrangement. From a count in October prior to the change of 46,460 passengers per week passing Pilrig this reduced to 19,900 three months later. Leith Council also made an approach to the Company regarding purchase of the lines within their Burgh, but this was rejected as Leith were only prepared to proceed on the same basis as had been contentiously offered under Mr Tennant's arbitration. Preparations were also under way for extensions in Leith which had been authorised before the schism. Horse bus routes in the City were being extended, but as tram feeders, not as competition to the other company's operations.

Subsequent events relative to the Street Tramways Company followed a comparatively straightforward pattern which can be related consecutively, before a return is made (at page 83) to record matters relative to the District Company until eventually the capital's last horse tram operated early in the following century – but even at that stage there are subsequent events which require to be noted.

The shrunken Street Company

Inspection of the new lines in Leith took place on 29 June 1895 with opening for traffic on 1 July; these were along Claremont Park from Restalrig Road to Seafield Baths, on Commercial Street to the Custom House and a short link line across the foot of Leith Walk. This coincided with the introduction of many new ½d fares which helped revenue. Track mileage increased from 6 miles 52 chains to 7 miles 33 chains, this including the lines to Portobello from Waterloo Place and represented the maximum run by the Street Company following the split. An interesting development at the end of the current year was the favourable response to a request to operate the Johnston mechanical motor tram on the Portobello route. This paraffin-fuelled car had been tried on the Glasgow tramways, but although the authorities were inclined to give permission – and even went through to inspect and travel on the car – a most unfortunate accident saw the machine badly damaged by fire before any Portobello trial could be arranged. New lines were planned from Portobello to Joppa and in Leith from Stanley Road to Commercial

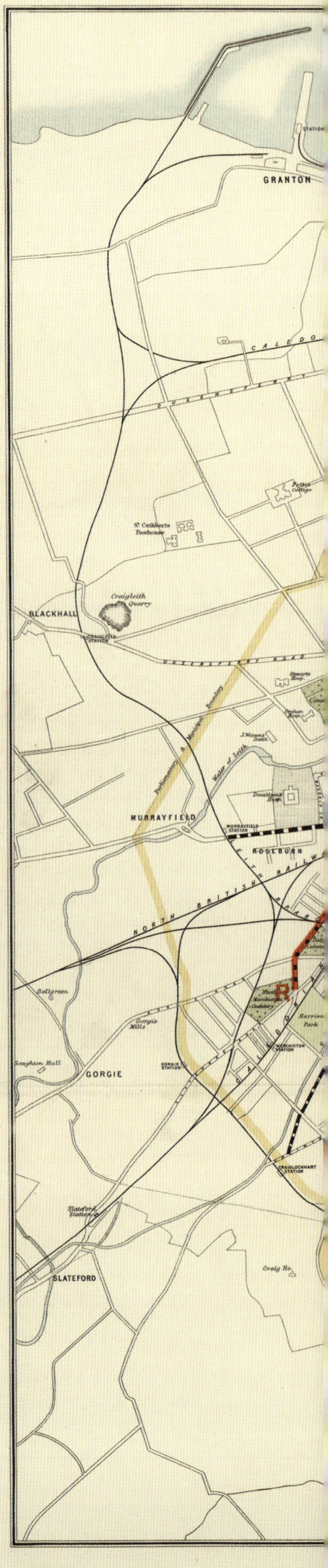

The Burgh Engineer's Plan of lines proposed to be cabled January 1895. (Reproduced by permission of the National Library of Scotland)

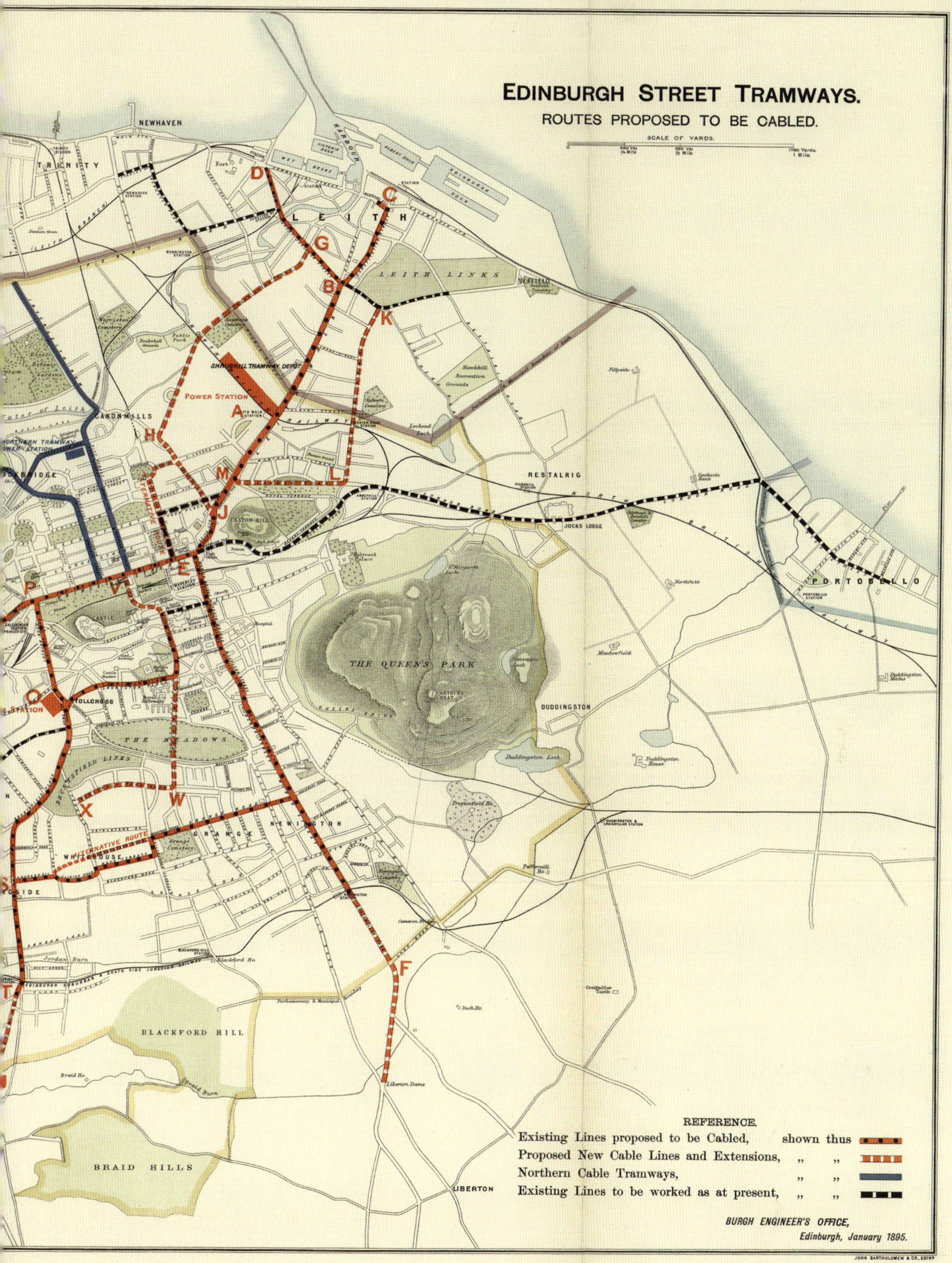
EDINBURGH STREET TRAMWAYS.
ROUTES PROPOSED TO BE CABLED.
SCALE OF YARDS.
NEWHAVEN
TRINITY
LEITH
LEITH LINKS
SEAFIELD
SHRUBHILL TRAMWAY DEPOT
POWER STATION
CANONMILLS
RESTALRIG
JOCKS LODGE
CALTON HILL
PORTOBELLO
THE QUEEN'S PARK
DUDDINGSTON
TOLLCROSS
THE MEADOWS
BRUNTSFIELD LINKS
GRANGE
NEWINGTON
ALTERNATIVE ROUTE
BLACKFORD HILL
BRAID HILLS
LIBERTON
A
B
C
D
E
F
G
H
J
K
L
M
O
P
V
W
X
REFERENCE.
Existing Lines proposed to be Cabled, shown thus
Proposed New Cable Lines and Extensions, ,, ,,
Northern Cable Tramways, ,, ,,
Existing Lines to be worked as at present, ,, ,,
BURGH ENGINEER'S OFFICE,
Edinburgh, January 1895.
JOHN BARTHOLOMEW & CO. EDIN

Street via Newhaven plus a short connection between the closely adjacent termini of Bernard and Commercial Streets. Mechanical traction options were being considered – cable was already considered to be obsolescent but '...results in America and elsewhere point in favour of electricity.'

Edinburgh Council made overtures to purchase, as was its right, the line between Waterloo Place and the former city boundary at Meadowbank and again Mr Tennant became involved as, again, the worth was disputed. The Company valued their lines at £15,955; the Corporation at £7953 – Mr Tennant at £13,615. The award was made on Friday 31 January 1896, the Corporation took the line at midnight of the following day with the District Company operating the service from first car on Monday 3 February. Staff and horse change-over was now at Meadowbank. From Monday 4 May 1896 the Company introduced a bus service between Haymarket and Grange Loan, using new vehicles specially built in London. The seasonal bus to Roslin recommenced on the same day while the Portobello to Musselburgh service now had two buses instead of one, much patronised by golfers. The Company now ran ten bus services, as described in the

EDINBURGH STREET TRAMWAYS COMPANY.

The EDINBURGH STREET TRAMWAYS COMPANY beg to intimate that the WORKING ARRANGEMENTS FOR THROUGH TRAFFIC BETWEEN LEITH AND EDINBURGH, in terms of the Award of the Arbitrator appointed by the Board of Trade, will Commence on MONDAY, the 24th instant.

On and after that date, and until further notice, the following Through and Local Fares in Leith will take effect:

THROUGH FARES.

Through Tickets will be issued for passengers travelling between

1. Bernard Street.........
2. Seafield (Lindsay Road)..
3. Junction Bridge.........

} and General Post Office, Edinburgh, at a uniform fare of 2d, Inside or Outside.

Passengers will retain their THROUGH Tickets until they pass the Leith Boundary at Pilrig, when they will give them up to the Conductor on the Edinburgh side, and receive a Penny Ticket in Exchange.

LOCAL FARES IN LEITH.

	Inside or Outside.
Newhaven Terminus and Pilrig, either way	2d.
Seafield (Lindsay Road) / Junction Bridge....... / Bernard Street.......... } & Pilrig. Do.	1d.
Newhaven Terminus and Junction Bridge, either way .... / Bonnington Terrace and Smith's Place, Leith Walk, either way.......... / Fort St. and Lorne St., either way....... / Commercial St. and Lorne St., either way.	1d.
Smith's Place, Leith Walk, and Pilrig, either way	½d.

SCHOOL AND MESSAGE TICKETS.

School and Errand Tickets available for any distance on the Leith section, without change of Car, and up to the Pilrig Boundary on the Through Route to Edinburgh will be issued from the Company's Offices in Leith at Morton Place, 149 Leith Walk, and in Edinburgh at 54 North Bridge, for one half-penny each—in Bundles of 60.

WORKMEN'S TICKETS AND CARS.

Tickets will be issued for Workmen on the Special Morning Cars at a uniform fare of one half-penny to or from Pilrig and any point within Leith where these Cars are run, and provision will be made for an Afternoon Service by the Ordinary Through Cars at the same rate of ½d (outside) within the Leith Boundary.

WORKMEN'S CARS.

The Arbiter's Award, which precludes horses and men going through, has rendered it impracticable to work the full service of Morning Cars between Leith and Edinburgh. A service has, however, been arranged between the two Companies which, with other local services, might be considerably increased but for the refusal of the necessary facilities for a more frequent interchange of Traffic at Pilrig.

PORTOBELLO SECTION.

A service of Through Cars from Portobello to Colinton Road, Edinburgh, will also commence on the 24th inst., as per Time-Table exhibited in the Cars—the local fares and special ticket rates between Waterloo Place and Portobello remaining the same as at present.

Time-Tables and Tables of Local Fares, &c., will be exhibited in all the Cars, and copies of these with any further information can be obtained on application at the COMPANY'S OFFICES at 149 LEITH WALK or at 54 NORTH BRIDGE, EDINBURGH.

By Order.

J. S. ADAM, Manager.

54 NORTH BRIDGE,
EDINBURGH, 21st December, 1894.

Scotsman 22 December 1894 Notification of arrangements after end of through running at Pilrig.

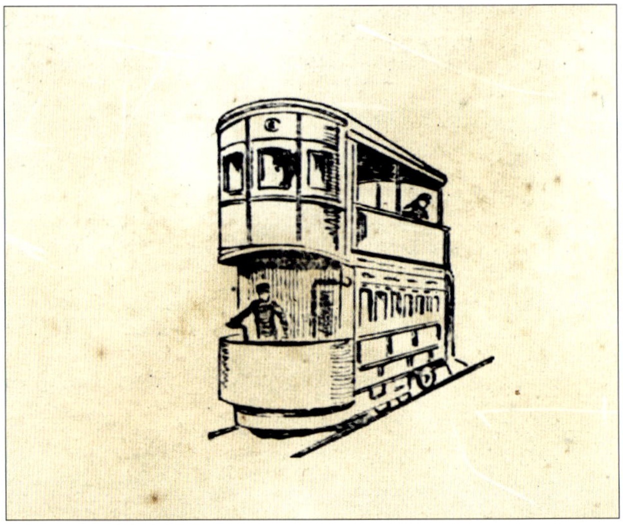

Contemporary sketch from October 1895 of the Johnston paraffin-oil fuelled steam car. Given permission for experimental use in Edinburgh, an unfortunate accident while in Glasgow saw it almost totally destroyed by fire. It would have been the first top covered tram in Edinburgh had these proposals come to fruition.

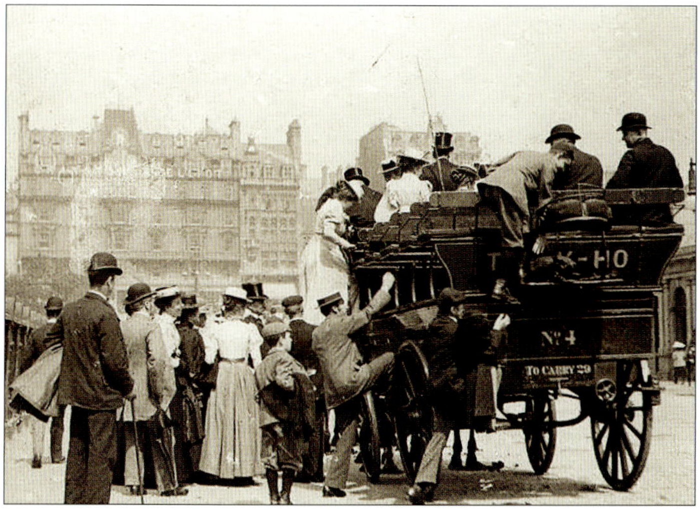

Left. The char-a-banc *'Tally-ho'* loading on Waverley Bridge with a private party heading for the Forth Bridge. The potential for a glimpse of ankle made the experience memorable for some.

Below. Many excursions made for the engineering marvel It stands as resolute in the twenty-first century as it did in the nineteenth. Perhaps over-designed following the failure of Bouch's Tay viaduct, it has nevertheless stood the test of time.

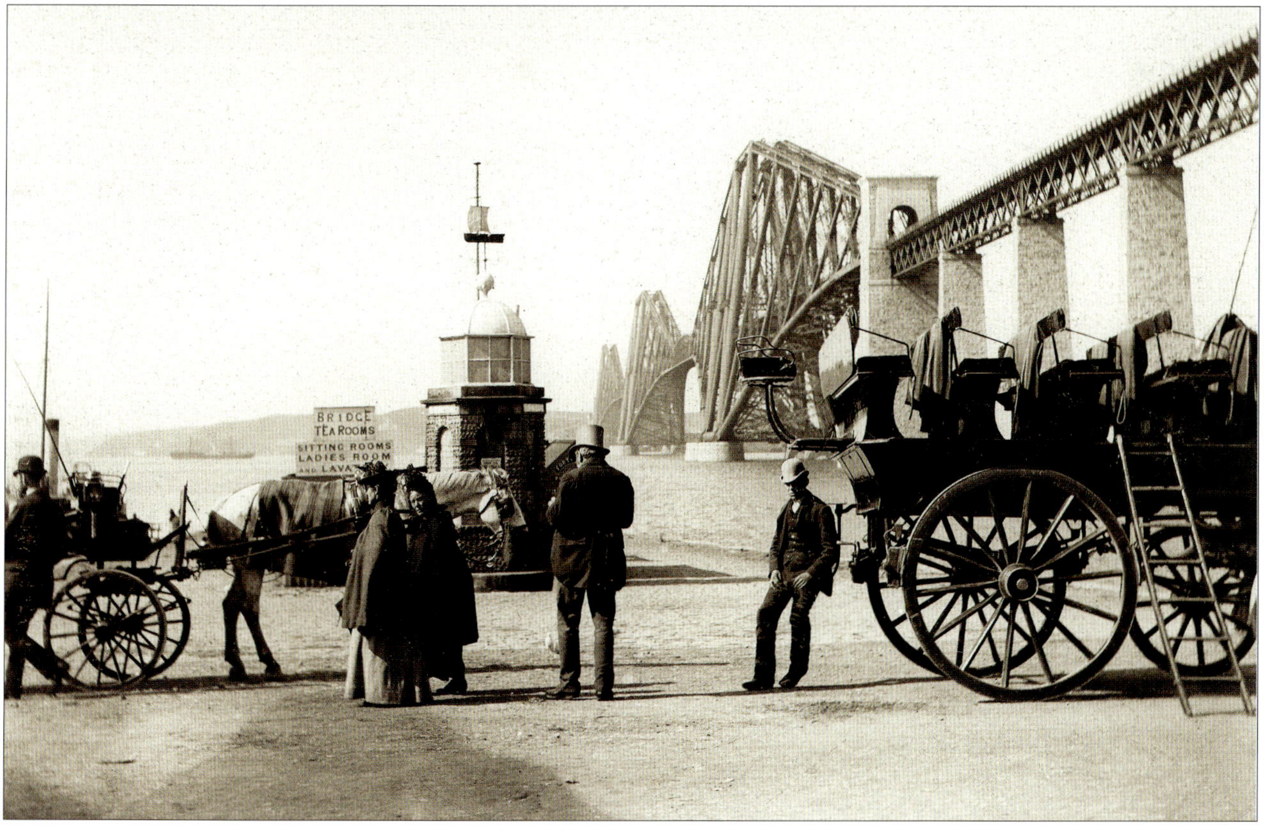

press advert on page 78; the reference numbers were not displayed on vehicles[128]. Shareholders were reassured that the Company was not trying to emulate the Glasgow situation and were not seeking to compete with the District Company. Their bus routes were described as 'cross routes', away from the tram lines and of course these did not involve any outlay for rails etc.

This side of the business now assumed much greater importance with, by the end of the year the number of omnibuses owned increased to 35 (then to

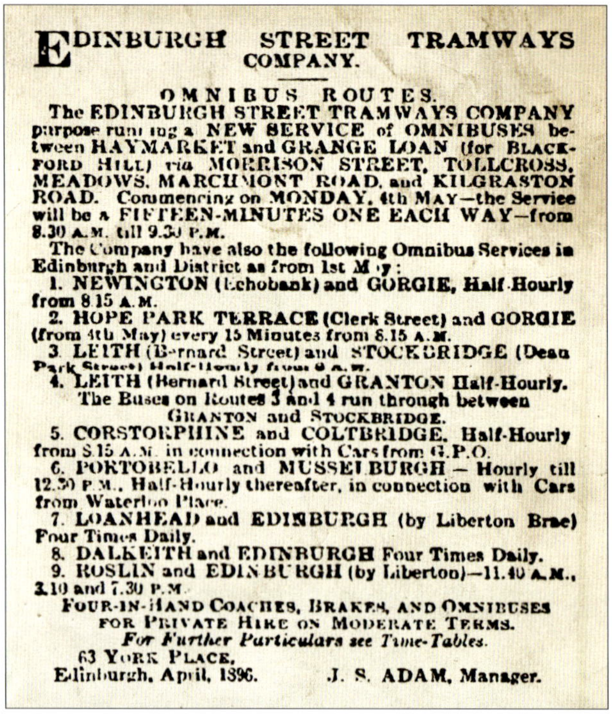

EDINBURGH STREET TRAMWAYS COMPANY.

OMNIBUS ROUTES.

The EDINBURGH STREET TRAMWAYS COMPANY purpose running a NEW SERVICE of OMNIBUSES between HAYMARKET and GRANGE LOAN (for BLACKFORD HILL) via MORRISON STREET, TOLLCROSS, MEADOWS, MARCHMONT ROAD, and KILGRASTON ROAD. Commencing on MONDAY, 4th MAY—the Service will be a FIFTEEN-MINUTES ONE EACH WAY—from 8.30 A.M. till 9.30 P.M.

The Company have also the following Omnibus Services in Edinburgh and District as from 1st May:

1. NEWINGTON (Echobank) and GORGIE, Half-Hourly from 8.15 A.M.
2. HOPE PARK TERRACE (Clerk Street) and GORGIE (from 4th May) every 15 Minutes from 8.15 A.M.
3. LEITH (Bernard Street) and STOCKBRIDGE (Dean Park Street) Half-Hourly from 9 A.M.
4. LEITH (Bernard Street) and GRANTON Half-Hourly.

The Buses on Routes 3 and 4 run through between GRANTON and STOCKBRIDGE.

5. CORSTORPHINE and COLTBRIDGE, Half-Hourly from 8.15 A.M. in connection with Cars from G.P.O.
6. PORTOBELLO and MUSSELBURGH – Hourly till 12.30 P.M., Half-Hourly thereafter, in connection with Cars from Waterloo Place.
7. LOANHEAD and EDINBURGH (by Liberton Brae) Four Times Daily.
8. DALKEITH and EDINBURGH Four Times Daily.
9. ROSLIN and EDINBURGH (by Liberton)—11.40 A.M., 3.10 and 7.30 P.M.

FOUR-IN-HAND COACHES, BRAKES, AND OMNIBUSES FOR PRIVATE HIRE ON MODERATE TERMS.

For Further Particulars see Time-Tables.

63 YORK PLACE,
Edinburgh, April, 1896. J. S. ADAM, Manager.

Evening News 29 April 1896

39 in 1897) plus 24 trams. In addition there were 12 'other coaches and carriages'. Good progress was made with the authorised tram extensions, with the line from Portobello to Joppa inspected on 13 May and opened – probably – on 24th (the Queen's Birthday holiday) this adding 50 chains, or ⅝ mile to the Company's tramway mileage. Additional stables were built at Livingston Place in the centre of Portobello.

During the second half of 1897 several meetings were held with the relevant local authorities, and agreement was reached for sale of the Company's lines in Leith and Portobello for £75,000 and £40,000 respectively. By this time Portobello had been absorbed by Edinburgh, effective from 1 November 1896. When negotiations were completed, it was proposed to make the District Company's lease include all lines, the intention being to extend Edinburgh's cable haulage system to (at least) the foot of Leith Walk. The matter appeared cut and dry, with an end in sight for the 'muddles' at Pilrig and Meadowbank – or so it seemed. A date was set – 30 June 1898 – the local press noting; 'the advantages to the public dependent on the speedy completion of both sales are too obvious for comment'[129]. On the first day of July Edinburgh, having paid its dues, took possession of the Portobello lines and passed operation over to the District Company. The changeover at Meadowbank ceased and frequency for most of the day was increased to a car every 7 minutes. Street Tramway shareholders benefitted from a payment of £1 per share.

However, the fly in the ointment – preventing a conclusion to the Pilrig tramway imbroglio, was now Leith Council – which on 14 April had determined to complete the purchase. Certain members of the Council appeared determined to frustrate the proposed extension of the cable system into Leith, as had been incorporated into the tentative agreement. The recent failed attempt to amalgamate Leith and Edinburgh was fresh in many minds; this extension of the tramway into the Burgh was now seen as just the thin end of the wedge towards achievement of such an end. Thus the purchase of the Leith lines, also scheduled for 30 June, did not take place. At a special Council meeting on 5 July the convenor of the Tramway Committee, Bailie Waldie, moved that the purchase be completed, but Bailie Gibson moved that the matter be held over for six weeks. This was carried, thereafter Waldie immediately resigned. As soon as this became public, Edinburgh Council wrote to Leith intimating that they now intended to make an offer for the remaining lines in Leith. Much of the dubiety in the minds of Leith Councillors was said to lie with the matter of just exactly who they were dealing with, and whether the leasing arrangement was completely above board. The Edinburgh lease was with Dick, Kerr & Co, but they were now being asked to sign up with the Edinburgh & District Tramways Co, an organisation which they believed had, in law, no standing. Some observers thought that this was Leith's way of attempting to avoid having to sign an agreement leading to the installation of cable power tramways in Leith. The matter should have been clarified when a letter was sent to Leith's Town Clerk indicating that the lease would be with the Tramways Company, but that Dick, Kerr would be cautioners for the lessees' obligations. It was even suggested that some Leith councillors had deliberately absented themselves from meetings so as to prevent achievement of a quorum.

Andrew Gibson took umbrage with the press coverage of the proceedings '... tramway affairs in Edinburgh are so backward and immature that there is abundance of time for the Leith part of the work ...'. This provoked a lengthy leader which seems, from this distance in time to be less than non-partisan. '... Mr Gibson's letter affords a very fair illustration of the muddle-headedness and misapprehension under which many members of the Leith Town Council appear to suffer. They have succeeded in bringing themselves into complete contempt, and it is not likely that Mr Gibson's letter will give the public generally any higher opinion of their manners or their intelligence.'[130] The Street Tramways Company's statutory powers of 1892 required them to adopt the same motive power as used in Edinburgh on Leith Walk north of Pilrig, just as soon as the Edinburgh section was converted. On 7 December 1898 Leith Council wrote to the Street Company '... the Council will not adopt cabling as the form of traction for the tramways in Leith [and] decline their consent to the Company's cabling the Leith Walk section.' Thus matters stagnated: the disruption to through traffic occasioned by the necessity of complying with the arbiter's decision on the horse tramways now became a substantial obstacle. Edinburgh had commenced conversion to cable haulage of the horse tramways within its boundaries, but Leith now steadfastly refused to have cable north of Pilrig. The Street Tramways Company directors saw no immediate prospect of a sensible resolution, so determined to make the best of a bad lot and to operate what they were left with to their best advantage. It was noted – perhaps with no little sense of irony early in February 1899 – that Aberdeen Corporation were to convert their Woodside line to electric operation.

Within Leith, reconstruction of the old bridge over the Water of Leith at the east end of Commercial Street was undertaken, the Dock Commissioners – to whom the bridge belonged – having extracted from the Tramways Company an agreement to contribute £3000 to the cost. A new swing bridge was duly constructed, complete with tram rails, the only problem then being that there were then no tram rails on the streets on either side. Eventually this was resolved and the short length joining the termini in Bernard Street and Commercial Street was completed, inspected, and opened to traffic on 31 July. Services were reorganised across the bridge to give a new double circular route. This ran from Foot of Leith Walk, by Bernard Street, Constitution Street and Junction Bridge back to Leith Walk, then ran up to the Post Office and round the 'Inner Circle' by the Bridges, Marchmont, Melville Drive and Tollcross back to Princes Street and the Post Office. The half-yearly report advised that the loss to the Company from the disruption resulting from the cabling of the Edinburgh lines had reduced earnings by some £400 per annum[131]. Final through horse car operation at Pilrig was on Saturday 21 October 1899; for the subsequent two decades the travelling public had to endure the inconvenient change from Edinburgh's cable operated line to Leith's horse, then electric, trams.

The Street Tramways Company was a reluctant participant in this drama, but were determined to maximise the benefits of their operations. At the end of March the tracks serving Newhaven were inspected by Colonel Yorke. Creating another circular route these lines ran from the former Stanley Road terminus, down Craighall Road then by Annfield to join the Commercial Street tracks. These came into use on 2 April 1900, used by a service from Pilrig back to Pilrig, by Junction Street, Stanley Road, Craighall Road and Commercial Street. With the end of through traffic at Pilrig, the Company now ran all services from that terminus; to Commercial Street, to Bernard Street, to Seafield plus the 'circular' service detailed above. This extension brought the Company lines to 4 miles 77 chains (just three chains or 198 feet short of five miles); six cars were added, purchased from the District Company, bringing the total to 26, plus also their 49 buses and 14 other coaches and carriages[132]. Further cars were obtained as passenger numbers increased, to a maximum of 29 in 1903.

A further approach to purchase was made by Leith Council in 1900, who yet again withdrew 'on the eve of completion'. An operating loss was reported, this attributed mostly to the effects of the Pilrig disruption being felt fully for the first time. Bus services now accounted for 57% of earnings. A new cross-town bus service, tapping areas not previously served was introduced on 29 October 1900, running from Ferry Road at Newhaven Road by way of Powderhall, Claremont Street and Broughton Street to Princes Street at the Mound. It lasted less than a year however.

In an unusually far-sighted move, when tracks were renewed in Leith Walk and Constitution Street during 1901, with the agreement (and at the cost) of Leith Council, these were bonded and cross-tied to be suitable for electric operation. They were also re-laid six feet apart, in lieu of the more usual four feet, to provide space for later erection of centre poles for overhead power wires. The Company's capital was increased by £15,000 in 5% Preference Shares to fund this (and other) expenses. While the tramway side of the business was now well defined, various modifications followed regarding horse bus operation, to accommodate the changes following cable tram extensions, also to adjust bus routes. A new service was introduced from Tron Church to Angle Park Terrace by Chambers Street, Tollcross and Fountainbridge. This was soon extended westwards to Robertson Avenue, then cut back to Tollcross; this end was later extended to Hope Park Terrace then further to Echo Bank (better known now as Cameron Toll). When any route became unprofitable, it was axed. Premises for stables were purchased at 125 Fountainbridge and 30 Upper Gray Street, the latter large enough for 50 horses and 12 vehicles.

The stock of buses peaked at 49, many of them manufactured in London and seating just 12 in and 14 out on garden seats. The country routes continued, to Loanhead and Roslin, while the long standing Corstorphine route was extended in to Haymarket. From Newhaven there were services to Granton and to the cable car terminus at Goldenacre. Company finances suffered greatly from the disruption at Pilrig with major dislocation of traffic at the busiest point of the entire operation. Prior to cessation of through traffic the Company averaged 11.22d income per car mile; after the schism this dropped to 8.17d – a reduction in earnings of 27.2% – a drop which led to the loss of dividends for shareholders. Operational costs amounted to just over 7d per car mile, so margins were exceedingly tight. Profits were greatly influenced by good weather increasing traffic – a factor over which the Company had no influence. Another such variable was the unforeseeable, and uncontrollable, price for fodder.

Leith Corporation's Horse Tramway

Having had no sensible contact with Leith Council since 1900, it was not until three years later that any move was made to take advantage of the statutory opportunity for purchase, which came in 1906. Subsequently a formal offer of £60,000 was tabled, which, after proper consideration, was accepted by the Company; ten years before this asset was offered for £155,000. The proposal required that, after the purchase, the Tramways Company would be wound up. After the formalisation of this by a Provisional Order dated 27 July 1904, events moved quite rapidly, with the last day of Company operation being 22 October. Mr Adam stepped down from his position and was replaced on a temporary basis by John Wilson, former traffic superintendent. An early change was the cessation of services up Craighall Road, ending the 'Outer Circle' route. On – probably – Leith's steepest gradient, and with little traffic potential, this made good sense, cars now terminated at Newhaven and Stanley Road.

Work on electrification proceeded rapidly, with new lines constructed along Pilrig Street (the northern track actually in Edinburgh, the southern one only in Leith, as the boundary ran along the centre line of the street as far as Ferry Road). A short lived horse car service used this line, along Pilrig Street to Stanley Road from 16 June 1905 until electric services commenced on 18 August[133]. However, Leith's horse cars were still to be seen running between Bonnington

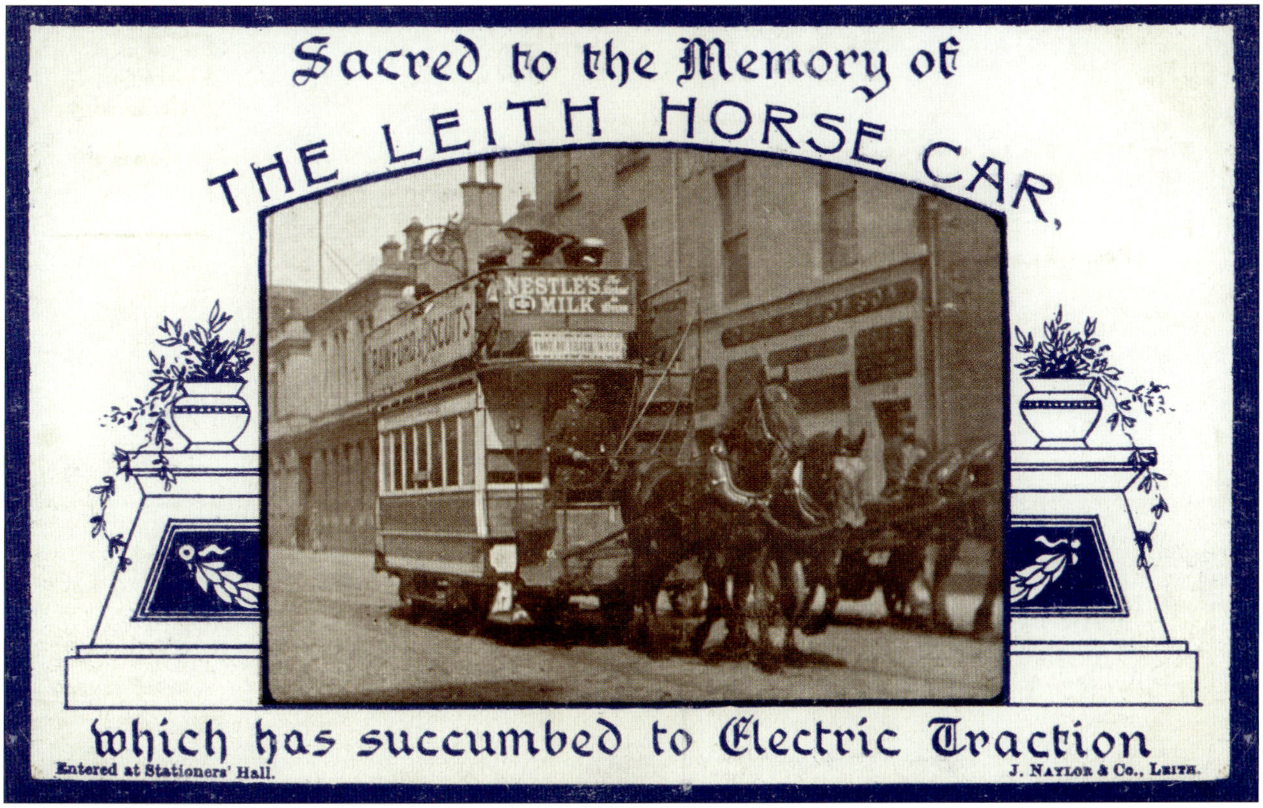

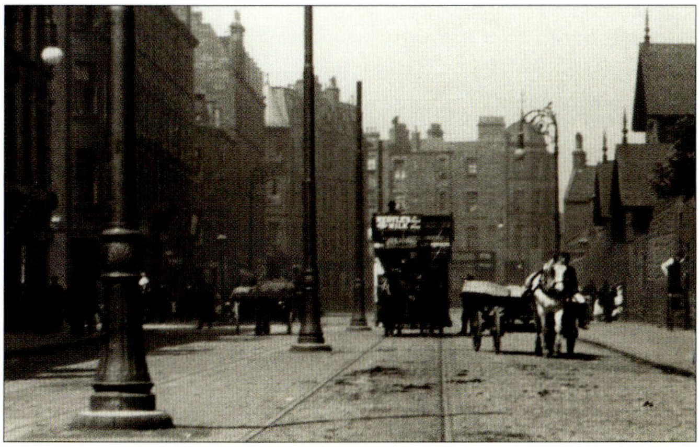

Above. Postcard marking the passing of the Leith horse trams.

Left. Horse car 7, now owned by Leith Corporation, on Great Junction Street after the track has been reconstructed for electric car operation. While the centre poles are in place, the overhead wires are yet to be added. Leith's poles were dignified with Burgh arms cast on the decorative bases.

Road and Seafield by Great Junction Street until 1 November – a special post card produced to commemorate the event.

After completion of the sale of their tramways the Company was required to wind up the rest of the business, as required by the Provisional Order. Why this inclusion was not disputed is hard to understand. Perhaps after more than 30 years of local authority acrimony, the directors were quite glad to call it a day. However, the bus element of the undertaking had the potential to be continued as a separate company, and the directors floated these assets for sale at £6750, open till 1 December 1904 but there were no takers.[134] Horses and remaining vehicles were retained until the following spring when improved prices were anticipated – whether that was justified when set against the

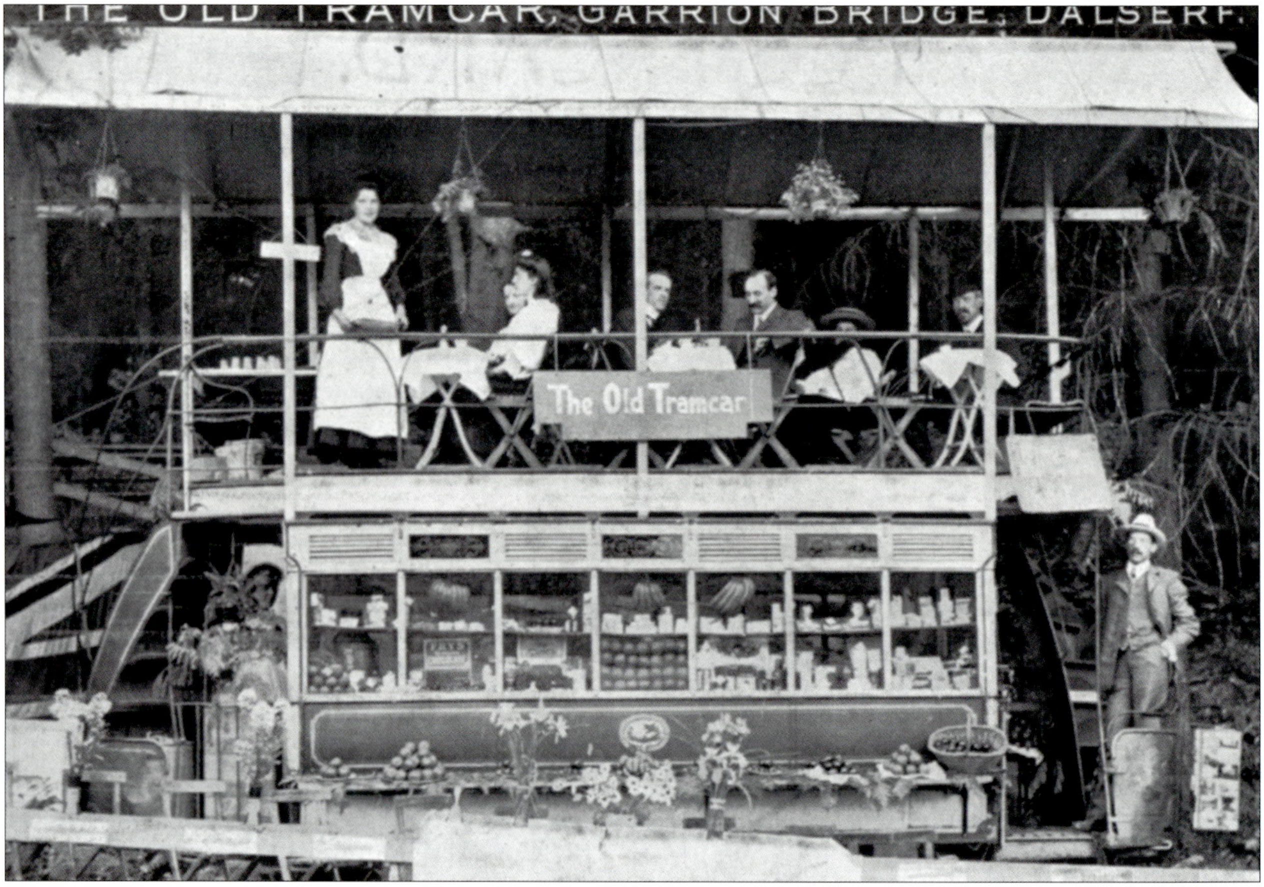

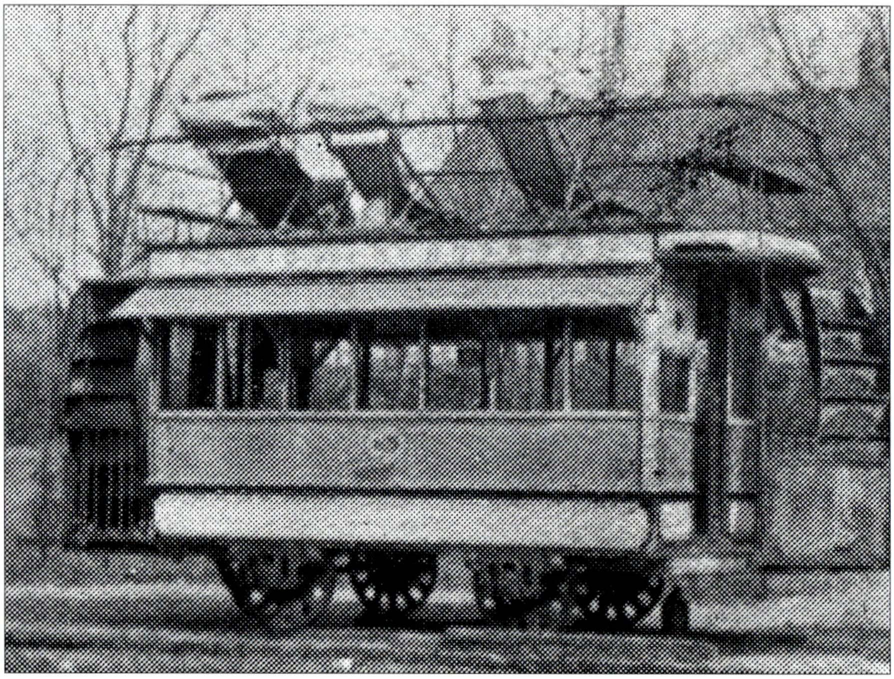

Above. Uses to which redundant horse cars were put were many and varied. This ESTCo car went to South Lanarkshire where it served near Garrion Bridge over the Clyde as a popular wayside tea-room and shop.

Left. A coarse screen press photograph, but recording another use for disused horse trams. Leith Corporation sold four to East Pilton Hospital as sleeping accommodation for patients suffering from consumption – but with most of the windows removed.

Leith Section.

Bernard Street to Newhaven (*via* Annfield)—7-56 a.m, and every 10 minutes till 11-16 p.m

Bernard Street to Pilrig (*via* Constitution Street)—8-18 a.m; and every 10 min. till 9-0 a.m, then every 5 min. till 7-0 p.m; then every 10 min. till 11-8 p.m; 11-18, 11-25, 11-35 p.m to Stables

Bonnington Terrace to Pilrig—12-23 p.m, and every 5 minutes till 10-13 p.m

Newhaven (Pier Place) to Pilrig (*via* Annfield and Bernard Street)—8-8 a.m. and ev. 10 min. till 11-8 p.m; 11-18, 11-28, 11-38, 11-43 p.m to Stables by Ferry Road

Newhaven (Pier Place) *via* Ferry Rd. and Junction St.—8-10 a.m, and every 10 minutes till 11-10 p.m.; 11-20, 11-30 p.m to Stables; 11-10, 11-20, 11-30, 11-40 p.m from Stanley Road to Stables

Pilrig to Bernard Street (*via* Constitution Street)—7-45, 7-55, 8-5, 8-15, 8-25, 8-35, 8-45, 8-55, and every 5 min. till 6-55 p.m, then every 10 mins. till 11-35 p.m

Pilrig to Bonnington Terrace—12-8 p.m, and every 5 minutes till 9-58 p.m

Pilrig to Junction Bridge—7-40, 7-50, 7-58, 8-0, 8-10, 8-13, 8-20 a.m, and every 10 minutes till 12-8, then every 5 minutes thereafter

Pilrig to Newhaven (*via* Constitution St. and Bernard Street)—7-45 a.m. and every 10 minutes till 11-5, 11-15, 11-25 and 11-35 p.m to Bernard Street only

Pilrig to Newhaven (*via* Junction Street and Ferry Rd.)—7-43 a.m, and every 10 minutes till 10-43 p.m, then 10-53, 11-3, 11-13, 11-25 to Stanley Road.

Pilrig to Seafield—7-50 a.m, and every 15 mins. till 12-5 p.m; then 12-17 and every 10 min. till 9-37 p.m; then every 15 min. till 11-20 p.m

Seafield to Pilrig—7-50, 8-5 a.m, and ev. 15 min. till 11-50 a.m; then every 10 min. till 9-42 p.m; then every 15 minutes till 11-5 p.m; 11-20 and 11-35 p.m to Morton Place only

Leith Section details, from *Murray's Timetables* of June 1901

cost of keep over the winter must be debatable. John Croall sold these off at various auctions in March and May 1905. The Company's stables and two acres of ground in Corstorphine were sold for £1000 at the end of April 1905.[135] Some routes were continued by operators who saw potential; the Corstorphine service was maintained for a time by George Hall, who had latterly acted as a contractor to the Tramways Company. With all mortgages and debentures paid off, shareholders received a final disbursement of 16 shillings per (£10) share whereupon the Company was wound up.

District Company horse tram operations

Returning to where matters were left in 1894, at page 74 above; after the split, the new (District) Company was the lessee and operator of 11 miles 70 chains of track with 70 assorted cars. Many new 1d fares were introduced, immediately popular, with increased usage and urgent need for additional rolling stock. Fortunately for the Edinburgh undertaking, the corresponding Glasgow Company had, at the end of its lease, been unable to agree terms with Glasgow Corporation and consequently had a large number of trams and horses to dispose of. While a number of vehicles changed hands, the horses were not considered of suitable quality for Edinburgh.

An element of the new lease was a requirement to reduce the platform staff working hours to a maximum of 54 per week. This was effected from 23 February 1895 – but with the natural effect also of reducing earnings. While no doubt the council had the best interests of the tramwaymen at heart, the consequences were that wages reduced by an average of 3s 0d per week for both drivers and conductors. Scales for drivers then started at 20 s 0d, rising to 23s 6d and for conductors from 18s 0d to 22s 0d; reductions of nearly 20% could not be accepted readily. Discontent was alleviated in July when a 1s 0d per hour increase was granted, and shifts were reorganised so that each pair of cars was worked by three pairs of staff, this resulting in each man theoretically working no more than the stipulated 54 hours. The change also required employment of 20 or 30 additional platform staff.[136]

After prolonged deliberation, at a special meeting on 1 March 1895 Edinburgh Council made the decision to convert their tramways to mechanical – i.e. cable – not electrical operation, a decision led by a reluctance to have overhead electrical wires disfiguring the aesthetic appeal of their fine streets. Other options considered included electrification using underground conduit or the surface stud contact systems, but these were rejected as too expensive. Councillor McRae, for the city, said '… the electric system had not been perfected to that stage where they could adopt it safely, as far at least as financial results were concerned.'[137]

Dick, Kerr, then an engineering company rather than a transport operator, was anxious to get on with what they saw as their real job – that of rebuilding the

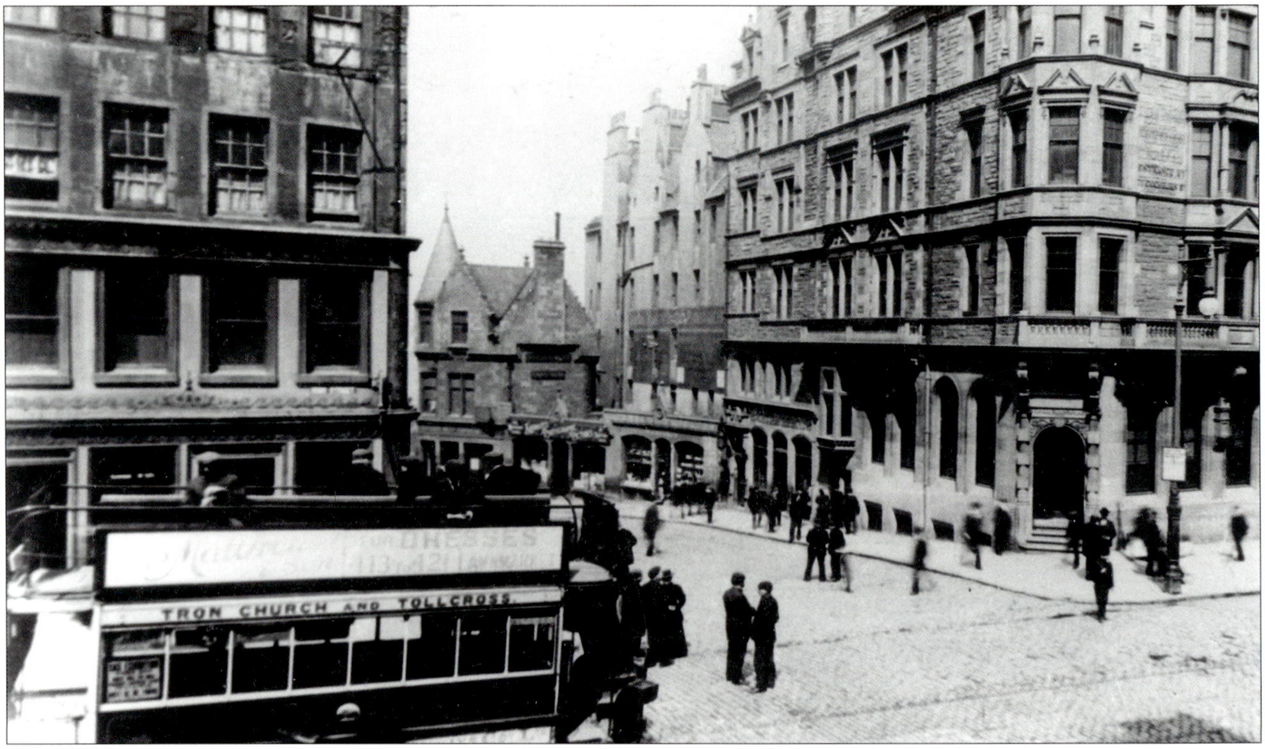

Above. The top of Cockburn Street from the High Street at the corner of Hunter Square. Most of the area seen is now entirely given over to tourist related outlets, Scotland's largest 'industry'.

Opposite. From the Crown Hotel again, the view of Calton Hill changed little, but the street scene was an ever changing one; this is the summer of 1886.

lines for cable operation and then installing the plant to drive the miles of cables below the streets. Initially the plan was to construct the cable lines from Pilrig to the recently extended city boundary at (or beyond) Nether Liberton, Braids, Murrayfield and Dalry, plus the cross line from Newington to Morningside. Provision was to be made for Edinburgh and Leith to be considered as an entity, with facility included for cable haulage to Bernard Street and Great Junction Street in Leith. New lines were planned; the Mound to Warrender Park Road, London Road to Easter Road, Broughton Street by Bonnington Road to Junction Street and along Fountainbridge, should it eventually be widened.[138] These extensions were authorised by an Act passed by Parliament on 7 August 1896 which (surprisingly) also included permission for electric operation. The line across the Meadows to Warrender Park Road was not pursued, an unfortunate decision which might have had major influence in future developments – however, it was not to be, and the idea was never resurrected.

Cable tram preparations

With all preparations complete, a ceremony of breaking of the ground was held on 9 September 1896 at Craigmillar Park, with Lord Provost McDonald using a silver spade for the special occasion. After the event two brand new horse trams took the official party to lunch in the Royal Hotel. Edinburgh seldom marked tram events in any special manner – this was an exception. Work on all new tracks soon commenced – in most cases starting from the outer terminus and working in

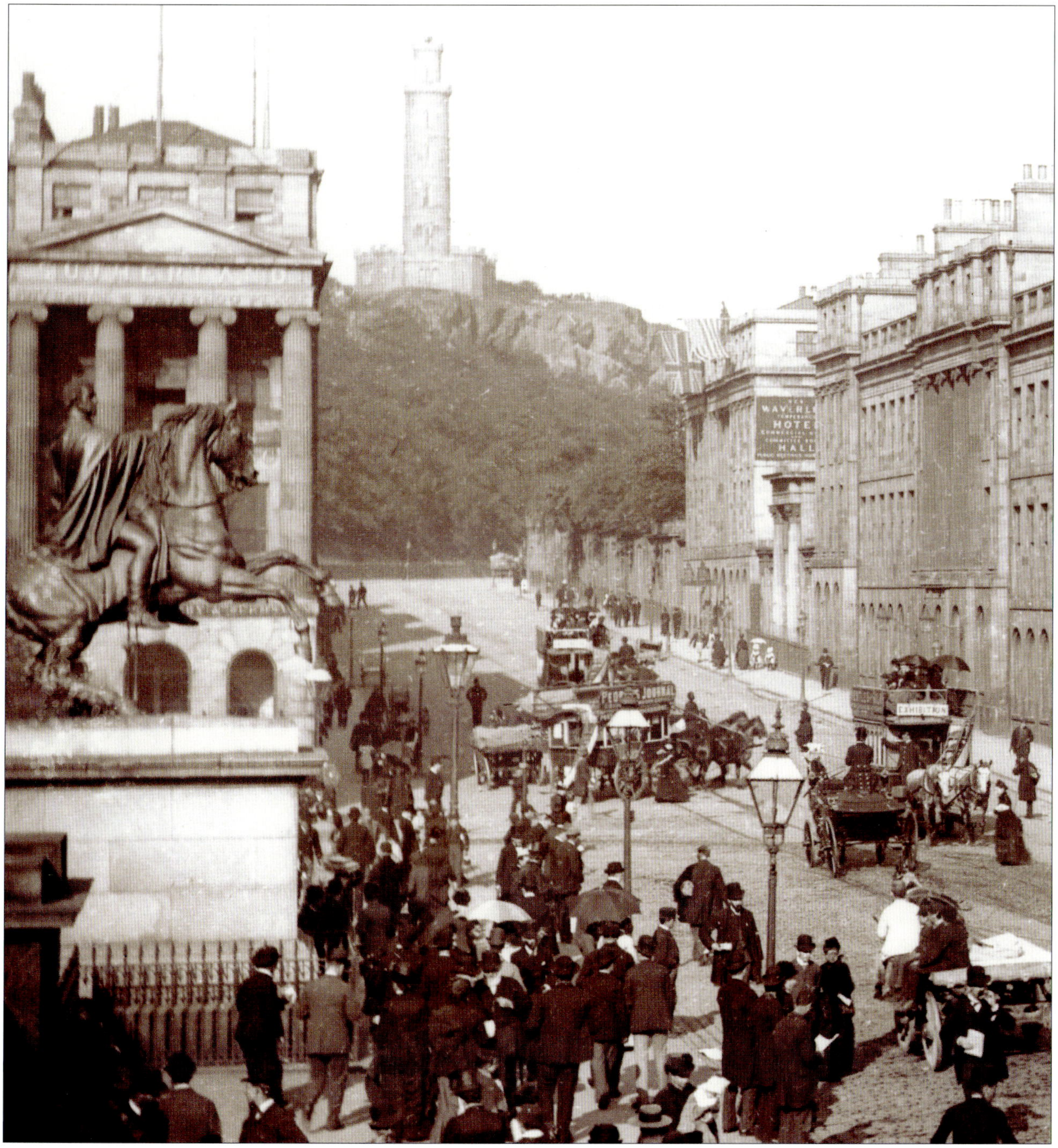

to the city. Outlay on the new cable power source was reckoned at £300,000 in 1896 – equivalent to over £35 million in 2016. Where operational horse tram lines were met, temporary tracks were laid to allow continuity. As the extended lines were completed they were made available for horse tram use until the new cable system was instigated.

Waterloo Place to Meadowbank (Jock's Lodge) passed to the District Company on 1 February 1896, followed by the remainder of the Portobello line on

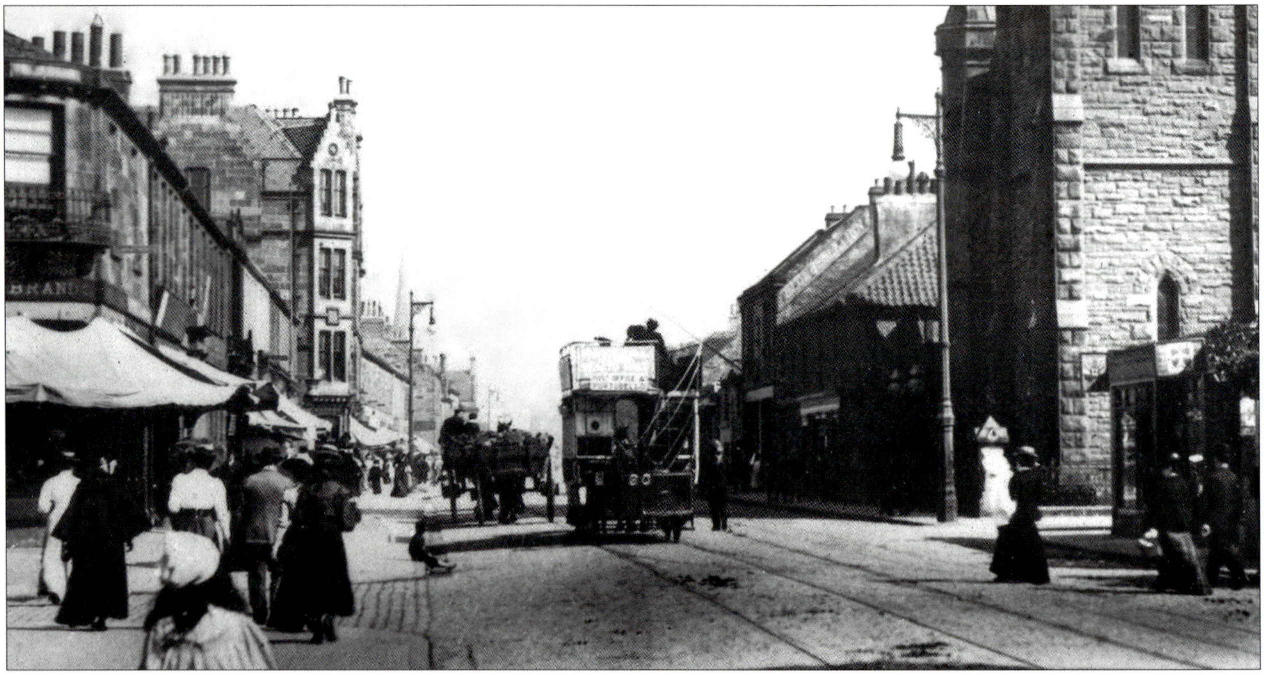

Above. Looking east along Abercorn Terrace at Windsor Place with car 90 about to reverse at the cross-over. This was the terminus until the track was extended to Joppa in 1897.

Right. Notice relating to traffic arrangements for the cabling of Princes Street, March 1897.

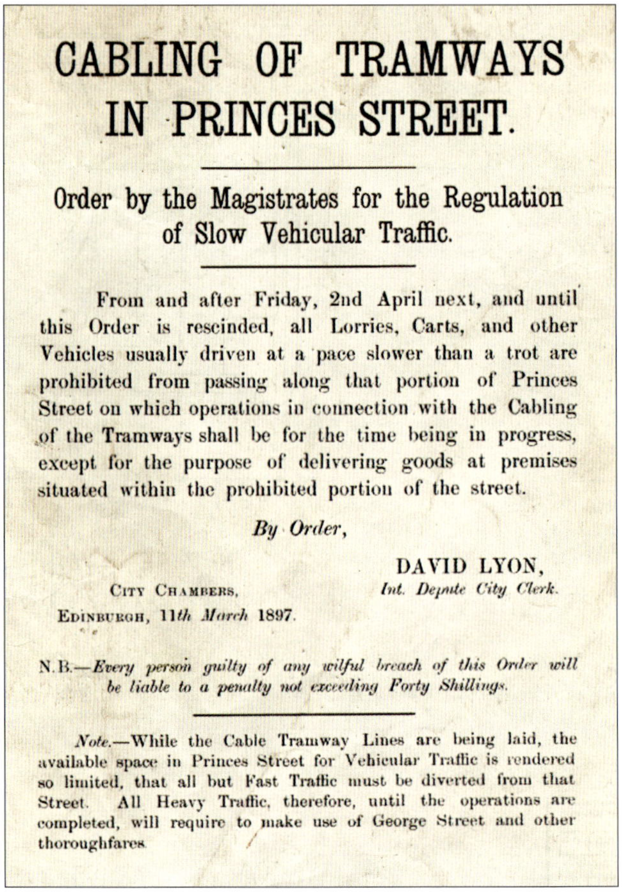

CABLING OF TRAMWAYS IN PRINCES STREET.

Order by the Magistrates for the Regulation of Slow Vehicular Traffic.

From and after Friday, 2nd April next, and until this Order is rescinded, all Lorries, Carts, and other Vehicles usually driven at a pace slower than a trot are prohibited from passing along that portion of Princes Street on which operations in connection with the Cabling of the Tramways shall be for the time being in progress, except for the purpose of delivering goods at premises situated within the prohibited portion of the street.

By Order,

DAVID LYON,
Int. Depute City Clerk.

City Chambers,
Edinburgh, 11*th March* 1897.

N.B.—*Every person guilty of any wilful breach of this Order will be liable to a penalty not exceeding Forty Shillings.*

Note.—While the Cable Tramway Lines are being laid, the available space in Princes Street for Vehicular Traffic is rendered so limited, that all but Fast Traffic must be diverted from that Street. All Heavy Traffic, therefore, until the operations are completed, will require to make use of George Street and other thoroughfares.

1 July 1898. By this date usage of the tramway lines had recovered from the hiatus caused by the Pilrig difficulty, and from a previous maximum annual figure of just over 16 million passengers per annum, the District Company had increased in 1896 to some 17,538,696 passengers, this allowing shareholders to receive a 6¾% dividend. Much of this recovery came from the new lowered fare scale.

As the suburban cable extensions were completed they were opened using horse trams. On 10 March 1897 a new service commenced between Braids (Braids Hill Hotel) and Craigmillar Park. The pull up from Morningside Station was a long hard drag for horses, with a trace horse or horses required for the full distance. During cabling operations services were maintained, and on Princes Street, where work commenced in April 1897, a temporary track was laid along its south

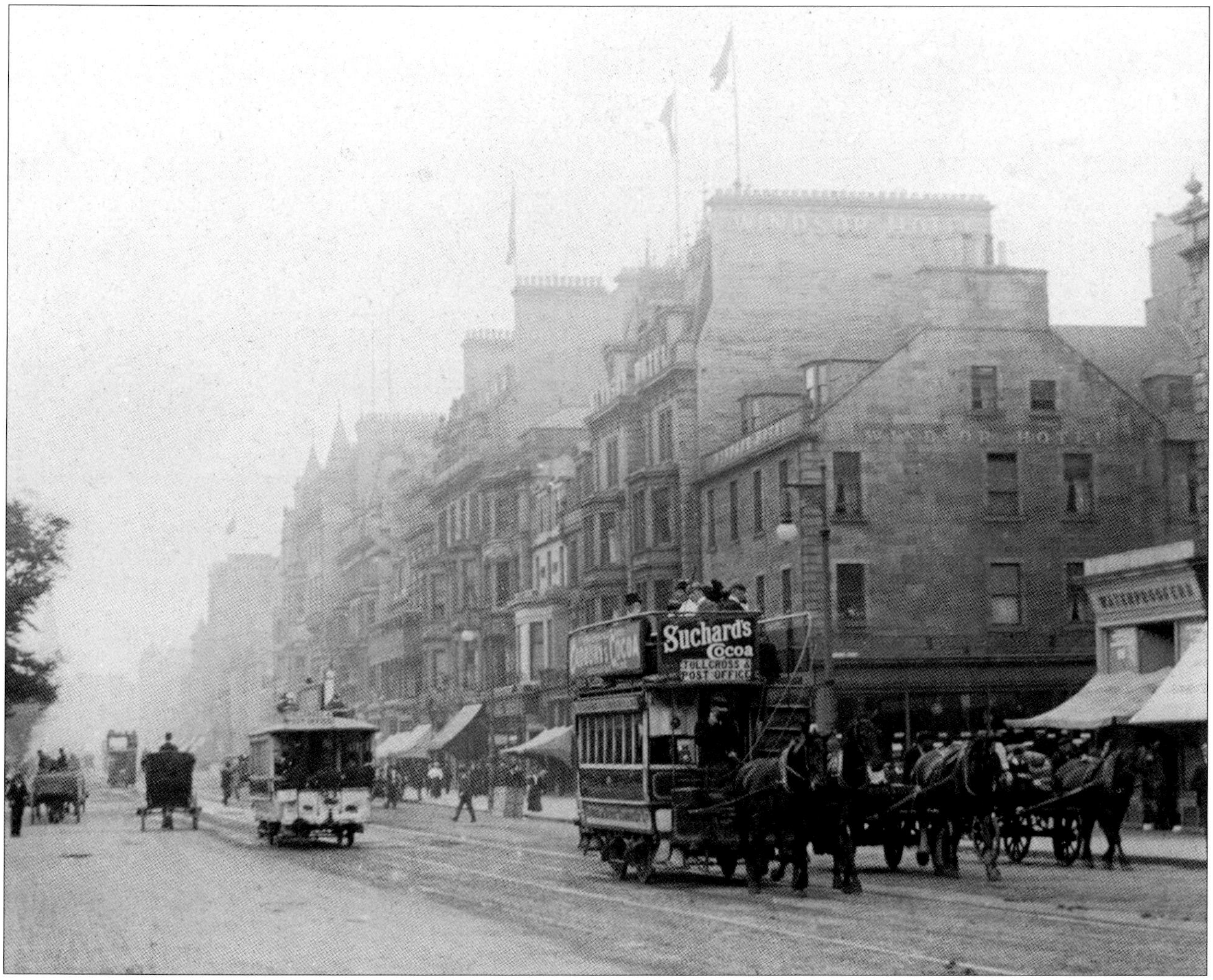

Looking west on Princes Street at South St David Street in the summer of 1899. Tram routes were adjusted to accommodate extensions built for cable operation and these cars (number 4 and canopy car 91) are both working on the recently introduced – and short lived – Post Office to Marchmont Road run. By this time the lines for cable operation were in place on Princes Street.

side. To allow work to proceed on the new cable power station at Shrubhill, temporary stables and car storage were provided at the north-west end of the site (some of these tracks were still to be seen when Edinburgh's electric cars were abandoned in 1956). Access to these facilities was by temporary track along Middlefield, James Street (now Spey Terrace) and Dryden Street. Further temporary stables were also built in McDonald Road. The new Gorgie line was inspected and opened using horse cars on 14 May 1897.

The cable operated lines of the Edinburgh Northern Tramways Company were purchased by Edinburgh Council (for £115,000) effective 1 July 1897 and immediately passed to the District Company, who then became cable car operators for the first time, with 18 cars on 2 miles 49 chains of track. The vesting date was taken back to be the start of that calendar year.

Major Marindin returned to the city on 13 August to inspect (and pass for use) the new cable lines in London Road, Melville Drive and Marchmont Road. Services put in place (from 18 August) on the new lines were Meadowbank to Braids via London Road, and Waterloo Place to Marchmont Road via Tollcross and Melville Drive. The latter service appears to have been

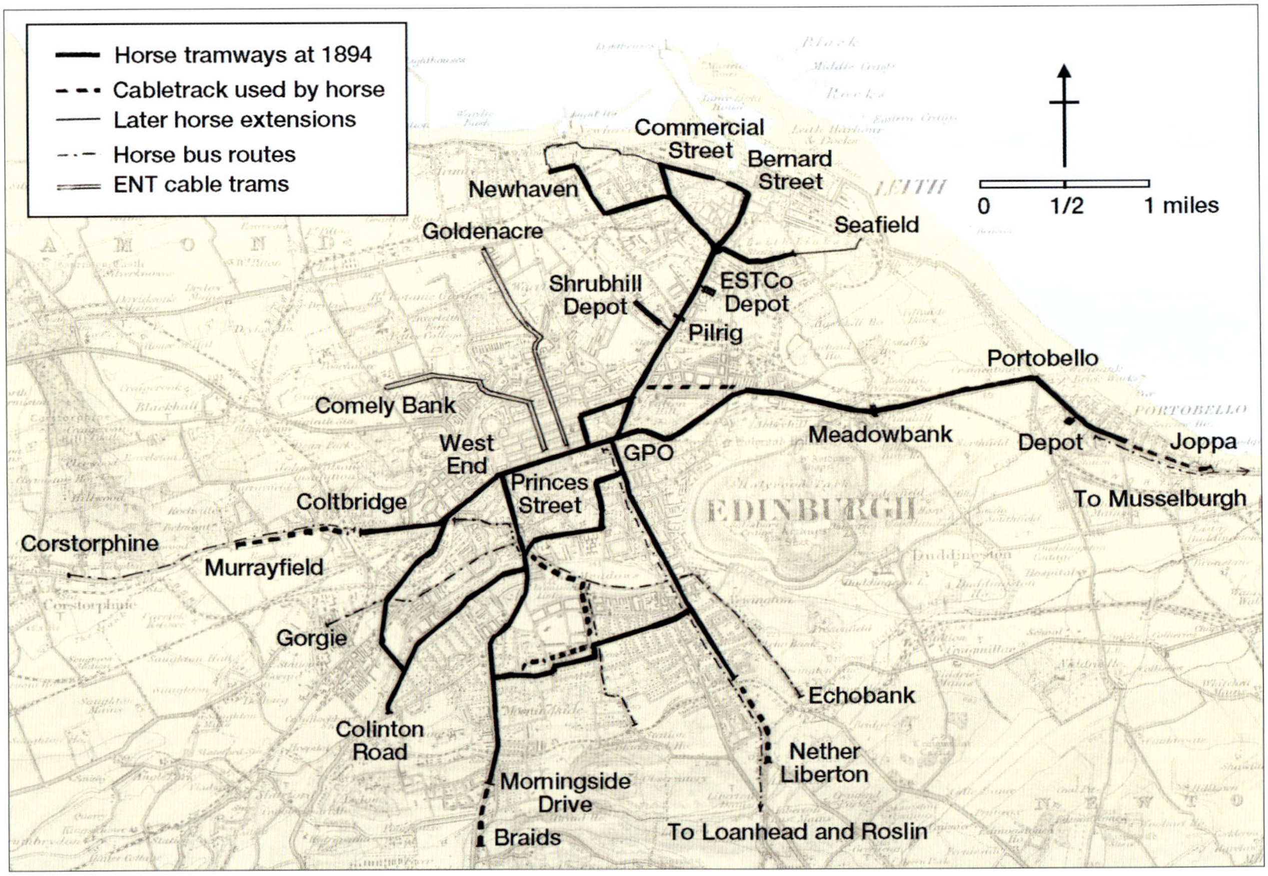

Above. Horse tramways in Edinburgh, Leith and Portobello.

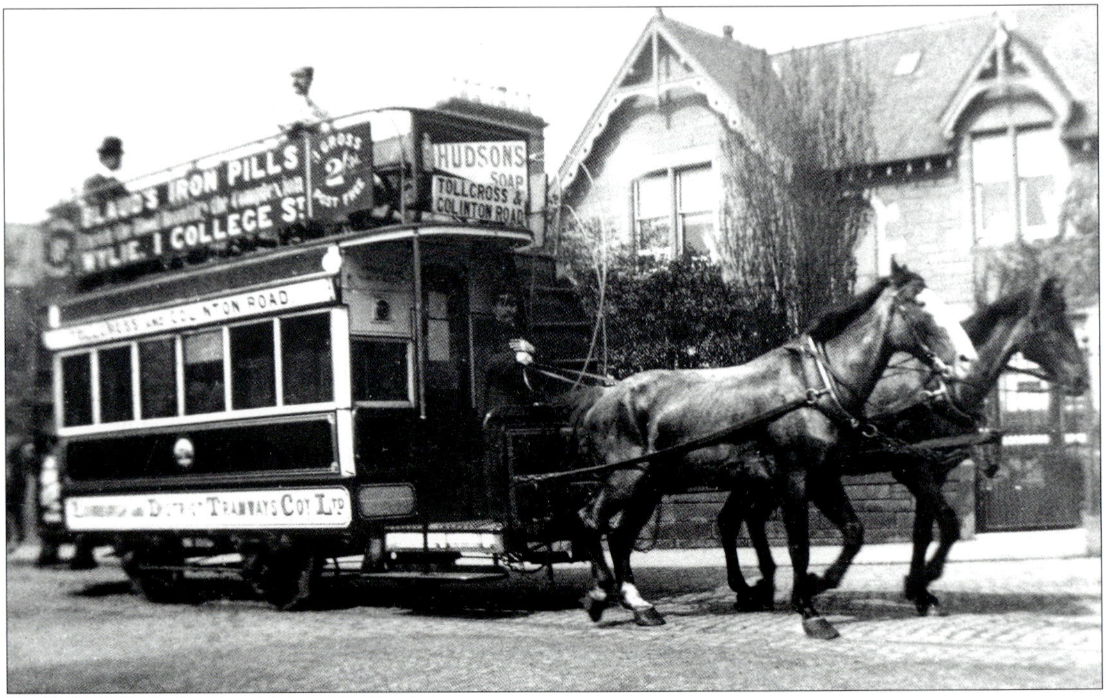

Right. Car 72 was one of the final three cars used on the Colinton Road route. It is seen here passing the junction of the tracks leading to the top of Harrison Road.

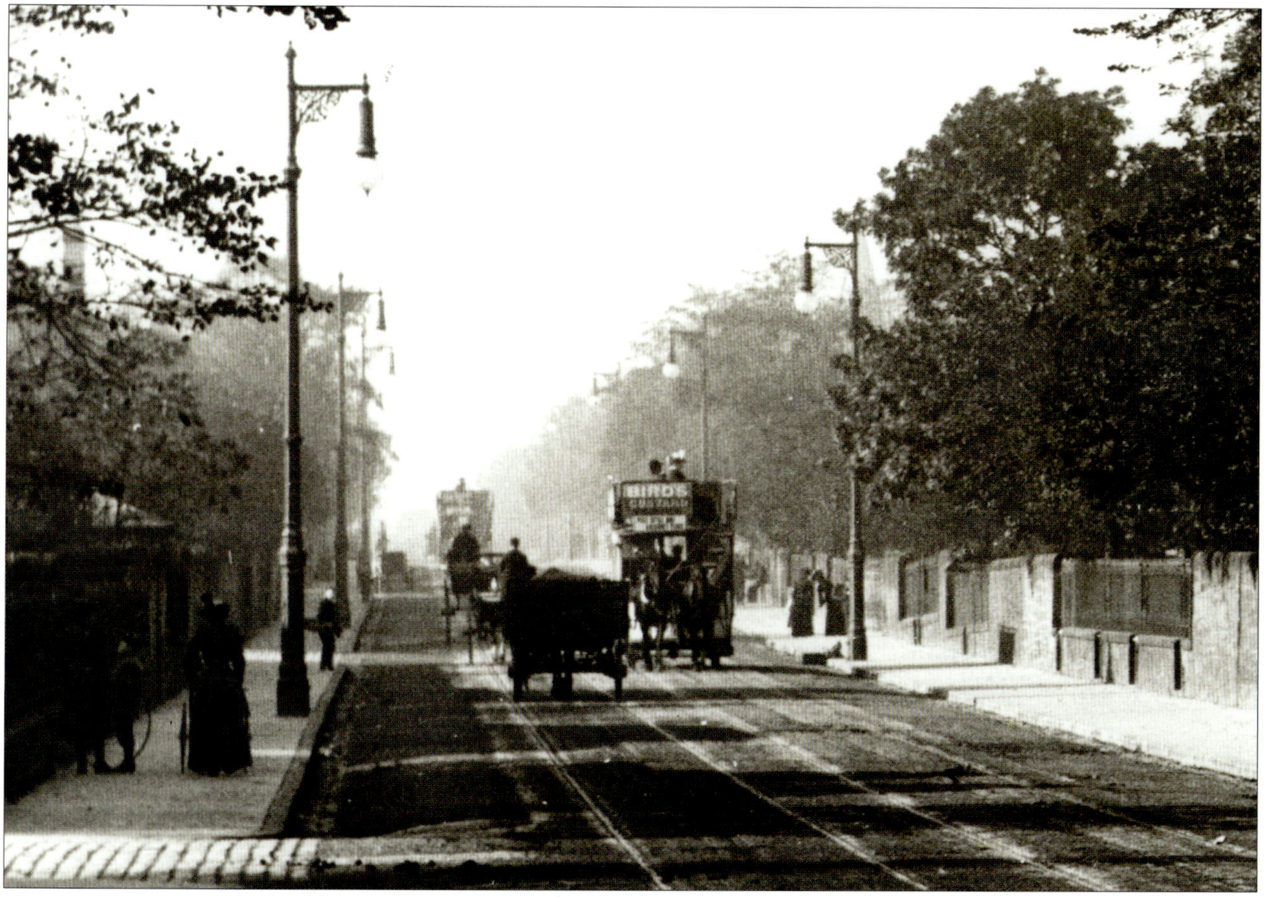

Strathearn Road at Findhorn Place has changed little in this scene from the end of the nineteenth century. The advent of the internal combustion engine has since removed the tranquillity associated then with a more measured pace of life.

provided mostly by single deck 'canopy' cars, with a trace horse provided for the gradient up to the terminus. Further new lines were inspected by Colonel Yorke on 11 December 1897; from Coltbridge to Murrayfield (Ellersly Road), Gorgie Road to Balgreen Road, Lady Road to Liberton Dams; and Greenbank to Braid Hills Road. It appears that the existing horse car services were extended along each of these new lines, probably from the following Monday, 13 December. Despite the major disruption caused by the track reconstruction, services were maintained, with passenger numbers increasing year on year, reaching over 23 million journeys in the year to 30 June 1898. This figure includes those travelling on the former Northern Company's line but was the last complete year before the new 'city' cable trams started. Shareholders benefitted to the extent of a 5½% payment on ordinary shares plus a 1½% bonus. To service this increased traffic the number of horses owned increased from 915 to 1030 and horse cars from 87 to 114.[139]

While good progress had been made on rebuilding the track, the highly complex underground arrangements at the thirteen major junctions were a different matter, and they appear to have been undertaken consecutively, rather than simultaneously. This may have resulted from the disruption each created. Generally street traffic was carried above the excavations, but at Salisbury streets were closed and the Morningside circle tram service was suspended. In lieu a service ran from the Post Office by the West End, Tollcross, and

Marchmont Road to Salisbury Place, with another operating between Salisbury Place and Churchhill.[140] This disruption was to be replicated when the twenty-first century Edinburgh trams were being installed; but on this later occasion, delays were partly caused by the apparent lack of knowledge of the existence of the cable tram junction pits which remained below Edinburgh's main streets. Colonel Yorke's next visit was on 1 June when he inspected the deviation line by Strathearn Road on the circular route. From 5 June horse cars resumed the Morningside Circle, now running by the new route. The disused Hope Terrace and Clinton Road tracks were soon removed, but their whin sett surfaces remain as a reminder of their earlier role.

The other major event – on the same day, but not apparently attended by Yorke – was the first official cable car operation, from Shrubhill to Pilrig then up to St Andrew Street. The car had been run down from York Place to Shrubhill late on the evening of 30 May using the cable, then after the official party had adjourned, the public were treated to three hours of free travel on the car. From 31 May 1899 – but only for a relatively short period – the Waterloo Place to Marchmont Road route was adjusted to become the 'Inner Circle' which existed as route 6 until the 1956 closure. It was, however, only operated in an anti-clockwise direction, with the clockwise circle operated by cars which formerly ran from Commercial Street to Churchhill via the Bridges. This service was now diverted down Marchmont Road then by Tollcross and the West End back to Leith, but only operated in this form until 21 October. By this time the distinctive route liveries had fallen into abeyance and many horse cars were painted brown to dash and waist panels. This extended to the new cable cars being delivered which were described as of 'chocolate' colour.[141]

On Thursday 12 October 1899 the completed cable lines from Pilrig to Braids were inspected by (now Sir) Francis Marindin, but his certificate was not issued until the 23rd. That same day was the first when citizens discovered that cars no longer ran north of Pilrig. Only trial cable cars were on the streets, intermingled with horse cars, but through services no longer ran, and all passengers faced an interruption to their journeys, a condition which was to prevail for the ensuing 24 years. Public use of the cable system commenced on 26 October, after an adequate number of drivers had been trained on the Northern lines. On that day also, cable cars ran amongst horse cars, their numbers increasing throughout the day.

From this time on cable cars were introduced as quickly as practicable throughout the system, with parallel reduction in horse car operation. However because of drivers' unfamiliarity with the new system, interruptions were not infrequent and horse cars, and horses, were retained to provide emergency services. In addition, at this stage, workers early morning services continued to be run by horse cars. To run the District Company's full service had required 80 horse trams; 30 cable cars on the Pilrig to Braids route took the place of 16 horse cars which had operated this route before. Cable routes were opened in 1900; Tollcross to Salisbury Place to Churchhill on 4 April; Post Office to Nether Liberton on 23 May; West End to Haymarket on 10 August, then on to Murrayfield on 10 September; then Morrison Street to Gorgie on 14 December.[142] This allowed the horse car fleet to be reduced by 27 cars – four scrapped, others sold, some to the Street Tramways Company for Leith, the total number being reduced to 57. The chairman explained 'They had had to keep a very large stud of horses [451] because they could not dispose of them until they were quite sure that the cable lines were to work properly ...'.[143]

During the following two years the remaining lines planned for conversion were undertaken, with the new Mound to Tollcross line opened on 11 September 1901 (resulting in immediate closure of the horse operated line on High Street between Lawnmarket and Tron Church), Waterloo Place to Joppa on 1 May 1902 then finally Leith Walk to Abbeyhill on 10 July 1902, leaving only the Tollcross to Colinton Road route operated by horse. It was considered that the limited traffic generated did not immediately justify the cost of cabling. The terminus for the Colinton Road line was cut back to Tollcross from 4 June 1900. This last remnant of the

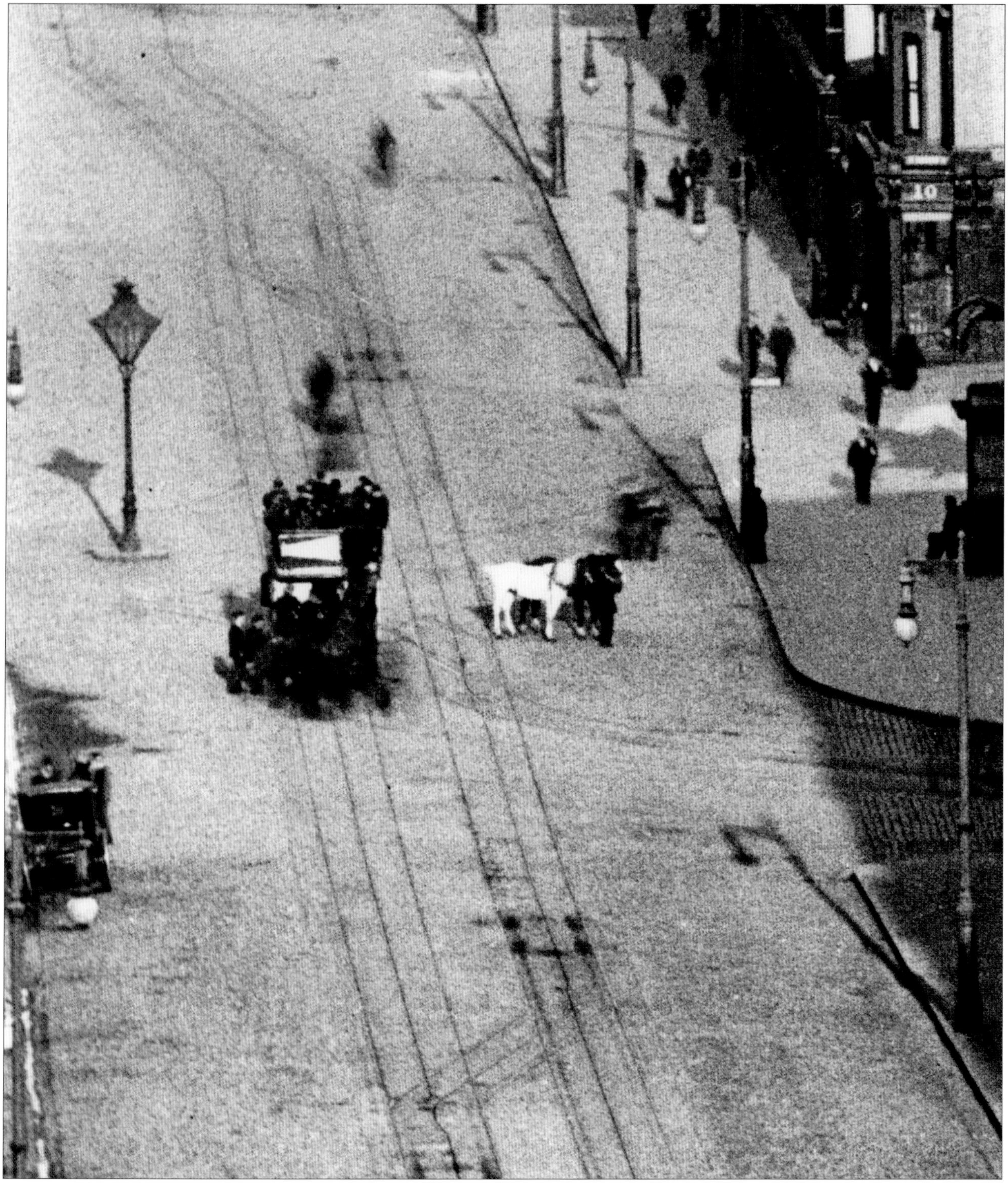

After commencement of cable car operation, early morning workers' services used horse cars. This long-distance view from Calton Hill records just this, with the trace horses having been taken from a car after its early morning climb up Leith Street (the lamp standard shadows act as time-pieces). That the cable tracks were then in use can be deduced from the oil stains on the cobbles where the cars paused at the Waterloo Place terminus for cars to Portobello.

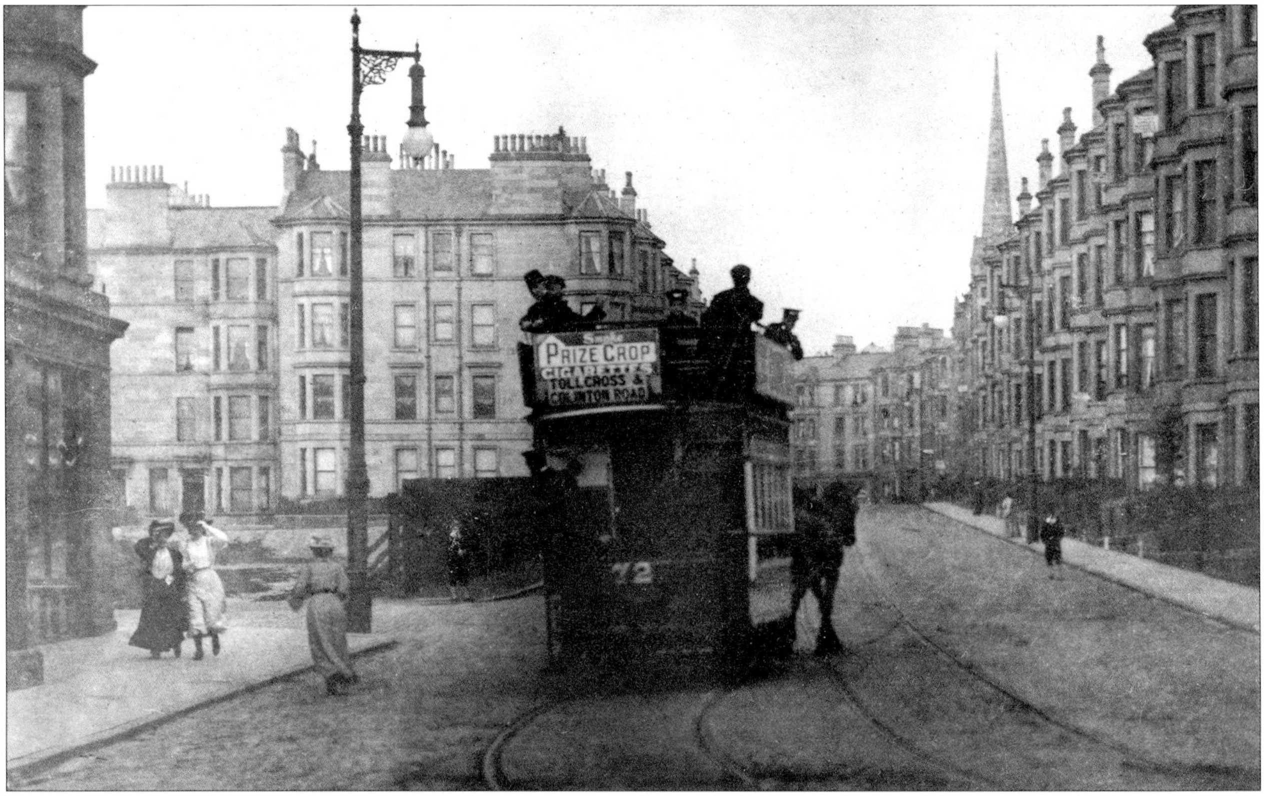
PRIZE CROP
TOLLCROSS &
COLINTON ROAD
72

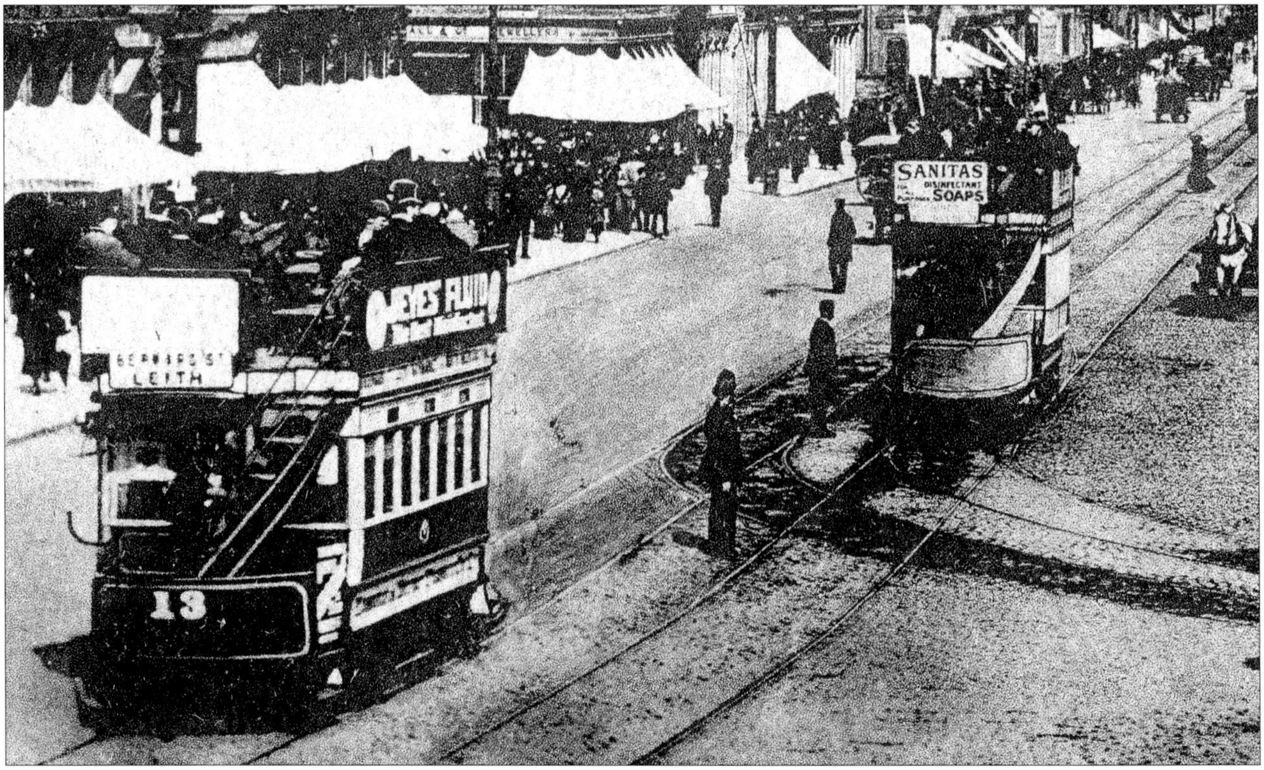
LEITH
13
SANITAS
DISINFECTANT
SOAPS

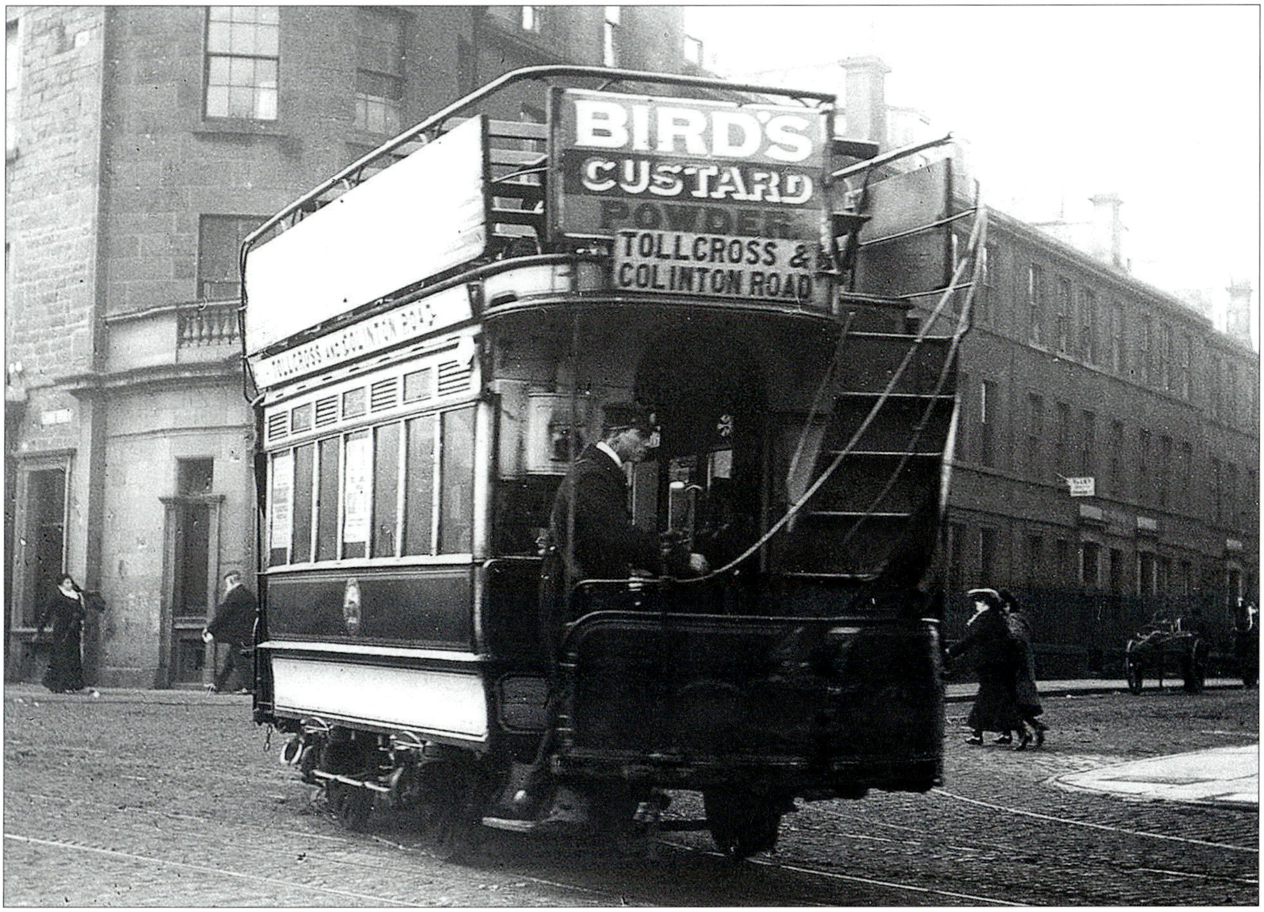

Opposite top. Car 72 again, but now in Polwarth Gardens, negotiating one of the twelve passing places encountered on its 1½ mile run to Home Street. Then followed some 200 yards of double track shared with cable cars, with its terminus in a short stub on the south side of Tollcross, this added in June 1900.

Opposite below. The easy way to update picture postcards was to convert the cars from horse to cable simply by removing the horses. Here are two horse cars so 'converted' at the West End.

Above. 47 was another of the numbers used for the final three horse cars (the third was 5, but so far no photograph of it has been found). However, the actual car carrying that number was changed at least twice in the last few years of operation.

past came in for a deal of criticism, with letters to the press of which the following are typical; '... the horse cars (which seem not to be housed during the night) are turned out in the morning with the seats on top all covered with snow and ice ... surely the height of bad management ...' and '... all along the [Gilmore Place] route the rails are so worn that it is no uncommon occurrence for the horses to drag a well-filled car along the causeway for several yards because the carriage has got off the track' then '... the line is a single one with frequent crossing places which were laid down for the Exhibition at Meggatland in 1890 and it has been allowed to deteriorate so much that it is quite common for a car to leave the metals several times in the course of a journey ... a car has to change from single line to double, or vice versa, some twenty-four times, and each time the car is swung and jerked to such an extent that anyone who happens to be on his feet runs a good chance of being violently deposited in the lap of some fellow-passenger, and that is exactly what frequently occurs ... the conductor, who was collecting fares, was thrown down on a passenger, whose hat he crushed

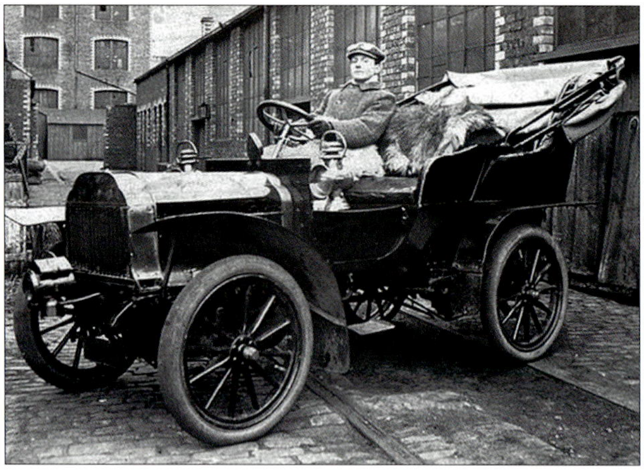

The least-known length of horse car track in Edinburgh was probably this, leading behind the coach-building department to the paint shop. This is thought to be Mr Pitcairn's (later) official transport, a 1907 Argyll 10/12 tourer with its chauffeur. Behind can be seen the five-storey 1882 granaary building.

with his elbow. That passenger claimed a new hat: he has not got it yet ... the old timetables of the various routes on which the cars were previously employed survived until quite recently, but they have not been replaced by timetables of the present service ...'.[144] 41 horse cars remained in stock at the end of 1901 (two having been rebuilt as cable cars); a year later 28 remained, in the next year this reduced to just ten licensed.[145]

Finally, after much debate, the Council decided that the Gilmour Place to Colinton Road horse car line should be upgraded. While many assorted electrical methods were considered, the Council plumped to persevere with the cable system. The last horse car ran, unremarked and unmourned, from Tollcross to Colinton Road on 24 August 1907. Latterly the horse car fleet had been whittled down to just three cars, and one of these survived to be transformed into a cable tram, then, in a third incarnation became an electric works car for the permanent way department. In this final guise it was in use (occasionally) until c1946, the last horse car. Or so it seemed until a remarkable discovery was made in a garden in the Borders. That part of the story is related in Part III of this work.

Recollections of horse car days

Years later his horse car reminiscences were recorded by 'John Mason'.

> 'My thoughts sometimes go back to those peaceful days in Edinburgh during the reign of Queen Victoria, when there was little to disturb the safety of the causeway, nothing to harass my lady as she swept majestically across the street, except an odd cab or a merchant's lorry or a horse-drawn car.
>
> Those cars – painted yellow and white, I think – had spacious windows through which you could see the passengers. They rolled along with a low-toned song humming in the wheels, the jangle of chains in front, and the regular beat of shod hooves upon the carriage-way.
>
> In the front of the car the car-driver was perched on his little one-legged stool, grasping the bent lever with his hand, winding and unwinding the chain which controlled the braking system, content as he softly sang the music-hall ditty of the day, the Irish labourer's dream of opulent ease:
>
> *No more rising up at half-past six,*
> *Climbing up the ladder with a hod full of bricks;*
> *No more clay pipes, nothing but cigars,*
> *For I am a driver of the tramway cars.*
>
> There was something very pleasing, something romantic, about those cars, especially in high summer. That was the time for the water-cart to appear, raising the dust, then laying it cool and damp under the hot sun; the time when laddies with barefeet and with their breeks pulled up well above the knee, welcomed the gushing water as they walked behind the water-cart to catch the spray upon their bare shanks.
>
> We used to put pins on the tramway rails

so that the wheels might flatten them: we used also to pull soft tar from between the causey stones where it had oozed up in the heat. We rolled it between spittle-wet palms, making pellets which we threw at one another.

In summer the tramway horses wore straw bonnets and ear hoods to protect them from the flies, blue bottles and clegs. Wise provision was made to slocken the thirst of the beasts. At regular intervals along the car route oak tubs containing a brew of oatmeal and fresh water were set at the pavement's edge. When the car was opposite one of these the driver would halt his horses, lift a pail from near his feet , plunge it into the brew, and give the thirsty beasts a drink.

I remember the trace horses going down the steep slope of Leith Street with laddies poised precariously on their backs. I also recall them straining uphill with the load they were helping to pull, the shod hoofs striking sparks on the granite setts.

Sometimes on the route the driver would ring his bell in warning when the car approached a distressed cyclist struggling feverishly to dislodge the slim solid-rubber tyres of his machine from the groove of the tramway rail; or when the high rider of a 'penny farthing' pedalled between the rails, fearing to swerve in case he might come a cropper; or when a private coach drawn by a pair of sleek, well-matched horses in shining harness, with a liveried coachman and footman on the box, moved at a slow trot along the tramway track to the evident enjoyment of the old lady reclining on the cushioned seat. In the autumn evenings, when the air was touched with frost and the gas lights were burning, how enchanting it was to watch the tramway cars go by, and see them pacing the hansom cabs that birled along beside them.

On Sabbath day there were no tramway cars to be seen on the city streets. The horses were all dovering contentedly in the dimness of the stable. On Sabbath morning the drivers were at home, smoking contentedly by the kitchen fire – there were no Sunday papers then – or daundering down the street with the bairn or with the dog, or to the chapel or the kirk, if they were so inclined.

J.M.'

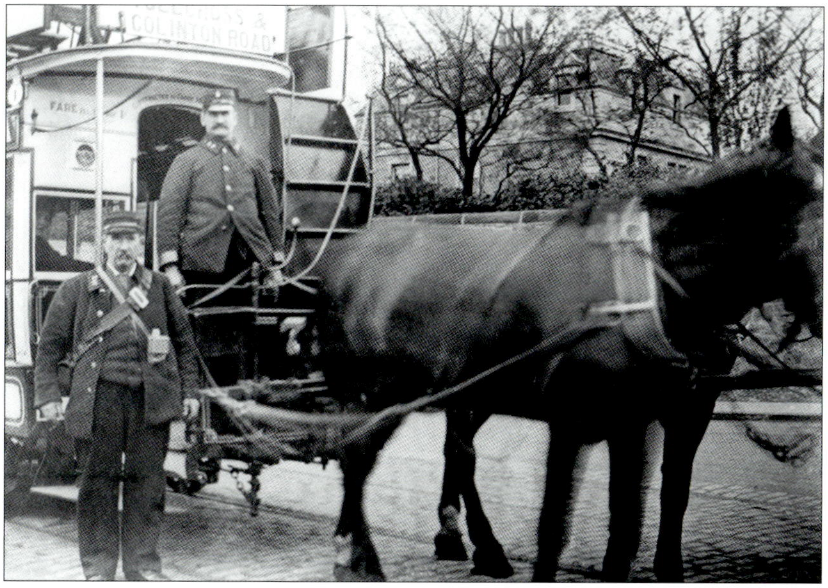

Car 72 at Colinton Road terminus during the last week of operation, with conductor John O'Neill and driver John Forbes.

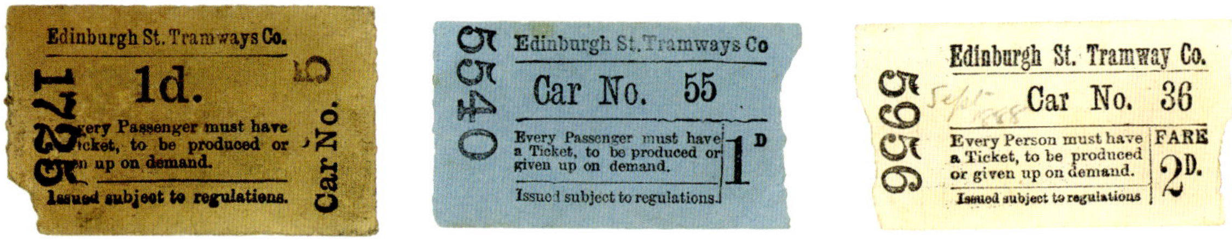

Edinburgh Street Tramways Company tickets

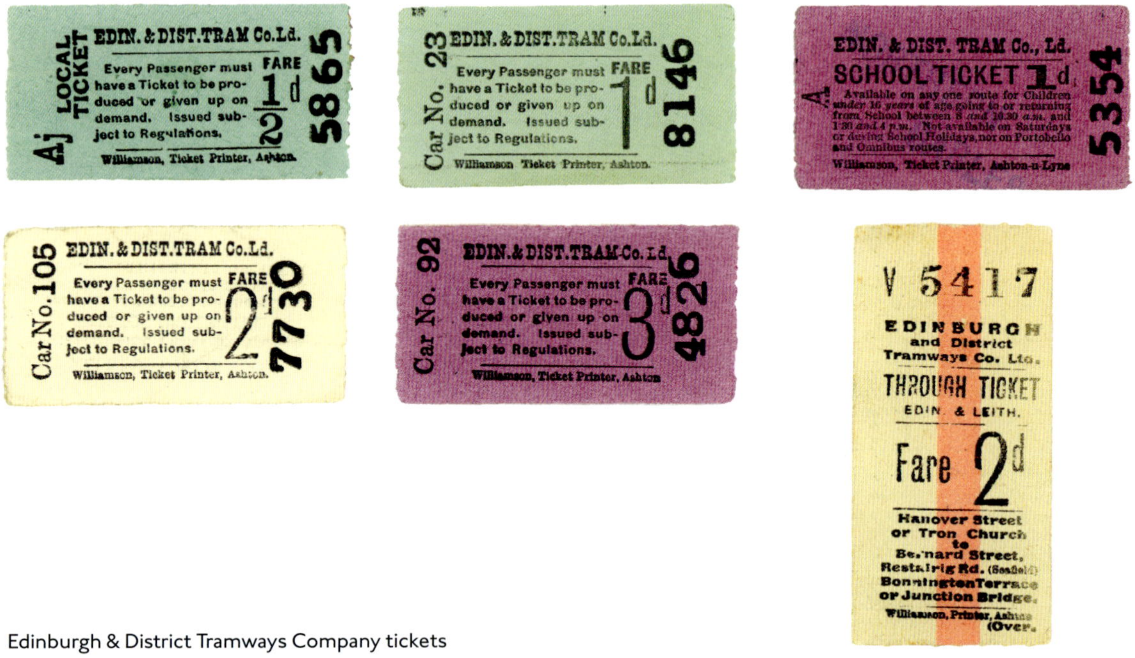

Edinburgh & District Tramways Company tickets

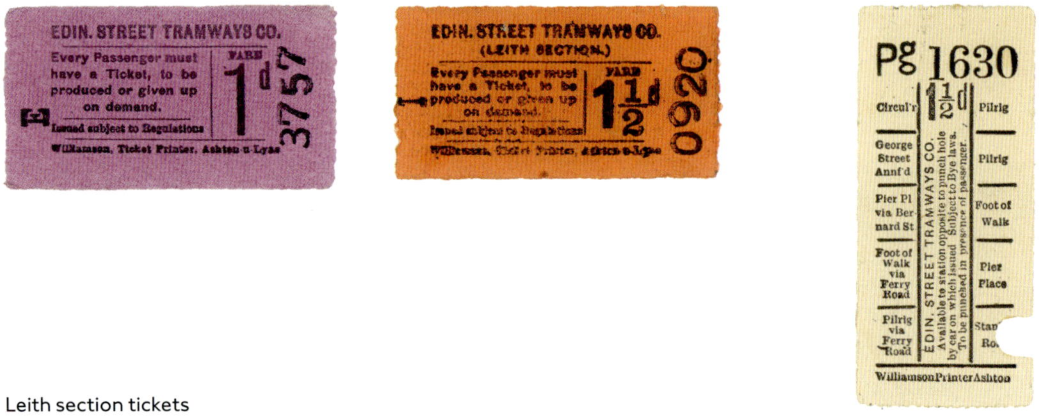

Leith section tickets

PART TWO

Rolling Stock

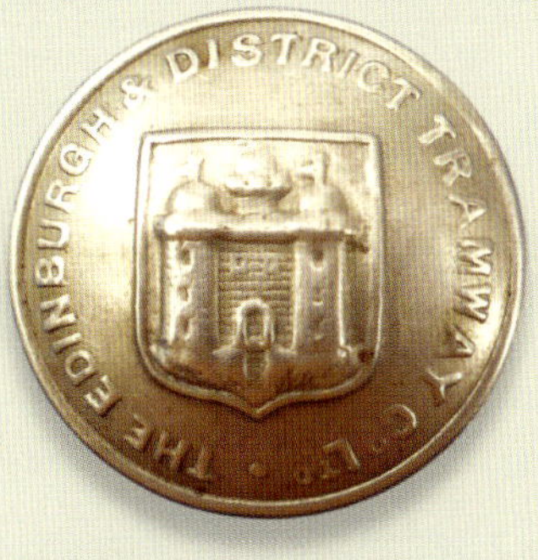

Uniform button of the Edinburgh & District Tramway (*sic*) Company Limited. (From the collection of Ashley Birch)

These coloured drawings are from the Thomson notebook. Although perspective seems beyond the illustrator, where details can be compared with photographs, a high degree of accuracy is evident. It is felt, therefore, that the colours represent competently the route liveries carried by Edinburgh's horse trams.

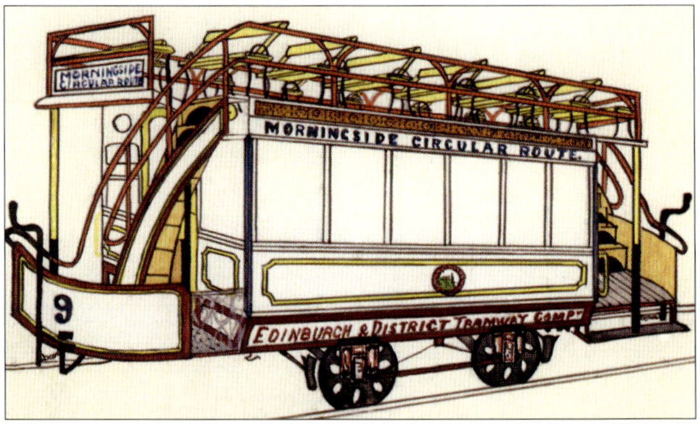

The white colour for the Morningside Circle route is represented by car 9, a light-weight garden seat car with double entrances in service from 21 April 1896. Ostensibly a rebuild, it bears no resemblance whatsoever to the previous car of this number which had a seven window saloon and knifeboard seats with waist panel of the 'Liverpool' style.

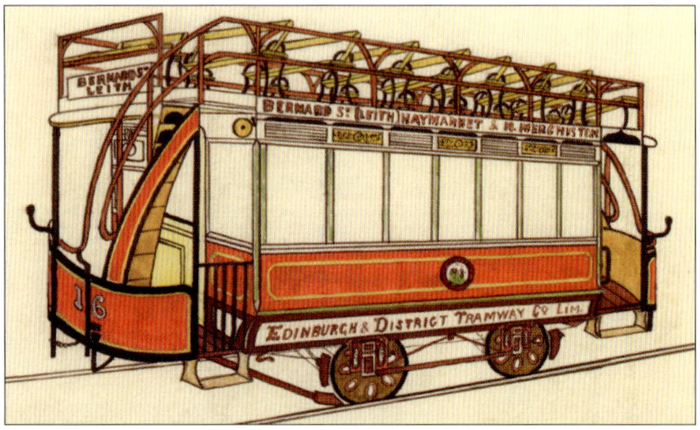

Car 16 illustrates the red livery of the Bernard Street to North Merchiston service. It is of the 'Exhibition' design, but with garden seats on top in lieu of the knifeboard seats of the car exhibited. This was the most numerous of the multitude of Edinburgh horse tram designs, with over 40 built at Shrubhill.

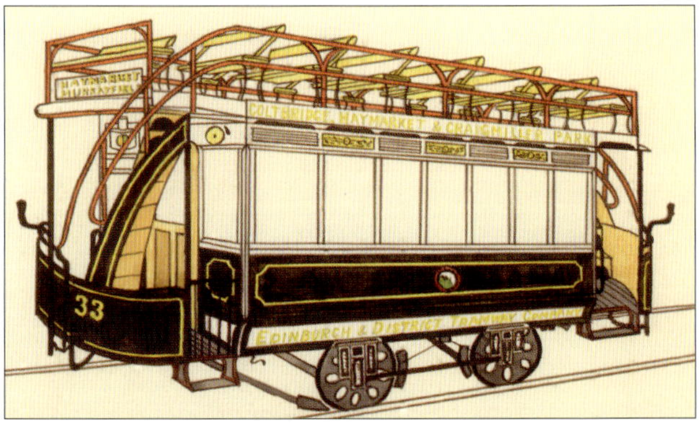

The livery of the 'trunk' Coltbridge to Craigmillar Park route was chocolate and buff, represented here on car 33. This is an 'Exhibition' design garden seat car. Those of this design carried 26 outside passengers, an increase over the 18 carried on knifeboard seats. Some of the earlier design were rebuilt with garden seats.

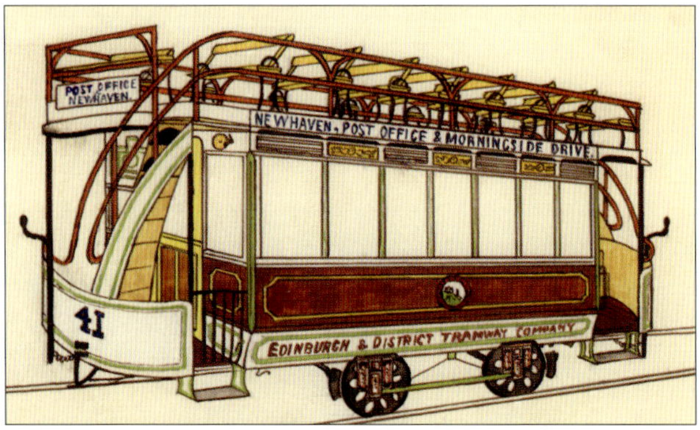

The Newhaven to Morningside route is represented by car 41 of the 'Exhibition' design. Here the main panels are described as 'oak' with white elsewhere. Car 45 of this design, but with knifeboard seats, was the car shown at the 1886 Exhibition and had electro-plated fittings plus cushioned interior seats.

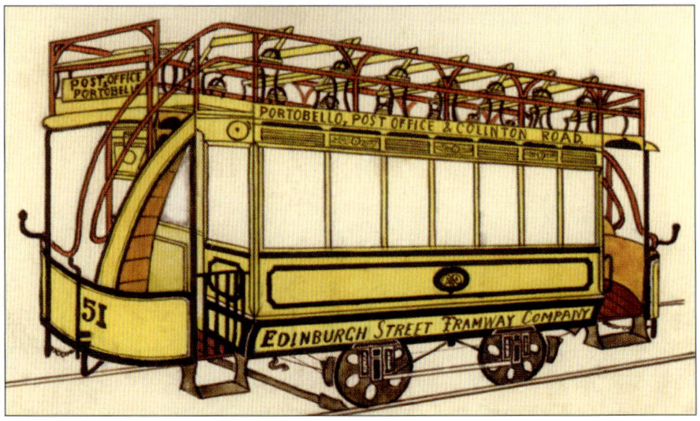

Portobello to Colinton Road cars used a yellow livery (which does not show well in contemporary photographs). Car 51 was one of the cars retained by the ESTCo for the joint running to Portobello, not transferred to the District Company until October 1899. It also is of the 'Exhibition' design.

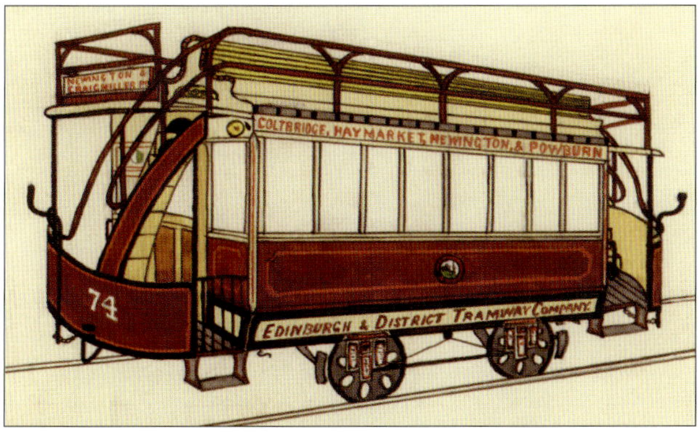

Car 74 is accurately represented as an eight-window, knifeboard seat design. It entered service in September 1894, purchased second-hand from the Glasgow Tramway & Omnibus Company, painted chocolate and buff for the Coltbridge to Powburn route. The Thomson book lists it as a 38 seat car, but it was licensed to carry 40, as were the other cars got from Glasgow.

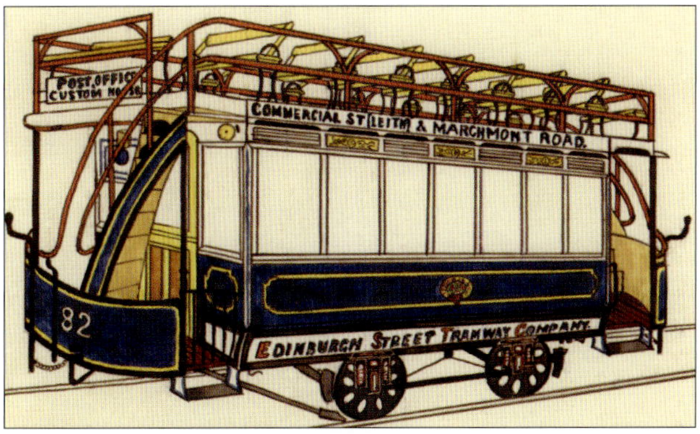

Car 82 is in the royal blue and white colours of the Commercial Street to Marchmont Road service; these were the colours of preserved car 23. Another 'Exhibition' design car, it was never used or owned by the District Company, remaining with the Street Tramways Company until it was passed to Leith Corporation in October 1904.

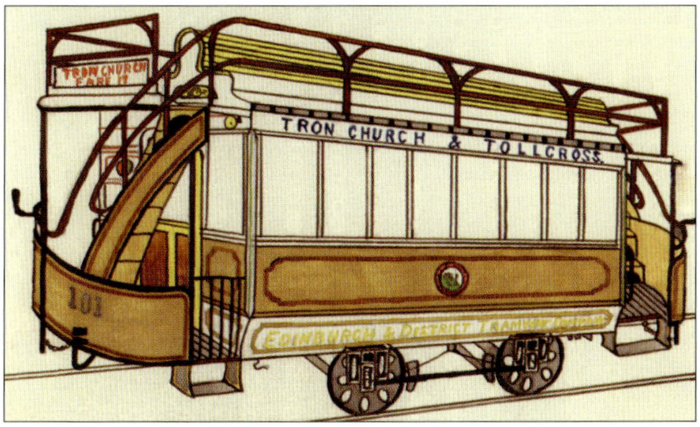

Ochre (defined as 'pale brownish yellow') and white was the livery for cars on the short route between Tron Church and Tollcross. Car 101 is correctly detailed as another of the thirteen purchased from the Glasgow Tramway & Omnibus Company, entering service in Edinburgh in December 1894.

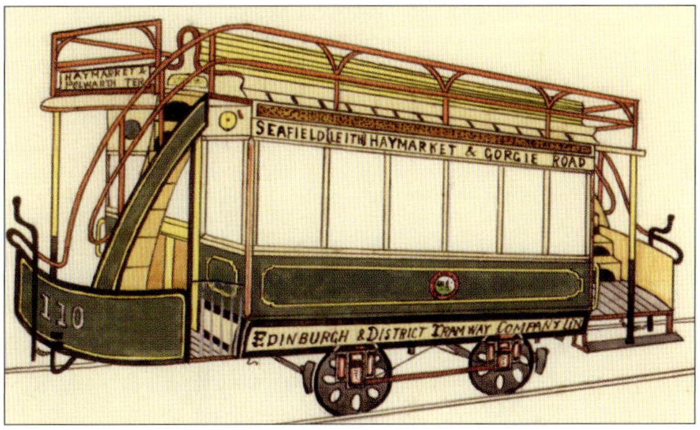

Car 110 was unique in the Tramways' fleet. New in January 1896, it appeared almost ten years after the last previous knifeboard seat car had been built and may have been the result of a 'tidying up operation' making use of assorted parts lying around the body shop. With double entrances, it was painted green and buff.

In July 1871 an order was placed for twenty cars from the Tramway Car and Works Company of Greenwich, established just a few months earlier as a subsidiary of the British & Foreign Tramways Coy. Both companies were floated by Messrs Ashurst and Morris, with some directors in common. (The Tramway Car and Works Company was not registered until 25 January 1872.) It has not proved possible to establish how many cars from the first order were delivered before cancellation of the balance, less than a week after the opening. Twelve were to hand by 7 November, with eleven in use on the opening day.[146] As sixteen replacement light cars were ordered, it seems probable that sixteen of these 'heavy' TCWCo cars were accepted. The 5 December timetable has six (1, 3, 5, 7, 9 and 11) running Bernard Street to Haymarket, and five (2, 4, 6, 8 and 10) running Bernard Street to the West End.

These first cars were described in detail; '... of a uniform size, the body of the car being 14 ft. long, and the length over all, including the platforms at the ends, 19 ft. The vehicle is carried on two pairs of wheels, placed within 5 ft. of each other, so as to admit of their moving freely round tolerably sharp curves. The wheels, which measure 3 ft. in diameter, are of chilled

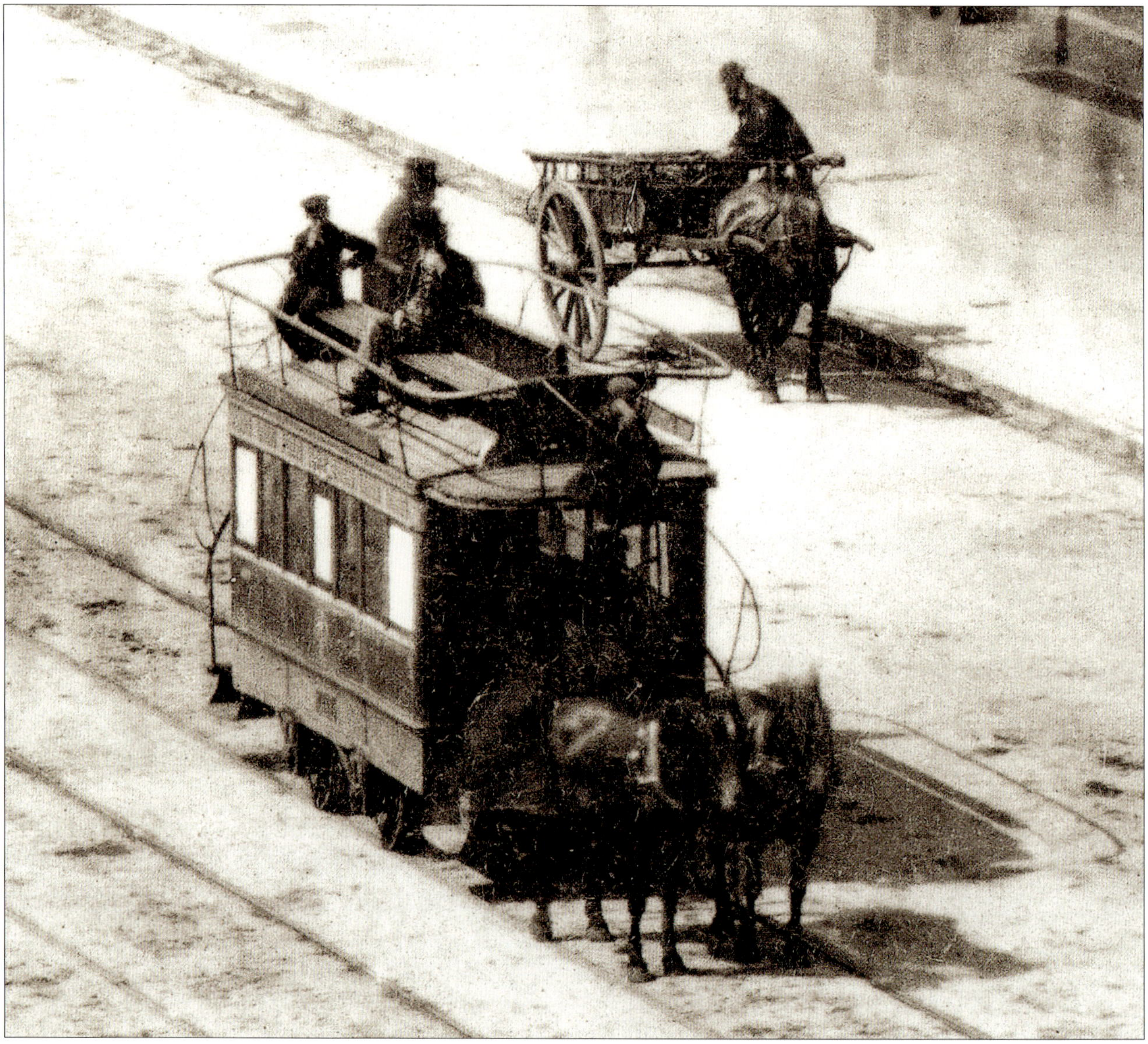

Probably the earliest type of vehicle supplied for Edinburgh's tramway. The flat-sided seven window saloon has basic style 'trunion' axle-boxes and the first design of flimsy iron spiral stair.

The destination board was used to prevent access to the leading end stair, on this occasion the vantage point providing a seat for a young passenger.

iron, each being cast in one piece … both ends being alike, there is no necessity to turn the car at the close of a journey; all that requires to be done is to shift the horses from one end to another, while the driver and the conductor change places. Of the body of the car, the lower part is painted after the fashion of a railway carriage, while the whole upper portion, both of sides and of ends, is formed of glass. The panes are fixed so as to avoid the clattering occasioned by movable sashes; but ventilation is amply provided for by apertures in the sides and top. Comfortably-cushioned seats are carried round the interior, numerous straps being hung from the roof for the purpose of assisting passengers to move steadily while the car is in motion. There are also cords carried along from end to end, by pulling which passengers may indicate to the driver and conductor

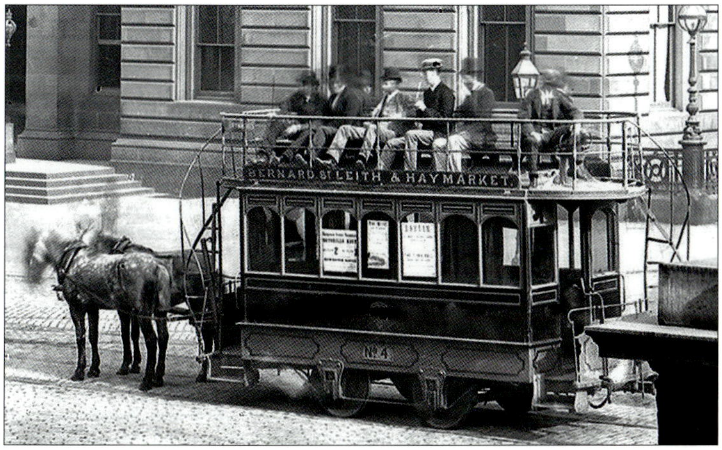

Left. Probably one of the lighter Leith cars. A window poster relates to the Portobello route, opened in May 1875. Again note the basic axle-mountings, the flimsy stair to the top deck, and the 'Liverpool' style of divided waist panel. It may be that this was the configuration adopted by Boyall of Grantham who built a number of early light cars. (G W Wilson Collection, Aberdeen University Library)

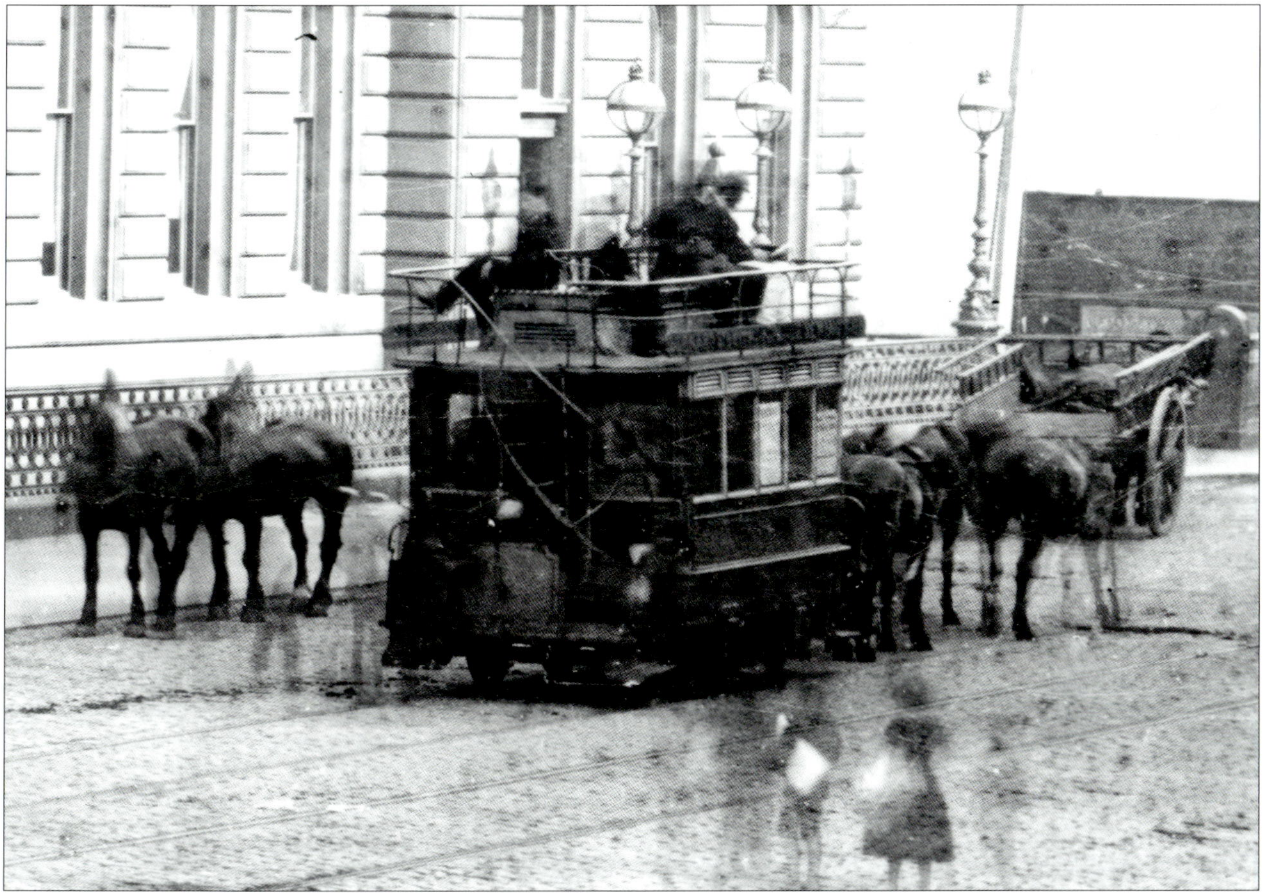

Below. From the same negative, a view at the North Bridge with a 5-window car – possibly one of the original 'heavy' cars down in length. The car is on the Bernard Street to Newington run. The 'ghostly' images are of children, one of whom appears to be a bare-footed newspaper seller. (G W Wilson Collection, Aberdeen University Collection)

when they wish to be set down. The lighting of the interior at night will be provided for by a large lamp at each end, showing a white light inwards, and a red or green light towards the street. In conducting the traffic it is proposed that the conductor shall give a slip of paper for every fare he collects, these being torn from a book where each leaves a counterfoil. Such a system will afford a perfect check upon the company's servants – that is to say, if the public can be induced to insist on having tickets every time they pay'.[147] Another report said that the cars were initially not seen to best advantage, being delivered 'perched on the frame of an old first class carriage' and noted the crimson plush seats inside – perhaps complementing the external paintwork; at this time North British Railway coaches were painted crimson lake.[148] [149] It was immediately found that these initial cars were considerably heavier than anticipated, and at the company's first meeting on 27 December 1871 the chairman advised 'as sufficient number of cars for the traffic ... could not be got in Scotland in time, arrangements were made with builders in England to furnish them. On the opening of the line ... ten of these were placed on the route. Although these have been constructed after the most approved model, and are similar to those used by existing companies, they are, however found to be somewhat heavier than had been anticipated. Still, they carry more passengers than lighter cars would have done. Meanwhile, cars of lighter construction are being built for the steeper gradients'.[150] In 1877 the Greenwich-built cars were described as 'proving more lasting'.[151]

Notice of the replacement cars was given in February 1872 'A trial was made yesterday of one of the new cars which have been constructed for the Edinburgh and Leith portion of the line ... lighter in actual weight by about 9 or 10 cwt. than the old car, the new vehicle also posess the advantage of greater ease in taking the curves and points, and presents a rather smarter appearance. The new car is seated for 14 persons inside and 16 outside, or six passengers less than in its predecessor. The run ... was made with two horses, but the car was comparatively little weighted, and it does not appear possible that two horses will be sufficient for the long incline from Leith to the Register House. The old cars will be used solely for the level route as soon as the new ones are ready to be put on the tramway, which it is expected will be in about a week's time.'[152] It is considered that four cars were obtained from four builders – Croall, and Drew & Burnett both of Edinburgh, Richard J Boyall of the Brownlow Carriage Works Grantham, and one other, possibly the Glasgow plant of the Tramway Car & Works Company (which operated 1872–5 only). Croall's locally built car attracted considerable interest 'it has a combination of improvements on those running at present. It weighs only 33 cwt., 14 cwt. less than the old cars. The body is mounted on steel springs in place of gutta-percha balls. The step, in place of the stirrup step adopted in the old cars, in addition to being somewhat lower, projects more prominently from the body, and being closed in at the back avoids any danger of the foot going through in a hasty attempt to get on. A seat is provided for the driver, ingeniously and simply contrived so that it can be unshipped and transferred to the other end easily. Access to the top is easier, and in the upper part of the protecting rail the slender iron rail is replaced by a stout wooden baton. There are crimson curtains in the windows, and the appearance is gayer than the others'.[153]

Dr Wood patented (211 of January 1872) a rail and snow cleaning machine. Drawn by a single horse, tines engaged in the rail grooves to remove stones, the resultant debris brushed away by rotating brushes; for use in snow, a plough was fixed ahead of the rail tines. At least one of these machines was built by James Bogie of 25 Thistle Street.[154] Winters then were snowier than in recent years, and clearance of streets – particularly when related to the large number of horses with their consequent by-product – in bad weather became a very necessary task. Men worked as crossing sweepers at fixed locations to keep crossings clear – particularly important when most women's clothing was ankle-length.

Wood's fertile mind was also exercised in trying to find a light alternative to the conventional tram. It was soon reported 'A new patent Rotunda car was tried yesterday on the Edinburgh and Leith tramways with the most satisfactory results. This is the invention of Dr Alexander Wood, has a highly ornate appearance, and yesterday created some interest and attention in the thoroughfares along which it traversed. As its name implies, the body of the vehicle is of a rounded shape. The form adopted, which is egg-shaped, admits of seating thirty persons in less space than the present cars. The trial car was weighed yesterday, and found to be 35 cwts, while the ordinary cars are 45 cwts; and it was

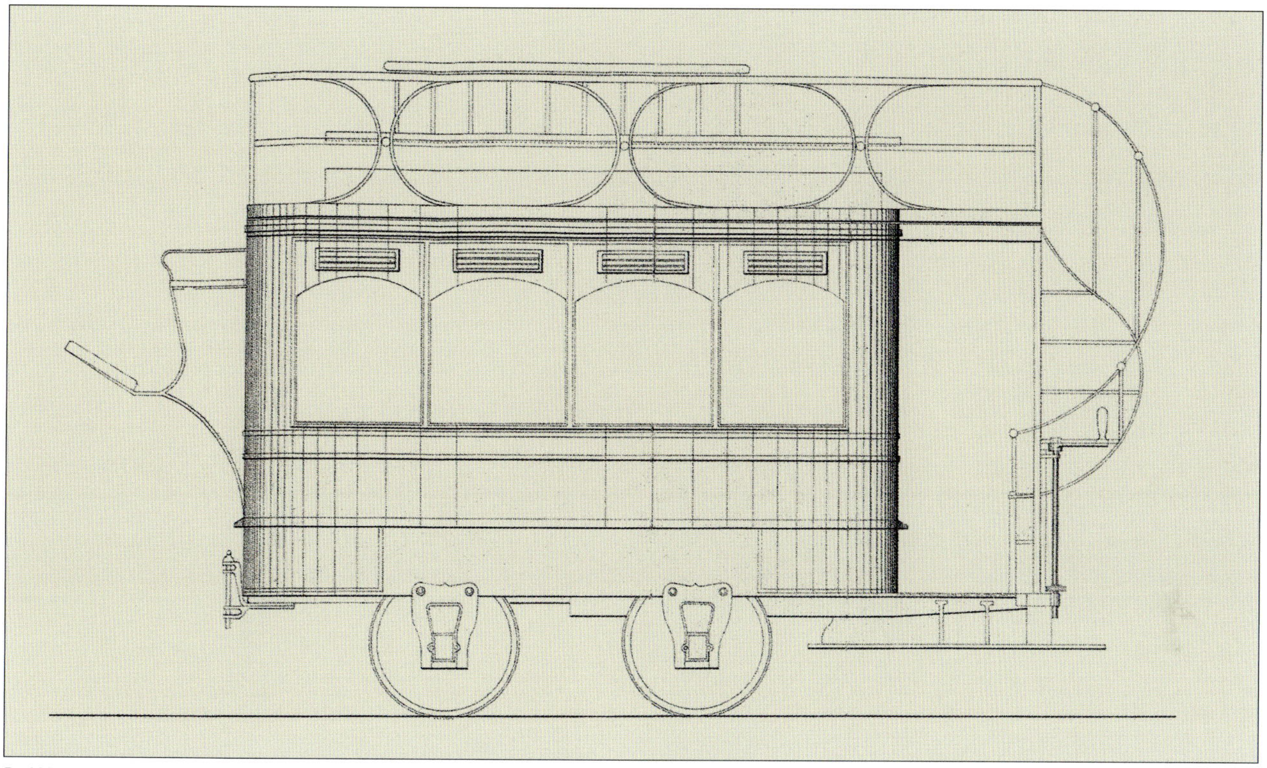

Dr Wood's patented 'Rotunda' design car, of which at least one specimen was actually built. This image shows an odd vehicle, with a saloon shaped in plan like a rugby ball.

Again we find the minimally sprung suspension and spiral stair access. The driver has a perch similar to his seat on contemporary horse buses.

easily drawn, even up the Leith Street and St Andrew Street gradients, by two horses. We believe that in future the Edinburgh Tramway Company will adopt the Rotunda car for their lines'.[155] Probably built by Croall, the 'egg-car' to Wood's patent (213 of January 1872), there is no evidence of any further cars to this unusual design being built. The patent described it as being constructed to accommodate more passengers and to bring the horses nearer to their work. 'The advantages of constructing the body of the car in the form of an oval or ellipse instead of with parallel sides, the greatest width being that at the centre, seats can be placed in the middle of the passage to accommodate 2, 4, or more other passengers, allowing a similar number to be taken off the length, not only diminishing weight, but also draught. Rounding of the ends of the cars enables the platforms to be made wider giving greater facilities for entering or leaving, while this form is well adapted for overcoming the resistance to the motion by the surrounding atmosphere. Constructed on two pairs of wheels, entrance and platform at the rear, driver's seat and coupling at the front'. The saloon had four windows and the driver's seat was at a high level, as on contemporary buses. Seats were carried entirely around the interior of the car except at the entrance and there was a ladder on the rear platform for access to the roof seats, plus a guard rail round the top of the car 'in the usual manner'. Alternative drawings with the patent showed a double ended version, with a 'drawbar below the body from one end to the other allowing horses to be attached avoiding the necessity of turning the car as in the first drawing'.[156] The contemporary report suggests that the single ended version was built. However, this would have led to problems at the existing terminals, where there were no facilities for reversal. Nor is any subsequent history of it recorded; no photographic evidence has been found nor any later mention. It is not even clear whether it was accepted

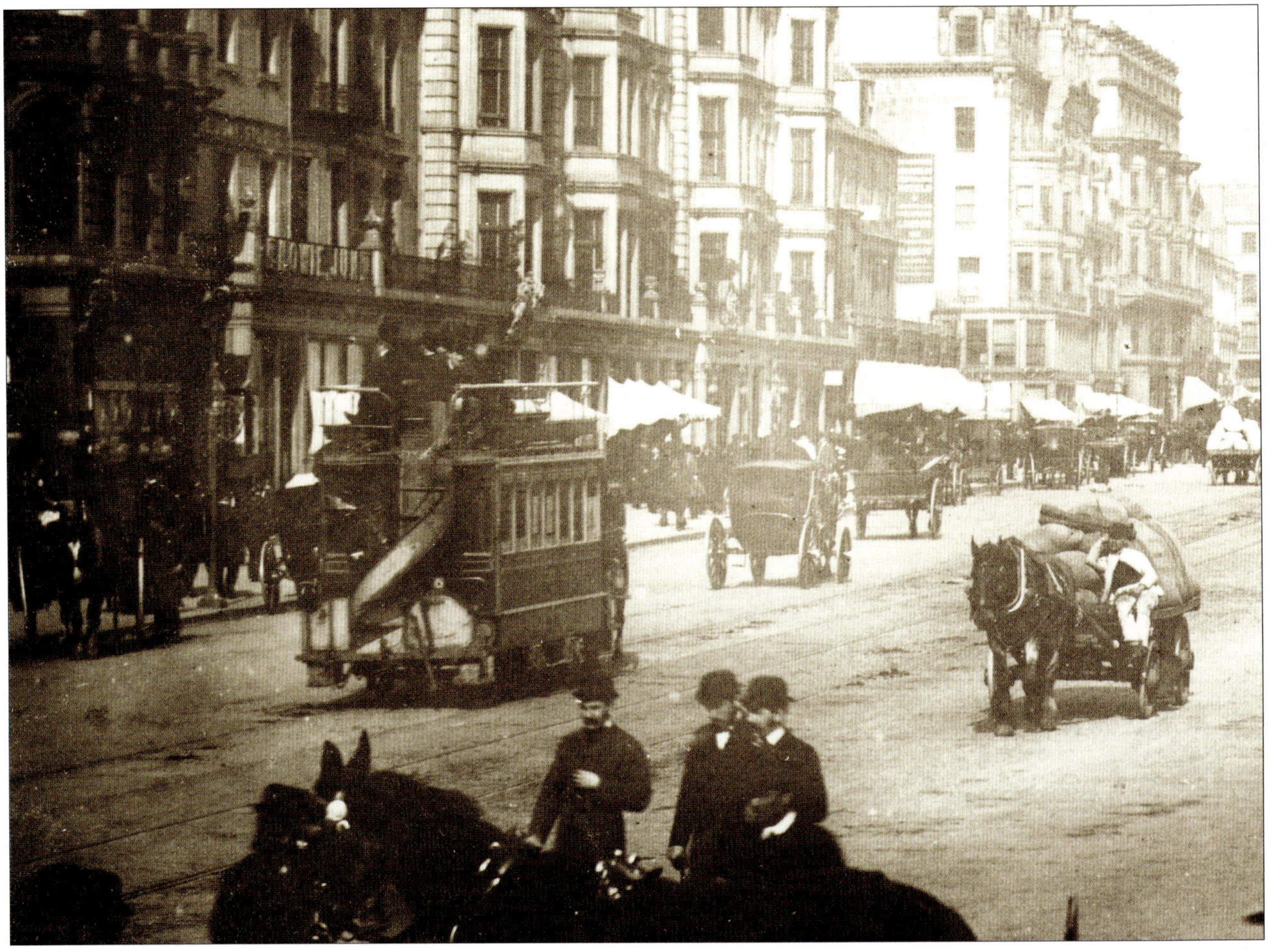

View along Princes Street in the late 1870s with one of the early cars, now fitted with an improved stair for top deck access. So far as is known, this style was unique to Edinburgh, and represented a considerable improvement on the open spiral design.

by the Company; perhaps Dr Wood retained it as his individual property. This leads to the speculation that he could have kept it as his private tram, used for professional calls around the city! In the 1890s two small cars existed (number 60 with 29 seats, and 66 with 30 seats). Could one or other of these be the little 'egg-car', still extant due to its limited use? It appears unlikely that this mystery can be solved unless new sources are found. Both numbers were used for replacement cars in April 1895.

The new routes on the south side of the city had 'timetable numbers' issued on 28 May 1872 for cars 17 – 20 running Post Office to Newington (Hamilton Place), with operation commencing the following day. On 14 June this altered to Post Office to Newington (Mayfield Loan) for cars 17 & 18; and Post Office to Grange Cemetery for 19 & 20,[157] this change not implemented until 6 July.[158] This may add credibility to the logic for 1 to 16 being the heavy TCWCo cars. Four new cars were added to the complement by the end of October; 'Messrs Drew and Burnett, Coach-builders, Fountainbridge, have recently completed some new tramway cars that are specially worthy of notice. They are the lightest yet constructed for the Company. Two of the cars weigh 37 cwt. each, being between 8 and 10 cwt. lighter than the cars purchased from the Greenwich firm, when the tramways were started in November last, constructed to hold 18 in and

20 out. The other two cars are made expressly for the Morningside route. This being circular, the necessity of changing the horses from one end to the other is avoided and accordingly the new cars are constructed on the omnibus plan. There is only one entrance, that of course being in the rear. The weight of these two cars is only 32 ½ cwt, the lightest which have as yet been constructed. The building of tramway cars has also now been commenced by a company specially formed in Glasgow'.[159] A reference was shortly made to wheel-guards for cars 23 and 24 built by Mr Drew of Drew & Burnett.[160] These four cars could *possibly* have had numbers 21 – 24.

There are a few references – most relative to lost property – to cars in these earliest days detailing them by number. However, as the magistrates in their wisdom approved timetables by individual car numbers (as they had done with horse buses) this soon caused working difficulties. At a very early date individual numbering of cars ceased (if ever actually used) replaced by the 'timetable number'. This related to the duties the car was timed to undertake, and was not painted on the car but was carried on a removable plate in a holder on the rocker panel. It was thus possible to switch the 'timetable number' between different vehicles to allow operational flexibility; this does not help to unravel details of these earliest trams!

Edinburgh's magistrates maintained a licence book, and while one of these large volumes still exists, with a single page for each vehicle (but giving only the date of issue of the licence and the seating capacity of the car), this starts at 1 August 1894.[161] There was obviously a previous volume (or two) which, if still extant, could throw much light on early matters. Nevertheless, with the information from this one remaining volume plus the detail from the Thomson notebook, much can be deduced regarding Edinburgh's remarkably convoluted horse tram fleet. Without these contemporary sources, the mysteries of Edinburgh's horse cars would be even more difficult to unravel.

The half-yearly accounts to 30 June 1873 show £33.12s paid for tramcar licences – conveniently equating to 32 cars at 1 guinea each.[162] Licences issued

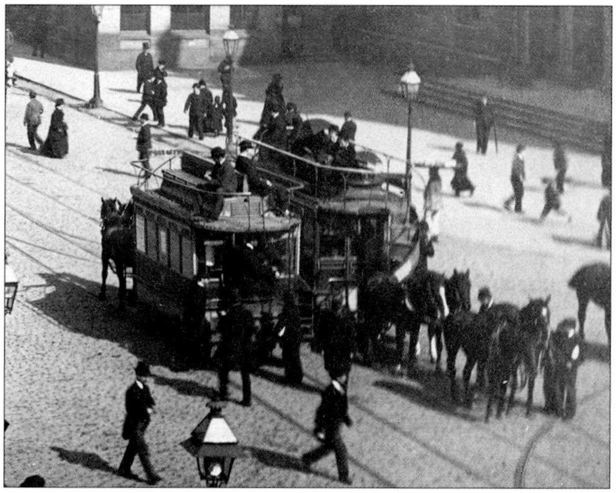

View from the Crown Hotel in West Register Street showing two early designs of car. On the left is one of the 5 window cut-down heavy cars, the other exhibiting the 'Liverpool' style waist and the improved stair design. Also noticeable are the two trace horses which have assisted the car up Leith Walk and Leith Street.

in January 1874 were for cars 25, 26, 27 and 28 on the Morningside Circular, plus 29, 30 and 31 running Coltbridge to Powburn, but by mid-August, licences on the Circle route were for, 'Inner' 21, 23, 25, 27 and 29; 'Outer', 22, 24, 26, 28 and 30. By 30 June 1874, rolling-stock totalled 43 vehicles, of which five were buses. Tramcars would thus number thirty-eight, of which thirty-four were required for timetabled operations. When the Portobello line opened in May 1875, licences were 33 – 35, with 36 added in October. Licences 38 and 39 were issued in July 1875 for a new route from the West End to Stanley Road. By May 1877, the Portobello route were licences 33 – 35 and 37 – 39.[163] The builders of these cars have not been identified, but could have been Boyall of Grantham.

The difficulty of tying timetable operation to specific vehicle numbers is readily apparent; the Company solution to this, by using a removable 'timetable-number' for each car, was possibly the only practical way to deal with these constraints. The never-ending attempts to ease the work of the horses resulted in an experiment being made in early 1873 using wheels of 3 ft 6 ins diameter. Although the benefit was said to be appreciable, most cars retained the original

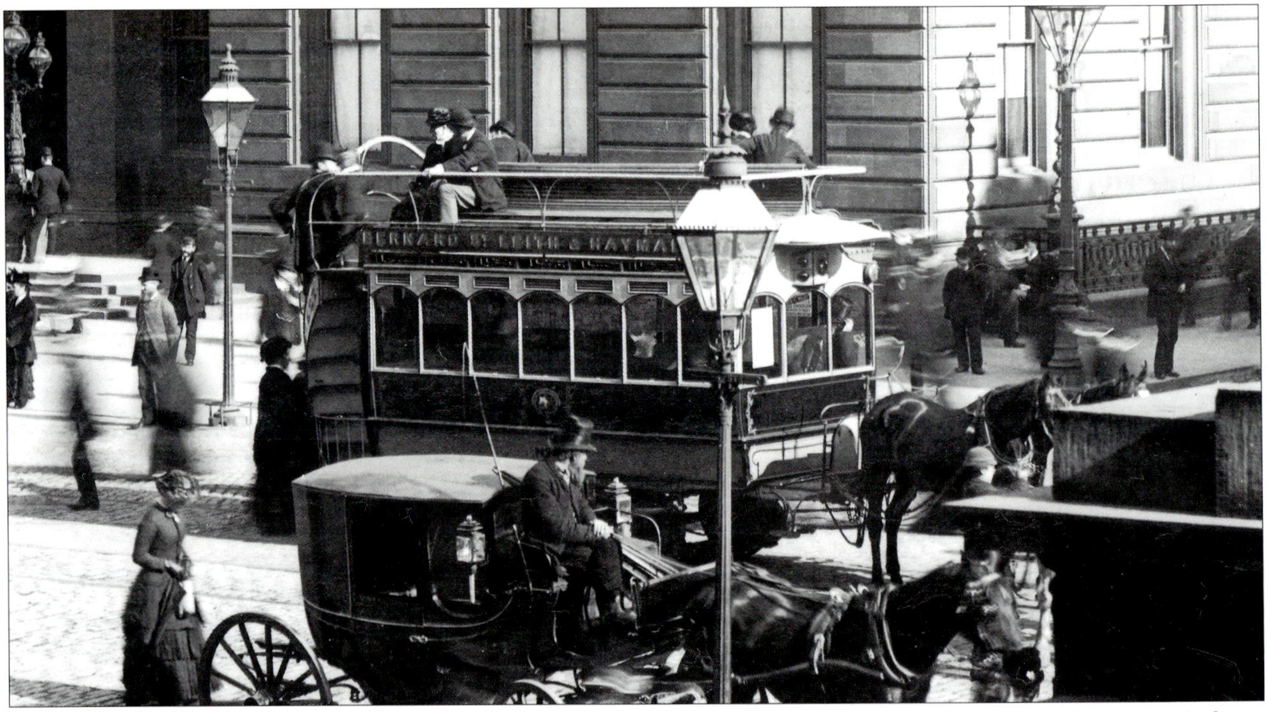

Reversible single-ended car built under licence at Shrubhill to Eades' patent. It has to be higher off the ground than normal to allow the body to rotate above the wheels. The cabbie in the foreground is showing a high degree of interest in the car, perhaps this indicates that he has not seen anything of this nature before. Edinburgh's reversible cars were first seen in April 1882. (G W Wilson collection, Aberdeen University Library)

wheels. Also tried at the same time was a wire safety grill around the wheels, both in front and at the sides.[164] Accidents where pedestrians fell under tram wheels resulted in court decisions against the Company, the financial penalties of which reflected directly on profitability. It is not surprising that another wheel-guard was tried invented by Henry Shiels, then rolling stock superintendent. A leather-covered board hung in front of the wheels was forced back when encountering an obstruction and pressed rubber blocks against the wheels to stop the car. By means of a foot lever the driver could also apply these as an emergency brake; the device was not generally adopted.

In January 1874 the weight of the Edinburgh cars became a *cause célèbre*, the matter raised as a major issue in the *Scotsman*, with weights defined; the New Car for 32 passengers [16/16] 30 cwt., Small Car 30 passengers [16/14] 35 cwt., Medium Car 40 passengers [20/20] 42 cwt., Large Car 38 passengers [20/18] 45½ cwt. By this early date there was already a variety of designs, as the directors struggled to find the lightest practical vehicle. The SSPCA demanded to be told why the heavy cars were still used on the Leith route while lighter cars were running to Morningside and Newington.[165] For his fifth shareholders' report Dr Wood had to advise that, '... by having lighter cars and additional horses, provision had been made for overcoming these difficulties. Experience has proved that even the lighter cars are too heavy, and a new set has been provided ...'[166] and to the subsequent meeting '... the cars have been twice lightened'.[167] But a month later the Lord Provost felt able to pacify Baroness Burdett Coutts '... with one or two exceptions, all the heavy cars had been withdrawn and lighter ones substituted, and that the heavy ones remaining were employed only on level ground ...'[168] The accuracy of this is debatable.

A committee of the Royal Scottish Society of Arts reported, comparing weights of the Edinburgh trams and buses, suggesting that the Magistrates should not merely license the vehicles, but should also determine

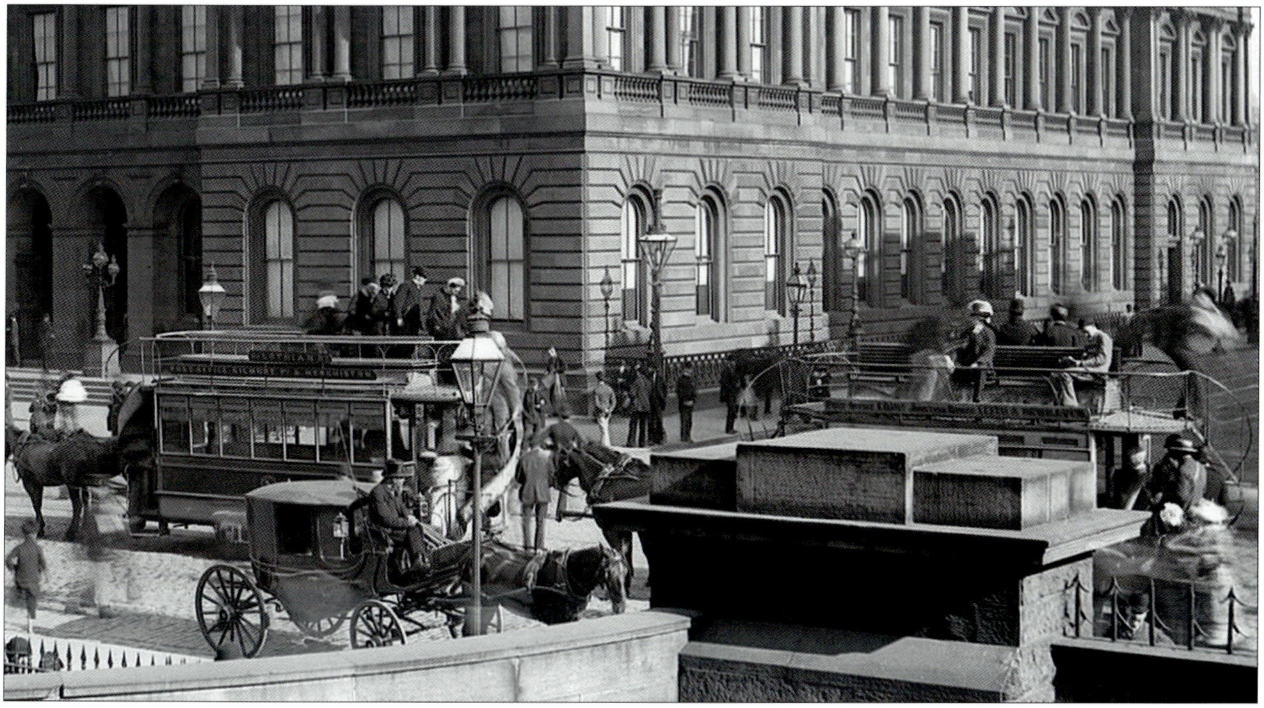

The same vantage point probably on the same day – with the same cabbie still waiting for custom. On the left, a seven window car with the 'Liverpool' style of bodywork, followed by a five window car (possibly one of the shortened heavy cars). The leading car has the revised stair design, protruding through the dash, much more substantial than the earlier variety. (G W Wilson Collection, Aberdeen University Library)

the number of horses required for each. Comparative figures quoted were:

	Weight (cwt)	*Passengers*	*Wt/ Passenger (cwt)*
Omnibuses:			
Large	36	36	1.00
Small	28	28	1.00
New	30	32	0.938
Tramcars:			
Large	45.5	38	1.2
Medium	42	40	1.05
Small	35	30	1.16[169]
[New	30	32	0.9375][170]

The magistrates in their wisdom had decreed the permitted seating capacity be calculated on a length of 18 inch per passenger inside each vehicle, but at 16 inches per passenger for the outside seats.[171] Perhaps this was to reflect the differing styles of clothing adopted by each gender, it being understood that ladies would not use the outside seats. However, it meant that cars which had been effectively built for 18 inside and 18 outside, were now permitted two more outside passengers. Thus the 'Large' cars referred to above were those original heavy Greenwich-built which had initiated the problem, the 'Small' cars those which had been lightened by chopping off the length of two inside seats per side (thus outside also) 20/18 hence becoming 16/14. The original seven window saloons were reduced to five windows length.

Pressure was maintained on the company to provide some form of 'life-guard' on the cars. After a fatal accident, Dr Wood wrote to the Lord Provost and explained measures adopted; '... The directors, previous to commencing running the cars at all, and at various times subsequent thereto, have seriously considered whether the wheels should not be guarded in some

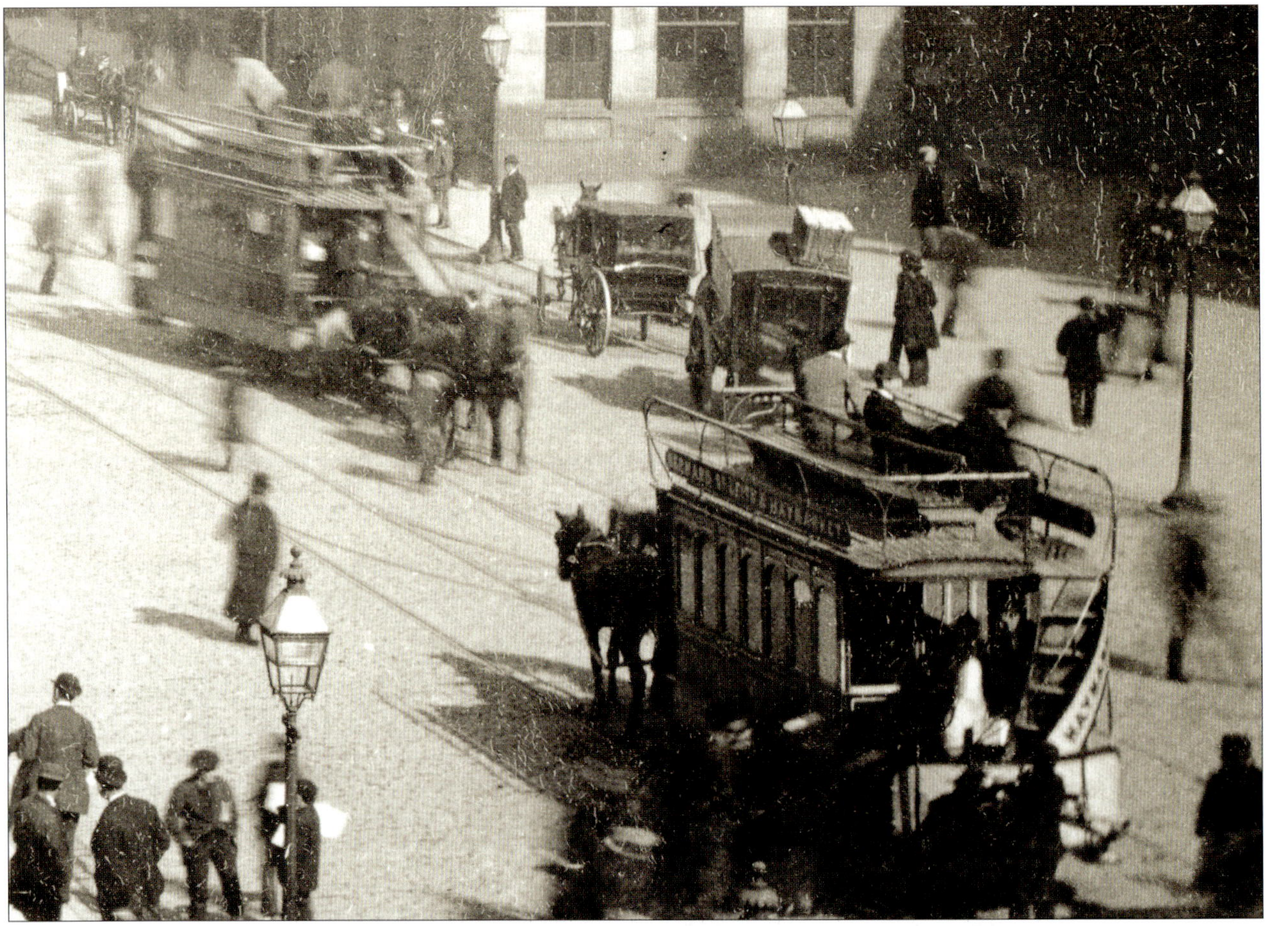

Another scene from the Crown Hotel, probably in the early eighties. The car on the right of the 'Liverpool' saloon design has been rebuilt with stairs which closely resemble those patented by Stephenson of New York, which were probably first seen on the cars imported in 1877. The other car appears to be one of those shortened, again with an improved stair.

efficient manner so as to prevent accidents'. ... Then quoting from a report prepared by John Macrae ... 'A wire railing is used in Glasgow and elsewhere, but neither here nor in Glasgow does evidence of its effects justify its use. The first shields were tried in 1872, and consisted of a piece of strong sheet iron attached to the brake bar placed in front of the wheels of the car ... in practice they only increased the danger and were discontinued. Colonel Davidson's suggestion was next tried ... the result was such that we came to the conclusion that it could not be wrought practically without the risk of increasing rather than diminishing the danger to those unfortunately falling in front of a car. ... The manager designed a padded bar ... which we found unworkable. Mr Irvine substituted a retarder which we had tested on one of our cars; it was found to work so clumsily that it also was discontinued. The brake invented by Mr Gillespie of Torbanehill was objectionable for its weight and clumsiness ... the result of my experience, and of experiments, is that no guard has yet been suggested that is likely to be of any service whatever in preventing accidents'.[172]

In the half-year to 31 December 1874, it was noted that nine cars had been 'made equal to new' with all others maintained in efficient order. These nine would be original 'heavy' cars shortened and made more usable. At this time, a tram – presumably one of the original unloved heavy batch – was loaned to William

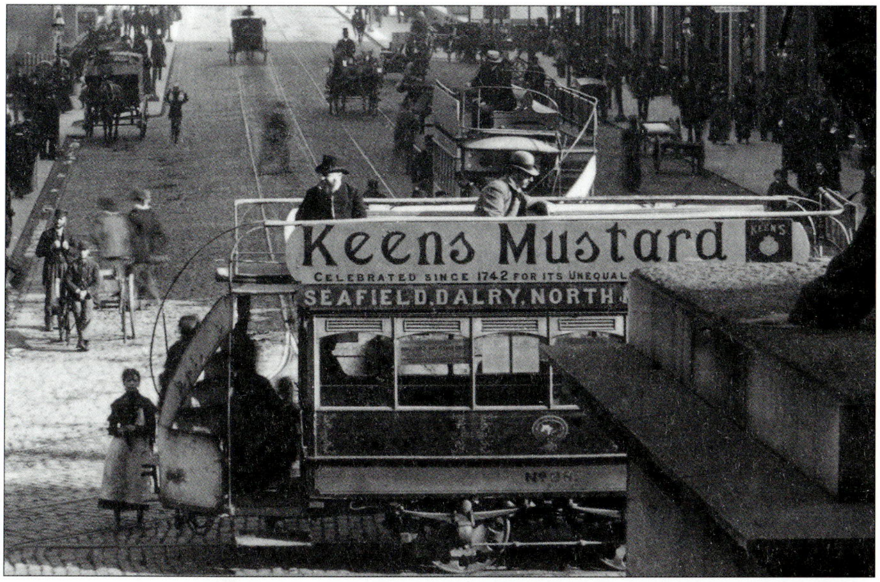

Left. A finely detailed view from Register House, but, as appears frequently, with the tram partly obscured. This has No 38 painted on the rocker panel, in the position occupied by the licence number plate. It seems therefore that this scene dates from when the plates were replaced by numbers on each individual vehicle. This car has leaf springs, not a common feature of horse trams.

Below. At Clifton Terrace (Haymarket) rests a car similar to No 38. The body has a seven arched-top window saloon in place of the six of the car seen above.

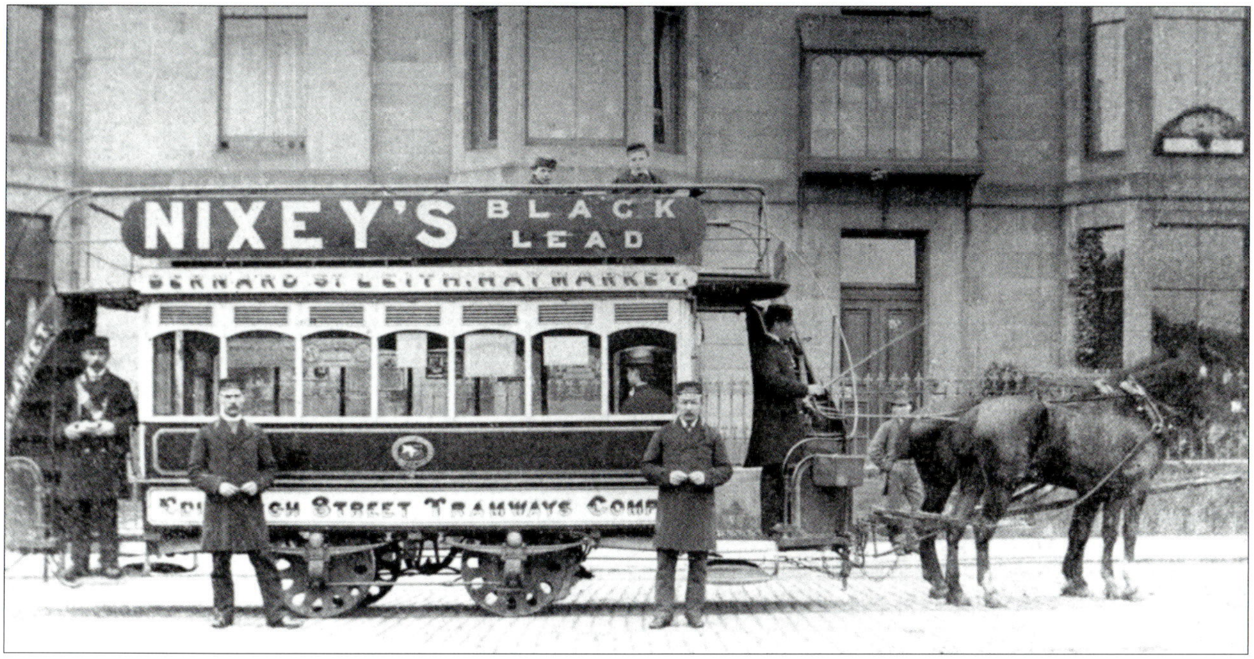

Dundas Scott-Moncrieff for his experiments using compressed air for propulsion. James Howden of Hyde Park Works in Glasgow constructed a self-contained under-frame with air receivers and driving cylinders. This was taken to Elder's shipyard in Govan where it was charged up with air under pressure, to prove that theory also worked in practice. The Edinburgh body was then put on this chassis, and the assemblage operated in Govan, with paying passengers, for two weeks in January 1876. It could be that the directors of the Edinburgh company thought this might answer their horsing problems. They were, even at this early time, anxious to examine every alternative with Dr Wood later saying that all options (compressed air, steam, and even clockwork) had been considered.

Mechanical traction for tramways was discussed at

From the Thomson book, this drawing appears to represent what first constituted a 'canopy car'. That was an 35 seat open toastrack with a light canopy cover, either of canvas or light timber. This is said to date from c1882, and by the time of writing had been broken up. This was probably one of the original open cars, with cover added.

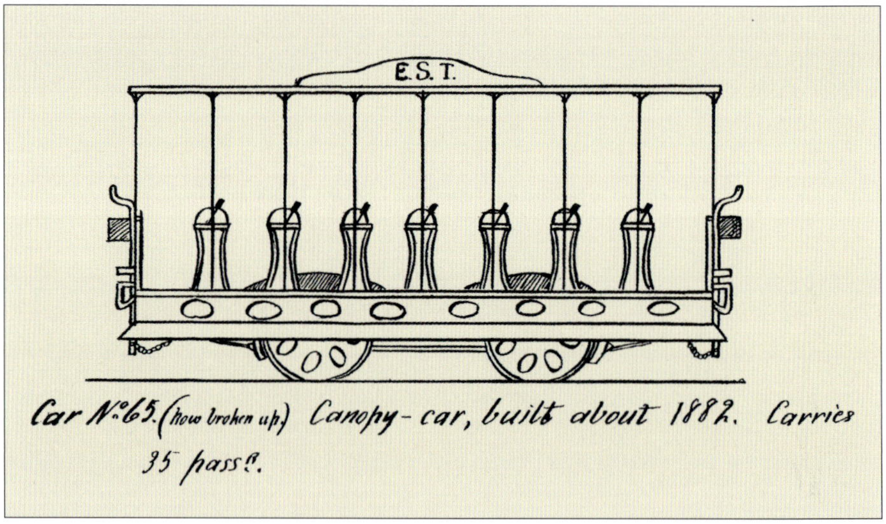

a meeting of the Edinburgh and Leith Engineering Society in October 1873, when a compressed air system patented by W S Taylor C E was debated. Plant and rolling stock for the Edinburgh lines could be got for £25,000.[173] Although noted by the directors, it was but the first of many schemes (some more practical than others) which were investigated over the ensuing years in an endeavour to placate the 'anti-cruelty' voices, and also to reduce the large costs of horse traction. Figures for other operators show just how excessive the Edinburgh horsing costs were. The first comparable statistics show, in Edinburgh, operating costs per mile of 13.82 pence; for the London Tramways Company the equivalent was 11.77 pence, and for Sheffield 10.14 pence.

By the end of 1874 34 cars were recorded in daily use.[174] Spare vehicles brought the total to 38. Of cars obtained over the next few years (bringing the total to 42 two years later)[175] details are sparse, but no single manufacturer has been identified. The chairman in mid-1876 said 'It was found quite impossible to run cars the same size as other towns (42 seat) and they had, even after reducing the size of their cars, been compelled to use four horses in place of two ...'[176]

Such was the immediate summer popularity of the Portobello route that in May 1876 the first open single deck car was put in service. It was reported to have 20 rows of seats for six passengers, but this seems highly improbable.[177] Illustrations show more plausibly seven rows of seats and since these cars were (latterly at least) licensed to carry 35, each bench would accommodate five passengers. Despite their light weight, two horses were always used. By 1883 there were ten of these, some with a light canvas roof. While the first (four?) examples were bought in, later such cars were built at Shrubhill. They appear to have had numbers at the end of the 'normal' series, being renumbered as required to maintain this situation. Thus there was an 'old' open car numbered 65, scrapped or re-numbered when 'new' 65 was licensed. The last six open cars in the late 1890s were 85 – 89, and 100.

A crisis in the rolling stock department developed by mid 1877, with the chairman advising '... when they commenced they purchased cars from a Greenwich factory and afterwards from local makers, but the cars purchased in Edinburgh and elsewhere in Scotland were not worth the money ...'[178] His next report returned to the subject '... In the past year the Company have put on seven new cars by three different builders; two from Starbuck, two from New York and two from Richard Boyall of Grantham (from whom they got some of the best of the original cars) for the Leith to Newington route, then another car from the same maker today for the Leith to Haymarket route. Three additional cars are in course of construction'.[179] The builder of these has not been determined,

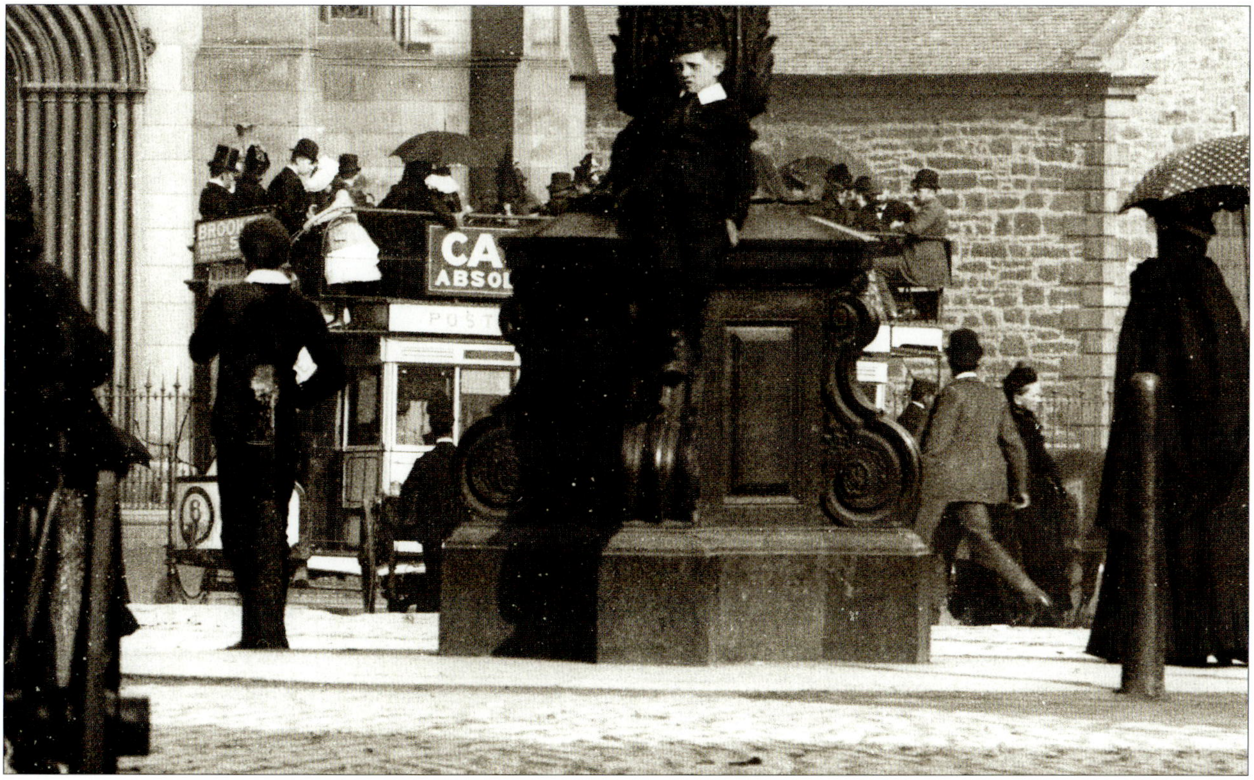

This is the only known identifiable view of one of the two trams built by Stephenson of New York and imported in May 1877. This scene shows car 6 (the other was 12) at the West End – obscured by the elaborate lamp which then graced the junction. Enough is seen to deduce that the saloon has eight flat-topped windows. Both cars were altered from knifeboard upper seating to garden seats; at one time these cars ran as single-ended.

but they could also have come from Boyall.

The New York cars were built by the prolific and long established undertaking of John Stephenson, who said that by use of home-grown timber they could undercut the cost of British-built cars. Intended for the Portobello route, they entered service in May 1877,[180] but were found too heavy(!)[181] and were moved to the Morningside Circle. Seating was for 44 passengers, presumably 22/22, and they had an improved staircase, '… more substantial and easy to mount than those of the smaller cars, resembling the plan of the Glasgow ones.' Platforms were larger, adding (it was later said) to traction difficulties,[182] the top deck seating division rail 'more comfortable' plus 'full provision for ventilation'. This latter feature called for comment 'The opening of the windows and the Venetian blinds show that [the cars] are intended for a warmer climate'. These two Stephenson cars must have been well constructed, as both lasted to the end of regular horse tram operation in Edinburgh. The Thomson book has them as Morningside Circle numbers 6 and 12; 'Altered several times. At one time stair at back end only, but now [both] have stair at each end; long seat on top substituted by cross seats'. They were large cars, with eight saloon windows, and while Thomson has them with 56 seats, they were latterly licensed for 30/22. A 'turnstile' passenger check was tried in 1877, possibly on one of these cars.[183]

The two cars from Starbuck were also described in detail; 'This week, two new cars built by the Starbuck Car Company of Birkenhead were placed on the Haymarket to Leith route. They seat 16 inside and 22 outside, the inside seats are of perforated American wood; the roofs are of alternate strips of alternate light and dark coloured wood. The roof is approached from the centre of a spacious outside platform by a staircase

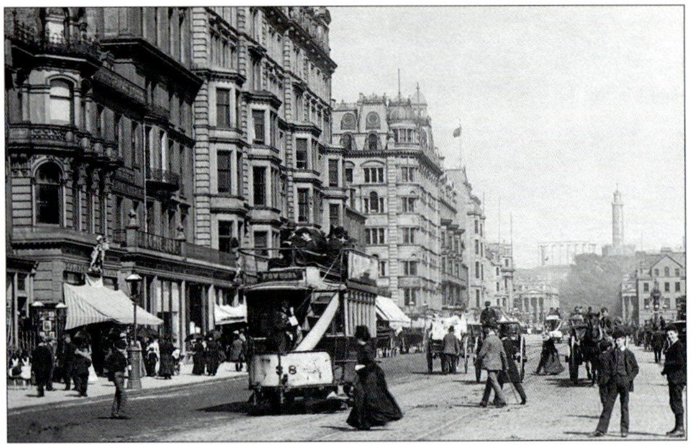

This 1880s Princes Street view, but with a different car numbered 38. This one has a seven window saloon (flat topped), that earlier of this number, had a six window saloon with arched tops to the windows. This car is also on a differing route, indicating how having numbers allocated to specific routes was restrictive.

(not a ladder) so that ladies can easily use it. The lamps are entirely outside, throwing light by a reflector through plate glass into the interior, hence there is no smell. The inside has a neat false floor of thin spars separated by vulcanite buttons, which can be rolled up for sweeping the floor. The bells are protected from the rough usage of passengers. The cars run very easily when their size is taken account of. They are very superior in finish and comfort, although less glaring colours might have been selected'.[184]

To complete the clutch of cars obtained at this time, a number were got from R J Boyall '... two new cars on the Newington to Leith route are from the well known workshop of Mr R J Boyall of Grantham, from whom the Company received some of the best of the original cars. They are good substantial cars on which not 1d has been wasted. A new car from the same maker was today placed on the Leith to Haymarket route ... In all these new cars the old-fashioned stuffed squabs are discarded and the seats are polished. Three additional cars are in course of construction'.[185] The supplier of these is not named, but the wording implies Boyall, making his total order six. These cars increased the stock from 42 to 52.

Dundee's new tramway line was complete by the beginning of August 1877, but with one minor problem; their new cars were not to hand and the company in Birmingham with the order advised a delivery date in October. To provide a vehicle for the Board of Trade's inspection, an Edinburgh car was borrowed which arrived in Dundee, complete with an experienced driver and two horses on 6 August. It was used two days later for the successful inspection.[186] As, no doubt, this would be one of Edinburgh's newest vehicles, it was returned promptly, so when the Dundee company hired two Edinburgh cars for public operation use these were probably of the original heavy type. They arrived in Dundee on 27 August and were shortly joined by three more, hired from Glasgow. Dundee's tramway opened on 30 August, the two Edinburgh cars remaining there for several months.[187]

In his January statement 1878 Dr Wood advised that car numbers had been increased to alleviate complaints of overcrowding. '... It had been found necessary to make extensive changes in the car repairing department, which entails greater expense at the outset, but will be economical in the end. The cars are being put in a state of thorough repair, and in addition to those required for the new route, three cars have been added to stock in place of the same number of old ones which have been put aside as worn out.' Four new cars had been placed on the new route from Junction Bridge to Tollcross.[188] At the following meeting he added '... the Directors decided to have the whole of the cars thoroughly overhauled and such as are capable of repair being repaired. Mr Clark, formerly with one of the largest vehicle body building establishments has been engaged as foreman of the car repair department, which has been greatly expanded and separated from the engineering department'. Extra ground was feued behind Shrubhill, where large stables and car workshops were built.[189] Clark does not appear to have stayed long.

The first annual statistical return (June 1878) of the Board of Trade credited 52 cars to the Company, but the following year this reduced to 49 (possibly reflecting two cars on loan to Dundee and one to Scott Moncrieff, still languishing somewhere on his compressed-air operated underframe). These statistics are sometimes suspect, reflecting on information provided by each company, who probably regarded the matter as a needless chore. It is known that the Glasgow tramway company owned more cars than they officially acknowledged; they only licensed those required to operate and avoided paying for cars under repair. Edinburgh probably acted similarly; for special events 'old cars' were dusted off to meet operational needs.

From March 1879 the car building superintendent was Harry Booth, a skilled coach-wright whose experience had been gained in England, possibly with Boyall. With his knowledge and the benefit gained from cars recently purchased from the industry's best-known builders he decided they could build just as good a car themselves. This, the first of a family of Shrubhill-built tramcars which continued until 1950, was completed by the end of May 1879. 'Yesterday afternoon a new tramway car, the first entirely built by the workshops at Shrubhill, was turned out for a trial trip, at which several directors of the Company and members of the Town Council were present. Drawn by four handsome grey horses with new harness it stood at Waterloo Place and attracted much attention. It then proceeded round the Circular route and was reversed in Clinton Road to see how it would take the curves and gradients of Whitehouse Loan … it will be put out today for regular traffic. Several improvements have been made and it is the intention to have others constructed with further improvements. The car is lighter than those at present in use and if found suitable the Company will construct further cars at their own works'.[190]

Considerable coverage was given to the next new tram. 'The Company have, it seems, discovered that they can themselves build, at a saving in price, cars which are in every respect suitable for the service. At their depot they have already completed two such vehicles, the first of the same design as those ordinarily employed, and the second, with which a trial trip was made yesterday, embodying a number of improvements expected to render it at once more commodious, and better adapted to the exigencies of locomotion. Intended for use only on the circular route, the new car is provided with but one entrance, this being at the back, the front is designed in semi-octagonal shape, the space which would otherwise have been occupied with a door and stair being turned to account as extra accommodation for passengers, of whom the car can seat 50 – 24 inside and 26 on the roof. The inside seats are 38 inches apart, thus offering a passenger 6 inches wider than hitherto – an arrangement which must conduce to the comfort of passengers both while seated and in entering and leaving the car. Though of the same length and weight as the two American cars which have been used on the Edinburgh system for some time, the new vehicle is said to be lighter in draught. The contrivance by which this advantage is secured consists of a rod, extending from the coupling gear to the centre of the car underneath, where it is connected with a strong steel and india-rubber spring, so that when the car is started the spring relieves the strain upon the horses, and prevents jolting'.[191] Other press reports give further details 'Improvements have been made in the interior ventilation and safer stairs … the car has a light and cheerful, appearance ..'[192] From this time the company built (and rebuilt) most of its cars in a well-equipped coach building shop behind the Shrubhill car shed.

On average, through the next two decades, the works produced about eight new cars annually, plus numerous rebuilds of older cars incorporating improved stairs, platforms and seating etc. For example, during the first half of 1880 four new cars were built to replace worn-out cars and three overhauled 'equal to new' while in the corresponding period of the next year three completely new cars were built plus two reconstructed. This is the first mention of cars replacing withdrawn vehicles, these at most nine years old, and probably refers to withdrawal of the remaining original 1871 cars. It was noted that use of larger cars had increased profitability.[193] About this time (c 1880/1) several six-window saloon cars were purchased from Brown, Marshalls of Birmingham. At least one of these (car 14) survived to have garden seats fitted in place of its knifeboard, and ran until mid-1900. In 1882 it was

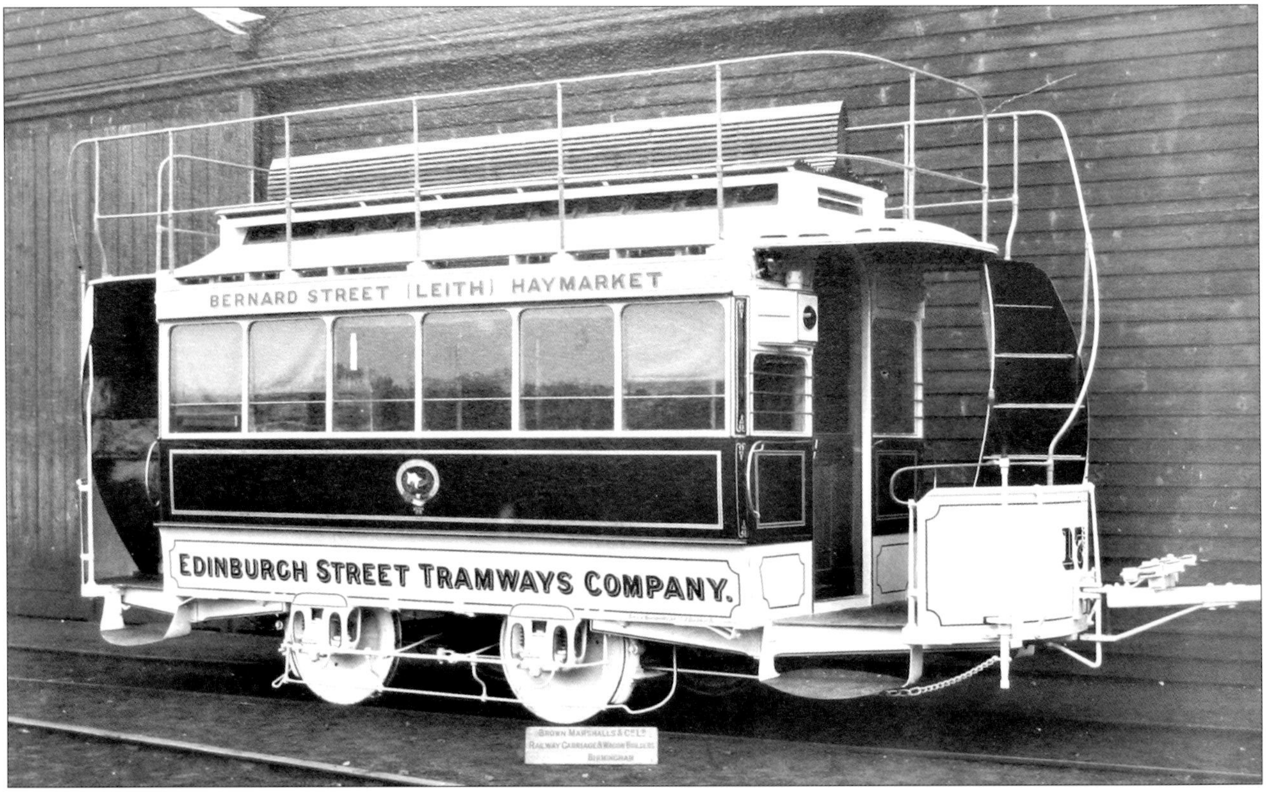
BERNARD STREET (LEITH) HAYMARKET
EDINBURGH STREET TRAMWAYS COMPANY.
BROWN MARSHALLS & Co Ltd
RAILWAY CARRIAGE & WAGON BUILDERS
BIRMINGHAM

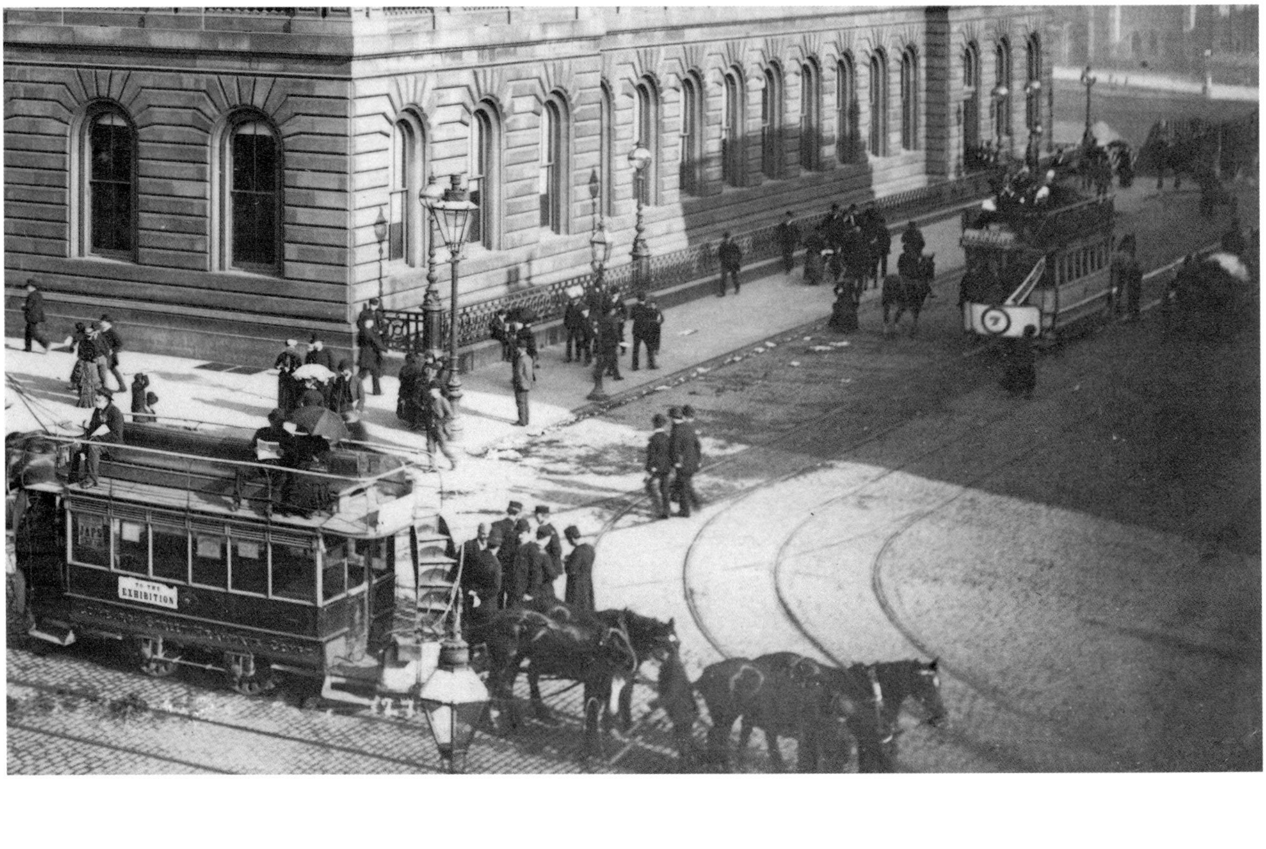
TO THE
EXHIBITION

announced that the company would henceforth built all their own cars.[194] Harry Booth at this time patented an improvement to the steel bar dropped to the roadway when a car stopped on an incline; this had a strong steel spring within a steel tube which was compressed when the car set back against it on a hill. When the car moved off, the spring assisted the horses. This earned Booth the Hepburn Medal of the Royal Scottish Society of Arts, but surprisingly was not universally adopted in the city.

By the start of 1882 the company acknowledged 60 cars and 15 buses, having by then built at least 15 new cars and rebuilt many others. Improvement and innovation continued, and in April a further variation appeared. This was to the patented 'Eades' principle, where a single-ended car body rotated on a pivot. 'There will be placed today, on the tramway between Haymarket and Leith, a new car, embodying what seem very desirable improvements. The body of the car is mounted on a bogey, made to travel upon a [horizontal] wheel, six feet in diameter, in such a way that it can be turned completely round. By this arrangement, the necessity for unshipping the pole and shifting the horses from one end to the other on reaching a terminus will be obviated, with corresponding diminution of the risk of accident from startling of the animals during such shifting. Instead of this it will only be necessary for the horses to pull the car round upon its pivot till their heads are in the right direction for the return journey. The driver will thus occupy continuously the same end of the vehicle, and, accordingly, a comparatively small platform, suitable for his accommodation, is provided. At the opposite end, where passengers will enter or leave, there is placed a platform at once lower and more spacious than that hitherto in use, and which is accessible not only from one side, but also from the back. The new car has been constructed at the company's works, under the superintendence of Mr Booth; and we understand that some half-dozen more on the same principle are forthwith to be built.[195] The car is built after the model of similar cars running in Manchester and weighs only 40 cwt. The platform can only be ascended from behind or from the left side of the door which opens on hinges like an omnibus door ... the stoplock is released by the driver pressing a spring-knob with his foot.[196] No record remains of how many of these reversible cars were built but there is no mention whatsoever of them in the Thomson note-book, commenced some twelve years subsequently.

Single deck 'Eades' reversible cars were apparently also constructed, seating 16. Six of this design were reported as being built at Shrubhill, the first two in service on 3 July 1882 between Commercial Street and Haymarket.[197] Surprisingly, not a single photograph with one of these has been found. This particular report adds that the Company also had in hand construction of 'several open cars, different from any in use, which will accommodate 32 passengers'. By the end of 1882 operating stock was 58 close and 9 open cars, some of the latter having light roofs.

Use of a removable number plate on the rocker panel, linked to the magistrates' timetable, ended by 1882, with each vehicle thereafter allocated a unique number. These reflected the 'timetable' numbers; ie 1 – 12 were for Morningside Circle and so on in route groups up to car 52. Cars numbered above this were additions, paid for from the capital account, rather than replacements. These took the numbers of cars they replaced and were charged to the revenue account. Spare (and old) cars took subsequent numbers, then came 'oddments' such as the open cars (popular in the summer on the Portobello route but also used for football specials and workers' cars at other times). Use of these in the winter for early morning workmen's cars caused complaint, and some old double deck cars were

Opposite top. Brown, Marshall & Co of Birmingham supplied a small number of cars of this design c1880, some of which survived to have the knifeboard seats replaced by garden seats ten years later. The six window saloons were recognisable by their curved top corners, a feature of these cars only.

Opposite bottom. Dated to July 1886, again from a vantage point on Register House, the scene includes two trams. On the left, an elderly vehicle, perhaps one of those brought out of store for the increased Exhibition traffic. On the right, car 7 of the Morningside Circular route.

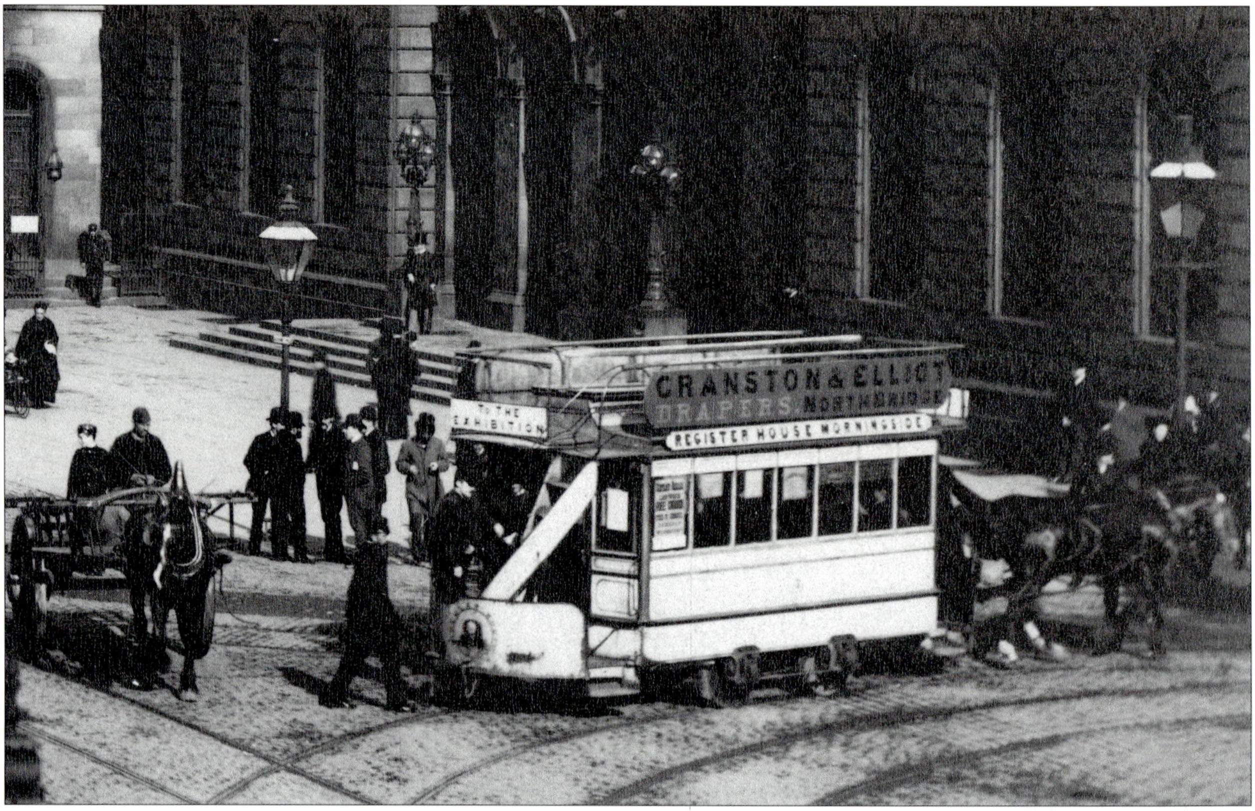

Above. Car 9 of the Circular Route at the GPO in the summer of 1886, indicated by its destination board 'To the Exhibition'. It is of one of the 1870s cars with the so-called 'Liverpool' saloon of seven windows, but does have signs of reconstruction, in particular that its original spiral stairs have been replaced by the substantial 'Stephenson Patent' style.

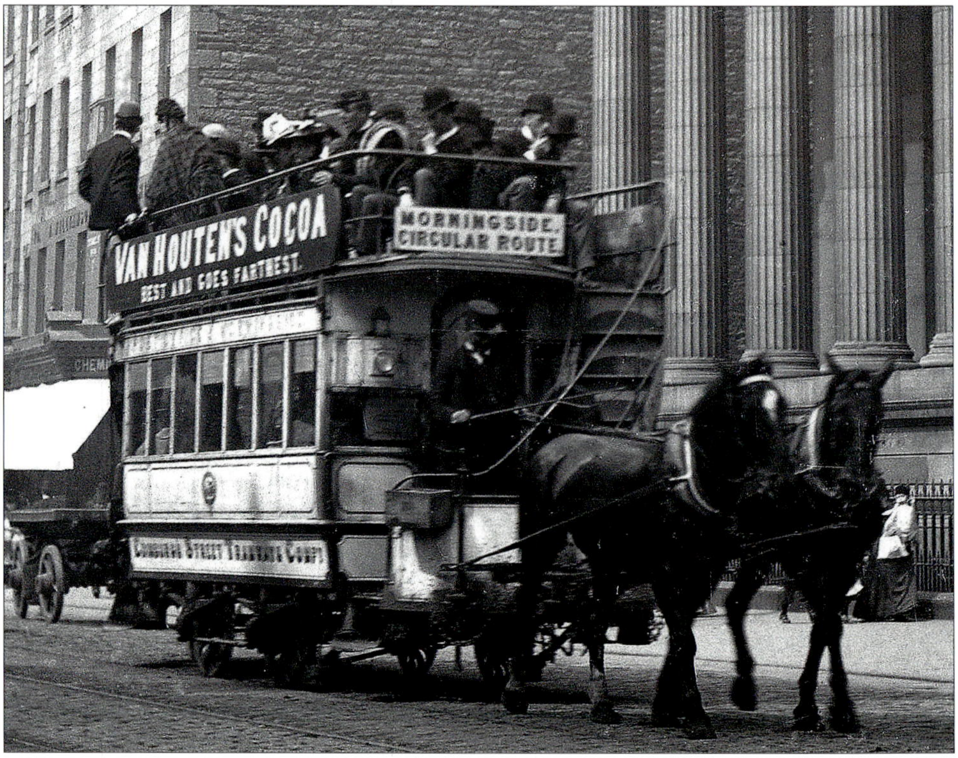

Right. White liveried car 10 (the number is on the sand box) passing Surgeon's Hall. In July 1898 this was replaced by a short-lived light garden seat car, so all that can be said with certainty is that this dates from before then and the car is approaching the end of its life. This car – which is of the same body style as preserved 23 – has leaf spring suspension.

retained for these workings. By the end of 1883 there were ten open toastracks, most painted yellow (the 'route' colour for Portobello also). Car numbers remained with these routes when cars were replaced, with numbers above 52 given randomly depending on whichever route the car was allocated to when placed in service. This did not, however, prevent cars being moved between routes, with consequent repainting (and potential renumbering).

Use of gas to illuminate cars was tried in 1882, with storage reservoirs below the lower saloon seats capable of providing three nights' illumination. Two cars were so fitted, number 16 on the Newhaven run and 27 on the Morningside route, but the experiment does not appear to have been extended.

James Clifton Robinson's appointment as manager in March 1883 brought immediate changes: from the end of April he reorganised most routes and introduced differing colours for their cars.[198]

cars 1–12 Morningside Circular; White (and White)
cars 13–16 Bernard Street to Haymarket; Red and White
cars 17–22 Bernard Street to Craigmillar Park; Blue and White
cars 23–25 Commercial St to Marchmont Rd; Royal Blue and White
cars 26–31 Seafield to Gorgie; Green and Buff
cars 32–37 Craigmillar Park to Haymarket; Chocolate and Buff
cars 38–46 Newhaven to Morningside 'Oak' and White
cars 47–52 Portobello to Colinton Road, Yellow (and Yellow)
Ochre and White was later used for cars running High Street to Tollcross.
(White, Buff and Yellow were applied to the lower (rocker) panels)

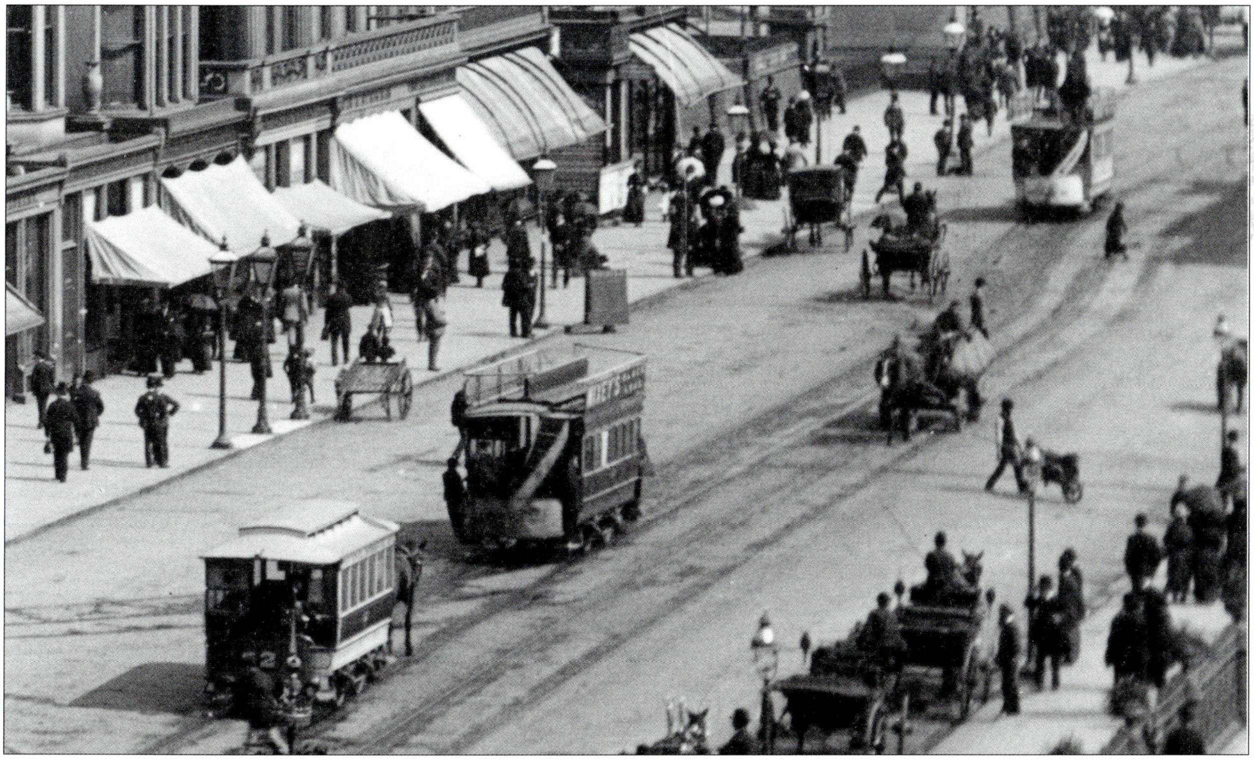

This view from the Scott Monument captures one of the light-weight single deck saloon cars built at Shrubhill expressly for the opening of the steeply graded extension to Morningside Drive in the summer of 1883. Apparently number 52 (why is there so often a passer-by in front of the number?). It seems probable that some, if not all, of these cars were rebuilt with top deck seats.

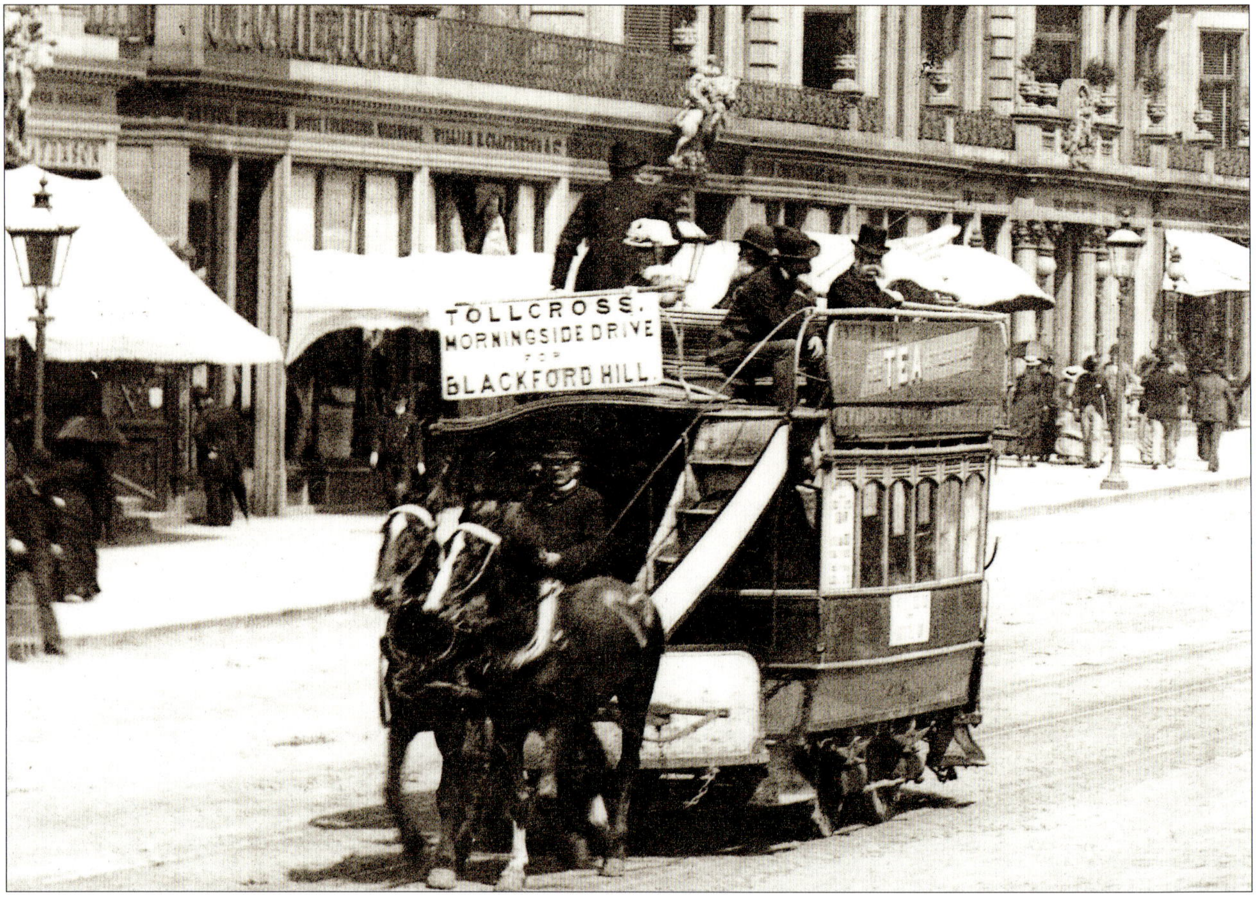

Little is known regarding this low set design of car. The sides – to judge by the shadow on the rocker panel – have a curve to them reminiscent of the 'Rotunda car' while the canopy resembles a contemporary horse bus. There is a photo of a car of this type numbered 42, but this specimen cannot be identified. Probably in 1886, the side poster for that year's exhibition.

In the summer of 1883 Shrubhill turned out some (probably four) small single deck saloon cars expressly for the Morningside Toll route. 'During the past week the company have introduced a number of cars, new in construction to Edinburgh. They are aimed at lightness, and for this reason have no seats on top. This is an American idea; the cars can be drawn by one horse on level routes. It is strange that the directors have not thought of this before, as Edinburgh has such steep gradients. The old cars require four horses plus trace horses; the new ones are served by two horses and require no assistance. These light cars are good also for investors; they have no empty seats, as in winter only one third of passengers use the outside seats. The cars recently put on to the West End to Morningside Toll route, built at Shrubhill, have all the latest improvements and weigh less than half of the other cars. They are neat, smart and very comfortable; light wood has been used in their construction, and they are unpainted except where absolutely necessary'.[199] Not only was this event 'strange' – it also ignores the reported (but perhaps unfulfilled) build just the previous summer of single deck reversible cars! The number of trams was given as 62 close and 10 open, also that '*cars of a lighter type*' were being built.[200] It is considered that this design (represented by our car 23) was built for the next three years, numbering at least twelve. Tenders invited for advertising (from 1 November 1883) specified 75 cars and 17 buses – but this probably includes the old cars kept for workmen, football and special occasions[201].

During October 1884 an experiment was undertaken using electricity as motive power. The International Forestry Exhibition held at Donaldson's Hospital on the west side of the city had seen demonstration of the pioneering electric system of Henry Bock Binko – which, at the end of the exhibition, was then used on one of the Tramway Company's cars. 'The electric motor which has been in use in the car within the exhibition grounds was placed in one of the ordinary cars of the Tramway Company. In the system here at work – that known as Binko's system – the electricity is generated in a dynamo-machine by steam-power. This machine … is at a considerable distance from the electric motor in the car; but the two are connected by underground cables with the rails on which the car is to run, or with some conducting plates set down parallel with the rails. From the rails or from these conducting plates the current of electricity, generated in the primary dynamo, and conveyed from it by the underground cables, is transmitted to the electric motor within the car, and by this current the electric motor is set in motion. According to the principle, the reversibility of the dynamo, 'the fact', is explained, 'that in the case of two dynamos at work at more or less distant stations, connected with each other, the current produced in one machine – its offspring, so to speak – sets the other to work, or becomes the parent of motive-power in its ally.' That is to say, in one dynamo is generated a current of electricity by steam-power, and this current, when transmitted to another dynamo, converts it into an engine, which may be stationary or locomotive, according as its mechanism may have been adapted. As the rails were not bonded together electrically, the current generated in the primary dynamo in the Exhibition grounds was not delivered to them, but to two copper strips laid on wooden planks in the centre of the tram line. The car was connected to these by a small trolley and cable. From the plates the current passed to the insulated wheel, then to the motor in the car. The current caused the armature of the electric motor to rotate, and the motion thus obtained was applied to traction purposes by belts communicating with the axle … The work of preparing the line for the experiment after the close of traffic on Friday night did not allow of the running of the car being commenced until Saturday morning was more than three hours advanced. With one car two journeys were made from the Exhibition to Haymarket Railway Station and back … An attempt was next made to run two cars by coupling one to that in which the electric motor was placed. This trial was not so successful but a portion of the road was run over at a lower rate of speed. The original intention was to run the car as far as the Post Office, but the cost would have been more than the directors considered it prudent to expend … no opinion was expressed as to the practicability of applying such a system to any extensive scheme of street tramway traffic'.[202] Power was generated by a ten horse power steam engine by Robey & Co of Lincoln.[203]

Binko had previously run his electric railway at the Crystal Palace in Croydon during the summer of 1882,[204] less than three years after the first ever practical demonstration of electricity for traction, by Siemens and Halske in Berlin in 1879. Binko was granted a provisional patent on 29 June 1882 and at Crystal Palace used his small locomotive *Volta* to pull three open trailers. In 1884 this demonstration line was moved to Edinburgh, now using a more powerful locomotive, the *Ohm*, with new trailer cars; operation of a half-mile circular line commenced on 17 July 1884.[205] On 22 August the line was graced by the Prince and Princess of Wales, travelling in a luxurious – but tiny – specially built saloon, the *Alexandra*. A week later this was used by Prime Minister W E Gladstone and his family. The diminutive coach was built in Edinburgh by John Hislop and Son of Antigua Street – it has been stated that Hislop also built tramcars, but no evidence of this has been produced. Binko was soon declared bankrupt, with a meeting of creditors held even before the end of the Forestry Exhibition. Notwithstanding this setback he relocated his operation to Great Yarmouth, running there for only six weeks.[206]

However, Binko and the Street Tramways Company achieved an important first in transport development, with the earliest operation of a tramcar in the

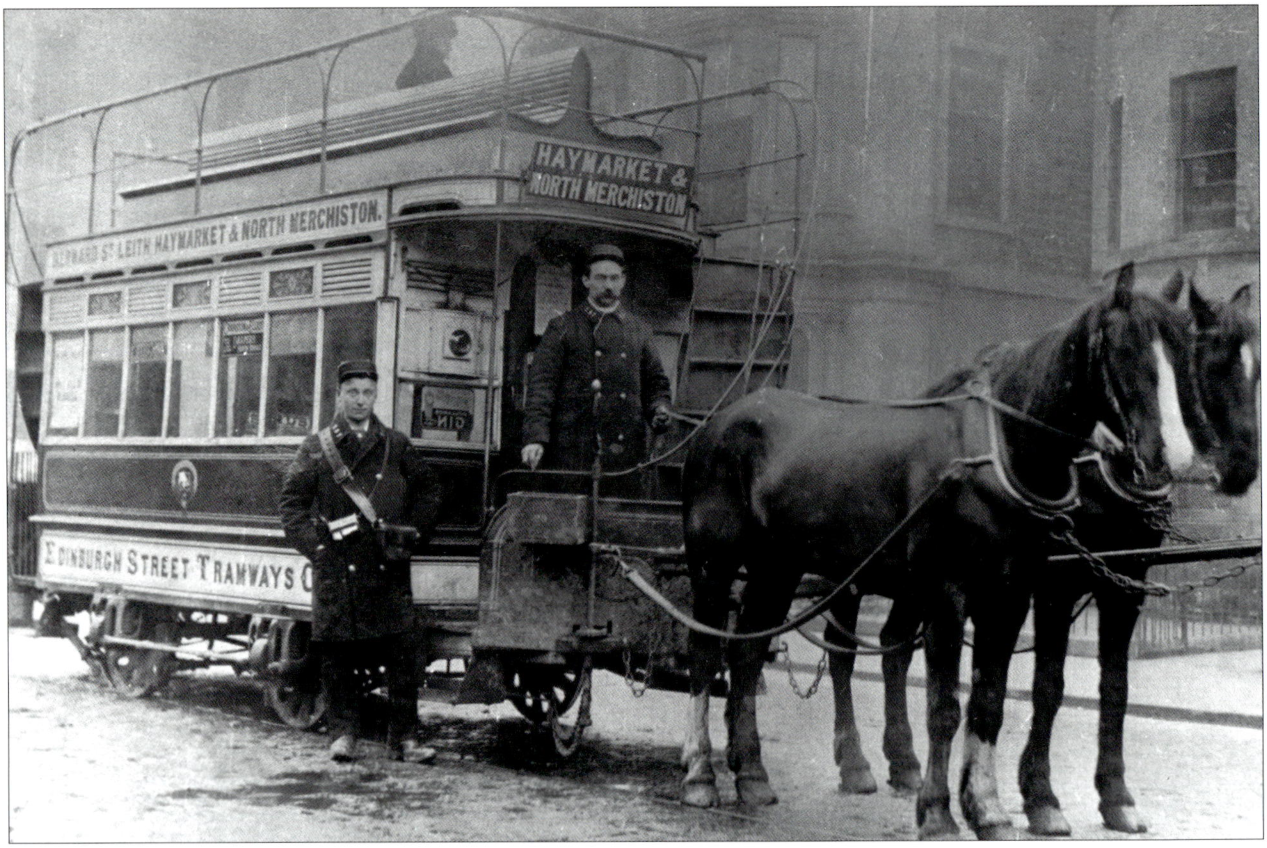

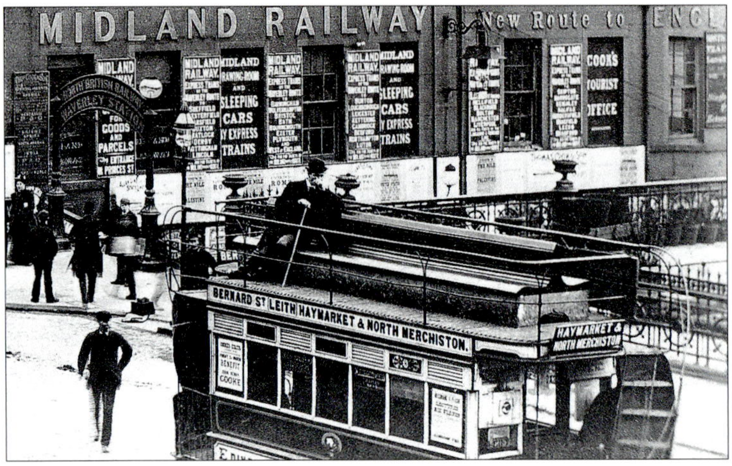

Above. Surprisingly no photograph appears to survive of the Gold medal winning tramcar exhibited at Edinburgh's 1886 International Exhibition (number 45). However it was of the same design as number 29, seen here at Bernard Street terminus, but with refinements such as electro-plated fittings and upholstered seats.

Left. A good detail view of one of these cars (probably 29 again) is provided by this photograph at the top of Waverley Steps. From the adverts in the car's windows the date can be given as March 1893. The far window advertises a benefit for John Henry Cooke, proprietor of the 'Royal Drawing-Room Circus' of Fountainbridge, held on 10 March.
(City of Edinburgh Council – Edinburgh Libraries www.capitalcollections.org.uk)

United Kingdom using power from a distant generation source.[207] If nothing else, this shows the determination Wood and his fellow directors exercised in their desire to leave no stone unturned in the quest for an effective alternative to their hard-pressed horses.

Reconstruction and replacement of both trams and omnibuses continued, until, for the 1886 Edinburgh Exhibition held in the Meadows, Shrubhill built a car which was awarded a gold medal. This then formed the basis of a design which was perpetuated, with little variation, for some six or seven years, with about 50 built; amounting to more than half the fleet.

The seven window saloon had coloured quarter lights, and was '... a handsome car, fitted with an electric bell, a patent life-saving guard, a rail cleaner, and a patent spring brake for emergency use. The car, which is all in light colours, with electro plated mountings &c, has been upholstered in an elegant way. It will be placed on the Morningside route after the Exhibition'.[208] In the Thomson notebook the car is identified as number 45 – the second of that number – and that it ran for some months on the Circle route, before being put on the Morningside Drive run. It seated eighteen inside and eighteen outside; but only the earliest examples had 'knifeboard' seats. Most had 'garden' seats outside, increasing the seating capacity accordingly.

28 July 1887 saw the first Shrubhill-built car with top deck 'garden seats' where passengers sat on cross seats with reversible backs facing the direction of travel. Put on the Coltbridge to Powburn route, it sat 24 on top and 16 inside. Of the 'Exhibition' style this car, possibly with six saloon windows, was soon superseded by the seven window design seating 26 on top and 18 inside, when it was found that the additional load of the increased number of passengers could be pulled without undue strain to the horses. Some old cars then had knifeboard seats replaced by garden seats.

Shrubhill's coachbuilders undertook continuous refurbishment of older stock where the condition warranted the cost, and improvements were frequently incorporated, the most beneficial being replacement of early stair designs. The imported Stephenson cars came with his patented stair, and as this patent applied only in the USA, several older Edinburgh cars had their spiral stairs replaced with his style. It may be noteworthy that in the chairman's report he would refer to 'serviceable' cars in the car fleet, and that at the time of the 1886 Exhibition said 'eight extra cars were running which previously had been the property of the Company, but had not been in use'.[209] This confirms that there were old cars kept for such occasions, and which did not feature in stock returns.

While continuous improvements and additions were made to the stock of cars, the total acknowledged remained fairly constant between 1883 and 1890, at around 62 'close' cars and 10 open cars. From that year returns split the fleet into three types; close, open and canopy. Latterly the description 'canopy car' appears to refer to any single deck car other than the open 'toast-racks'. The small single deck saloons (probably four) built in 1883 (the Thomson book has 'canopy' car 82 built in 1883) were not differentiated from close cars. An early photograph with one of these six-window saloon monitor-roof single deck Morningside cars *appears* to show it numbered 52. The term 'close car' then referred to any double deck car. At the end of 1889 stock was given as 63 close and 10 open cars; a year later this was 63 close, 8 canopy and 6 open. In the two intervening half-yearly reports, the changes recorded at end of June 1890, '3 cars have been added to capital and 4 cars and 1 omnibus charged to revenue',[210] then at end of December 1890 'one car added to stock and 5 cars charged to revenue'.[211] Thus in calendar year 1890, thirteen new cars were built and put in service, nine replacing older vehicles while the number of toastracks was reduced from ten to six. The charge on the capital account for each new car built at Shrubhill at this time was £158, while a bus cost £163.

Several single deck saloon cars were added at this time, with numbers 95, 98 and 99 built in 1890.

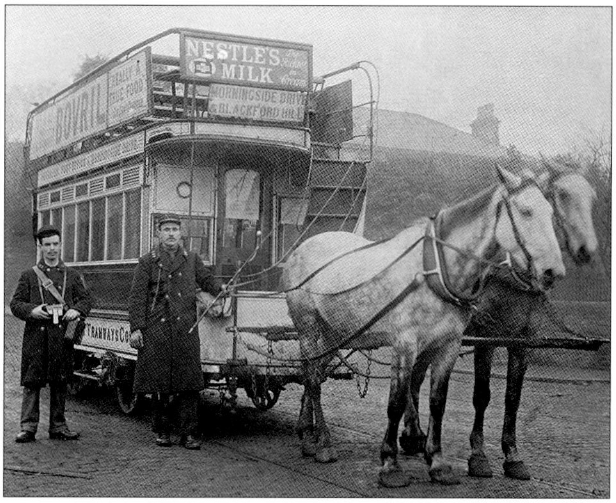

Car 83 at Newhaven terminus (at the top of Craighall Road) on the long (jointly operated) route to Morningside Drive; the livery for this route was oak and white. Under magnification the number is distinguishable on the sand-box.

Line drawing of 24-seat canopy car 82 built 1883 (according to Thomson). It does not feature in his notebook, and no photograph of a car of this style has been found.

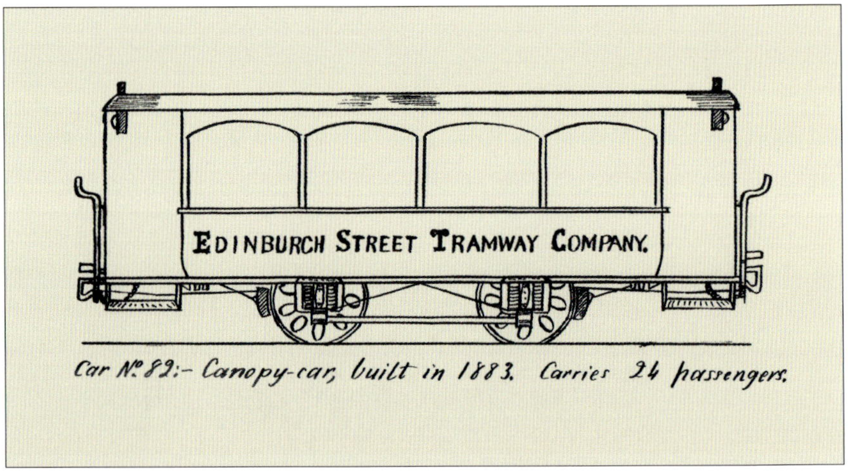

Yet another variant on the 'canopy car' theme. Thomson drawing representing car 95, said to be a 24-seat canopy car of 1890. Elsewhere in his record he has it as a 34 seat canopy car, while it is licensed by the magistrates as a canopy car seating 32 inside plus 3 on each platform.

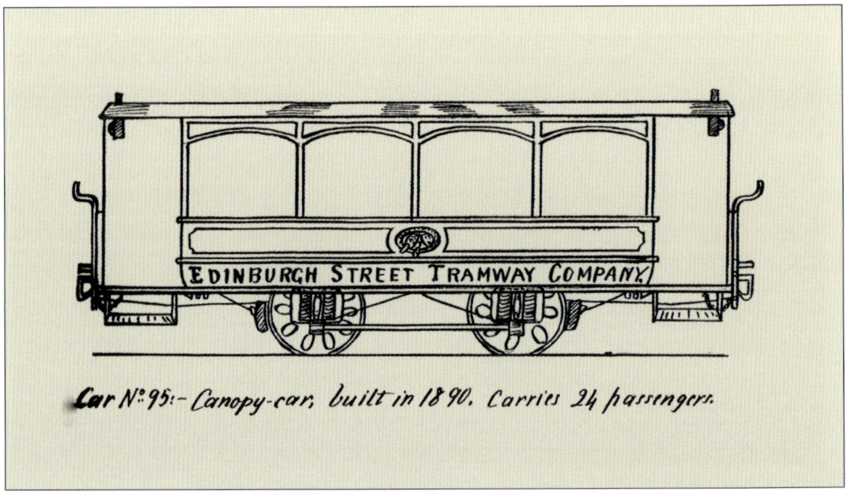

Thomson line drawing of car 99 *Faraday*. If reference is made to the photograph of sister car 98 on page 59, it will be seen that – despite the lack of proper appreciation of perspective – it seems quite accurate. Note the seat on the platform.

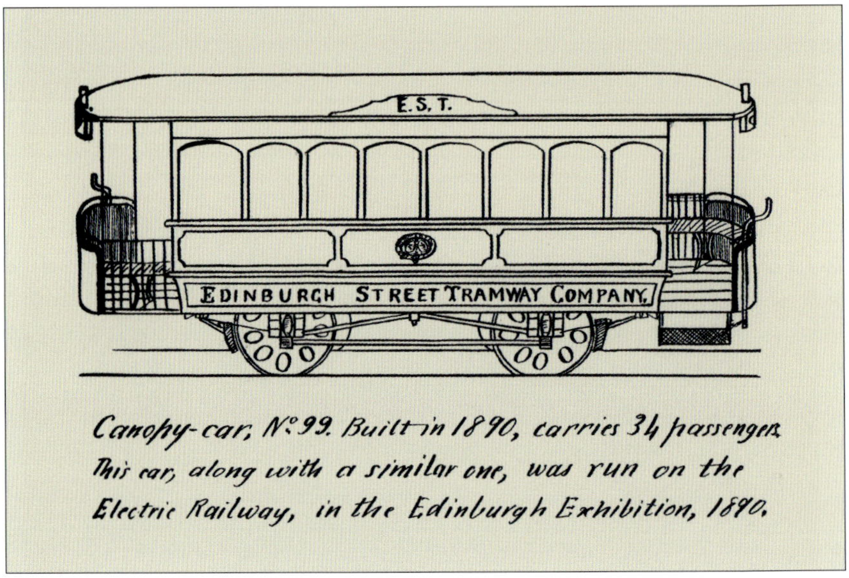

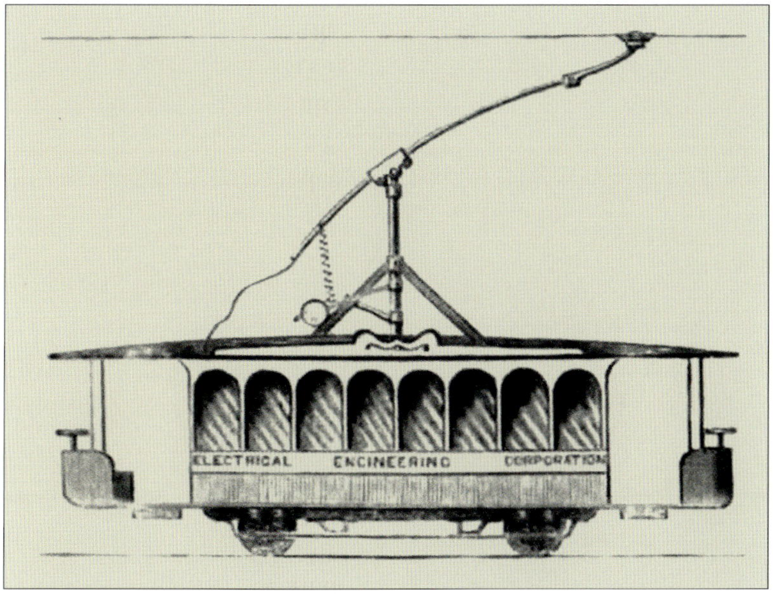

Contemporary illustration of the 1890 electric car *'Faraday'*. Inside seating for 26 passengers was 'fore-and-aft' (or across) not longitudinal.

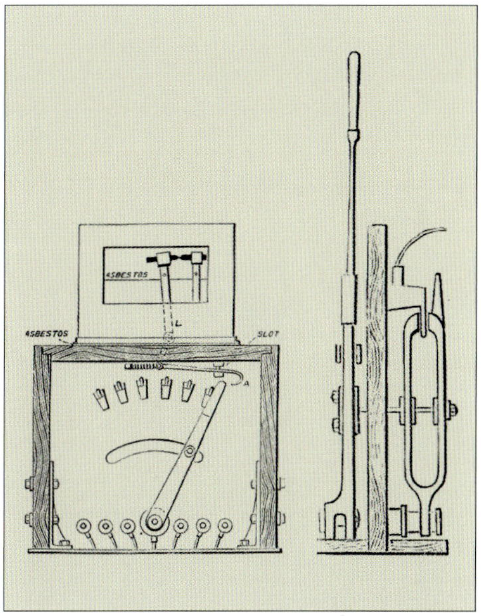

Side and end view of the controller mechanism. The contact studs were gun-metal on slate.

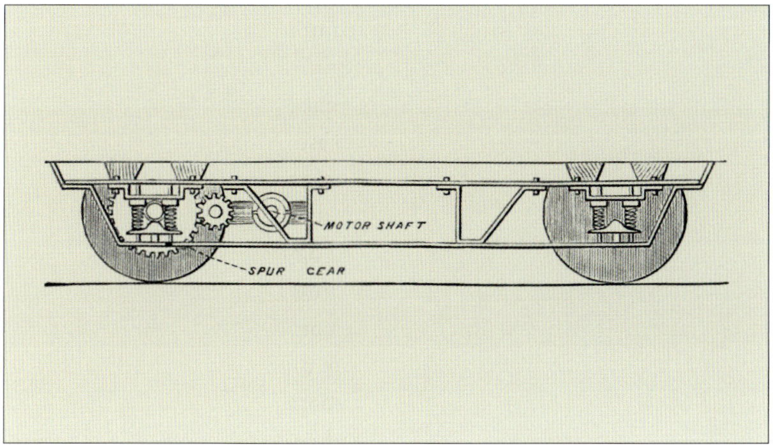

Detail of underframe with motor and drive shaft. The single Stetter motor was connected to the axle by double spur gearing.

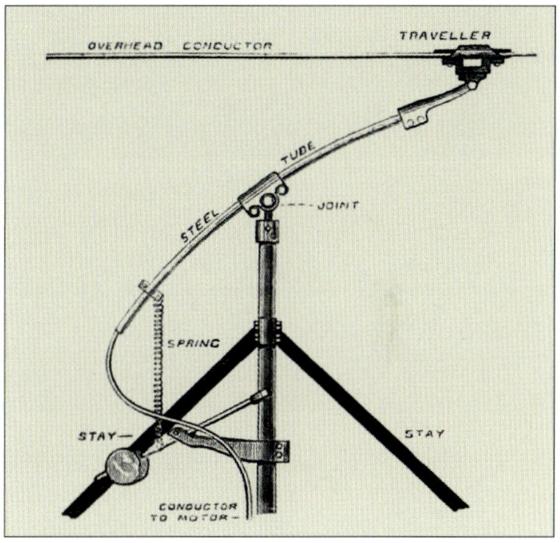

The arrangement of the pick-up from the overhead conductor wire. This was of phosphor-bronze, with the current at 300 volts.

Canopy and open cars were numbered at the end of the series, and renumbered as required to maintain this position. Thus the Thomson book has a sketch of car 82 as a four window saloon 24-seat single deck 'canopy' car of 1883, but in the numerical list (and from a photograph) 82 was an 'Exhibition' design garden seat car, of the Commercial Street to Marchmont Road route. At the time of creation of the District Tramways Company the canopy cars were numbers 90–99; some had cross seating for 32 passengers, plus seats for three on each platform, but 93 is noted as 'old style', and 91 is undefined. The final two canopy cars were added in 1891. When the Thomson book was commenced cars 90 and 94 had been withdrawn and then in 1895 were replaced by two ex-Glasgow cars.

Cars 98 and 99 require particular mention. Completed in June 1890, they were initially used on the electric tramway constructed for the International

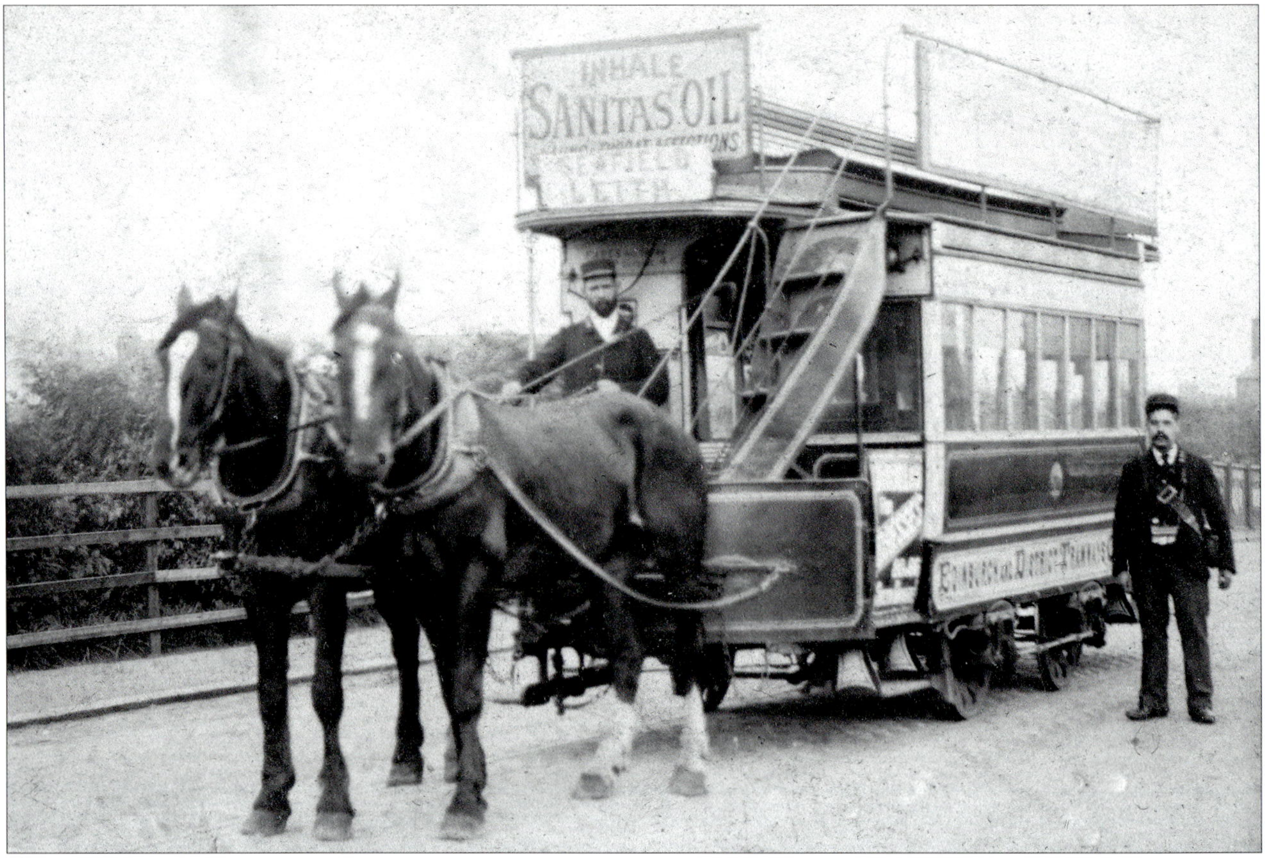

Above. A 36 seat car of the type represented by preserved car 23. This is most probably car 70 of the Seafield to Gorgie route, which was 'rebuilt' (or replaced almost entirely) in May 1896 to a garden seat car with the same number.

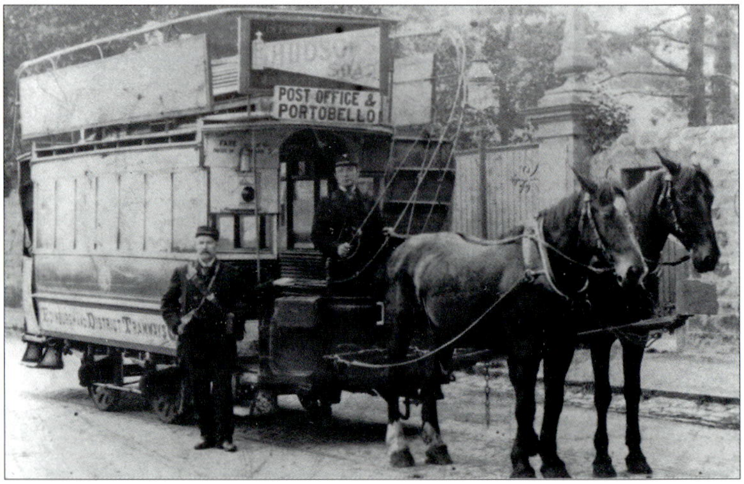

Right. Another 36 seat knifeboard car, but at Murrayfield terminus, probably in mid 1900 during the last days of horse operation before cable running started. It can be seen that the car is standing on track which has the cable centre slot. Much renumbering of old horse cars took place at this time, but from the magistrate's licence records, this has to be a car then numbered 16.

Exhibition held at Meggetland, north of the Union Canal. 'This addition to the numerous attractions of the Exhibition, is worked upon the American trolley system, and has been furnished by the Electrical Engineering Company. The permanent way measures about ½ mile in length and extends from the Caledonian Railway Exhibition station to the Suburban line in rear of Mr Ross' Tea Rooms, with an intermediate station near the Switchback. It is similar to an ordinary railway, while the two elegant cars have been named the *Clerk-Maxwell* and the *Faraday* – after the eminent scientists – have been constructed by the Edinburgh Street

Tramways Company. Yesterday afternoon the opening run was performed, the cars moving with great smoothness ... Mr Bennet, convener of the Electrical and Lighting Committee, said it gave him great pleasure to be able to invite them to the opening ... When the Committee decided to have an electrical railway at the Exhibition, they determined, seeing the great extent to which electrical tramways and railways on the overhead conductor system had been adopted in the United States, where the mileage exceeded 1000 miles, to have an electrical tramway of that type. That was the first electrical tramway in Great Britain powered via an overhead conductor. The executive Council considered that the railway would be of considerable utility in conveying passengers from the Caledonian Railway to the centre of the Exhibition. The cars were well patronised by the public'.[212]

Both cars were powered by a single 300 volt Statter motor via a six-notch stud controller. Power was from a single overhead wire, with pick-up by trolleys of a different design on each car.[213] This pioneer line was the very first in Britain to take power from an overhead supply, more than a year ahead of the next such, at Roundhay in Leeds. The Edinburgh local authorities would not permit their streets to be defiled by overhead wires, so when the time came, they demanded perpetuation of the outdated cable haulage system.

As end of the Street Tramways Company lease approached, much effort was devoted to maximising the value of assets for transfer to the new undertaking and the number of close cars acknowledged increased from 68 at the end of 1892 to 84 just one year later. In correspondence with the Board of Trade in 1892, the Company detailed by route the number of cars required. Thus for Newhaven to Morningside Drive there were 9 full day plus 4 half-day cars required; Commercial Street to Marchmont, 3 full day; Bernard Street to Marchmont, 3 full day; Bernard Street to Powburn, 6 full day; Bernard Street to North Merchiston, 6 full day; Seafield to Gorgie, 6 full day; Powburn to Coltbridge, 6 full day and 3 half day; Morningside Circle, 8 full day plus 4 half day; Tron Church to Tollcross, 2 full day; and Portobello to Colinton Road, 9

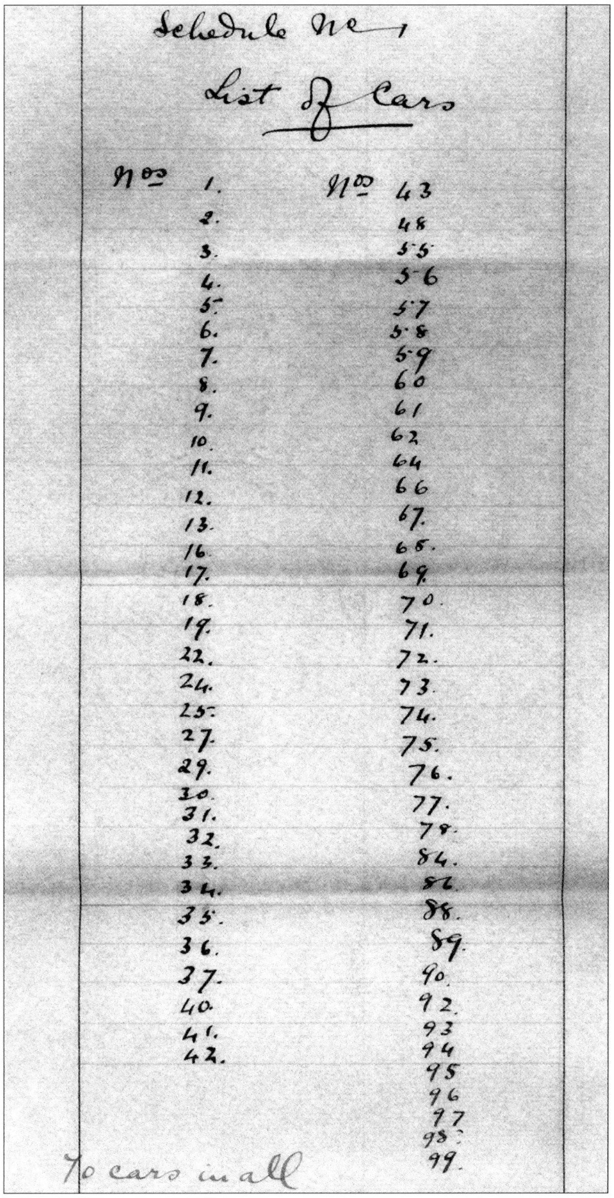

Schedule No 1

List of Cars

Nos	No
1.	43
2.	48
3.	55
4.	56
5.	57
6.	58
7.	59
8.	60
9.	61
10.	62
11.	64
12.	66
13.	67.
16.	68.
17.	69
18.	70.
19.	71.
22.	72.
24.	73.
25.	74.
27.	75.
29.	76.
30.	77.
31.	78.
32.	84.
33.	86.
34.	88.
35.	89.
36.	90.
37.	92.
40.	93
41.	94
42.	95
	96
	97
	98
	99.

70 cars in all

The list of cars contained within the documents relating to the division of assets. 'Schedule no 1'.

full day. This totalled 69 cars in daily use, to which had to be added further 13 closed, 10 canopy and six open cars, for workmen or football and holiday requirements. Thus when the division happened, the Street Tramways Company conveniently owned precisely one hundred trams. At this date, close cars (of all types) were numbered 1 – 84, open cars were 85 – 89 plus 100, while canopy cars were 90 – 99. It appears that,

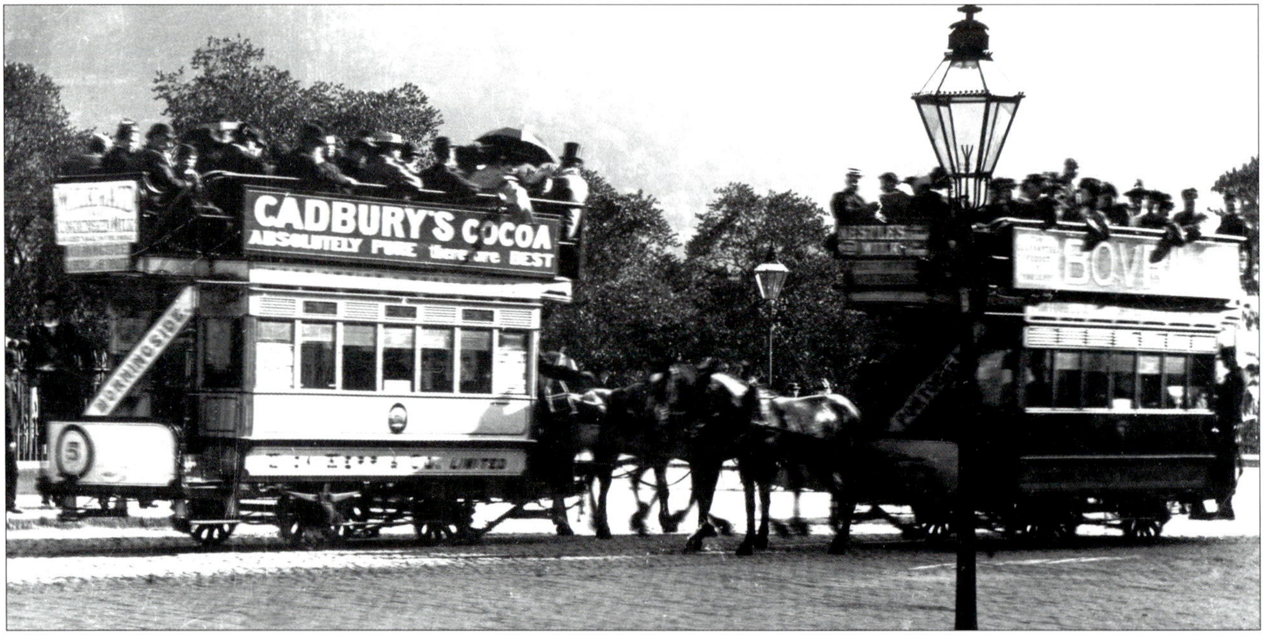

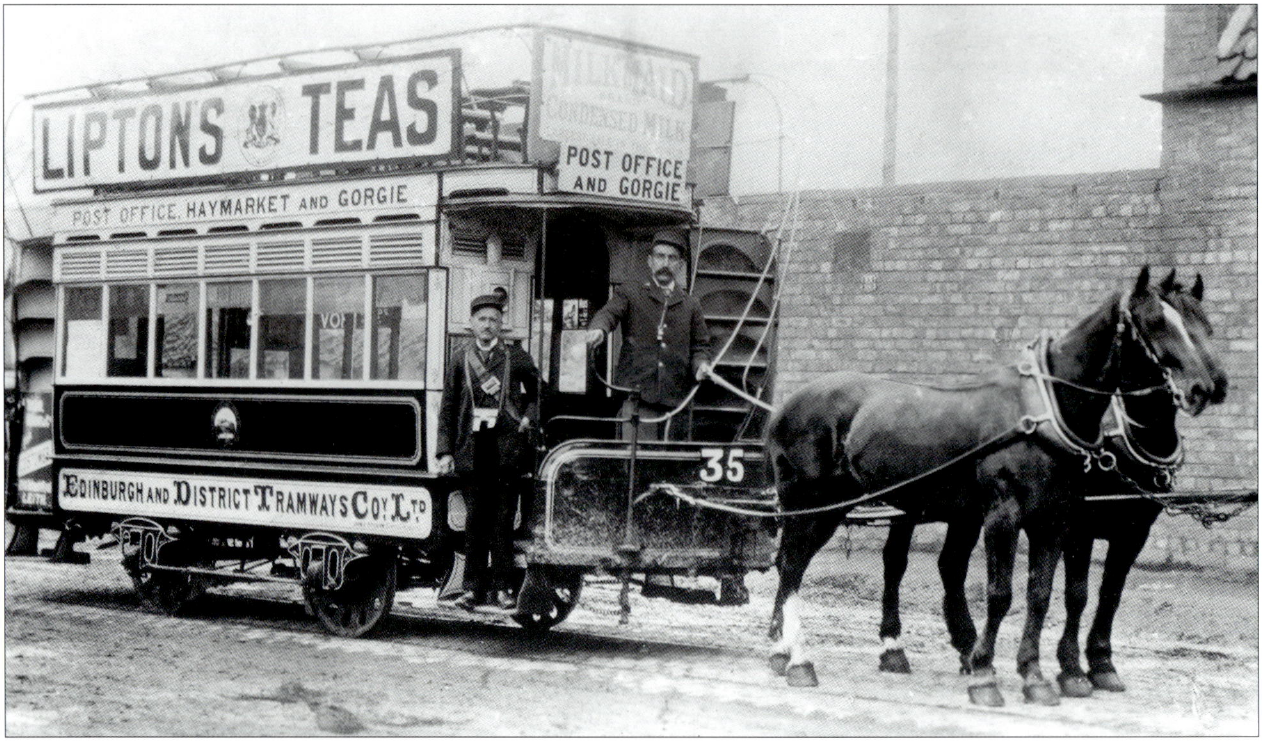

Top. Two 'Exhibition' design cars pass at the foot of Hanover Street in the summer of 1894. Car 5 of the Morningside Circular route has (unusually) leaf spring suspension, while the car on the right heading for Portobello lacks the three glass quarter light panels above the saloon windows. Car 5 has on the rocker panel the name of the lessee company, rather than the operating company.

Above. Within a short period the design was modified to incorporate garden seats on the top deck, which, in addition to being an improvement in comfort, also increased the carrying capacity on the top deck from 18 to 26. Although a standardised design, car 35 omits the engraved and coloured glass quarter-lights which on most cars were fitted between the above-window ventilators.

since the lease was about to end, the increase from 68 to 84 was achieved by dusting off and licensing the 16 old cars kept in reserve for occasional use.

To run on the routes of the new operating Company, the Corporation purchased, then passed to the lessees, some 70 cars, leaving 30 with the Street Company. The division was logical, based on which cars ran on which route. All cars used on self-contained 'District' routes went to the new Company, while cars on joint routes were shared according to the length run by each enterprise. Thus the Street Company retained close cars 14, 15, 20, 21, 23, 26, 28, 38, 39, 44–47, 49–54, 63, 79–84, plus 85 & 87 (open) and 90 & 95 (canopy). This is as detailed in the Thomson book (and could have been the reason for its creation) but needless to say the distribution and valuation was not achieved amicably, ending in court. The schedule provided with that action differs in detail, allotting cars 65, 91 & 100 to the Street Company and 84, 90 & 95 to the District, but this appears incorrect. This must have been a time of considerable confusion, with the division taking effect from midnight on Saturday 9 December 1893. Superficially life continued much as before, with financial accounts simply proportioned at 75% to the District Company and 25% to the Street Company. Both continued to use Shrubhill and both were initially managed by John Pitcairn. Henceforth both companies served Edinburgh separately, but necessarily closely interwoven. Edinburgh's magistrates decreed that cars operating within the city would have one sequence of numbers and we now follow the District Company, then return to the Street Tramways.

An early initiative by the new company increased the number of 1d stages, with an immediate boost in passenger numbers. To service this, additional cars were obtained, with the convenient availability at this precise time, of a large number from the Glasgow Tramway and Omnibus Company whose lease had just ended. Negotiations with Glasgow Corporation having failed, instead of the existing 200 plus cars being transferred, the Corporation put in place an entire replacement undertaking, with new horses, cars and depots. The District Company took advantage of this opportunity, purchasing several, all large eight-window saloon cars with knifeboard upper deck seats, seating 20 inside and 20 outside. The first four were put in service between

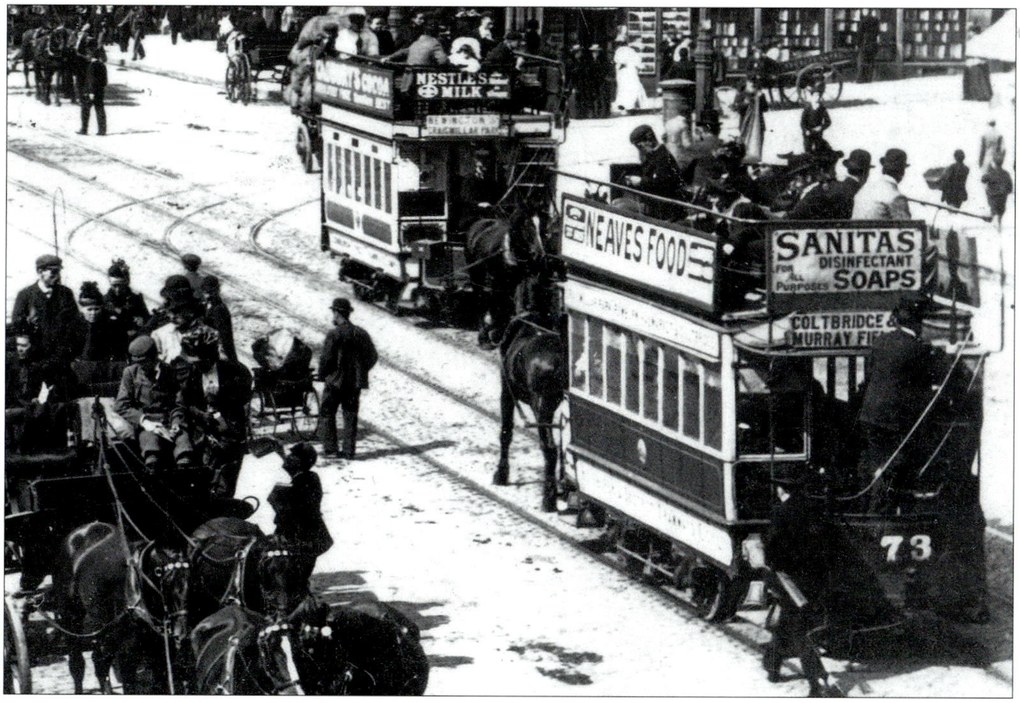

To cope with an increasing number of passengers, the District Company required additional vehicles. Coincidentally in Glasgow the incumbent operator was displaced by the Corporation, and a significant number of vehicles came timeously on the market. The District Company bought thirteen of these, number 73 was in service from 15 October 1894, the photograph dating from the summer of 1896.

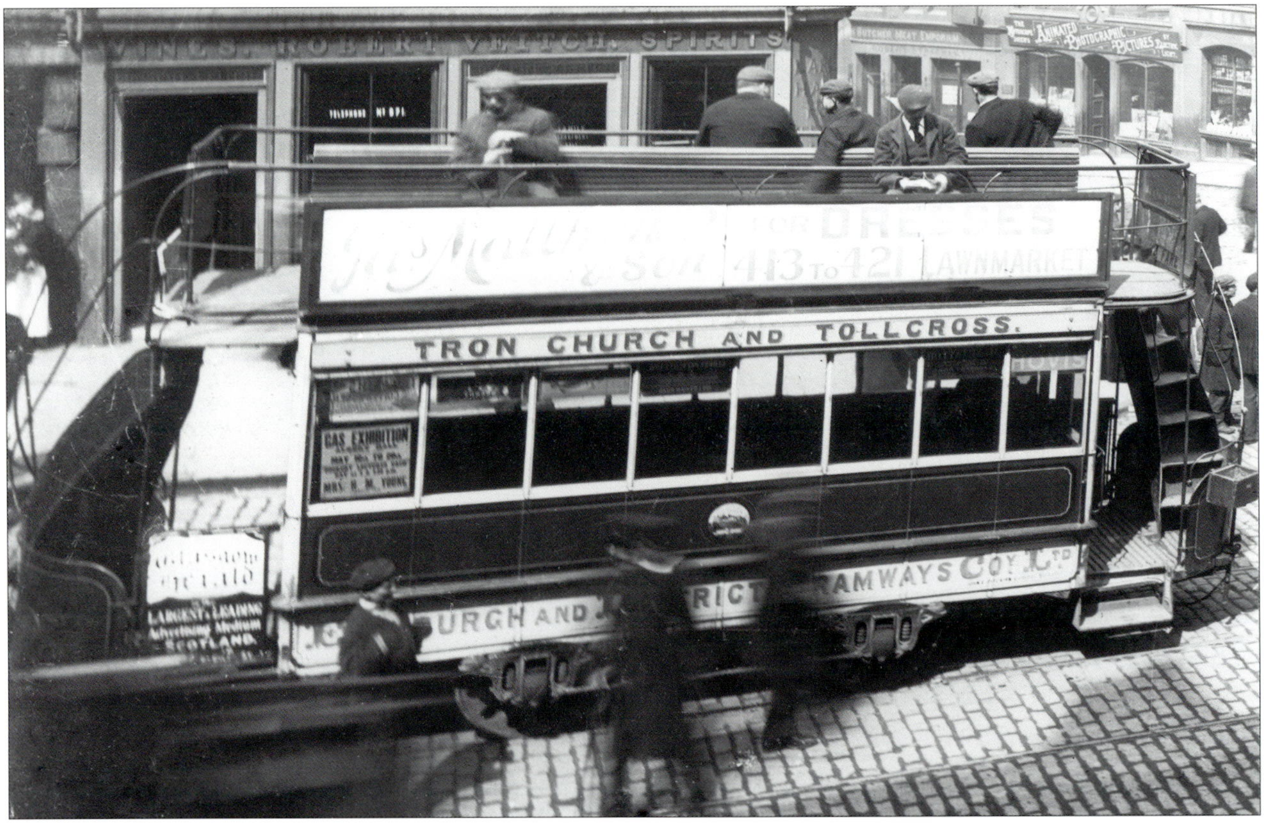

Above. Tron Church and Tollcross car 101 was another of those purchased from Glasgow, coming into use in Edinburgh on 31 December 1894. Although of a dated design, and with knifeboard seats, they were a bargain purchase and served the capital well. It was given a brown and white livery, which was replacing the assorted route colours.

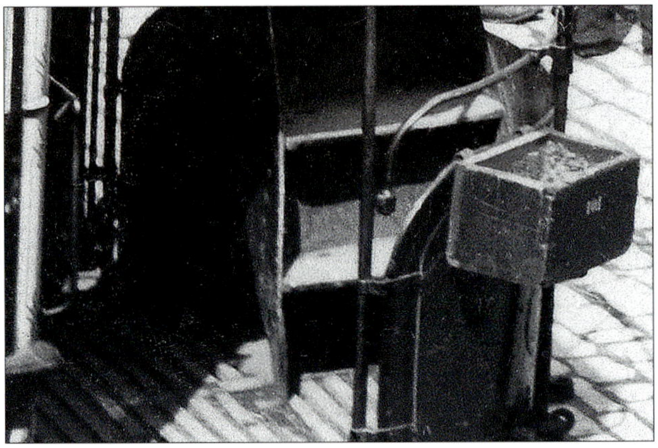

Right. Identification of this tram – as with many others where the fleet number is obscured – can sometimes be derived from the sand box. This, hung over the dash, held sand for the driver to cast below the hooves of his horses if they were in difficulty. It also was individual for each car, and carried the appropriate number. This enlargement from the above, shows this.

September and November 1894 taking the numbers of cars replaced (74, 73, 76 and 25, in that order). Some work was necessary before these were suitable for use; they had to be re-gauged from Glasgow's 4 ft 7¾ in to Edinburgh's 4 ft 8½ in, also new stairs and upper-deck handrails were fitted. However the price must have been right, as five more (101 – 105) were got, then another four (60, 61, 66 and 94), licensed on 5 April 1895.[214] The last six were fitted in Edinburgh with 'double entrances', a wider platform step with a central handrail, directing inside passengers left and outside passengers right, to speed up loading and unloading.

In July 1895 four cars (106 – 109) were purchased from the Metropolitan Railway Wagon & Carriage Company of Birmingham. These six window saloon cars were almost identical to the Glasgow Corporation

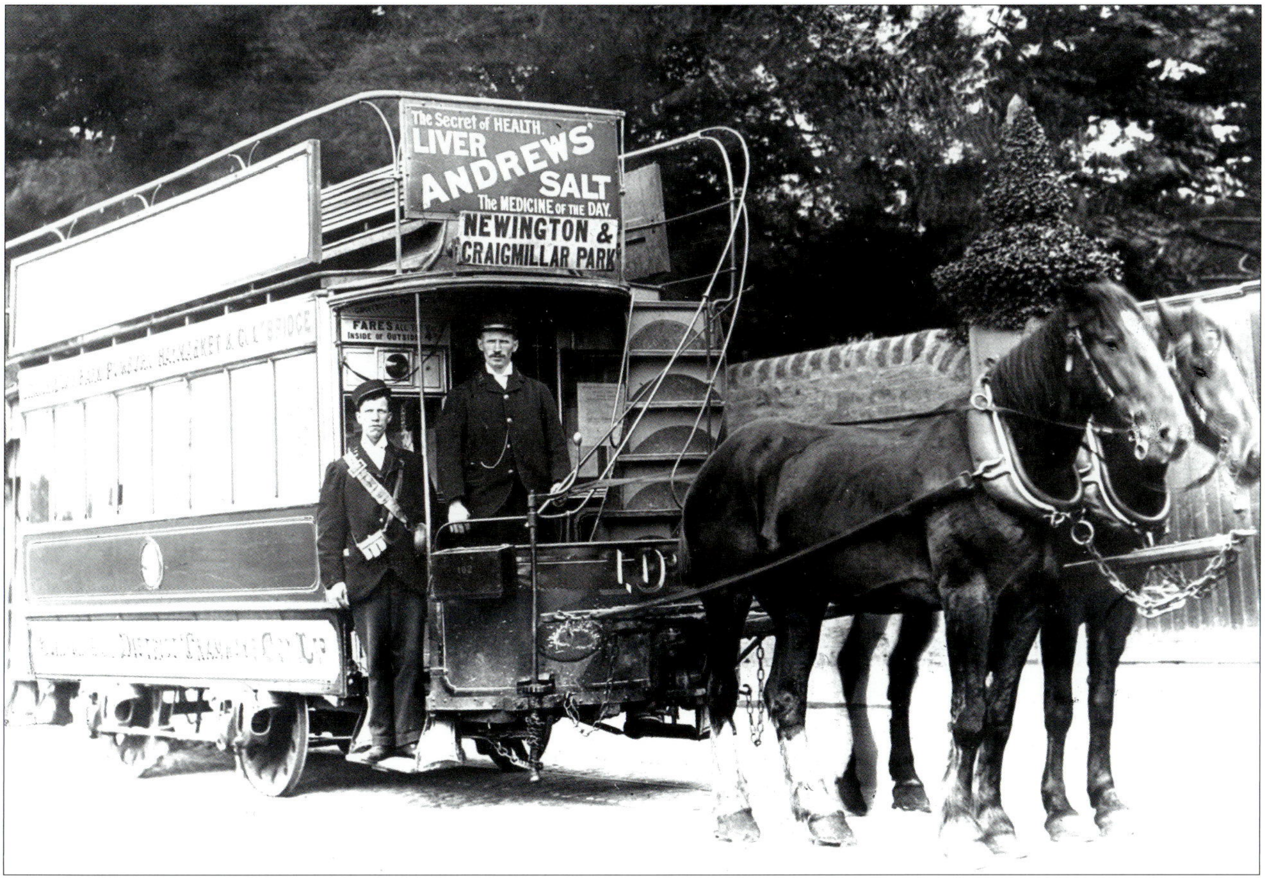

Another record at the Murrayfield terminus, this of car 102, an acquisition from the Glasgow Tramway & Omnibus Company at the end of December 1894. It seems to have been painted immediately after purchase in what appears to have become a uniform livery of brown with cream or off-white rocker panels and windows. It was licensed until mid 1903.

standard horse car, seating 22 out and 18 in. Details of both Edinburgh and Glasgow styles exist, the Edinburgh cars seemingly direct copies. The wheel back to back size on both drawings is 54 $\frac{3}{16}$ ins - correct for Glasgow but wrong by $\frac{3}{4}$ ins for Edinburgh. Glasgow's cars' wheels were at 5 ft 3 ins centres, Edinburgh used 5 ft 6 ins. Glasgow had wheel guards, sprung drawbars and battery operated electric lighting, features not provided in Edinburgh.

The next Shrubhill product was an oddity. Entering service on the Seafield to Gorgie route on 1 January 1896, car 110, for some now unfathomable reason, was built with top deck knifeboard seats, ten years after the last new car of this type. With a six window saloon, seating 18/18, but with double entrances, it remained unique. After this blip, from 1896 Shrubhill-built cars closely followed the Metropolitan design, but with seven saloon windows and seating 26/18; eight appeared in 1896, in order of build, 88, 89, 100, 71, 72, 55, 75 and 111. To cope with increasing patronage the company continued to build new cars, but the final products had seats for 24 outside and six (some three) window saloons, seating 24 outside. In year commencing July 1897 eight were added; in order, 44, 113, 29, 114, 78, 30, 10 and 53. The final two were licensed on 2 July 1898, the last horse cars built at

Overleaf. Closely following the Glasgow Corporation standard horse car design were the four cars built by the Metropolitan Company in 1896. Of lightweight construction, numbers 106 – 9 saw service on the long climb up Comiston Road to the Braids terminus, an extension from Morningside Drive built for cable operation which commenced on 26 October 1899.

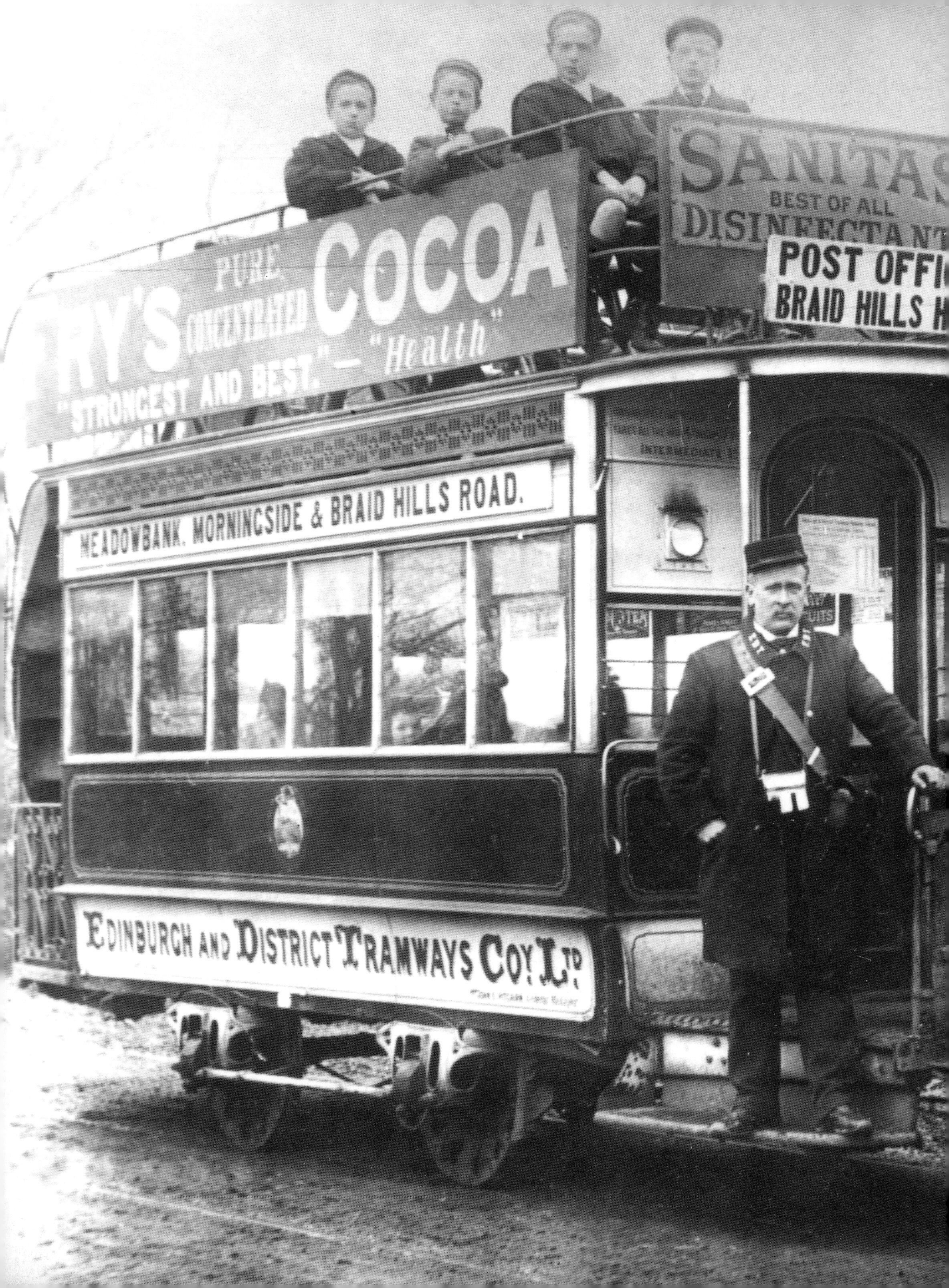
SANITAS
BEST OF ALL
DISINFECTANT
POST OFFIC
BRAID HILLS H
RY'S
PURE CONCENTRATED
COCOA
"STRONGEST AND BEST." — "Health"
MEADOWBANK, MORNINGSIDE & BRAID HILLS ROAD.
INTERMEDIATE
EDINBURGH AND DISTRICT TRAMWAYS COY. LTD

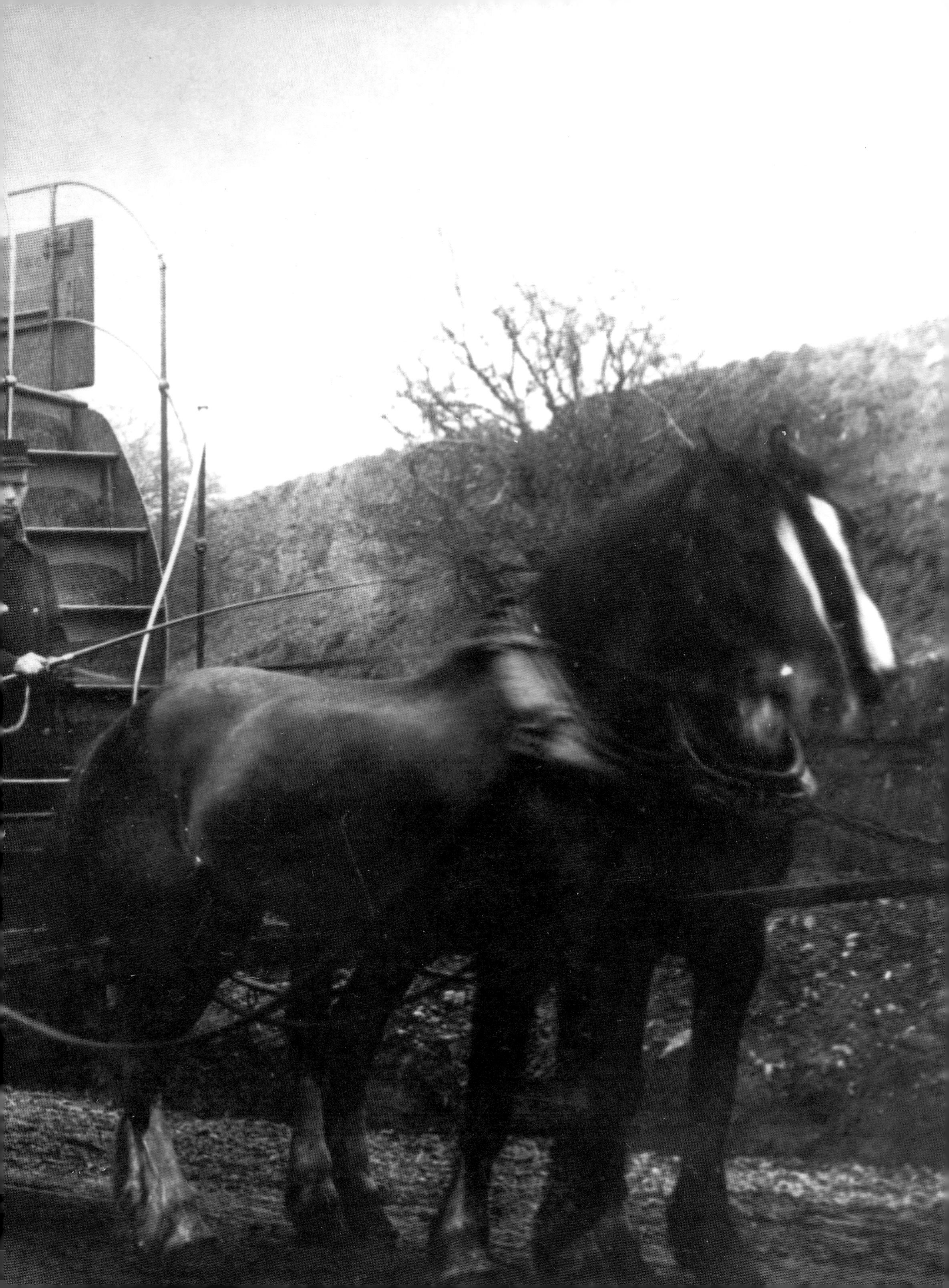

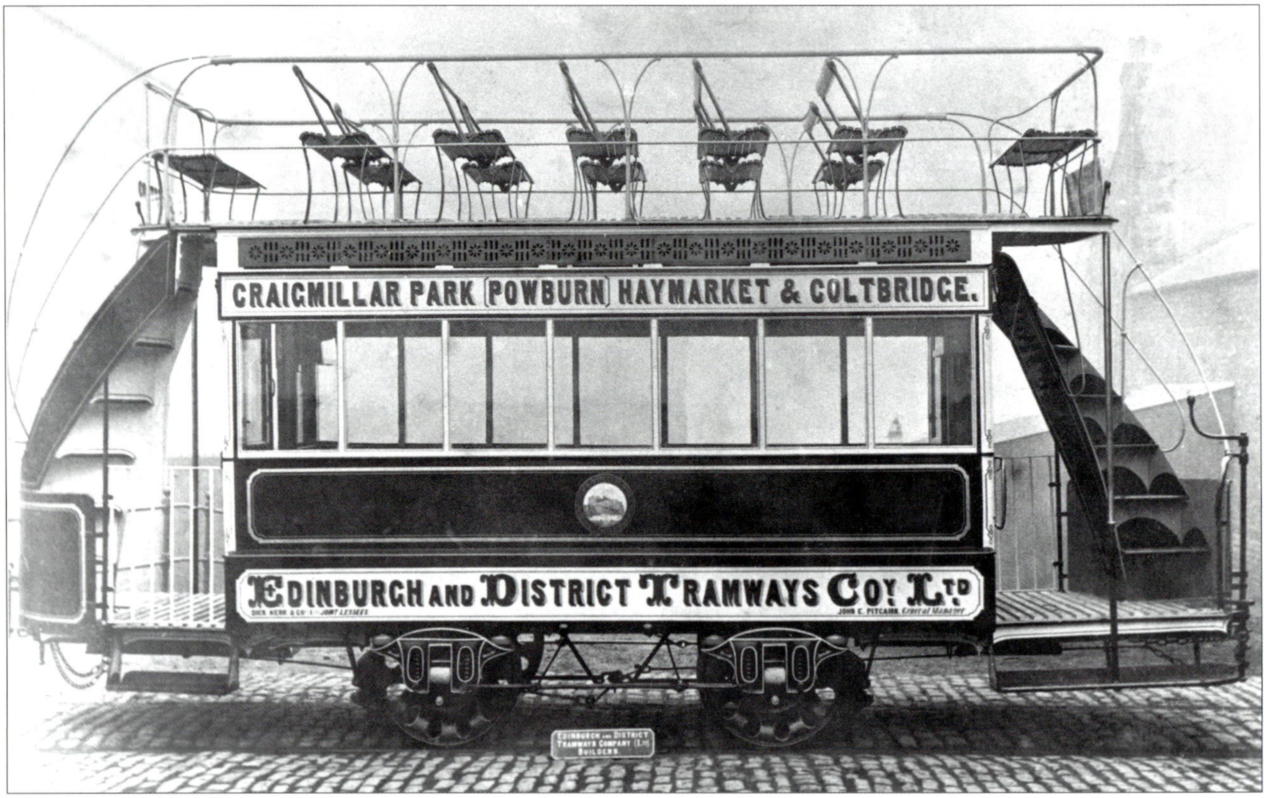

Shrubhill soon started building cars very similar to the Metropolitan design, with seven, then six window saloons. This newly built example was posed outside the body-building workshop at the north end of the works. A double-width entrance was used on these cars, speeding up passenger loading and unloading.

Shrubhill. On 31 January 1896 the line from Waterloo Place to Jock's Lodge passed to the District Company, and with it went the six cars used, 23, 44, 49, 52, 53 and 85. The rest of the line was transferred on 1 July 1898, with cars 47, 50, 51 and 80.

As the end of the horse tram era approached, the company, well aware of the limited life for new horse cars, constructed cars which could be readily rebuilt as cable cars. Some of these had saloons with three large side windows. Having built cable 112 (licensed from 13 October 1897) this made good sense but in the event only five were so rebuilt. 'The new [cable] cars will have a capacity about the same as the present horse cars, seating 18 inside and 26 out, and in external appearance the body of the cars will be much the same as those put on the circular route some time ago, having only three large panes of glass, instead of smaller panes, in each side. Indeed the bodies of a number of the present cars will be adjusted to meet the requirements of the cable system. There are now over 70 horse cars on the lines and it is likely that when the cable comes into operation the number will be considerably increased ...'[215]

Horse car numbers reduced as cable routes opened with, in 1900, 23 sold and four broken up; in 1901 14 sold, then in 1902 further 15 were disposed of, and by the end of 1903 only 21 horse cars remained with the District Company. At this period remaining cars were frequently re-numbered, newer cars replacing older models, taking their numbers – probably for accountancy reasons. Some such cars had their new identity for a few weeks only.[216] By 1904 seven horse cars remained, reducing to three (numbered 5, 47 and 72) for the final horse route to Colinton Road – but not one of these was the original of that number.[217]

There was little demand for second-hand horse

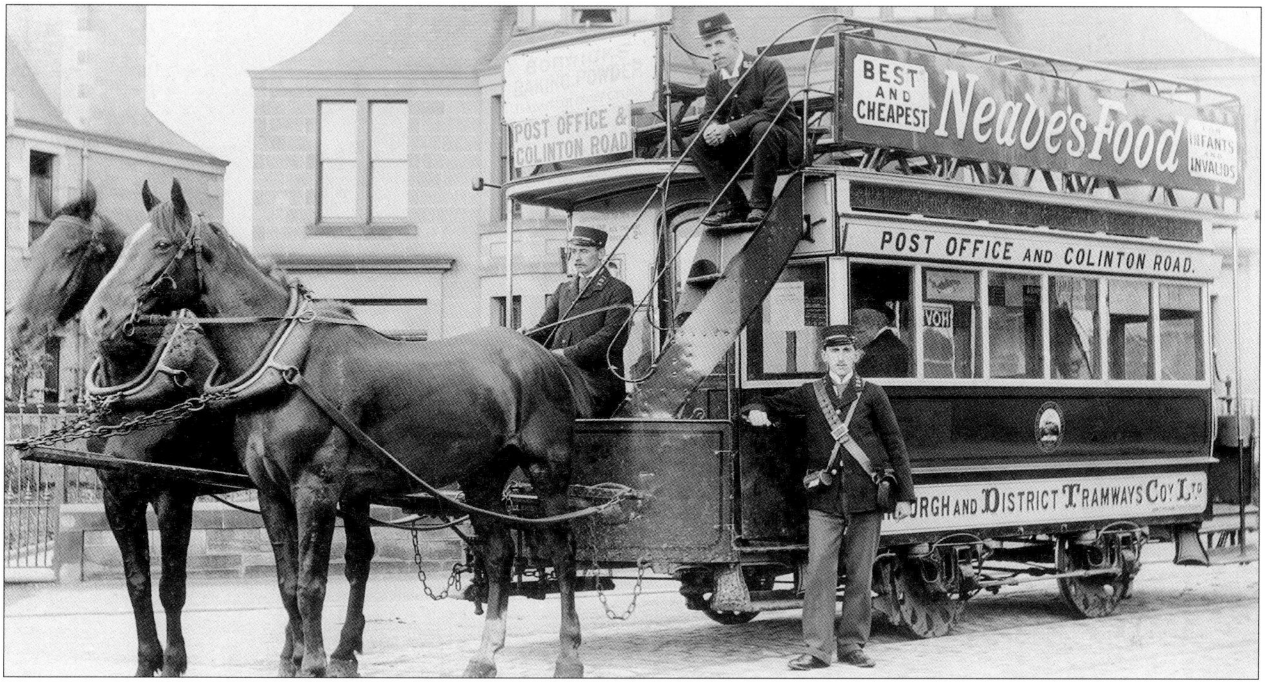

Colinton Road terminus was actually at the end of Polwarth Gardens, where this scene was recorded of car 89. The car was new in June 1896 and took the number formerly carried by an open toastrack. A Shrubhill product, it is similar, except for small detail differences, to the standard tram design evolved for Glasgow Corporation's fleet of 1894.

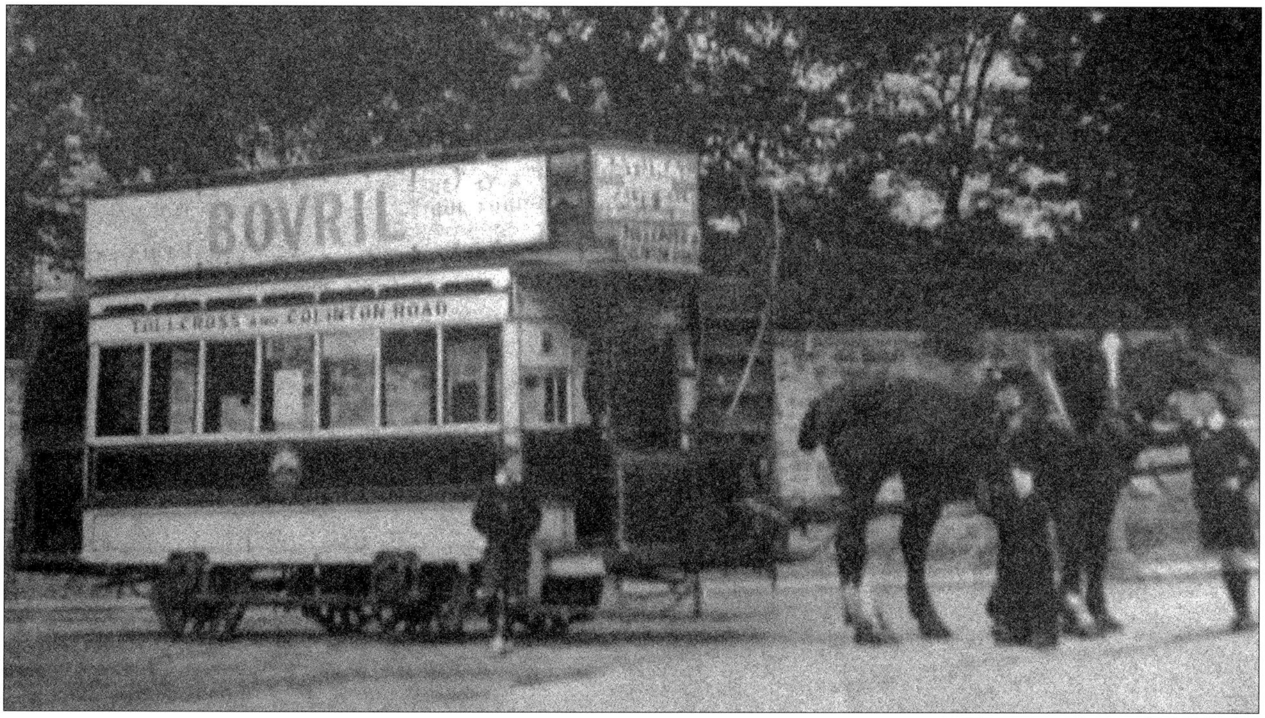

Now as 'Edinburgh's Last Car' this car (former car 170) reappeared on 21 July 1906 as '47' replacing an 'Exhibition' design car of that number on the Colinton Road shuttle (along with cars 5 and 72).

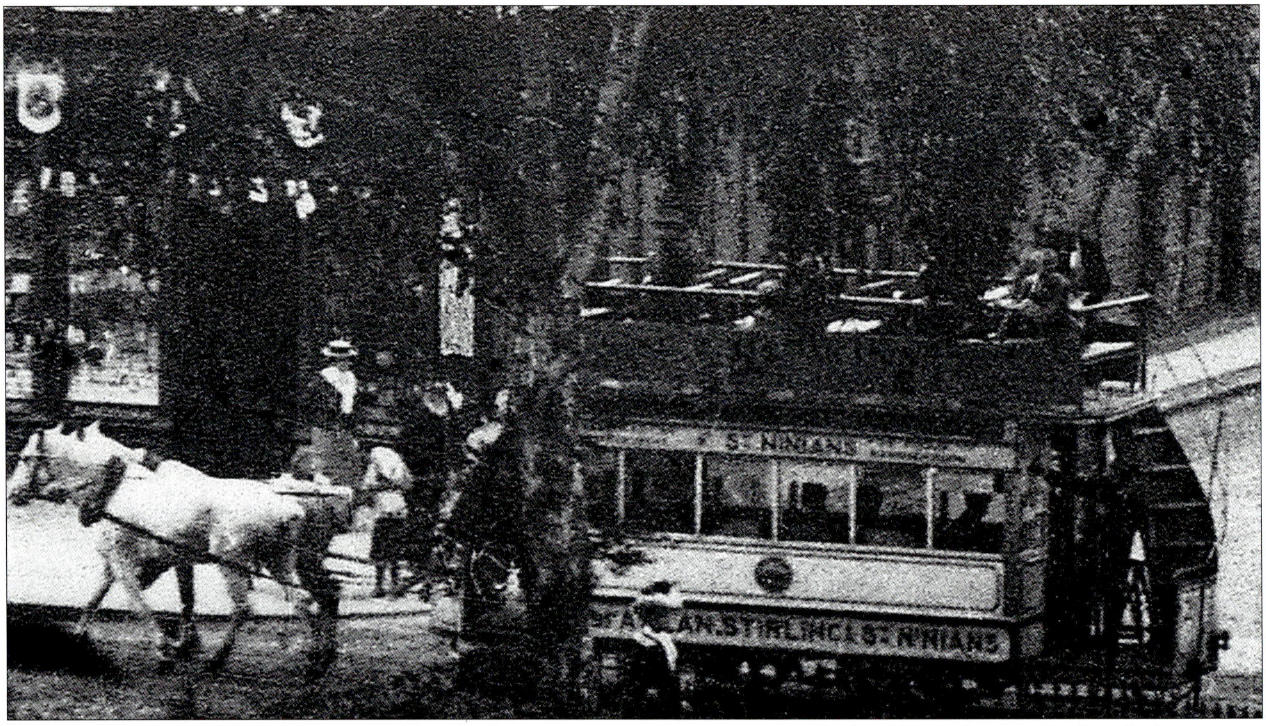

Above. Three Edinburgh horse cars were sold to the Stirling tramways in 1900, this view showing one – still in the livery of the Morningside Circular route – in Bridge of Allan in August 1902. The EDTCo badge has been replaced by that of the local company, the 'Wolf on the Rock'. It is one of Edinburgh's newest light-weight cars. Further purchases were of the 'Exhibition' design.

Opposite top. Said to have been photographed on the last operating day of Leith Corporation's horse cars. The car is on a shortened route from Seafield to Bonnington Terrace at the foot of Restalrig Road. The Corporation did not repaint the horse cars – a board indicating their ownership was screwed to the right hand end of the rocker panel.

Opposite bottom. An enlargement of the photograph on the post card of 'Leith's Last Horse Car'. With no similarity to any other Edinburgh horse tram, this is knifeboard seat car 170, a number issued to the EDTCo in May 1900. It was with the ESTCo by mid-1901, passed to Leith Corporation in October 1904 then sold back to the EDTCo in June 1906 where it became the final '47'. Its origin is unknown.

trams, hence only a small number from the large fleets being disposed of in both Glasgow and Edinburgh found new homes. Surprisingly perhaps Aberdeen, of all places, considered purchase of some Edinburgh open cars, but decided against, as they were '… not of handsome appearance'.[218] Six cars were sold in 1900-2 to the Stirling and Bridge of Allan Tramways, while the Street Tramways Company, working the Leith lines, was able to replace old cars with newer vehicles. Six changed hands in 1900 then further three (7, 75 and 170) the following year. The last of these brings to note that, when new cable cars to fleet number 169 had been delivered, two horse trams were then given numbers 170 and 171, the former a knifeboard seat car, the other a garden seat car. The identity of 170 changed yet again after it was sold and the number re-used for a toastrack. When through running at Pilrig ended in 1899, the need for one sequence of fleet numbers ended and some duplication with new cable cars followed.

Rolling stock of the ESTCo reached a minimum (20) in July 1898, after handing over the final four cars of the Portobello line, but they also had 44 buses and 13 'other vehicles'. Car numbers increased to 26 in

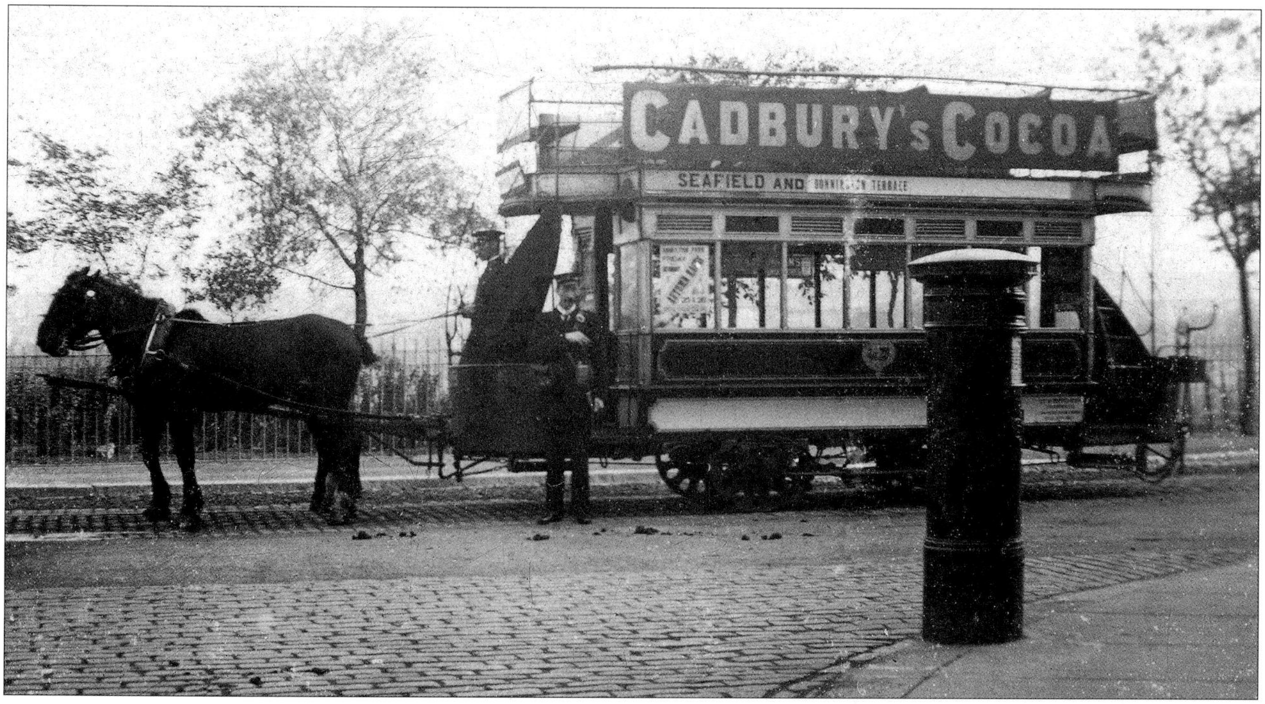
CADBURY's COCOA
SEAFIELD AND

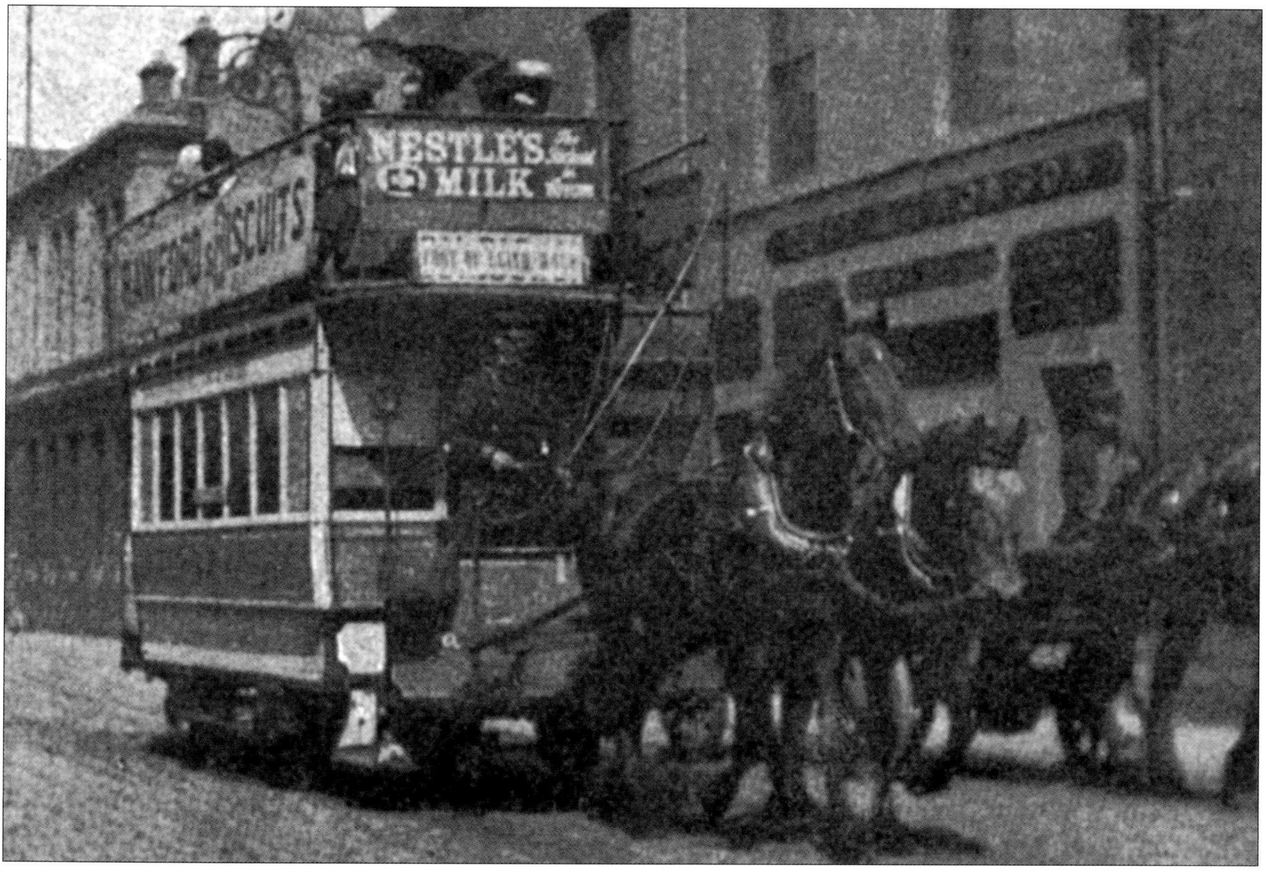
NESTLE'S
MILK

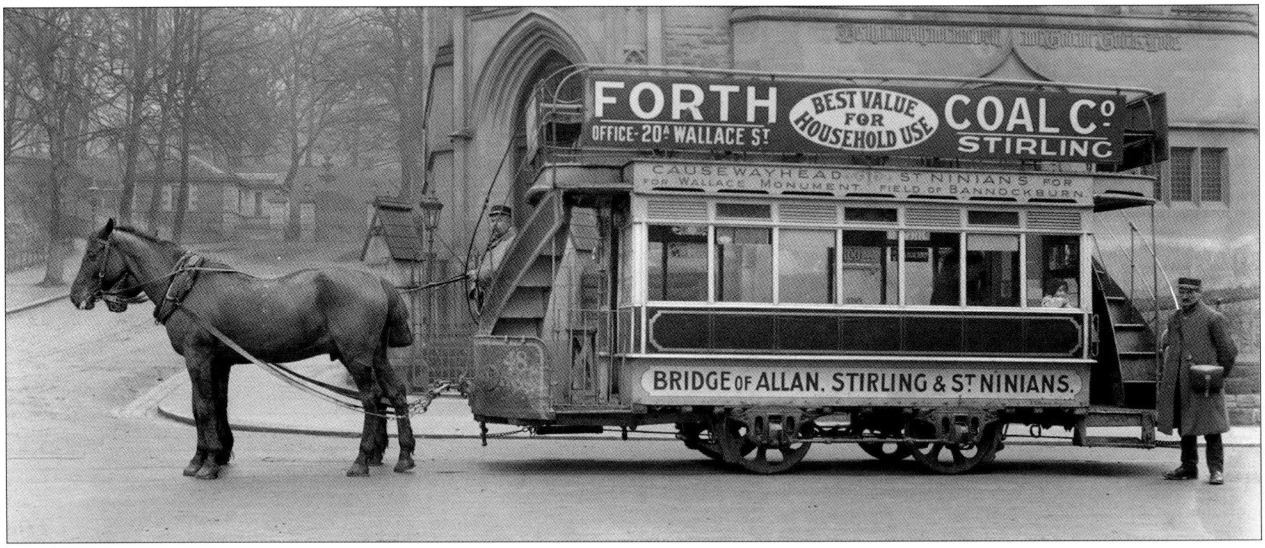

Leith Corporation sold two of their cars (39 & 83) to Stirling in December 1905 where they became 47 and 48. The latter is seen at Bridge of Allan terminus in December 1913, its Edinburgh antecedents fairly obvious. The 'Exhibition' design is quite distinctive, apparently constructed only by the EDTCo. The car ran in Stirling until ending of the horse tram service on 5 February 1920.

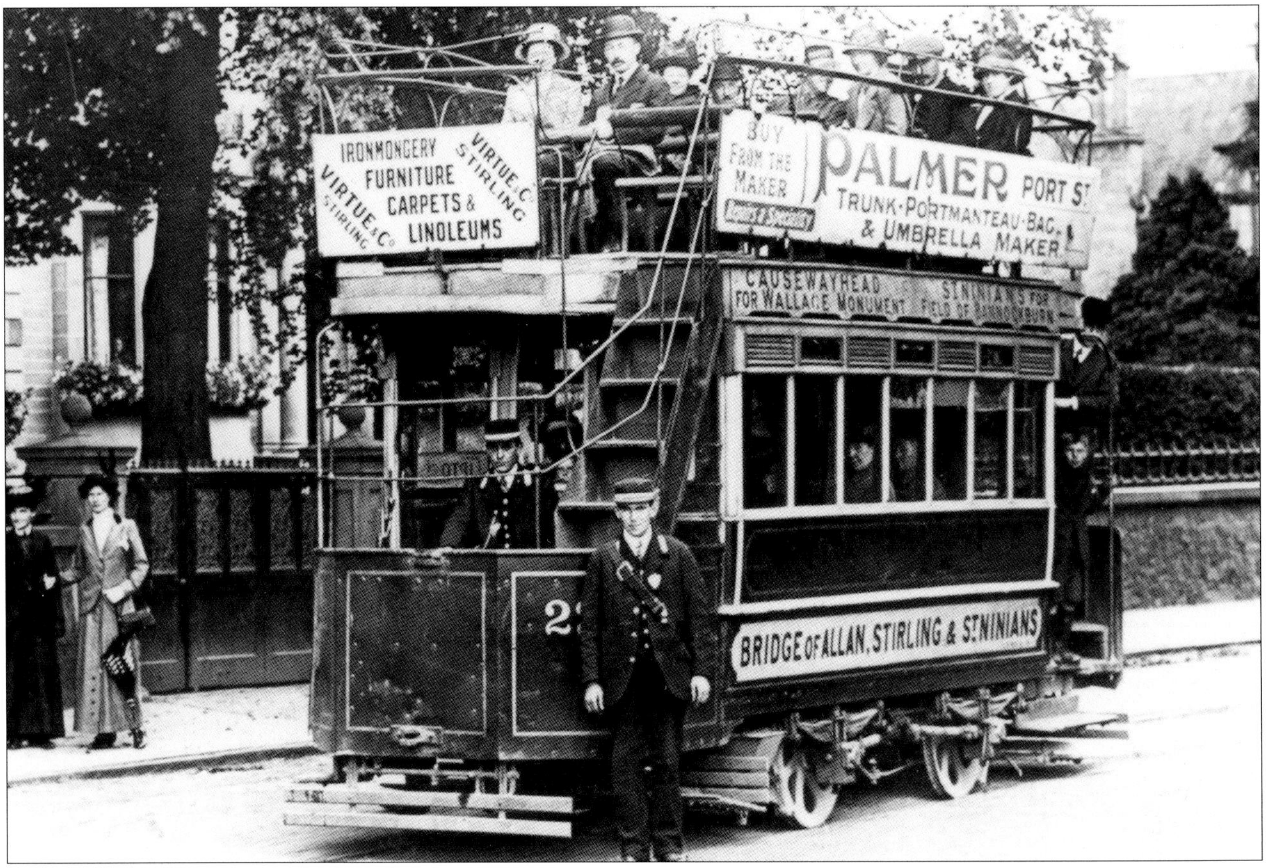

Stirling's horse tram 22, from the 1902 purchase of three Edinburgh cars, was fitted in 1913 with a petrol engine and ran – relatively successfully – until the tramway closed in its entirety on 25 May 1920. For the last four months it was the only tram operated on the line. Again its Edinburgh pedigree is apparent, but by 1917 it was looking rather tired.

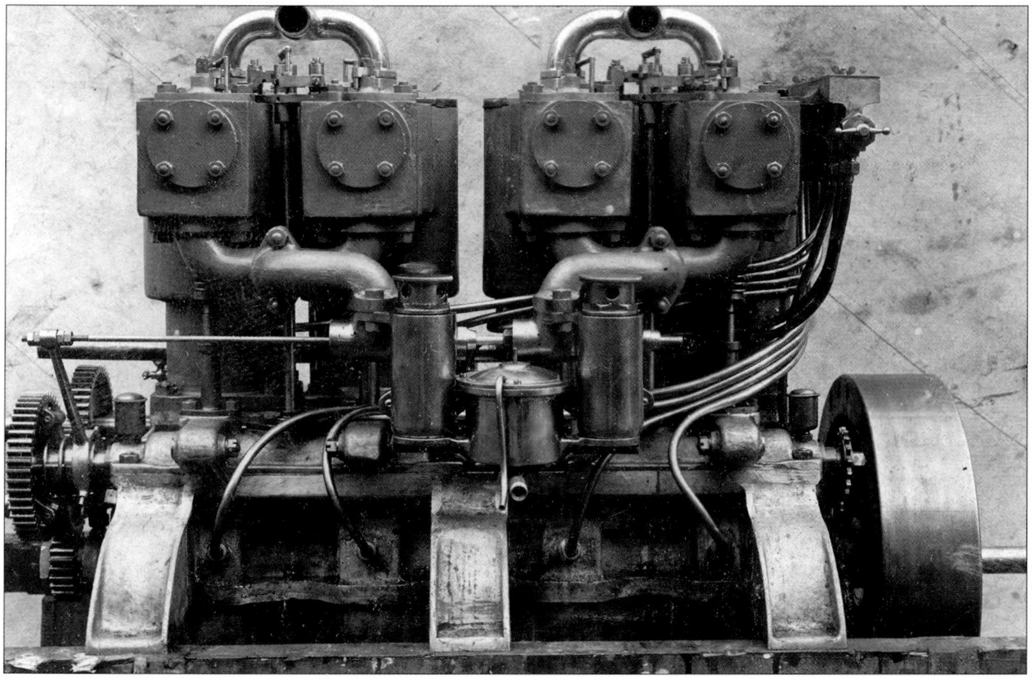

The redundant EDTCo horse car sold to the Stirling's Motor Construction Company was used to demonstrate that Company's petrol engine for tramcars. This shows the four cylinder engine, as also used in buses built by the company.

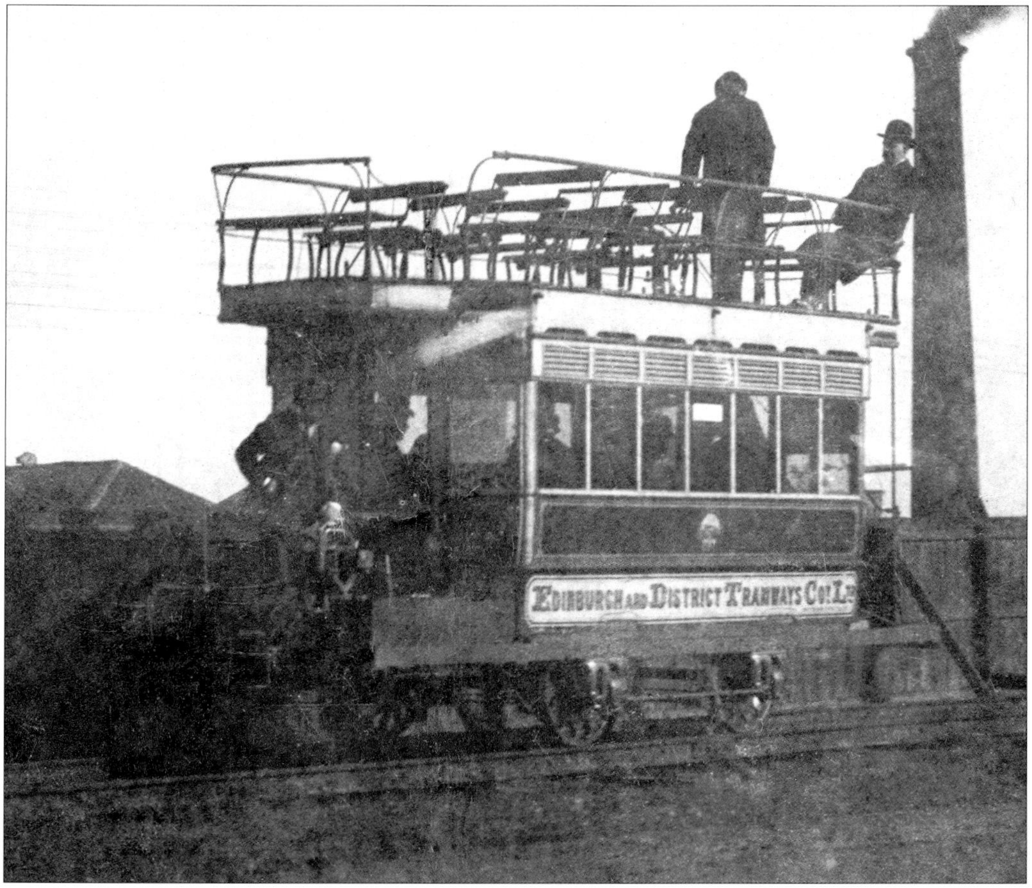

This is the first petrol tram on the test track at Stirling's Granton works. The factory was originally built in 1897–8 for the Madelvic Motor Company and used for motor car fabrication, and the (still standing) building is the oldest such specialist structure in Great Britain, and possibly the world. The tram has had the stair at the nearest end removed with the engine fitted here. The body is on a new underframe with the wheels off-centre to balance the uneven weight.

1900 then to 29 by 1902.[219] This figure was constant until the October 1904 sale to Leith Corporation but, during this period, older cars were replaced by bargain 'hand-me-downs' from the EDTCo. Leith horse cars are listed below, and the Corporation's Minutes give some detail of sales. For some reason Leith 26 went back to the EDTCo – less wheels and axles – in February 1905 for £4.10s. This car 26 was probably built by the ESTCo before 1893, passed to the EDTCo in 1894, was re-sold to the ESTCo c1901, went to Leith Corporation in 1904, and then finally returned to the EDTCo in 1905! Finally, in July 1906, Leith's 110 and 170 – both knifeboard seat cars – were sold back to the EDTCo in running order for £6 each.[220] They were then placed on the Colinton Road final horse route, for which they were given numbers 5 and 47, the previous cars of these numbers presumably beyond repair! Two more, 39 and 83, were sold in December 1905 at a slightly better price of £12.10s, to the Stirling tramway (becoming 47 and 48 there). Both were used until final horse operation on 5 February 1920, while Stirling 22 from the earlier sale (which had

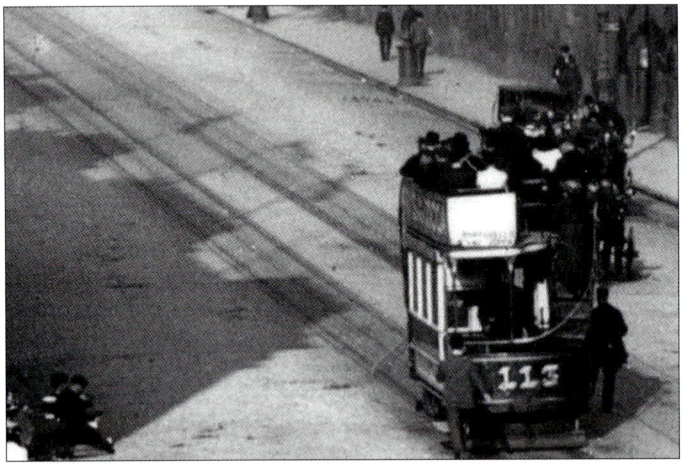

Seen in Waterloo Place, running as a (fairly) standard open-top cable car is number 113. It had only a short life as a horse car, from July 1897 to 1901. Several of the last horse cars built at Shrubhill had three large side windows to the saloon, and sat nine a-side against ten of the standard cable tram.

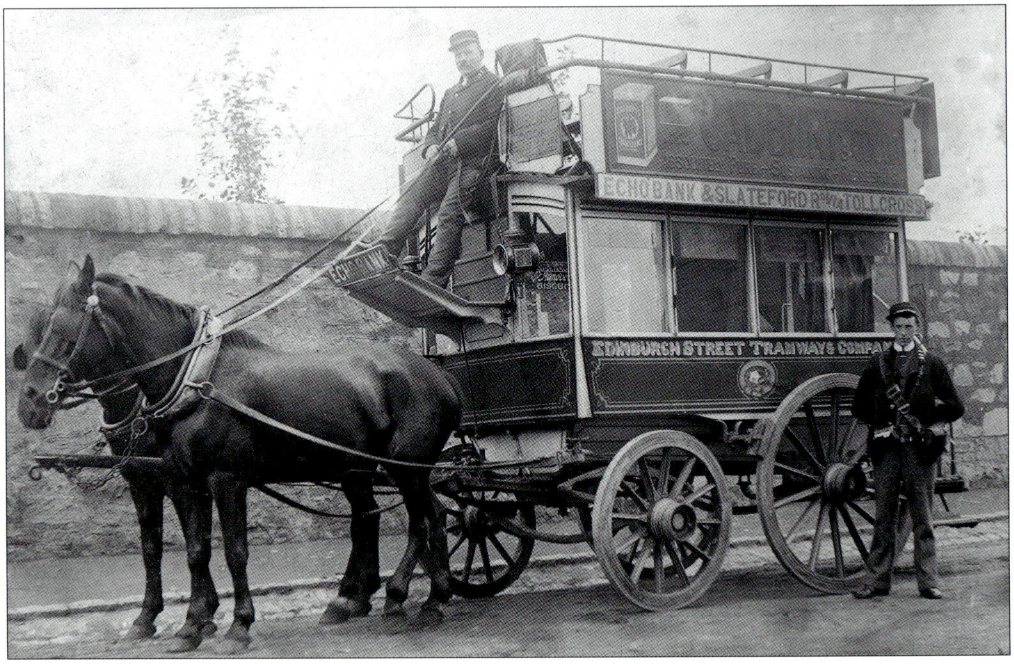

In its latter years the ESTCo expanded its bus and coaching side, but was quite careful to avoid competition with the other company. This view shows an ESTCo bus at Echobank – a destination which might puzzle some of today's travellers – but they would recognise Cameron Toll. This is the foot of Dalkieth Road (at Newington Cemetery) from where the bus ran by Tollcross to Slateford.

been fitted with a 25 hp Commer petrol engine in 1913) ran until final abandonment of that line four months later. Horse cars retained by the District Company reduced to ten by the end of 1903, then to six (5, 17, 35, 47, 72 and 75) by 1906 – some of these being cars purchased from Leith at the end of horse operation there.

Final horse car operation in Edinburgh was on 24 August 1907, and in the following year the last horse to cable car conversion was licensed – as number 17 – from 16 May 1908; this would be the former (and final) 72, by then the only remaining garden seat car. The newest horse cars had been designed for easy conversion, but in the event, only five were so treated. Horse 53 and 113 (then just two years old) re-entered service as cable cars of the same numbers on 1 August 1901. Two conversions were licensed as cable 15 and 19 on 23 August 1905, also from late 1898-built horse cars, probably numbers 44 and 114. With fewer seats than the norm these five, plus pioneer 112, were normally found on the Portobello run, all surviving to the end of cable operation. In January 1924 15 and 17 were rebuilt as departmental cars, plus 19 in July; 53 and 113 were scrapped. In 1935 the survivors (15, 17 & 19) were renumbered 4, 3 and 5, all being scrapped in the early 1940s; with number 3 – the last remaining ex- horse car – replaced by works car 10 (itself the former 112) in 1946.

One former Edinburgh horse tram had a surprising further use; in 1904 Stirling's Motor Construction Company of Granton purchased one and fitted it with a four-cylinder petrol engine of their own make. A short test track was laid behind the factory and Leith Council sent a deputation to see it, considering this instead of electrification; the demonstrations failed to convince. A further tram was built by Stirling's, to 3 ft 6 ins gauge for Perth Corporation. Relations became strained after delayed delivery of the body (from an English builder). When it eventually reached Perth, trials soon proved that their track was largely unsuitable. While tram horses learned to pull to the correct line at junctions, a self-propelled car had no such nous,

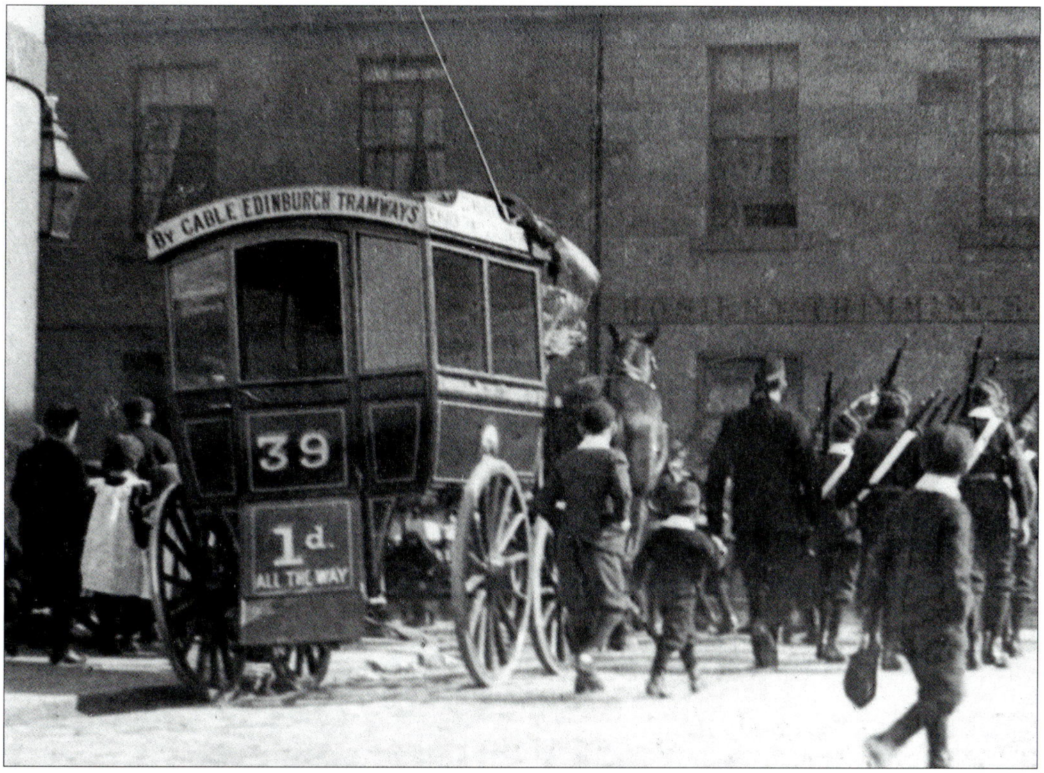

This small bus was run by the EDTCo from Newhaven's St Andrew's Square (now Fishmarket Square) up to Goldenacre to meet at their terminus the cable trams for Princes Street. Marching past is a detachment from the local Boys' Brigade – complete with rifles.

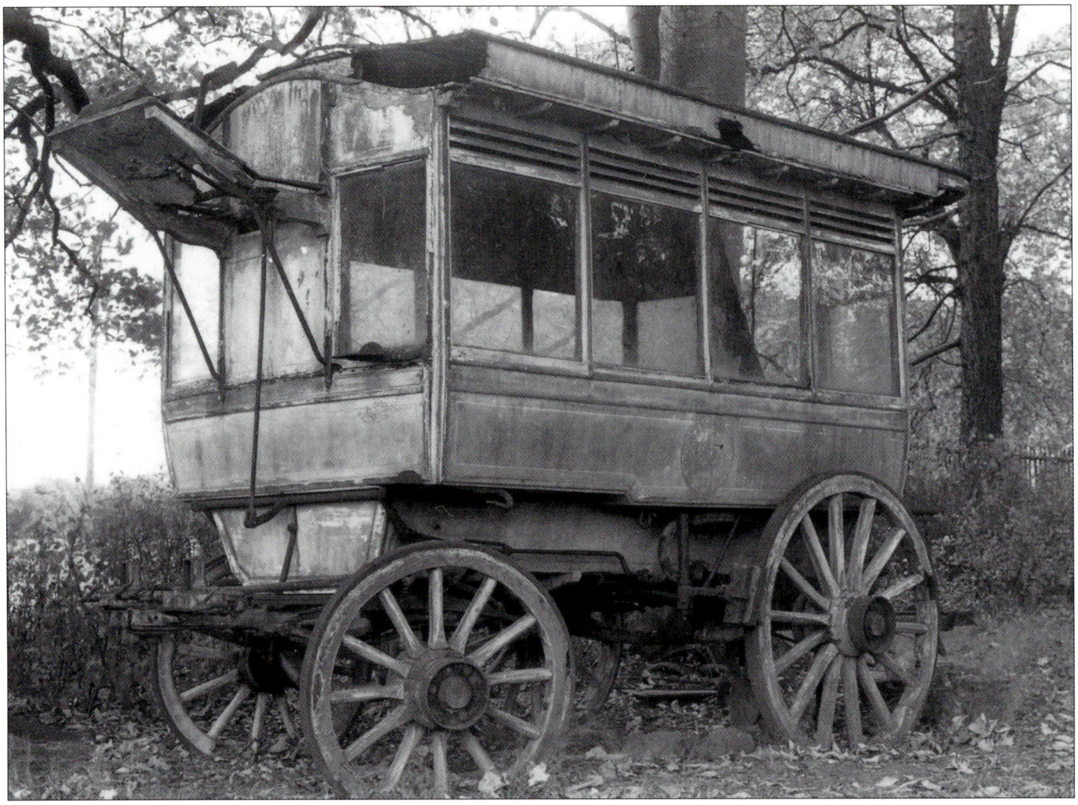

In the 1950s this old Edinburgh horse bus (number 83) was located on a farm near Pencaitland. Remarkably complete, it was restored by the Transport Department and was much in evidence during the week prior to operation of Edinburgh's last (first generation) electric trams.

hence it frequently derailed when confronted by points without a moveable tongue.

So far as is known, these two trams were Stirling's only attempts to break into this market. It was suggested in the contemporary technical press that an order had been obtained from Australia; this *could* relate to a 2½ -mile line of 3 ft 6 ins gauge at Leonora in Western Australia. On the other hand, this report *could also* have resulted from a journalist's misinterpretation that the 'Perth' which he had heard referred to was the capital of Western Australia, rather than the Scottish city. No record has been found of operation of any Scottish-built petrol trams in the antipodes, although the Stirling Company did export several *buses* there ... but that is another story.

The Street Tramways Company was required, when it gave up the powers for the Trinity lines, to operate horse buses in lieu of the authorised tramways, and their first five buses were those obtained in November 1874 from Croall for this purpose. As more omnibus services were introduced, so numbers of such vehicles increased until in 1881, 14 assorted buses and coaches were licensed, the newest built at Shrubhill. As all Edinburgh's horse buses and coaches were numbered in one series, the licence number was used as a 'fleet number'. Some had this painted under the driver's footrest while others used the outer stair stringer. Numbers allocated to Street Tramway buses included 39, 57, 60, 66, 83, 102, 105, 110 and 127. Probably, as with the trams, when a vehicle was replaced it would take that number vacated by its predecessor.

At division of assets in December 1893, the Street Company owned, and retained 13 buses plus 4 tourist coaches. This side of the business was then rapidly expanded and by 1900 non-tram stock had increased to 49 buses and 14 other vehicles, with many of these additions built in London. When their tramways were sold to Leith Corporation the Company had to liquidate the business; all remaining vehicles were consequently auctioned off in early 1905.

Street Tramways Company cars, 1871–1885 (from contemporary sources)

Date	*Builder*	*No off*	*Seats*	*Notes*	*Total*
[Seating indicated thus: outside seats/saloon seats]					
11.71	TCWCo	16?	20/18	'Large car'; nine(?) shortened: three loaned 1877	16
02.72	Croall	4?	16/14	'Small car'	20
03.72	Croall?	1	30	'Rotunda car'	
?.72	Boyall	4?	?		24
?.72	TCWCo?	4?	20/20	'Medium car' 'cars built elsewhere in Scotland'	28
10.72	Drew& Burnett	4	?	2 Single ended; 2 Double ended	32
06.73				[License fees]	32
?.73	Unknown	6	16/16	'New cars'	38
06.74				[43 vehicles total, less 5 buses]	38
by 12.74				[Nine (original) cars rebuilt 'equal to new']	
05.76	Unknown	4?	0/35?	Single deck open 'toastrack' cars	
08.76				'Average number of cars in use, 41½'	42+
During 1877				'Three worn-out cars replaced'	
				Two cars loaned to Dundee, one to Scott-Moncrieff	
05.77	Stephenson	2	30/24		
12.77	Starbuck	2	22/16		
12.77	Boyal	6?	?/?		
?.78	Brown, Marshalls	4?	16/16?		
06.78				[First annual Board of Trade Return]	52
06.78				[License fees]	55
05.79	ESTCo	1	?/?	First Shrubhill built car	
06.79				[Board of Trade Return]	49
08.79	ESTCo	1	26/24	Second Shrubhill built car (Single ended)	
06.80				[Board of Trade Return]	54
06.81				[Board of Trade Return]	56
01.82				[Report]	60
04.82	ESTCo	2?	?/?	Eades patent reversible car	
07.82	ESTCo	6?	0/16	Eades patent reversible cars (single deck)	
07.82	ESTCo	4?	0/32	Single deck open, some with light canvas roof	
12.82				[Report] 58 close + 9 open =	67
06.83				[Board of Trade Return]	72
07.83				[Report] 62 close + 10 open =	72
07.83	ESTCo	4?	0/24	Single deck cars for Morningside Toll route	
01.84				[Report] 64 close + 10 open =	74
06.84				[Board of Trade Return]	72
07.84				[Report] 62 close + 10 open =	72
01.85				[Report] 63 close + 10 open =	73

ROLLING STOCK DETAILS (from Thomson note book, licence books, press reports etc) after c 1893

[Grouped by seating capacity – probably an over-simplification]

'A' 18/18 (Knifeboard seats) Varied designs, including '1886 Exhibition style'

Many Shrubhill built cars incorporated reusable parts of earlier cars, while continuous upgrading saw suitable old cars rebuilt with new stairs, seating etc.

7 window saloon. Total 26

1	
2	
3	
4	
9	21 April 1896 re-licensed as GS, DE 26/18 [Type 'P']
10	
11	24 December 1895 re-licensed as GS, DE 26/18 [Type 'P']
20	21 April 1896 re-licensed as GS, DE 26/18 [Type 'P']
23	**Preserved Car**
24	
25	scrapped 1894
29 *	scrapped 1897
30 *	scrapped 1897
40	
45	Exhibition Car 1886
53	
56	scrapped 1898 [per licence records]
57	
61	scrapped 1894/5
63	scrapped by 1896
65	
67	
69	4 May 1896 re-licensed as GS, DE 26/18 [Type 'P']
70	21 May 1896 re-licensed as GS, DE 26/18 [Type 'P']
75	scrapped 1896
76	scrapped 1894

* seats 20/18
GS = Garden seats
DE = Double width entrances
[re-licensed cars were probably essentially new cars, see 'P' below]

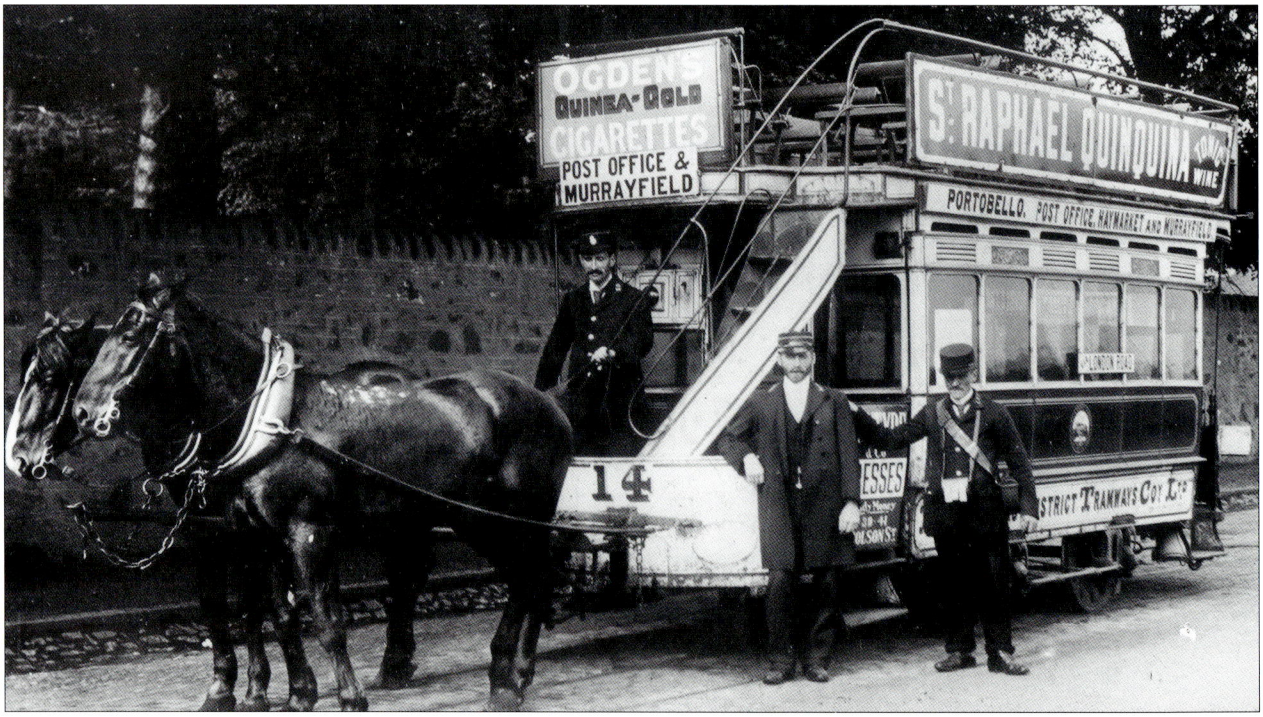

This car 14 is probably a derivative from the Brown Marshall built car shown on page 114. This particular vehicle, seen at Murrayfield in May 1900, was licensed from the end of November 1899 and is identified by the rounded window corners – these do not appear in other designs built subsequently at the Company's Shrubhill workshops.

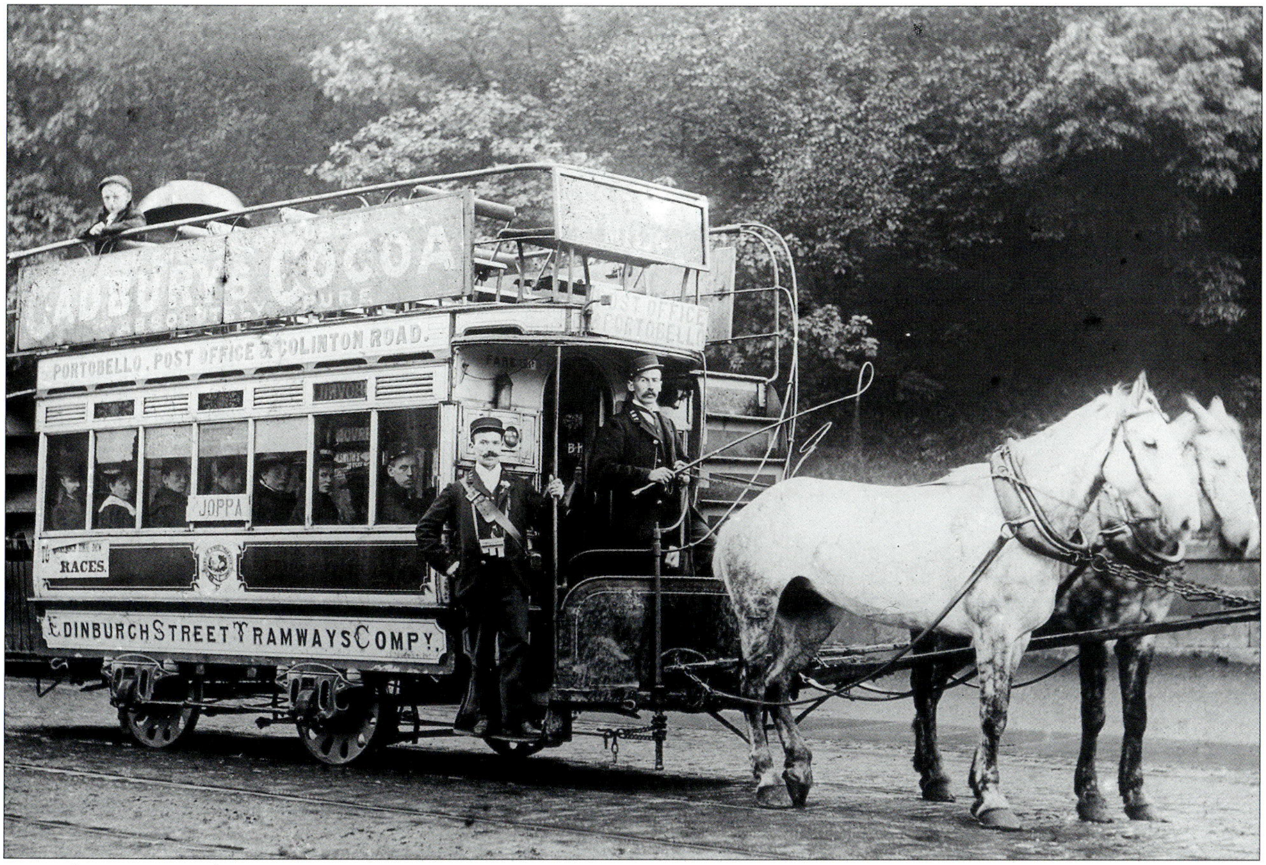

Car 80 (most probably) in the summer of 1898 at Colinton Road terminus on the long route to Portobello and Joppa which was operated jointly with the District Company from 1893 to July 1898. The extension to Joppa was opened in May 1897. The cars on this route used yellow as the indentifying colour, showing up on orthochromatic film as the dark panels on the waist and dash.

'B' 26/18 Shrubhill '1886 Exhibition design' with garden seats. Total 44

7 window saloon (some had 6 or 8 window saloons with seat adjustment)

5, 7, 8, 13, 14, 15, 16, 17, 18, 19, 20, 21, 22, 26, 27, 28, 31, 32, 33, 34, 35, 36, 37, 38, 39, 41, 42, 43, 46, 47, 48, 49, 50, 51, 52, 58, 59, 62, 79, 80, 81, 82, 83, 84.

'C' 30/22 Stephenson New York 1877. Total 2

8 window saloon
'Altered several times. At one time had stair at back end only, but now have a stair at each end' Originally knifeboard (22/22) later rebuilt with garden seats
6, 12

'D' 30/20 Garden seats. Total 1

77 (Thomson has 52 seats total)

'E' 22/20 (as licensed – Thomson has 18/18) Knifeboard seats. Total 2

71, 72 both scrapped 1896 (possibly the Starbuck built cars)

'F' 16/16 (as licensed – Thomson has 18/18) Knifeboard seats. Total 2

54, 55 (possible rebuild of Morningside single deck saloons.)

'G' 18/16 (as licensed – Thomson has 44 as 18/18) Knifeboard seats. Total 4

44, 64, 68,
78 rebuilt to single deck canopy (6/18) 1895

'H' 32 seat (16/16?) Knifeboard seats. Total 1

73 scrapped 1894

'I' 30 seat (16/14?) Knifeboard seats. Total 1

66 scrapped 1894/5 (possibly the 'Rotunda' car?)

'J' 29 seat (??) Knifeboard seats. Total 1

60 scrapped 1894/5 (possibly another 'Rotunda' style car?)

'K' 35 seat open toastrack [maximum number, 10 in 1883.] Total 6. Introduced from 1876

85, 86, 87,
88 scrapped by 1895
89 scrapped by 1896
100 possibly original number 90, later re-numbered 110

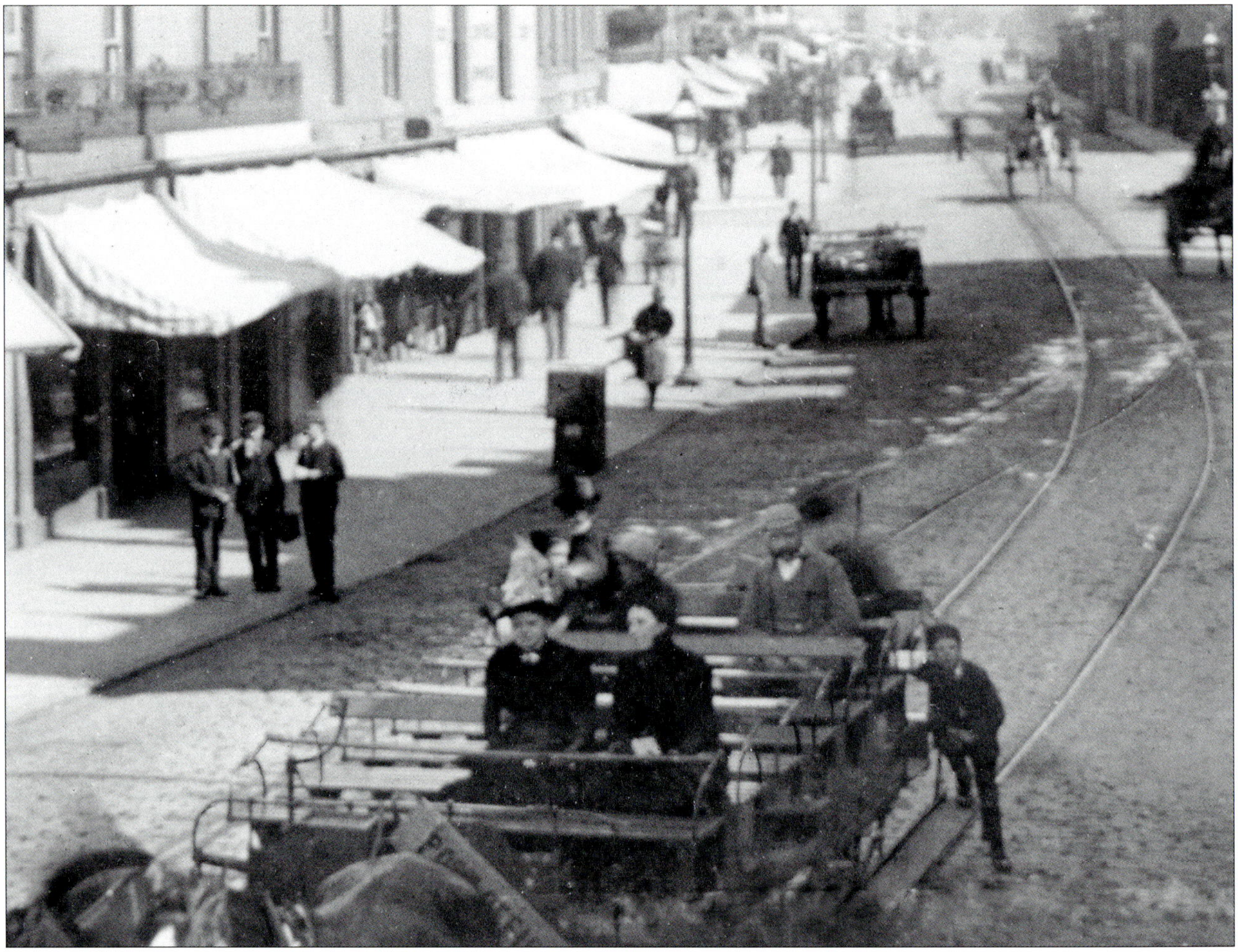

Before the introduction of the first 'canopy' cars, from the summer of 1876 the ESTCo ran these open 'toastracks'. Popular in the summer on the Portobello run, they were less popular in cold mornings when used for early workmen's operations. Eventually ten were owned; at the split, one of the six then remaining in stock was passed to the ESTCo.

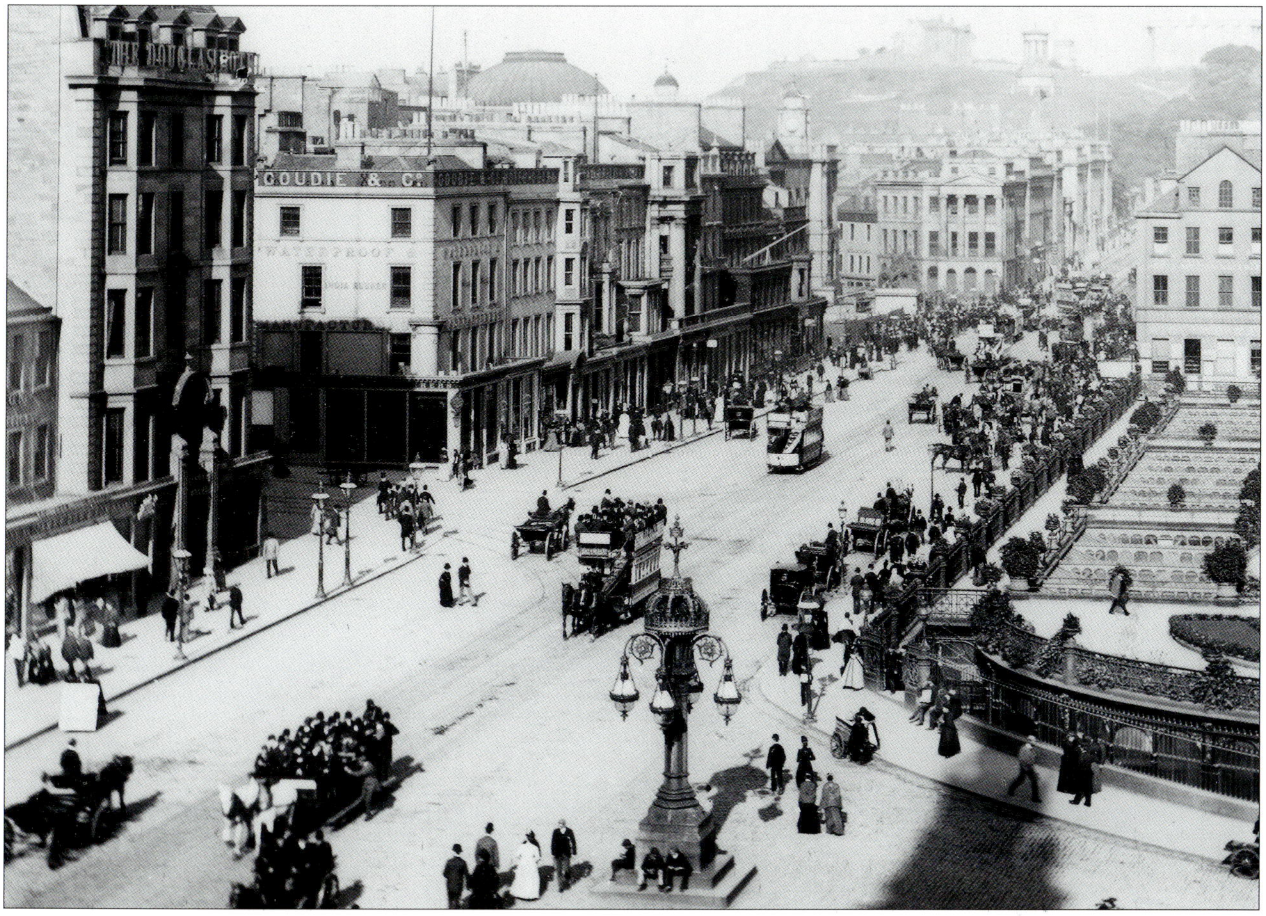

'L' 'Canopy' Cars, single deck (+3 seats on each platform). Total in 1894, 10

[Memorandum of August 1891 implies cars 60, 61 & 62 then canopy]

63 0/38 = 6/32? possible nominal 'rebuild' from 18/18
90 0/38 = 6/32?
91 6/28
92★ 6/32
93 6/28? 'Old Style' (T)
94 6/28? scrapped 1895
95★ 6/32 built 1890 (T)
96★ 6/32
97★ 6/32
98★ 6/28 built 1890 as electric car named *Clerk Maxwell*
99★ 6/28 built 1890 as electric car named *Faraday*
65 35 seat canopy car – roofed toastrack – of c1882, broken up (T)
82 24 seat canopy car – six window saloon with monitor roof built 1883, this possibly last of those for Morningside Toll route

★ cross seats inside

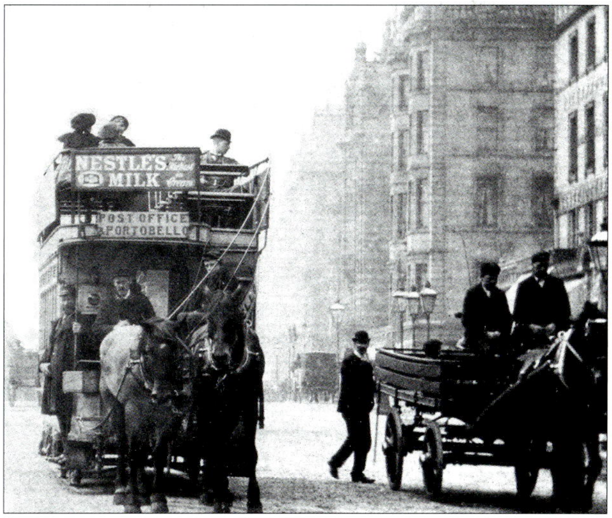

Top. Busy Princes Street scene with a fully laden open toastrack car hastening westwards – perhaps with a load of supporters heading for Tynecastle?

Above. 'Exhibition' design car at the east end of Princes Street.

'M' 20/20 ex-Glasgow T&OCo Knifeboard seats. Total 13

8 window saloon
74 21 September 1894
73 15 October 1894
76 26 October 1894
25 30 November 1894
101 7 December 1894
102 31 December 1894
103 31 December 1894
104* 22 February 1895
105* 22 February 1895
60* 5 April 1895
61* 5 April 1895
66* 5 April 1895
94* 5 April 1895

* rebuilt in Edinburgh with double width entrances

'N' 22/18 Metropolitan Co Garden seats, Double entrance. Total 4 (of Glasgow Corporation 1894 design).

6 window saloon
106 24 July 1895
107 26 July 1895
108 26 July 1895
109 31 July 1895

'O' 18/18 Shrubhill build Knifeboard seats, Double entrance. Total 1

6 window saloon
110 1 January 1896 [renumbered '5' in July 1906 then ran till end of horse traction]

'P' 26/18 Shrubhill 'rebuilt' cars as noted above. Total 5

(probably more new car than rebuild, but incorporating parts from original cars of these numbers for book-keeping purposes)
6 or 7 window saloon, Garden seats, Double entrance
11 24 December 1895
9 21 April 1896
20 21 April 1896
69 4 May 1896
70 21 May 1896

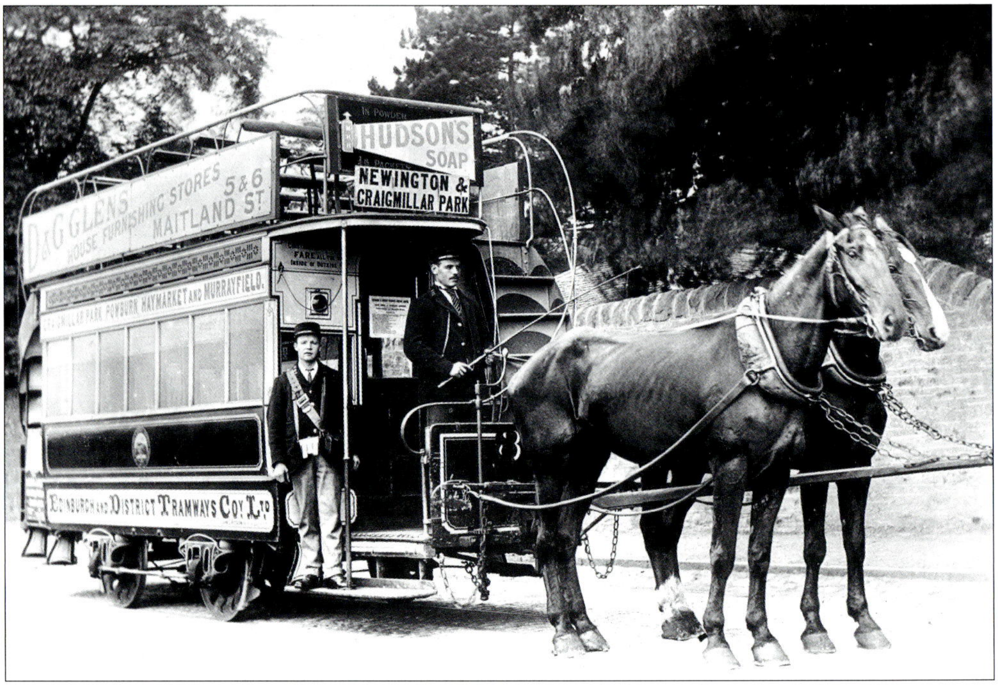

Car 88 is seen at the end of horse operation to Murrayfield (foot of Ellersley Road). It was new in service at the beginning of January 1896, but had a relatively short life, replaced by a cable car of the same number on 5 November 1900. Track for cable operation is in place.

'Q' 26/18 Shrubhill build Garden seats, Double entrance. Total 8

6 or 7 window saloon
88 2 January 1896
89 6 June 1896
100 29 June 1896
71 9 September 1896
72 9 September 1896
55 7 December 1896
75 16 December 1896
111 24 December 1896

[Prototype cable car]

112 13 October 1897 Shrubhill built, seating 28/18

'R' 24/18 Shrubhill build Garden seats, Double entrance. Total 8

6 or 3 window saloon

44	13 July 1897	Probably sold to Stirling 1900
113	16 July 1897	Rebuilt as cable car August 1901, retaining number 113
29	27 Nov 1897	Probably sold to Stirling 1900
114	31 Dec 1897	Possibly rebuilt as cable car August 1905, number 15 or 19
78	31 Dec 1897	Probably renumbered 72 28 May 1899, then as cable car 17
30	25 Jan 1898	Probably sold to Stirling 1900
10	2 July 1898	Probably renumbered 5, September 1901
53	2 July 1898	Rebuilt as cable car August 1901, retaining number 53

(Dates given are for issue of first licence)

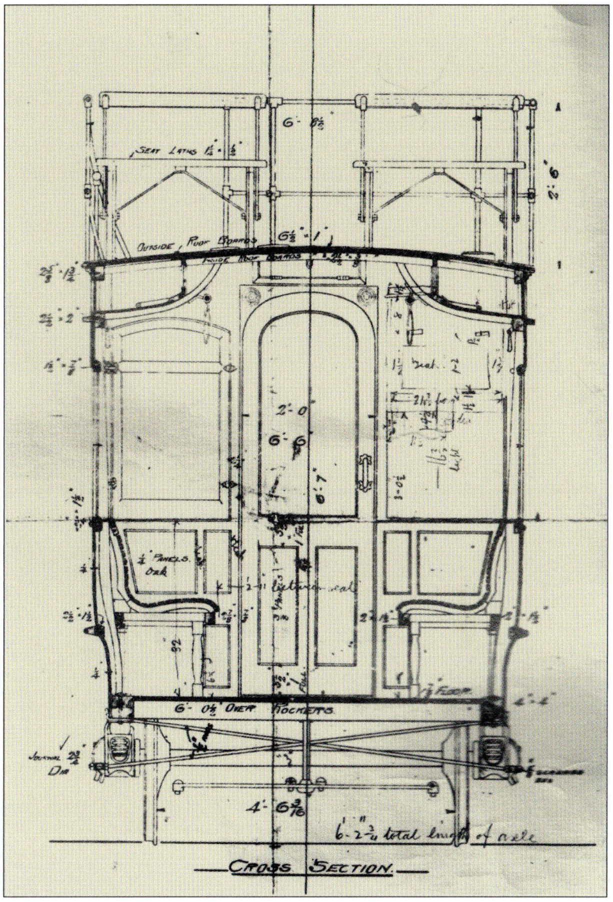

Cross-section drawing of the four 1896 horse trams (106 – 109) supplied to the EDTCo by Metropolitan Railway Carriage and Wagon Company of Birmingham in July 1895. All four were put initially on the Morningside Drive to Post Office route.

Horse cars retained by the ESTCo in 1894; 14, 15, 20, 21, 23, 26, 28, 38, 39, 44, 45, 46, 47, 49, 50, 51, 52, 53, 54, 63 (C), 79, 80, 81, 82, 83, 84, 85 (O), 87 (O), 90 (C), 95 (C). TOTAL 30

Transferred to the EDTCo in January 1896 from the above thirty were; 23, 44, 49, 52, 53, 85 (O). Total 6

Transferred to the EDTCo in July 1898 from the remaining twenty-four were; 47, 50, 51, 80. Total 4

Numbers 170 and 171 were issued to horse cars on 28 May and 7 July 1900 respectively. 170 was an 18/18 seven window knifeboard seat car, licensed until 28 May 1901 when it was then apparently purchased by the ESTCo for use in Leith. From 8 May 1901 to 28 May 1902 number 170 was then carried by a toastrack. 171 was a 26/18 garden seat car licensed until 28 May 1902. Both cars seem to be renumberings when their original numbers were re-issued.

Horse cars licensed (in Edinburgh) to end 1903; 5, 13, 17, 19, 25, 27, 35, 47, 49, 51, 52, 66, 72, 75, 76, 87, 90, 92, 97, 102, 108. Total 21

Final EDTCo horse cars, licensed to 28 May 1908; 5, 47, 72. Total 3

This last car 5 was the former 110 (seating 18/18), re-purchased from Leith Corporation in June 1906 and re-licensed by EDTCo from 12 July 1906. The final 47 was former 170 (seating 18/18) also re-purchased from Leith in June 1906 then re-licensed from 21 July 1906; the previous 5 and 47 had been 'Exhibition' design cars (seating 26/18).

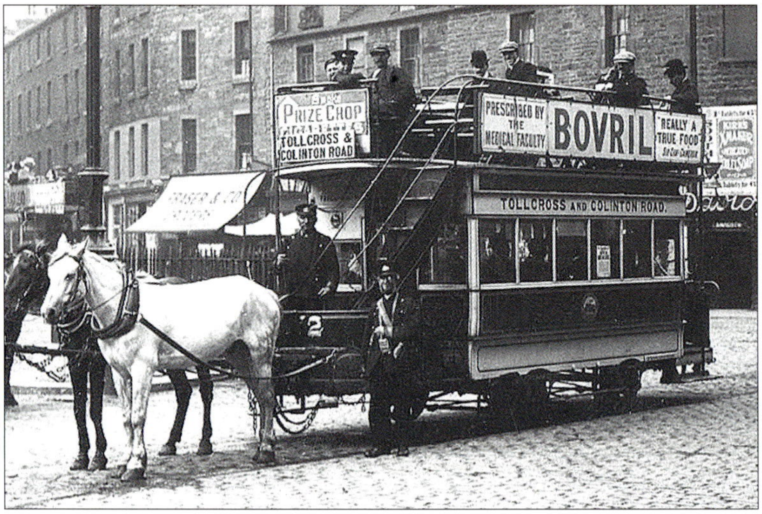

The last horse tram on the last day of operation in Edinburgh. Car 72 on its Tollcross siding, photographed on 24 August 1907. Behind in Earl Grey Street can be discerned one of the cable trams. This particular horse car had its life extended, rebuilt, to run as a cable car number 17. (City of Edinburgh Council – Edinburgh Libraries www.capitalcollections.org.uk)

Route colour details

As at 1894, from Thomson book
(First colour on waist panels, dash plates and stair stringers, second colour generally on rocker panels)

White and White: 1–12, 77
Red and White: 13–16, 29, 30, 67, 73
Blue and White: 17–25, 53, 63, 65, 81, 82
Green and Buff: 26–28, 31, 58, 59, 70
Chocolate and Buff: 32–37, 61, 62, 74
Oak and White: 38–46, 54–57, 64, 68, 69, 83, 84, and canopy cars
Yellow and Yellow: 47–52, 71, 72, 75, 76, 79, 80, and most open cars
Green and Yellow: 60, 66, 78

Later cars were painted;
White and White: new 60, new 71, new 90, new 94, 103, 104, 111
Red and White: new 75
Blue and White: new 100
Green and Buff: 110
Chocolate and Buff: new 73, new 74
Yellow and Yellow: new 55, new 61, new 76, new 89, 105
Ochre and White: new 25, new 66, 101
Dark Brown and White: new 72, new 88, 102, 106 – 109
Dark Brown and White (probably): Final eight horse cars built 1897–8

Individual car colours altered – plus others not recorded;
2 White to Blue and White (Feb 1896)
3 White to Oak and White (Aug 1895)
4 White to Blue and White (Nov 1895)
9 White to Blue and White (Nov 1894) when rebuilt with garden seats and double entrances; then White (April 1896)
11 White to Dark Brown and White (Dec 1895) when rebuilt with garden seats and double entrances
23 Blue and White to Dark Brown and White (Sept 1896) [no trace of second livery found on physical examination]
24 Blue and White to Green and Buff (Sept 1896)
32 Chocolate and Buff to White (1895)
33 Chocolate and Buff to Dark Brown and White (Oct 1895)
34 Chocolate and Buff to White (March 1896)
36 Chocolate and Buff to Dark Brown and White (Sept 1895)
37 Chocolate and Buff to Dark Brown and White (1895)
38 Oak and White to Red and White (1895)
39 Oak and White to Dark Brown and White (May 1897)
45 Oak and White to Dark Brown and Buff (1895)
46 Oak and White to Blue and White (1895)
47 Yellow to Orange-lead and Buff (1895)
49 Yellow to Orange-lead and Buff (1895)
50 Yellow to Orange-lead and Buff (Feb 1896)
52 Yellow to Orange-lead and Buff (1895)
62 Chocolate and Buff to Oak and White (1895)
64 Oak and White to Blue and White (July 1896)
68 Oak and White to Red and White (Nov 1895)
69 Oak and White to White (May 1896) when rebuilt with garden seats and double entrances
70 Green and Buff to Blue and White (May 1896) when rebuilt with garden seats and double entrances
72 Yellow to Chocolate and Buff (no date)
75 Yellow to Blue and White (June 1895)
78 Green and Yellow to Ochre and White (1895) when rebuilt as canopy car
79 Yellow to Red and White (Feb 1897)
80 Yellow to Orange-lead and Buff (May 1897)
93 Ochre Yellow to Oak and White (1892)
95 Oak and White to Ochre and White (1895)
98 Oak and White to Ochre and White (1895)

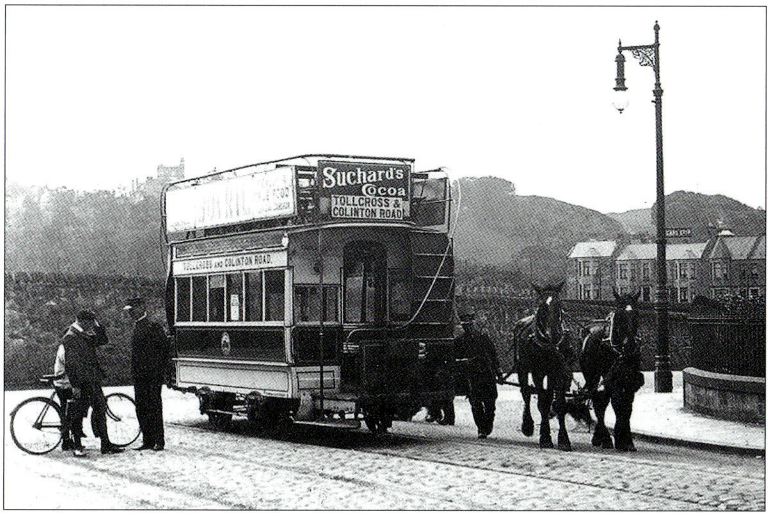

The driver of car 72 walks his horses round at the Colinton Road terminus on the last day of horse operation in Edinburgh, 24 August 1907.
(City of Edinburgh Council – Edinburgh Libraries www.capitalcollections.org.uk)

Route colours		*Approximate number of cars*
White and White	Circular Route (Morningside)	20
Red and White	Bernard Street and North Merchiston	10
Blue and White	Bernard Street and Craigmillar Park	8
Royal Blue and White	Bernard Street and Marchmont Road	8
Green and Buff	Seafield and Gorgie Road	8
Chocolate and Buff	Coltbridge and Powburn	12
Dark Brown and White	Meadowbank and Morningside Drive	12
Oak and White	Newhaven and Morningside Drive	18
Yellow and Yellow	Colinton Road and Portobello	17
Orange-lead and Buff	Colinton Road and Portobello	5
Ochre and White	Tron Church and Tollcross	5
Dark Brown and Buff	Post Office and Portobello (car 45 only)	1
Green and Yellow	Coltbridge and Powburn (car 60 only)	1
Green and Yellow	Register House and Haymarket (car 66 only)	1
Green and Yellow	Newhaven and Morningside Drive (car 78 only)	1

Orange-lead is a highly toxic lead based pigment of bright red/orange hue.
'Oak' can probably best be interpreted as varnished natural wood.

Leith Corporation

Horse cars at 23 October 1904;

7, 14, 15, 17, 22, 26, 28, 38, 39, 54, 63 (C), 67, 75, 79, 82, 83, 84, 87 (O), 90 (C), 95 (C), 100, 110, 170, plus six unidentified by number. Total 29

(Probably 20, 21, 45, 46, 81, and one other.)

Of these 7, 17, 22, 67, 75, 100, 110, 170 and the one unidentified car were most likely obtained by the ESTCo from the EDTCo during 1900–1.

Leith Corporation cars sold for further use:

39 and 83 to Stirling Tramways Coy in December 1905 (£12.10s each) becoming their 47 and 48.

26 (£4.10s, February 1905) 110 and 170 (£6 each, June 1906) to EDTCo

Two cars to the Motherwell Wagon & Rolling Stock Company

Four cars to East Pilton Hospital (later Northern General Hospital) for use as accommodation by patients with consumption – two patients per car – with some windows removed (for the benefit of their recovery!).

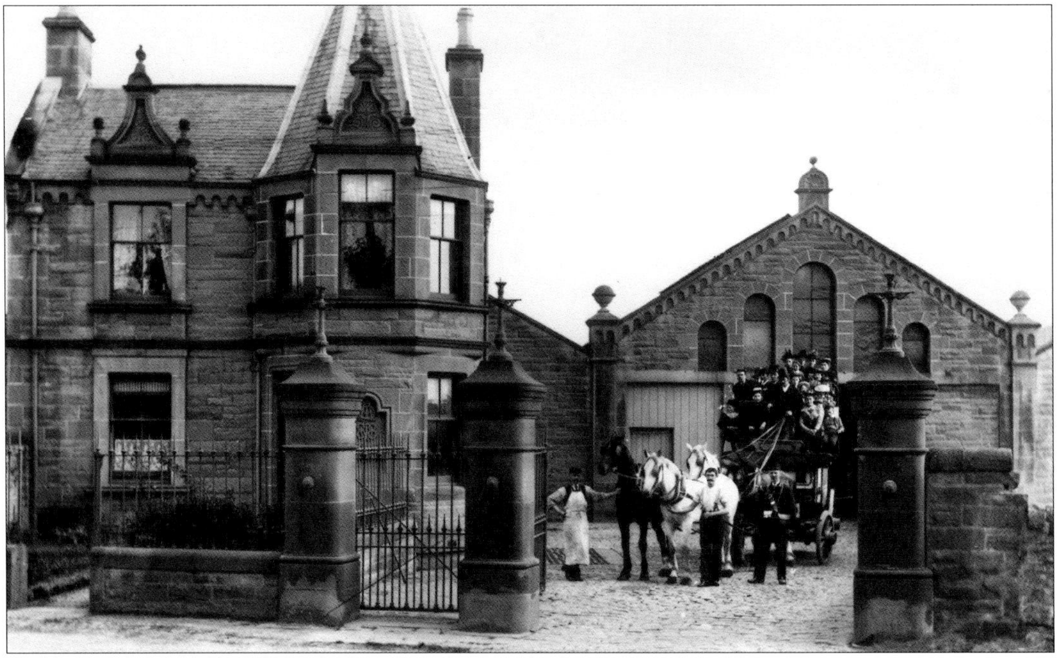

Corstorphine Stables. (courtesy Corstorphine Trust)

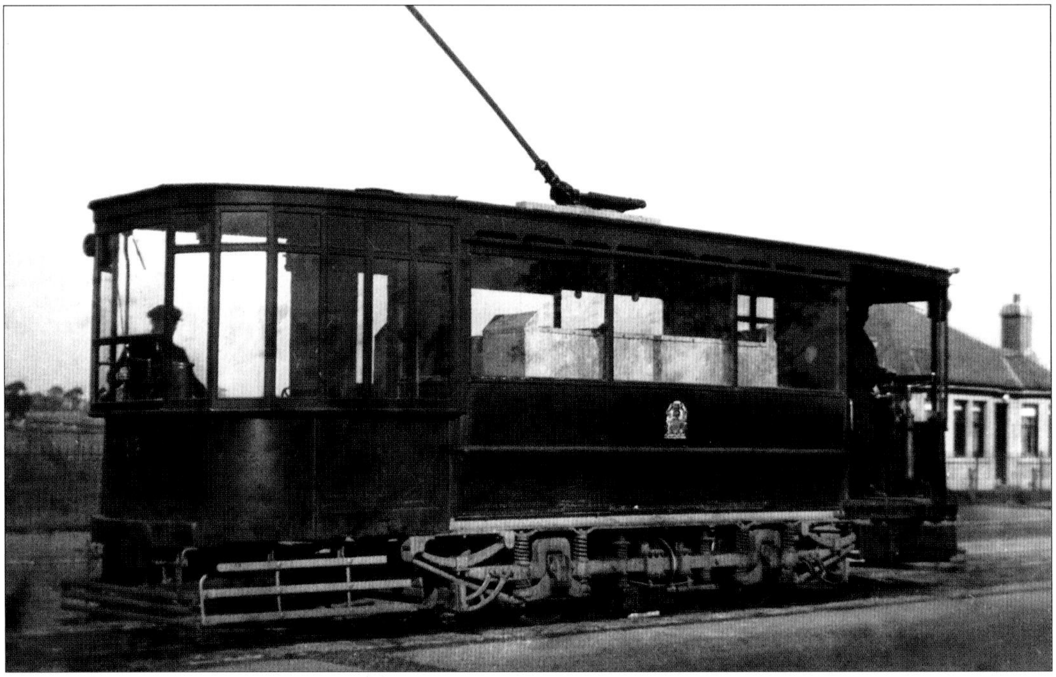

Final horse tram manifestation; grinder 17 working on rural Glasgow Road on 24 September 1934. The final horse car conversion to cable operation in May 1908, it survived to be electrified in November 1924.

It soon became a rail grinder, renumbered 3 in February 1935. In this guise it survived until c.1946, the last remaining operational horse tram relic until the discovery of the body of the former car 23.

PART THREE

Restoration of horse car 23 in the twenty-first century

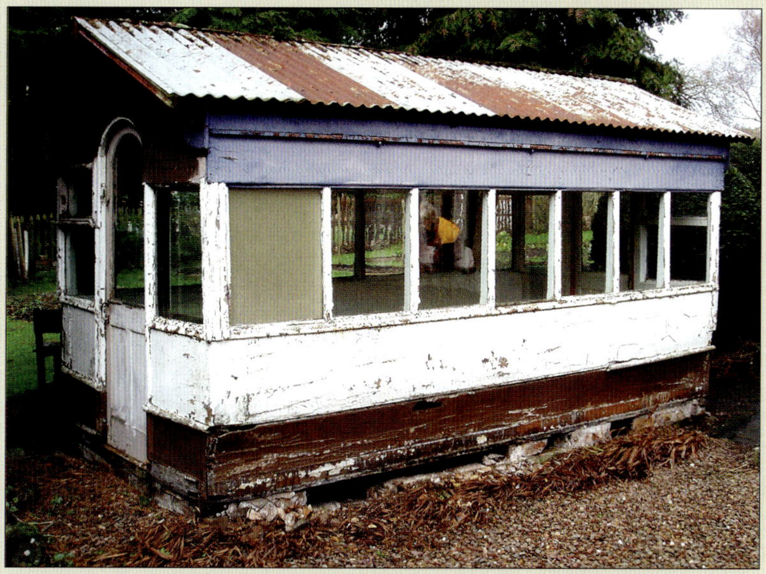

First sight of the tram in October 2005. The brick under-building and the corrugated iron roof (plus many layers of paint) are all factors in the amazing survival of the nineteenth century transport relic.

Car 23 appears to have been purchased by Mr Adam Hall, of *Fairfield* in Newtown St Boswells. Mr Hall was proprietor of the local Langlands yarn mill – an enterprise founded by him in 1880. The car was placed on a well ventilated brick foundation and given a pitched roof of corrugated-iron. These features – which suggest that considerable care was taken – plus many coats of protective paint applied through the years – ensured that the venerable tram-now-garden-shed survived there, undisturbed, for more than a century. As a garden summer-house it was well used – tradition suggesting it was for a time the meeting place of the local 'Wee Free' Church. *Fairfield* was purchased in 2001 by Roger and Gill French, who were much intrigued by the odd little summer house which they had acquired along with their other purchase. A visit by their son to the Scottish Railway Museum Society at Bo'ness led to Gill writing in August 2005 to the late John Burnie, then the Railway Museum's collections officer. Photographs sent with her letter were passed by John to the writer, who arranged to visit *Fairfield*, to determine if this was indeed an unexpected relic of Edinburgh's first generation trams. On 7 October 2005 the initial inspection confirmed the antecedents of their venerable garden shed, and established that what remained was remarkably sound and that restoration was achievable.

It soon became apparent that there was considerable enthusiasm for restoration of the relic. Initial discussions with the Heritage Lottery Fund in Edinburgh highlighted the major hurdles to be overcome before this project could be even considered for grant aid from that source. As these would result in both delay to progress and considerable unnecessary additional cost, this approach was abandoned. A decision was made to proceed independently, and a trust was created early in 2007, with its stated objects the restoration and display of the old vehicle. Both former owners of the tram became trustees, and have maintained a positive interest in the project since then.

The first Edinburgh horse tramcar numbered 23 was probably built by Drew & Burnett in early 1872. This seems to have come to the end of its useful life about 1885, when a replacement was built by the Tramways Company in the coach-building department at Shrubhill works. In the financial accounts of most tramway operators, replacement vehicles were charged to revenue, while those increasing the number in stock were funded from capital. 'Replacement' cars were given the number of the car being replaced; cars increasing the stock were added at the end of the numerical list.

A 'lighter and improved' design of knifeboard-seat car was introduced by Harry Booth, superintendent of the coach building department, in the first half of 1883, with a number – possibly twelve – built of this type. It is thought that our car 23 is from this group, with an 1885 press article giving a detailed contemporary description of cars then being built. '[The Company] have seen the advantages of building their own cars and omnibuses. They had no new cars in the shops when we visited them, but we had the pleasure of seeing one in use that had been turned out the previous day, and a good specimen of workmanship it was, not only light, but comfortable, well ventilated and substantial. The framework of the cars is constructed of best home grown ash; the bottom sides are of English oak; body, baywood and teak, and the average cost of the 36-passenger car is £140. A good stock of timber was shown to us consisting principally of English oak, ash, and American pine. The Car-Superintendent, Mr. H. Booth, is not content with running in the old stereotyped groove and taking advantage of other people's brains, but strikes out a line of his own: he not only believes in strength for his work but also has an eye for the beautiful, and is an inventor to wit: He has recently invented an automatic Chain Brake and Car Starter ...'[221] This design (which included our car 23) was superseded in 1886 by his 'Exhibition' award-winning design which became the most numerous of the many differing styles of horse tram in the city.

Contemporary sources of information on individual Edinburgh horse cars give few details of tram 23. To quote directly from the Thomson notebook: '23. Commercial St Leith & Marchmont Rd, painted blue

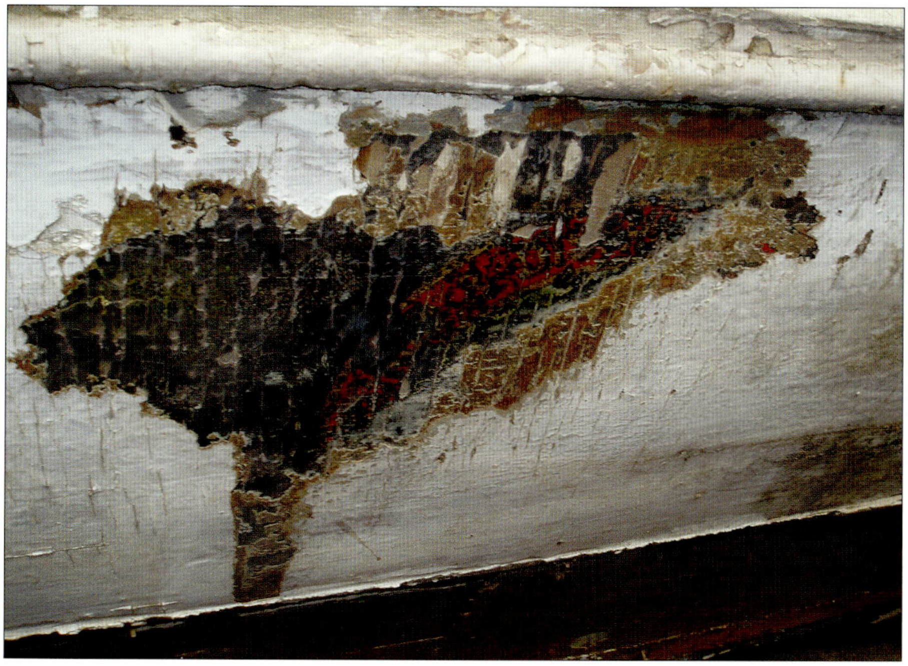

An early task was to attempt to identify 'our' tram. An investigation of the centre of the waist panel soon uncovered (below eleven coats of paint) the crest of the District Company – on a blue coloured waist panel. The brown above showed no trace of lining or crest to suggest that the car had ever run in that condition, despite the description in the Thomson notebook.

& white, built at Shrubhill by E.S.T.Co., carries 36 passrs, long seat on top. Put on Spare in 1895 (October) R.D. 2/4/94. Transferred to E.D.T.Co., on 1st February 1896 and is again plying on its original route. R.D.3/9/96, painted dark brown & white, plying between Coltbridge, Haymarket, Newington & Craigmillar Park.' The Magistrates' Licence Book records 23 licensed for 18 inside and 18 outside passengers by the Street Tramways Company from 1 August 1894 (when that volume commenced) until 5 April 1896, then by the District Tramways Company from 7 January 1896 until 28 May 1900. A cable tram 23 was licensed from 4 November 1900. Car 23 was renumbered *c.*May 1900, and ran as 22 until 28 October 1900. The Portobello route where 23 was on spare was transferred from one company to the other from 31 January 1896.

While the Thomson records can frequently be confirmed by other evidence, no trace was found on car 23 of a brown livery. The badge of the District Company was found, but on a royal blue background, not brown. On other panels there was evidence of a lined out paint scheme on blue panels, and while there were several coats of roughly applied brown colour, none of these carried any indication of lining, as should have been expected had this been a 'livery'. Also the blue paintwork was deeply scored, presumably to give the next coat a key; this would be unlikely if the car was to remain in service. 'R. D.' is thought to indicate 'Repaint Date' which was probably applied on the car in a visible position. Whoever compiled the Thomson notebook must have had access to all cars, as he correctly identified the builders of many, noting 'Exhibition' car 45, the two 1877 Stephenson cars 6 and 12, and the cars used on the 1890 electric railway, 98 and 99. Stephenson as builder would have been identified by his company's trademark 'ribbon' above both saloon doors, and it seems that Shrubhill identified their work (and possibly their rebuilds also) in like manner.

Car 23 was probably withdrawn – as one of the oldest then running – in October 1900; possibly when the Morningside Circle was converted to cable operation and newer horse cars became available. With a glut of surplus vehicles, some were retained for use in the event of cable breakdowns, but many were sold off. There were few takers for them as working cars, but the Street Tramways Company took some of the better vehicles for use in Leith. Six such were acquired in 1900 then further three the next year; these retained

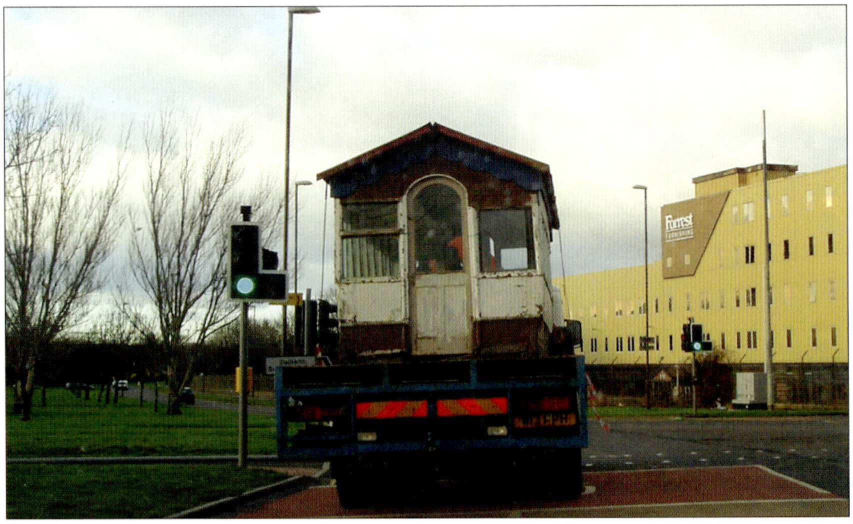

Horse tram meets traffic lights for the first time. Safely extricated on 10 January 2007 by the expert haulier from its resting place of over a century, the tram travelled up the A68 at speeds never dreamed of when it operated.

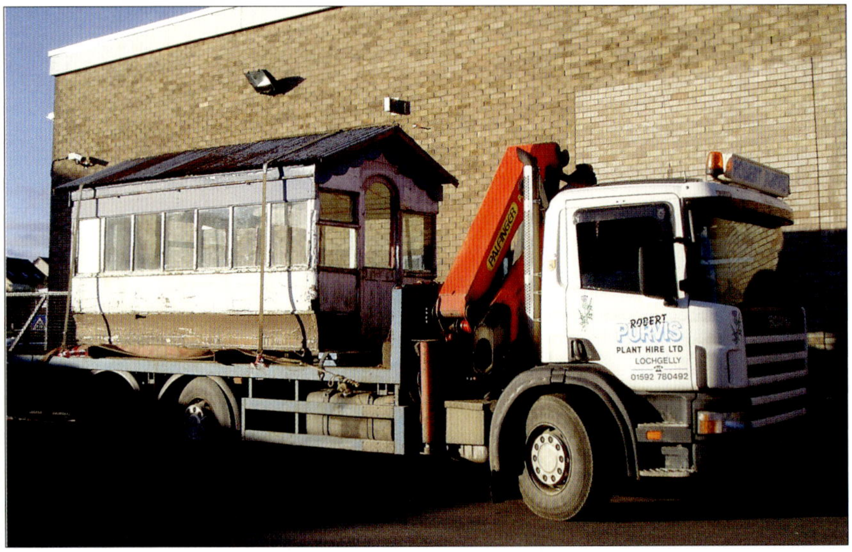

It was with an enormous sense of relief (to the writer at least) that the journey was completed safely, without the old tram disintegrating into a pile of wood dust by the roadside. Here the precious load has arrived at the Seafield facility of Lothian Buses who generously made space available for the safe storage of the tram, and to allow exploratory work to commence.

their original numbers. The only other *known* sale was to the tramway between Stirling and Bridge of Allan which purchased three cars in 1900, three in 1902 then further two (from their final owner, Leith Corporation) in 1905.

The tram body was carefully removed from its foundations on 10 January 2007, and lifted on to a flatbed lorry with a Hiab loader-crane from Purvis Plant of Lochgelly. The northbound journey was undertaken at speeds which the old tram had never ever before achieved in its existence. As the fundamental integrity of the tram was, at this stage, completely unknown, it was with considerable relief that the destination was reached with it still in one piece. Space was generously made available by Lothian Buses in their workshops off Seafield Road. With the tram safely unloaded adjacent to the stored Edinburgh cable tram 226 body remains, the first task undertaken was to remove everything not part of the original build. This included the corrugated iron roof, the floor and internal side boarding. A more accurate conditional assessment was now possible which showed that nothing original remained below floor level, the corner pillars had rot at waist level, and that the headstocks below the

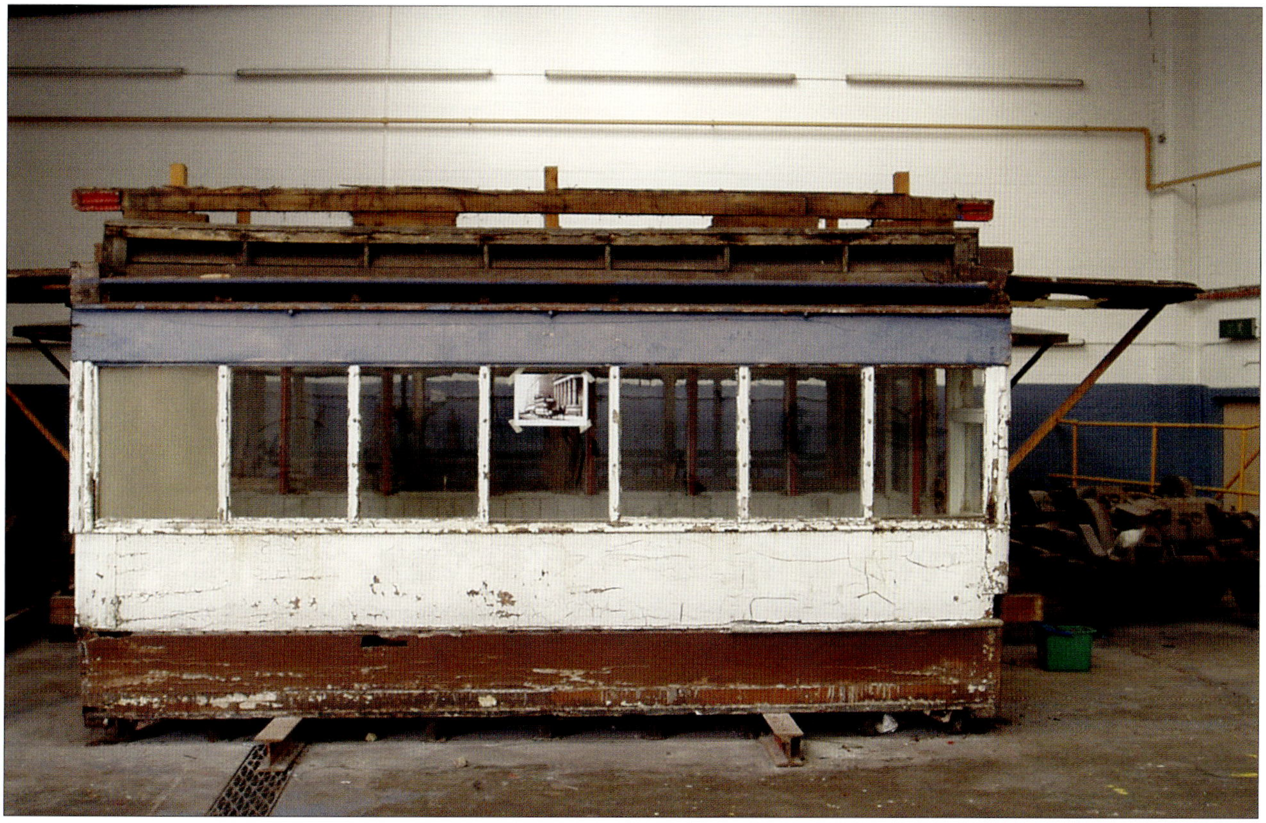

Safely unloaded, the corrugated iron roof which had afforded many years' protection was removed. Until this point it was not known whether or not the original top deck seats remained, and if the roof had been fitted over them. Unfortunately no trace of these remained, but it was now possible to make an accurate assessment of structural condition.

bulkheads were totally decayed – indeed the journey north had reduced that at one end to dust. However, most other areas were in remarkably good order, confirming the original opinion that restoration incorporating as much of the original fabric as possible was definitely feasible. An early decision was that no unnecessary dismantling would be undertaken, and that integrity of the old vehicle should be maintained, with re-use of original components where possible. During this period several decayed tickets were uncovered from hidden corners and from the roof area behind the clerestory windows were retrieved some pieces from a doll's tea set and a very old (empty) purse.

An advert in *Tramways and Urban Transit* magazine at this time offered to a good home a 'narrow gauge horse tramcar'. This resulted in a visit to Stuart Rivers in Llandudno where retired horse car 46 from the fleet of Douglas Corporation was marooned following an unsuccessful project to operate it in North Wales. Having been on offer as an operable tram for some time, and with zero interest shown, Stuart was pleased to transfer his tram to the Trust for a nominal sum (a framed pristine Scottish banknote), knowing that we proposed to use the running gear in restoration of our tram. During May the body above floor level was dismantled in Llandudno, revealing in the process considerable timber decay. The floor and running gear was brought to Seafield on 20 May 2008 where it remained for a short period.

By this time progress at Seafield had been made with the removal of paint from the body of the car, inside (five coats) and outside (at least eleven coats), to the point where original lettering, lining and livery were all clearly visible. The route details uncovered and

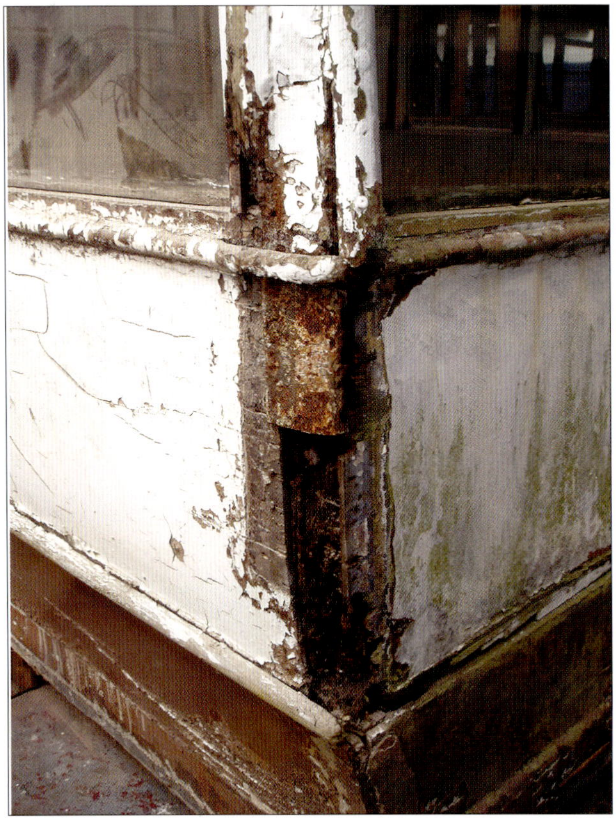

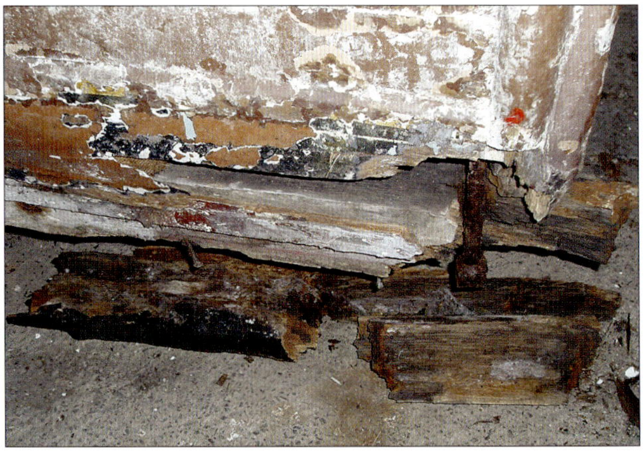

Above. The oak sole bar below both bulkheads was rotten and such little as remained rapidly disintegrated. While much original timber survived remarkably well, where oak had been incorporated, it had generally not lasted as well as other woods. On the working tram, areas subject to wear were covered by sacrificial boards. One of these can be seen here, made from a panel from a scrapped car; nothing wasted.

Left. It was soon found that the oak corner pillars were considerably rotted. This had apparently been obvious when the car was in use as thin metal covers had been fitted over rotted areas, then painted to match the rest of the car. This shows the condition of one of the original posts.

the style and seating capacity of the car led to the conclusion that there was only one car in the entire Edinburgh fleet which satisfied all criteria – car 23. This was the first positive identification of the old car.

Further examination of the timber work indicated both bulkhead headstocks were badly decayed, with replacement of these becoming one of the earliest tasks. Also severely rotted were the four oak corner pillars, probably as a result of water ingress into the many screw holes necessary for handrails etc. It was apparent that this decay must have been recognised while the car was operational, as some wasted areas had been 'disguised' with thin sheet metal covers – but with the livery applied to conceal the patch. It is probable that cars, which in normal circumstances would have been scrapped, were kept in use to maximise the asset value at the time of ownership transfer. New corner pillars were made and fitted in place. Skilled joinerwork throughout was undertaken highly successfully by Douglas Scoular for the Trustees.

With pending redevelopment of the paint shop area at Seafield, space was kindly made available by Lothian Buses in the disused rifle-range at their Longstone Garage, this move undertaken by them on 15 October. The new working area provided was ideal, being lock-fast, heated and well lit. Douglas recommenced here on new timber work, with assistance on unskilled work from various enthusiastic amateurs. A contract was agreed with the Shed 47 Group at Lathalmond to re-gauge the wheels and brakes of Isle of Man 46 from 3 ft 0 ins to Edinburgh's 4 ft 8½ ins. The under-frame was removed to Lathalmond on 1 November 2008.

Douglas 46's four wheels had been cast by Miller & Co, London Road Foundry, Edinburgh with the date of manufacture on each one. This specialist company operated for over one hundred years, from 1867 until 1991, supplying railway and tramway wheels and other high quality iron and steel castings to all corners of the globe. Under the work schedule agreed

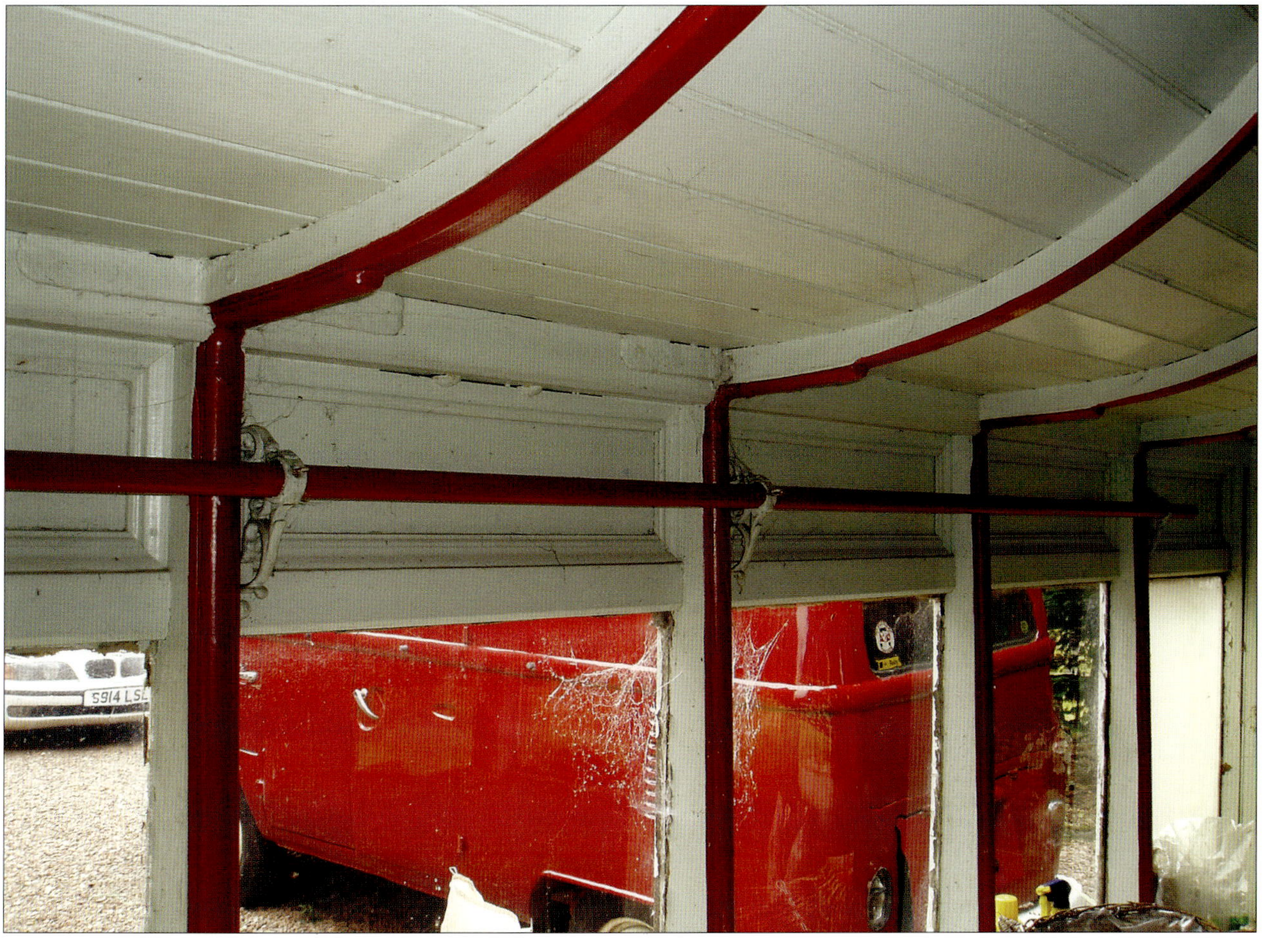

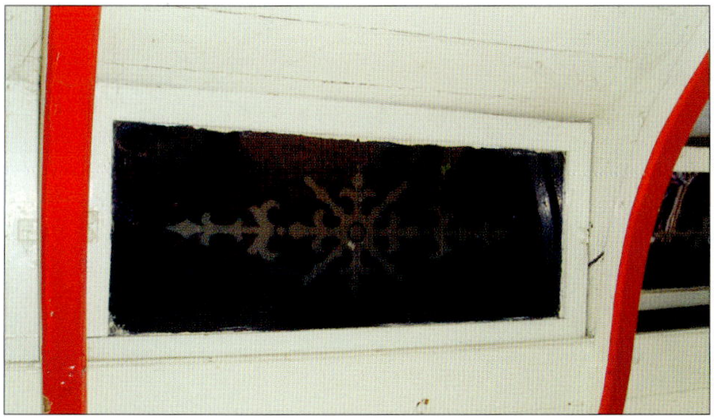

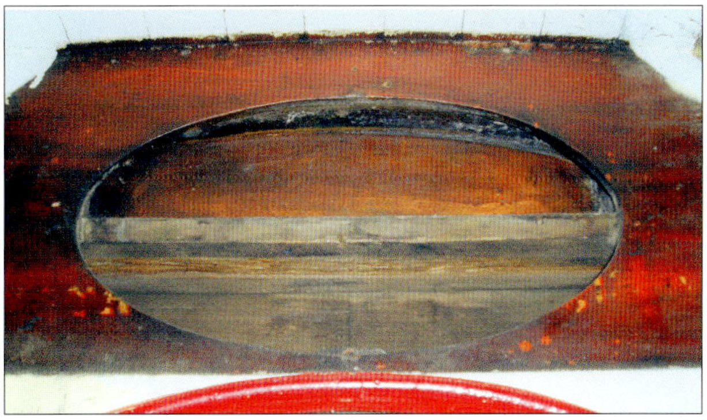

Top. Inside the car while it still lay in Newton St Boswells. This shows the care which had been lavished – helping wonderfully to preserve the fabric. The 'curtain rail' is in fact the roof hand rail, and the painted brackets are the finely detailed brass fitments to hold it in place. When these were removed was it realised that the back was curved, and fitted the roof sticks perfectly.

Above left. Detail of the ventilator blue glass windows. Of fourteen required, remarkably twelve were undamaged and in place. Replacements for the missing two were made, and can (with a little knowledge) be identified today. These have been fixed not to move or trap little fingers.

Above right. Panels above doors showed that they had been recycled from earlier vehicles; a philosophy which, while perhaps not surprising, was not anticipated. These panels show earlier lettering, cut into for subsequent different use. The shape retained and indicated by the unpainted area shows where the number panel was fixed above the door.

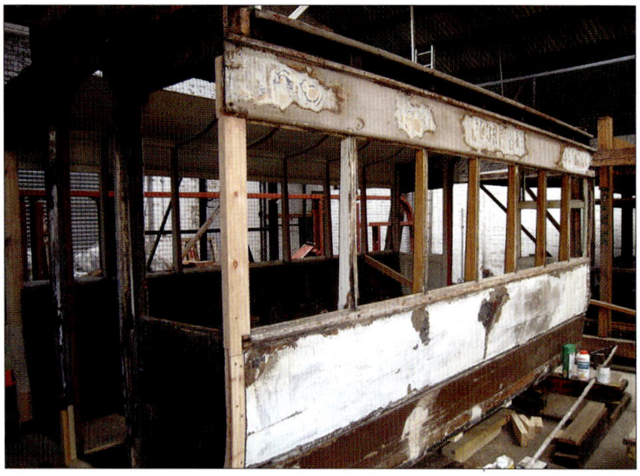

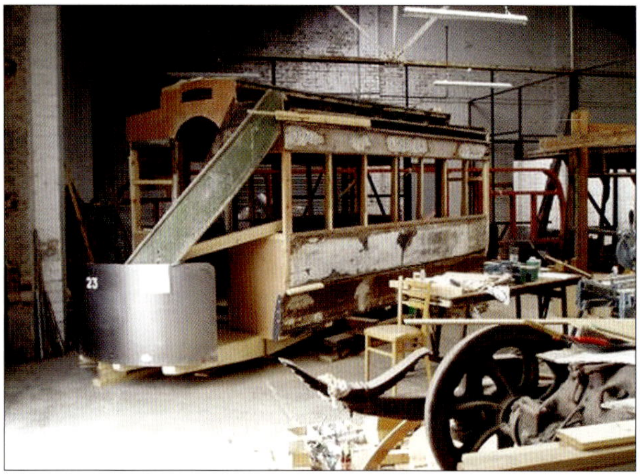

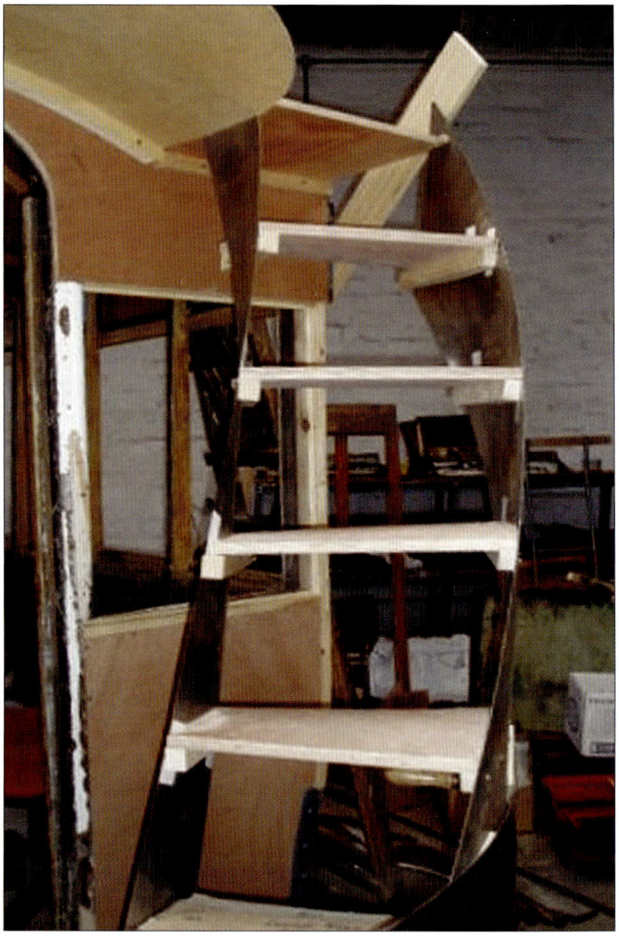

Top. An early decision was to try to retain as much as possible of the integrity of the old vehicle by avoiding disturbance to major undamaged panels. The rotted corner pillars were replaced with preserved timber cut to the original profiles. Investigation into the lettering of the side destination is under way in this scene.

Above. Here the platform is well under construction. To permit understanding of the geometry of the stair, a similar stair from an Aberdeen tram was put in place in order to get the details correct. This (with green stringer) is in position, as is the new dash plate and beams supporting the platform.

Above right. Construction of the stair is under way, with the stringers in place and each individual tread shaped and fitted.

Opposite. Much can be seen in this view; new pillars are in place, the stairs are taking shape and a flexible piece of hardboard is in place to start to derive the shape of the canopy (or 'bonnet'). The original route description is now seen on this side.

with the Shed 47 Group, all re-usable original components were refurbished. The wheels were removed from their axles and refitted to longer axles machined by Roemac Ltd, also based at Lathalmond. The brake gear was reassembled, with the brake tie bars lengthened to suit; the wheelbase reduced from 7 ft 0 ins to 5 ft 6 ins. Steel angle under frame members were provided to carry the saloon, distributing the car's weight evenly rather than supporting it directly on to just four trunnions. This was considered prudent, as the existing timber side members were much holed, compromising integrity and load bearing capacity. The new assembly was gauge tested on Shed 47's track at Lathalmond before being returned to Longstone.

The major elements of the tram which had been discarded when sold were the platforms and stairs, and work commenced to replace these. As no contemporary

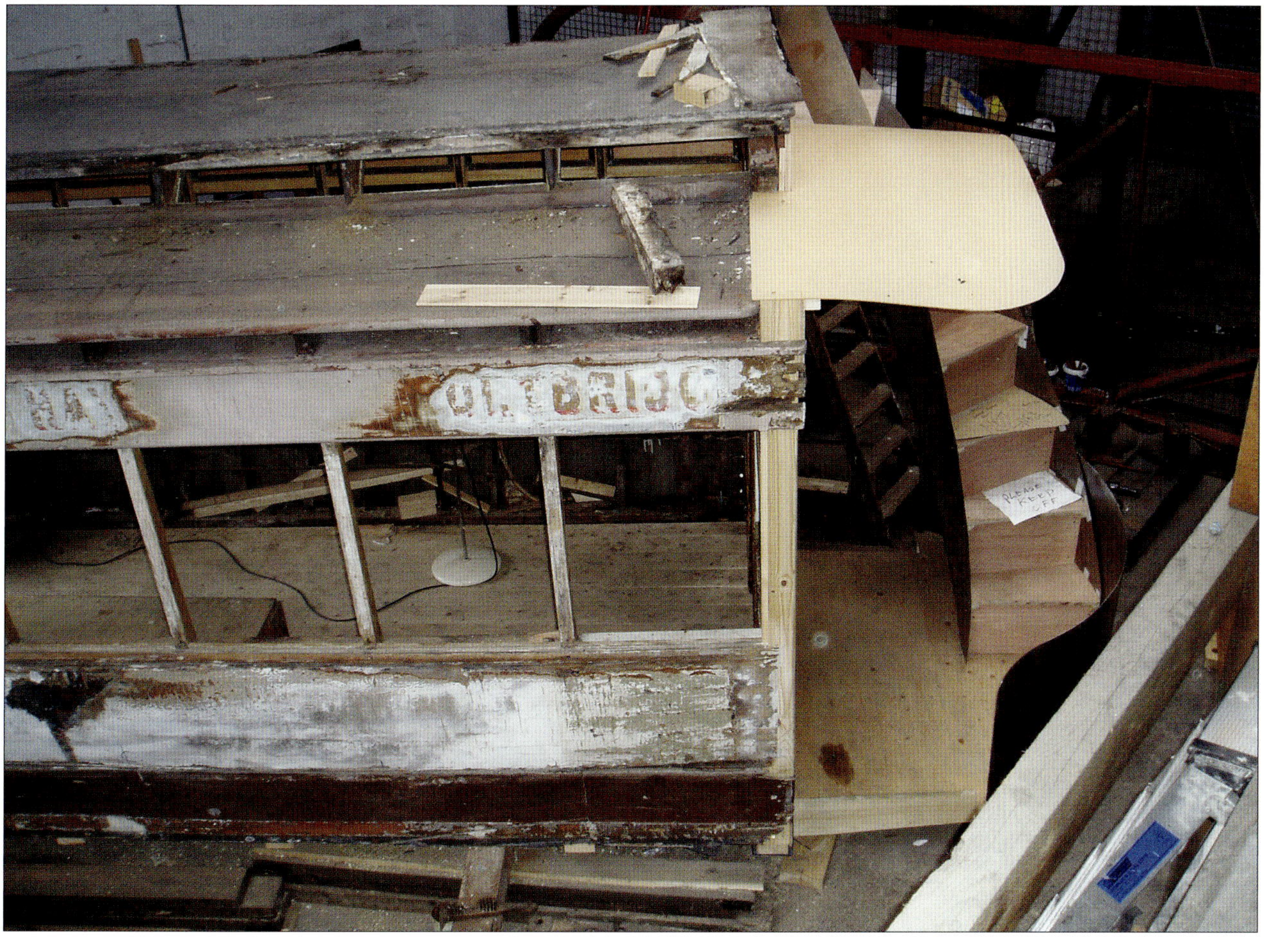

drawings of the car are known, new designs for all missing elements were prepared by reference to contemporary drawings of other horse cars aided by photographs, confirming the principles used – which tended to be standardised to a considerable degree.

Work progressed steadily during the following year achieving: new saloon flooring, new external bulkhead panels both ends, new canopies constructed, truss rods removed and refurbished, saloon interior stripping of all paint, old paint to waist and rocker panels removed, original lettering exposed on route boards and rocker panels where remaining. Many original brass fittings were, remarkably, still in situ and responded well to professional refurbishment. The highly decorative handrail brackets along the ceiling were still in the car, but were being used to support the poles which had re-used as curtain-rails above the windows. Two small (Kelly) paraffin lamps were purchased for use in the saloon light boxes.

By mid-November 2009 both platforms were designed and constructed, dash plates were cut from sheet metal and rolled to the required curve. Stair design was then undertaken, with a 90-degree turn stair ex-Aberdeen electric tram 14 put temporarily in place to determine the shape of the stringers. A mock-up was made using hardboard, and adjusted until the correct geometry was achieved. Treads and risers were then measured, with a distance piece keeping the stringers in the correct position. This mock-up was then used to create the final shapes, with stringers of sheet steel, treads and risers of timber. Using one of the cast iron tread plates from the Aberdeen stair as a template, fourteen tread plates were cast for the new stairs. With stair and dash at number 1 end well advanced, number 2 end stair was undertaken. During the next months work continued on the internal woodwork to remove all old paint. This was a time consuming task, with the grooves of the pine ceiling planks being cleared using a dentist's probe! The end result was well worth the considerable effort. The four main external panels of the saloon were originally each of a single half-inch thick mahogany board, but on one side – apparently as a result of accident damage, the lower panel was in three sections. Behind this were damaged or missing ribs, probably a consequence of the same accident. A replacement was made from marine quality ply for this damaged panel, and new ribs were made and fitted as necessary. On the original, the unseen inner face of all timber panels was covered with paint saturated hessian (to minimise the risk of the splitting and to act as sound-deadening). Again following the evidence, this was painted in a flat purple-red colour – as indeed were most unseen wooden surfaces. Other than this one replacement area, all main panels remain as original 1880s solid mahogany.

New steel corner tie pieces to take the ends of the truss rods were made, replicating the originals, and fitted to newly fabricated corner posts. The refurbished internal metal truss rods and their supports were tied through these corner pieces and tensioned. All were undercoated in red oxide and finished black. All other internal metalwork – other than brassware – was stripped and treated similarly.

At the beginning of July 2010 work commenced on the 'foot boards' for upper deck passengers above the roof. The originals were split from end to end, probably having been subjected to heat build-up below the corrugated iron roof. Both boards were removed from the tram and glued, with strengthening plates screwed from below. As several of the shaped supports for this foot board were decayed, replacements were manufactured and fitted prior to puting the repaired foot board back in place. Before fixing, the waterproofing canvas was replaced, bedded in paint. The upstands at each end of the foot boards were reconstructed to the original patterns. Ties were fitted around the top outside corners of the saloon to add strength and provide positive support. During August the water proofing canvas from the roof area below the seating was removed and replaced, with the new layer bedded in paint (red oxide – not white lead as was originally used). A piece of original canvas was kept for exhibition. New light boxes were made by Roemac Ltd, and fitted to the saloon ends, replicating the originals. Dioptric lenses for these lights were purchased.

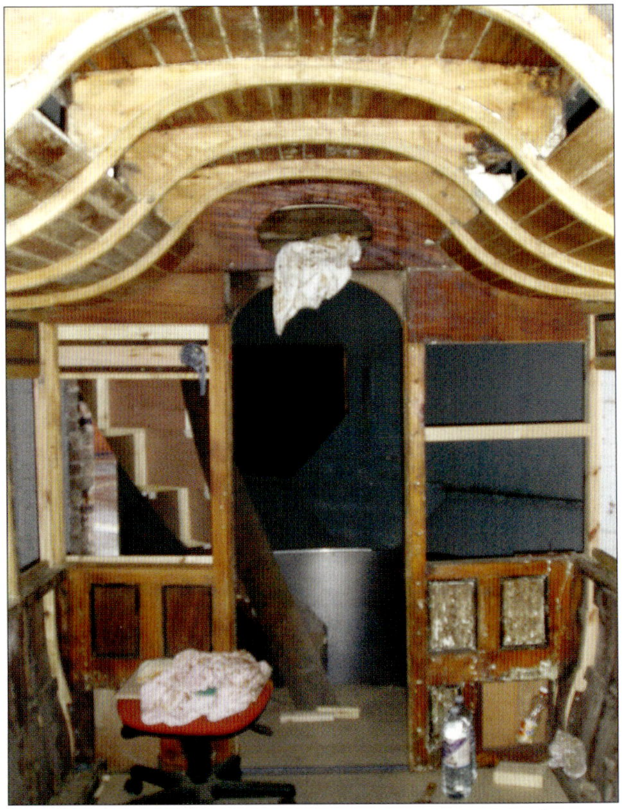

Work in hand inside the saloon on removal of old paint. A time consuming and laborious task, particularly in the longitudinal grooves of the ceiling timbers where a dentists' probe (redundant!) was used. However the finished job is considered to be well worth the effort. On the left side of the bulkhead are the rails supporting the roller at the edge of the door.

During September preparations commenced for uniting the body and the running gear. This involved dismantling the stairs and platform and raising the body to permit the under-frame to clear the tops of the wheels. Steel angles were fitted behind the timber bulkhead headstocks to provide additional support. The running gear was moved into position and the body lowered carefully. Heavy rubber strips were introduced

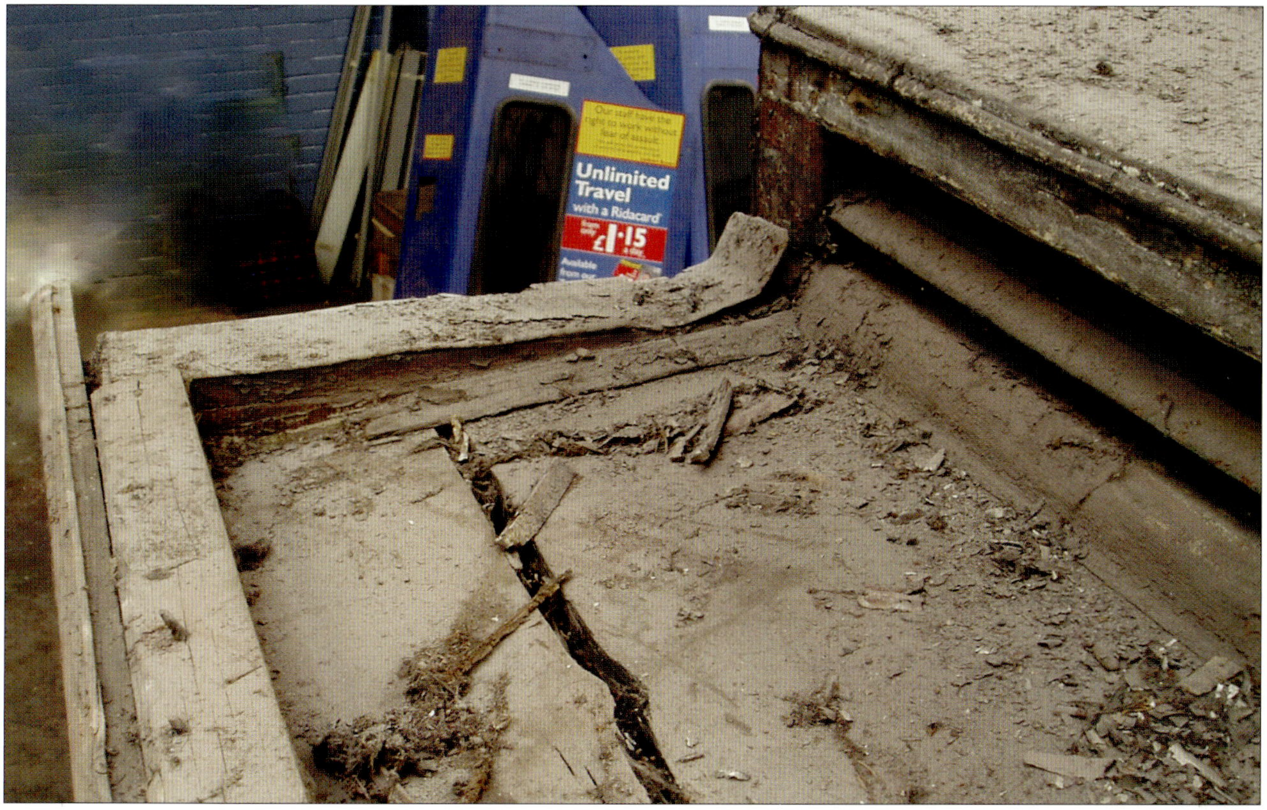

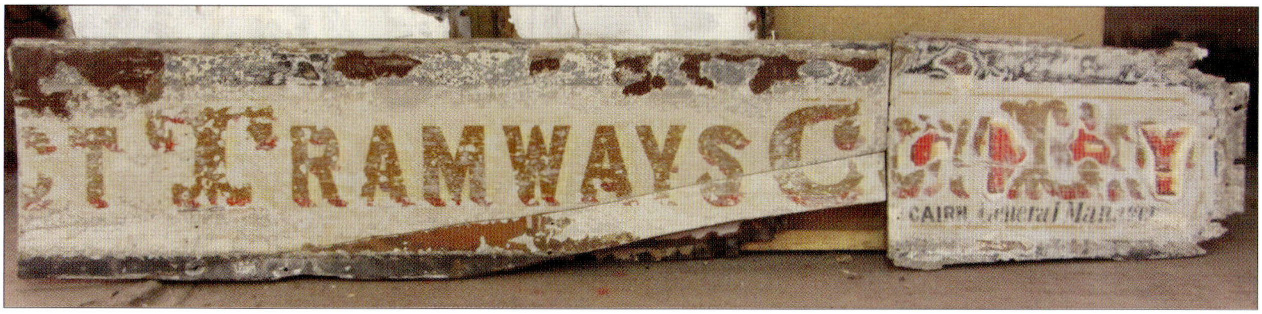

Top. Removal of the corrugated iron roof allowed access to the top deck; this showing what was found. The main 'walking board' – which surprisingly showed no sign of protective wearing strips – exhibited a massive shake from end to end. It is thought that this resulted from heat build-up under the protective iron roof. To the right can be seen one of the saloon ventilator windows.

Above. At some time in its operating life car 23 had sustained accidental damage, with parts of the rocker panel and several ribs affected. New ribs were fitted then the rocker panel was repaired. Opportunity was taken to determine and examine lettering details. Some of the pieces are shown; the lower lettering of the ESTCo is not present on the larger, newer, replacement section.

between these steel angles and the side frame members. As the tram body is not precisely the same width at each end, this was taken account of in the support structure. The opportunity was taken to treat the underside of all platform members with wood preservative. By the end of September 2010 the body and the running gear were bolted together; platforms, stairs and dashes were then re-assembled.

At the beginning of October 2010 the panels from above the doors were examined by Jacqueline Ridge, head of the Conservation Department of the National Galleries of Scotland. Ultraviolet light and infra-red

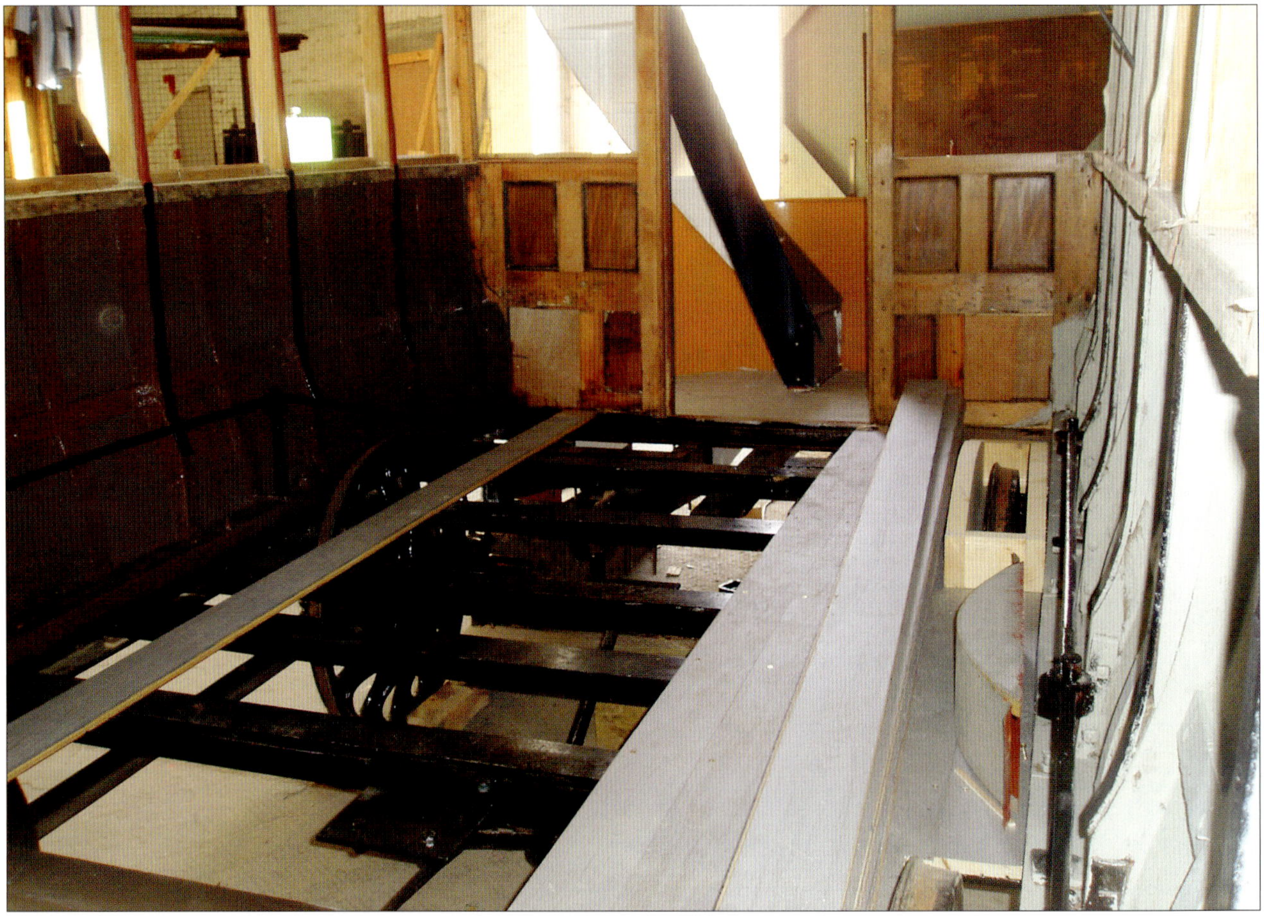

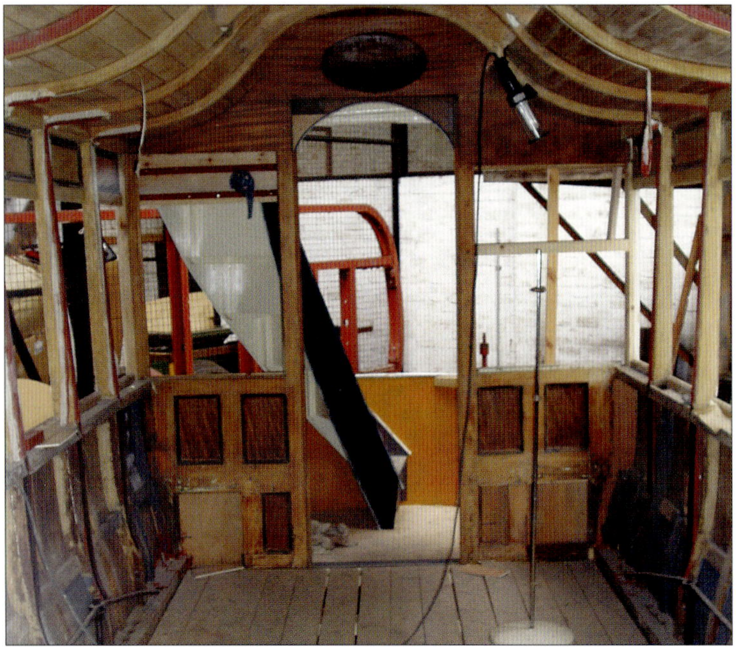

Above. Work proceeding on flooring. The stairs have advanced and the restoration of the panels on the interior bulkheads progressing, with the differing woods used apparent. The wheel covers are seen under construction on the right.

Left. When the car was removed to the old rifle range at Longstone Garage most of the interior woodwork had been stripped of five layers of paint. This had preserved the finely figured panelling, which when exposed, was found to be in very good condition.

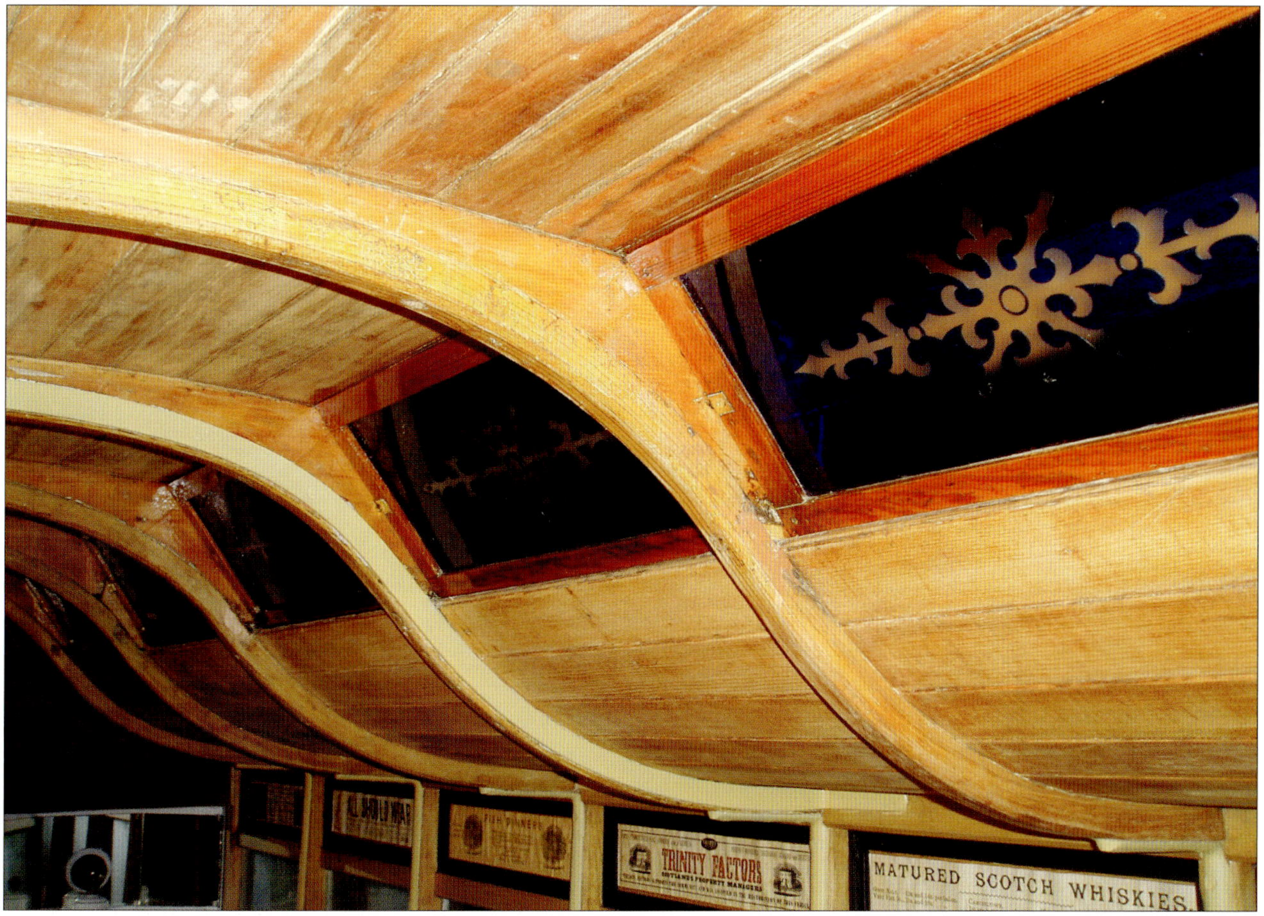

Two new engraved quarter light window glasses were made to match the originals (these, being hand engraved, had slight variations of design) by a stained glass artist – plus a spare.

reflectography techniques were applied, and using the latter the lettering became discernible and the findings recorded. These showed the figure 'No 23' had been altered to become 'No 22'. While this may appear contradictory to prior conclusions regarding the identity of the tram, recourse to Edinburgh's (fortunately still extant) licensing records show that car 23 (seating capacity 18/18) was licensed until 28 May 1900, with car 22 (seating 26/18, ie a garden seat car) also licensed to 28 May 1900, but with a substitute car (18/18) licensed between 17 February 1900 and 28 May 1900. This in turn was further substituted by a third 22 (also 18/18 seating) from 28 May to 28 October 1900. All this confirmed the infra-red examination of the 'number board' as being from the original 23, with the figure '3' altered to '2'. No satisfactory explanation for this series of short-term re-numberings can now be suggested. We are most grateful to Ms Ridge for undertaking this examination.

Prior to reinstatement of flooring, all work to brake-gear etc below floor level was completed. The flooring was then put in place and the underside treated with aluminium based sealer, undercoat of dark grey and finished in dark maroon, this maroon apparent on original timberwork. All metal work below floor level was finished with black gloss, as were all timber platform support beams and intermediate beams supporting floor boards. New wheel arch protectors were made and fitted.

In January 2011 toughened glass was fitted to the

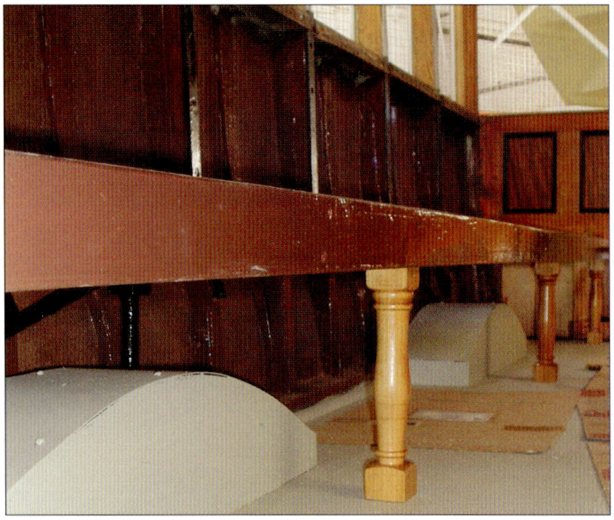

Left. One of the first tasks undertaken at Lathalmond was fitting the interior longitudinal seats. The finely turned legs were fitted to a supporting frame. The insides of all panels forming the saloon were covered in hessian (to act as sound deadening) and all unseen areas were painted a matt reddish- purple colour – as had been the original.

Below. Longitudinal seats to replicate the originals were made and fitted. Alternate laths were of contrasting wood – again reflecting the originals, which used pine and sequoia. This view shows the roof handrails with their ornate brass brackets. These remained in the car, supporting the rail while it was used as a curtain rod above the windows.

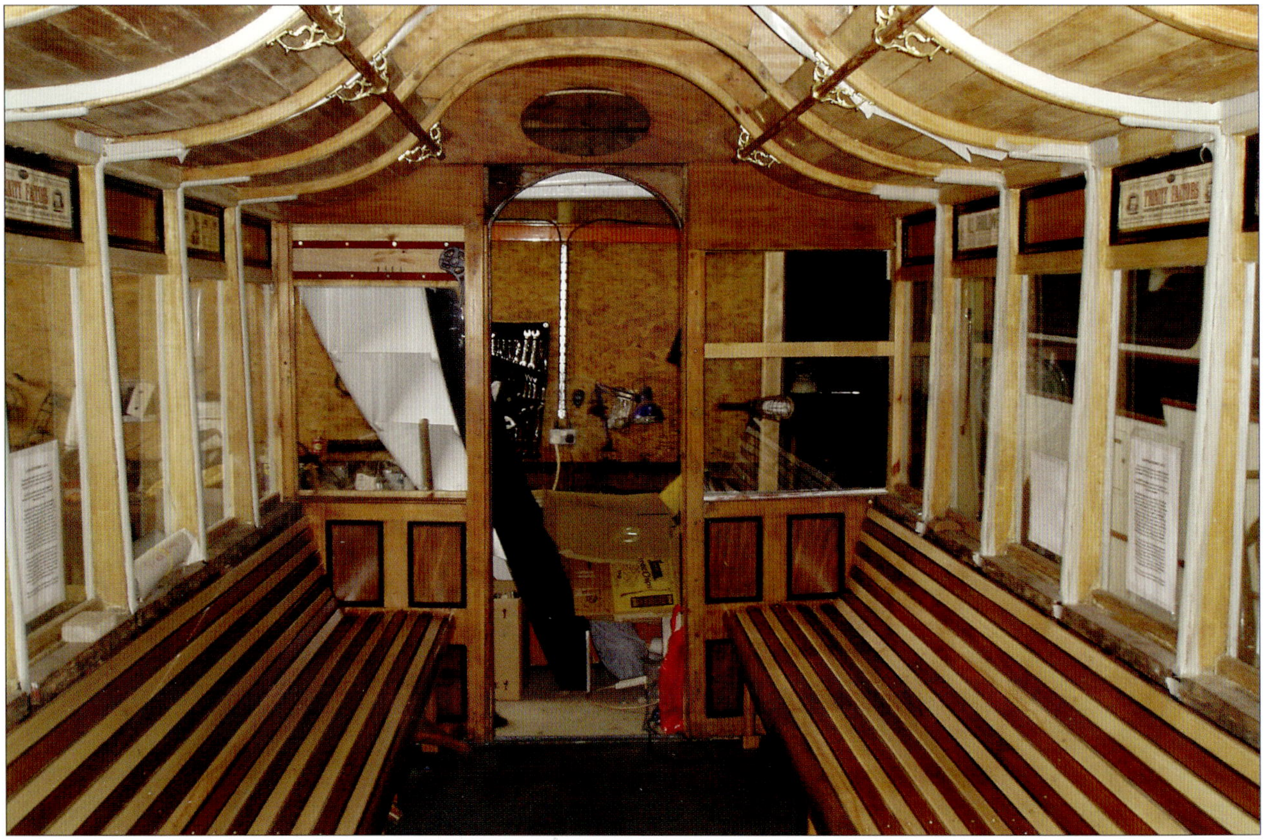

saloon side windows. This was made without the BS 'kite-mark', as this would have presented an incongruous, un-authentic for the period, appearance. Certification of the glass was obtained. Substitution for the surviving Victorian plate glass (which all remained in-situ except one pane) was deemed necessary in order that the vehicle might at some future time be allowed to run on the public highway. (Informal confirmation that the vehicle would comply with current Regulations was given by the Ministry of Transport.)

Off site restoration of various small components was undertaken. The blue glass clerestory windows were removed, cleaned, old paint and varnish removed and they were then re-varnished. Of the fourteen such windows, twelve retained their original engraved blue glass and close inspection revealed that, although similar, the hand-made designs differed slightly. Stained glass artist Emma McGarvie was commissioned to make new glasses to replace those missing (a third, spare, was also made). To enable identification of these two new glasses, the design incorporates a hidden horse-shoe. As the roof of the tram has a pronounced 'dip' in the centre, these small windows are not truly rectangular and each one fits a specific opening. All have an identifying number stamped on top of the frame, in Roman numerals, from I to XIV. They are hinged about the centre line, with hand-made brass pins, also specific to each window. These windows have now been fixed closed, to avoid any possibility of members of the public trapping a finger (the new fixings can be easily removed if required). The saloon doors and associated brass-ware were also stripped and refurbished. While suffering quite badly from age wear and tear, it was decided to restore the doors as they existed. Metalwork on the doors was cleaned, when the fore-edge roller support (one only) was found to carry the name and patent details of John Stephenson, New York. This may suggest that patented elements were imported, or that copies were made using the originals as patterns. The exposed metalwork of the doors was grained – as were the originals – to match adjacent woodwork. Strengthening metalwork to the roof arches and window pillars was refurbished in-situ and finished with a grained effect, as they had been originally.

Canopy cant rails were fabricated, the canopies floored, and waterproofing canvas was fitted in place, with the whole assembly then liberally treated with undercoat paint. Temporary supports were provided for the canopies at the corners of the dashes. The new light boxes were fitted in position on the bulkheads. Drawings were prepared for the upper deck handrails, it being noted that the roof boards rose at 6 degrees.

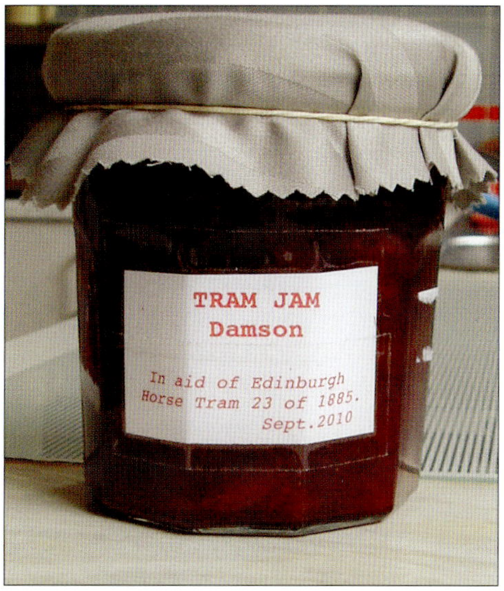

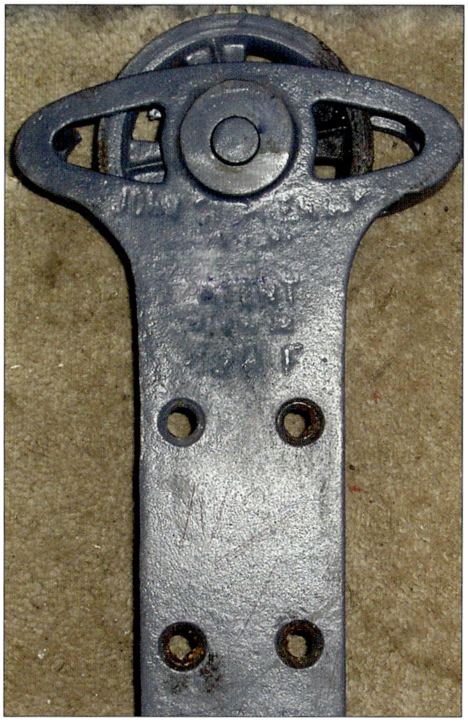

Top. Fund raising to cover the cost of restoration was entirely by voluntary donation and sales. One unusual, but rewarding money raiser, was sale of 'Tram jam' made by Mrs Marjorie Mackenzie.

Above. Interesting finds were made during the cleaning of original components. This is a hanger for the saloon door, and is inscribed (and can just be deciphered) 'John Stephenson & Co New York Patent'. Either the Company imported such components, or copies were made even including this detail.

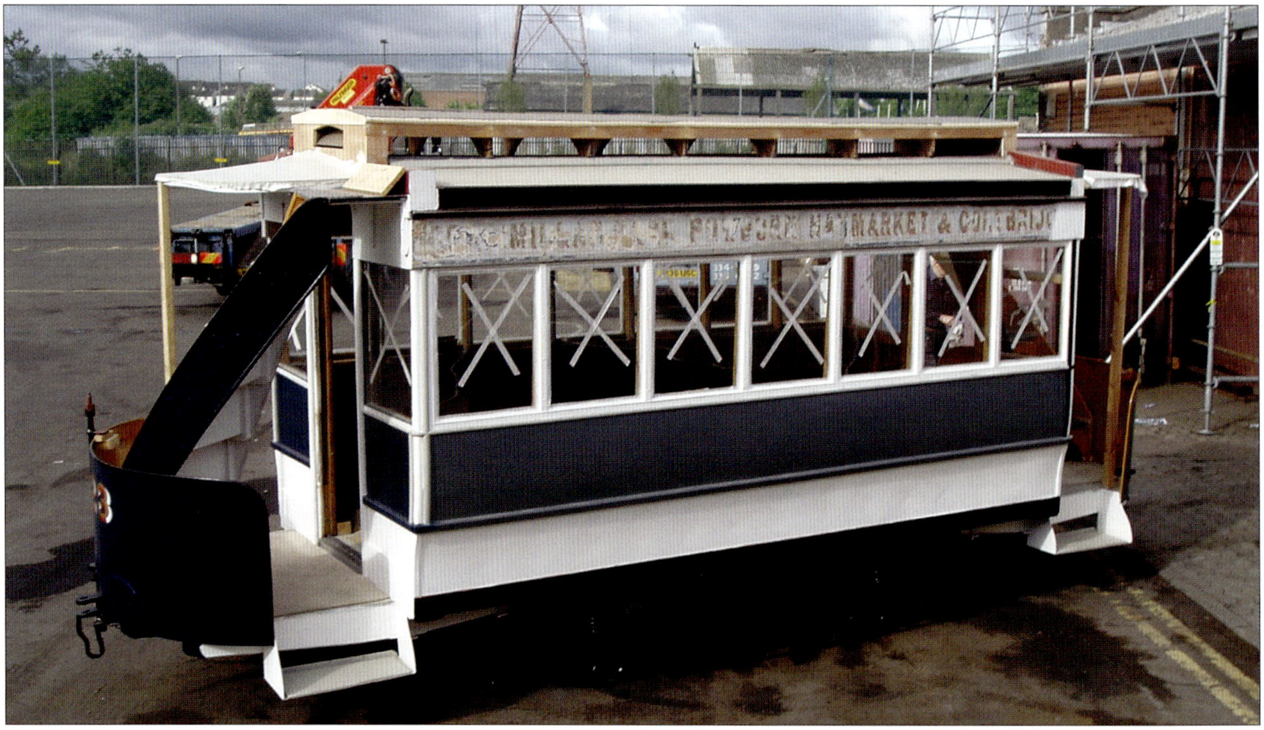

Above. Considerable progress was made prior to the removal from Longstone to Lathalmond. The car saw the light of day for the first time in many months on 17 May 2011. Safety glass had been fitted to windows and basic paintwork had commenced, but there still remained much to complete.

Left. This removal included a crossing of the Forth Road Bridge – surely the first occasion when it was used by a horse tram.

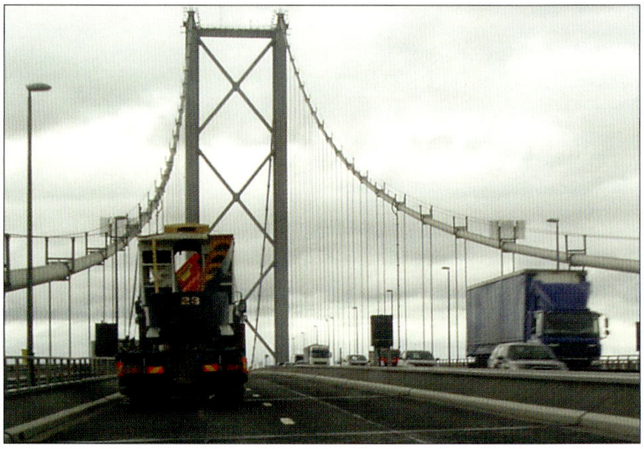

Lower saloon seat frames were fabricated and fitted in place temporarily.

Due to redevelopment of Lothian Buses' Longstone facility, it became necessary to move the car again, and on 17 May 2011 it was removed to the Scottish Vintage Bus Museum's workshop at Lathalmond in Fife. Here progress continued on all fronts, initially on fabrication of upper deck railings and new top deck 'knifeboard' pattern seats. A trickily shaped piece of brass casting was undertaken to form new commode handles. These fit on the bulkheads and provide a grip for boarding passengers, but are a complex shape. A left-hand sample was obtained on loan from the Ipswich Transport Museum, originating from the Cambridge horse tram in their collection, which is currently undergoing restoration. From this a pattern was made, plus one to the opposite hand. Four new handles were cast successfully by Laing & Sons, this cost generously met by the Scottish Tramway and Transport Society.

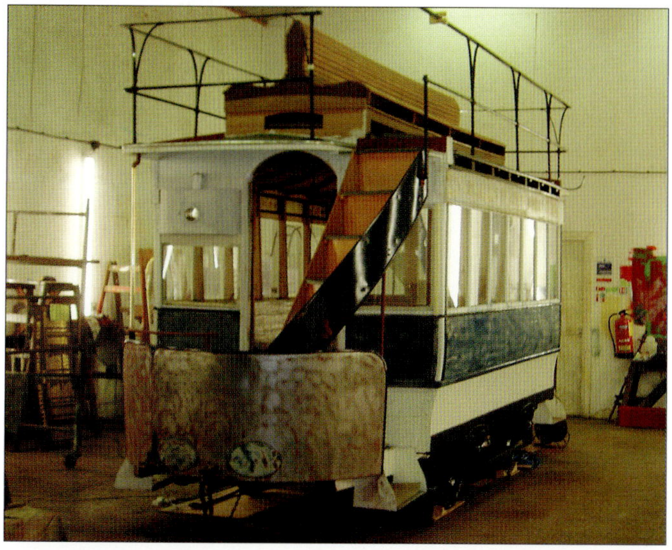

Left. With most restoration work complete, the tram was moved to the paint shop at Lathalmond – a facility which many vehicle fleet operators would appreciate. Filling and rubbing to form a proper base for subsequent coats of paint were time and labour intensive. This is just the starting point ...

Below. The top deck seats and handrails are now fitted, and route lettering exposed as much as possible.

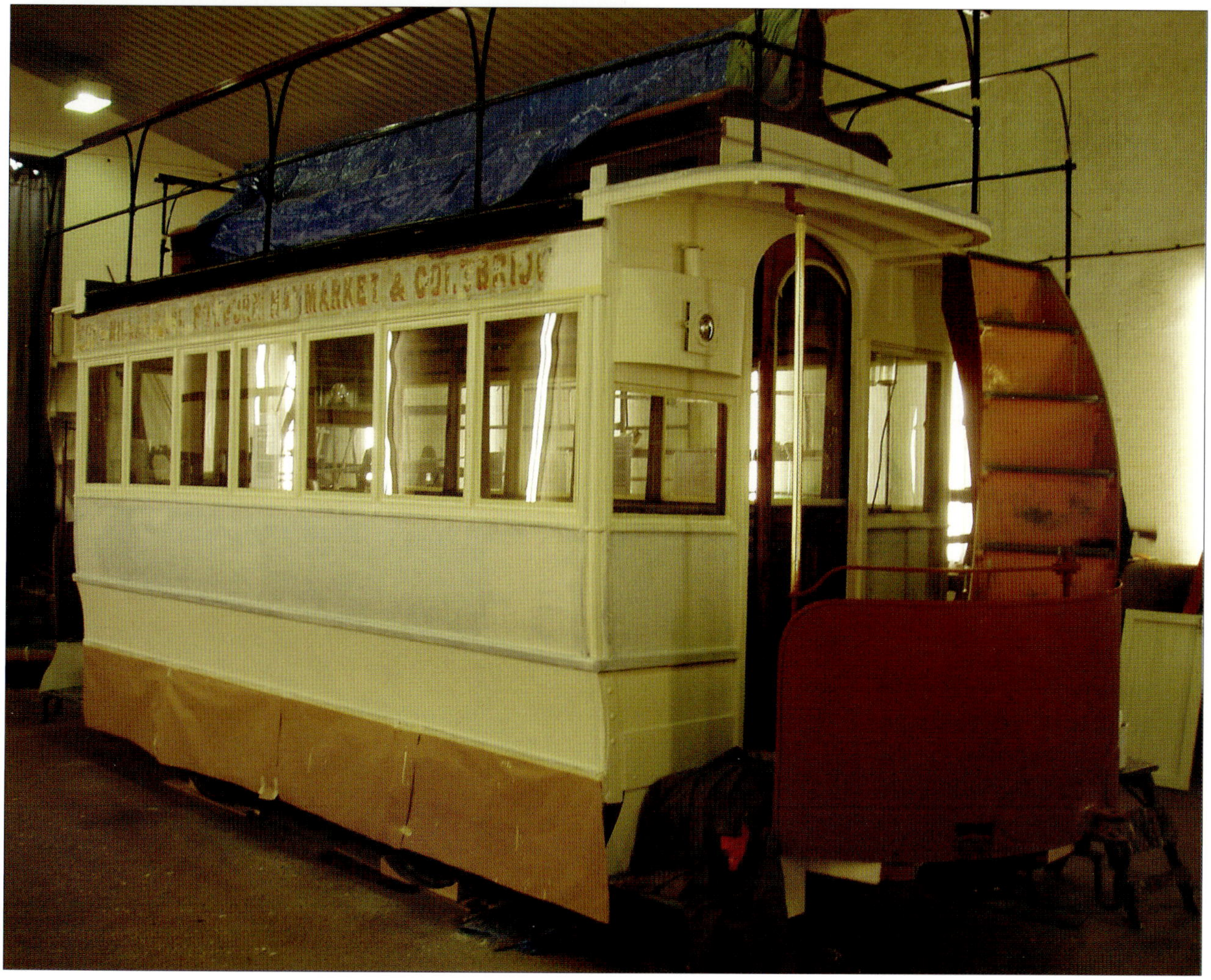

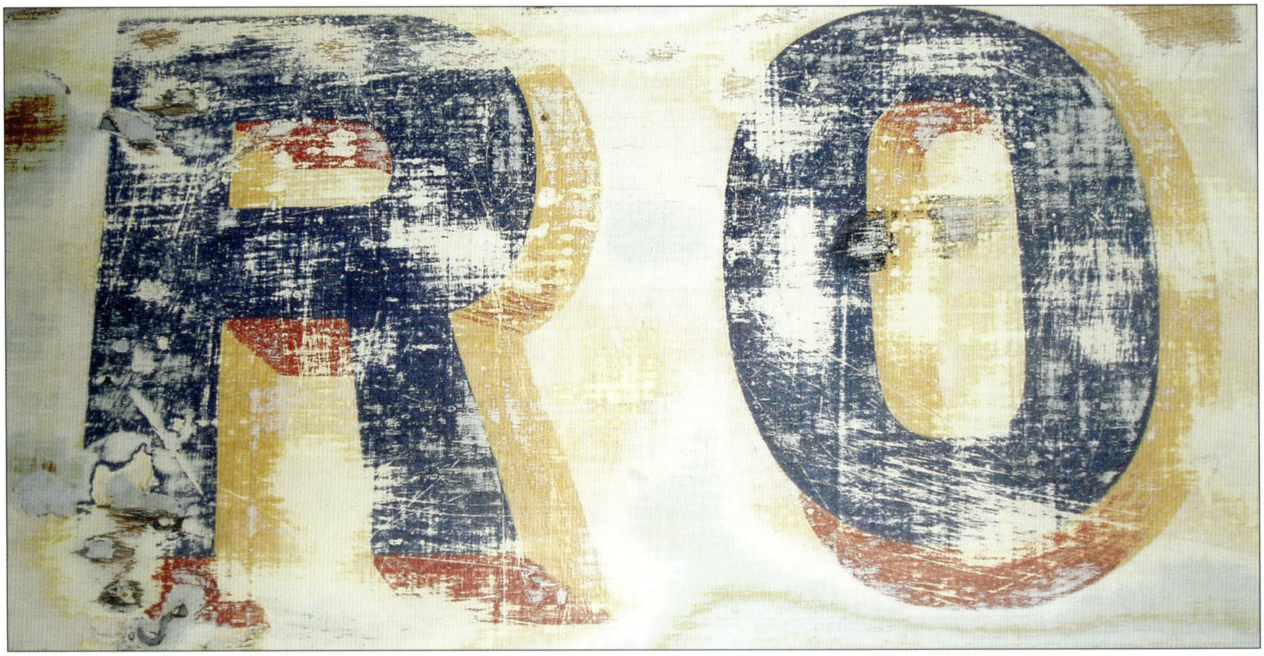

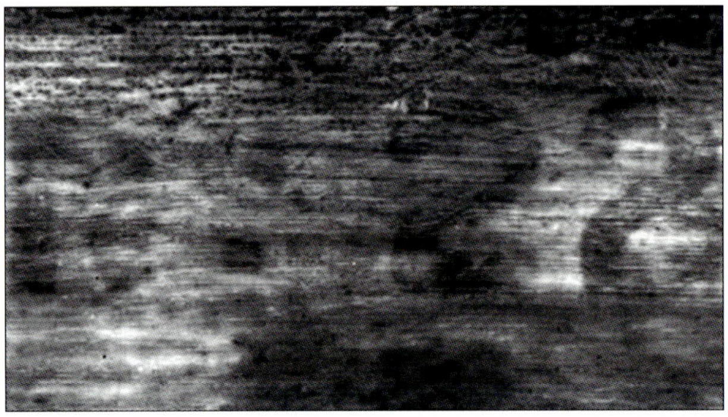

Above. Route lettering details as uncovered from below at least eleven coats of paint. Highly effective protection, but also very difficult to remove without simultaneously removing the lowest layers covering these details.

Left. The number boards from above the doors appeared bare of lettering, but when subjected to scanning by infra-red light at the conservation workshops of the National Gallery of Scotland, traces were uncovered. The figure '2' is visible on the right. Our car was changed from 23 to 22 in May 1900, this achieved simply by altering the lower part of the figure. It ran as 22 until withdrawn.

Before the August 2011 open days at Lathalmond when 23 would be on public display for the first time, some cosmetic paintwork was required. The waist panels were given two coats of blue, having previously been undercoated and rubbed down; the rocker panels had cream applied, after similar preparatory work. The dashes and stair stringers were painted blue at this time and under-floor paintwork was completed. The internal seating was varnished prior to the tram being accessible. The coach-painting was all undertaken in the most highly skilled professional manner by Peter Mitchell.

Knifeboard seating for the top deck was designed and constructed, then lifted into place. Prior to this all areas below the seats were painted to their final condition. The top deck seating bearers were located on solid rubber strips to take up any irregularities, as the roof structure is bowed, both outwards and longitudinally. By the end of 2011, all clerestory windows had been put in place, and in February the car was moved into the paint-shop. By this stage, most coach-building work had been completed, with final efforts directed to handrails, advert and route boards. Other work (non-painting related) undertaken at this stage included fitting the wooden handrail on to the top deck railing, fitting of floor wearing slats to platforms and saloon, making, fitting of blocks to carry bells and manufacture of side advert boards. Wearing slats for top of canopies

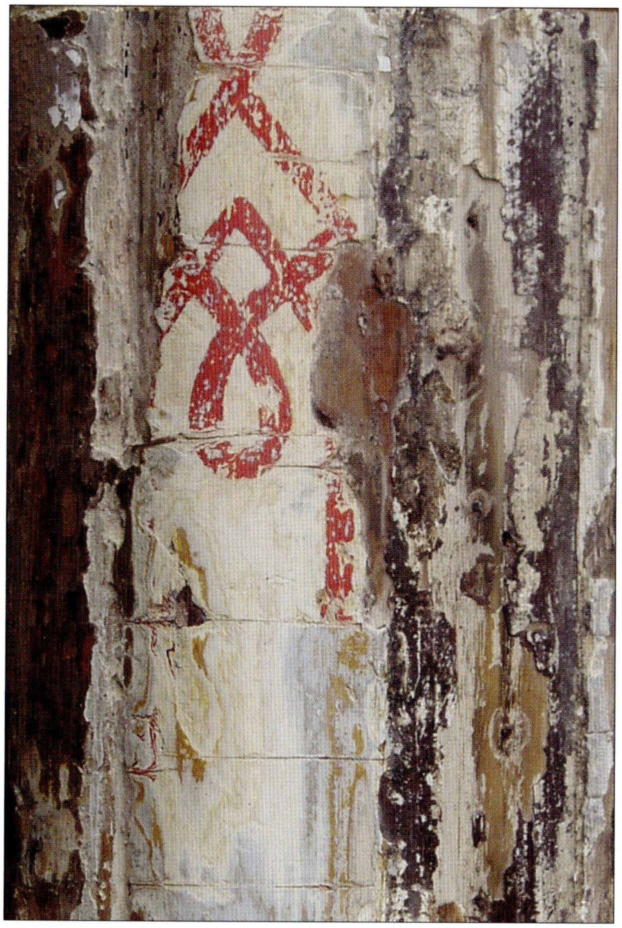

Lining detail from one of the corner pillars which had to be replaced. It is considered that rot in these elements (made from oak) was accelerated by rain water penetration via the large number of screw holes fixings for hand rails etc

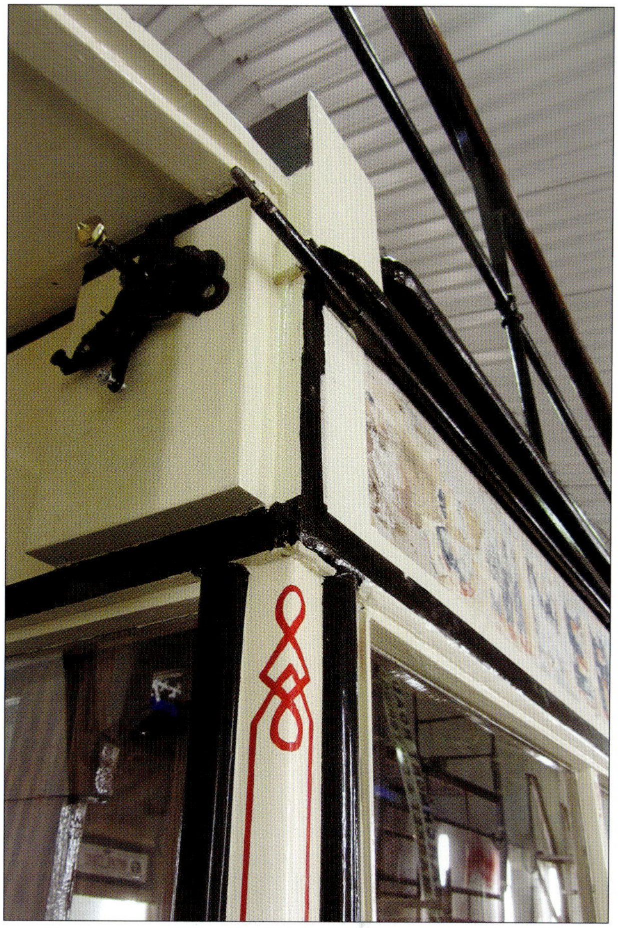

The same detail reproduced on the restored tram's corner pillar. Also seen is the mounting board for the bell. The mechanism of the bell is fitted, with the brass cover to be added. This fitment was recovered from another tram body many years previously.

were made with laths screwed to heavy rubber strip bearers to accommodate the curvature. All areas subject to foot traffic were painted with at least two coats of heavy duty dark grey flat paint. The saloon, internal and external seating were given two coats of varnish.

To ensure accuracy of reproduction of lettering, careful 'archaeological' examination of panels from the tram was undertaken. This involved removal of several coats of protective paint, applied through the century plus which the old car had stood exposed to the elements. This degree of protection had been to a large degree the salvation of the antique vehicle, and beneath these many layers remained the original liveries and lettering. From the remaining parts of the rocker panels, authentic details were obtained of both District and Street Tramways liveries. From this evidence, and from photographs, enough was known to re-create both styles. Similarly the route boards above the windows had two distinct inscriptions; these also were carefully exposed to allow reproduction. It was decided to retain this original lettering, and to reproduce the wording on boards over the originals. This followed precedent, as the car was fitted with brackets to carry removable boards – from the Thomson book this took place in October 1895. The original lettering is thus still visible on the tram.

Further investigation of external panels gave details of lining, and proved that on the royal blue areas this

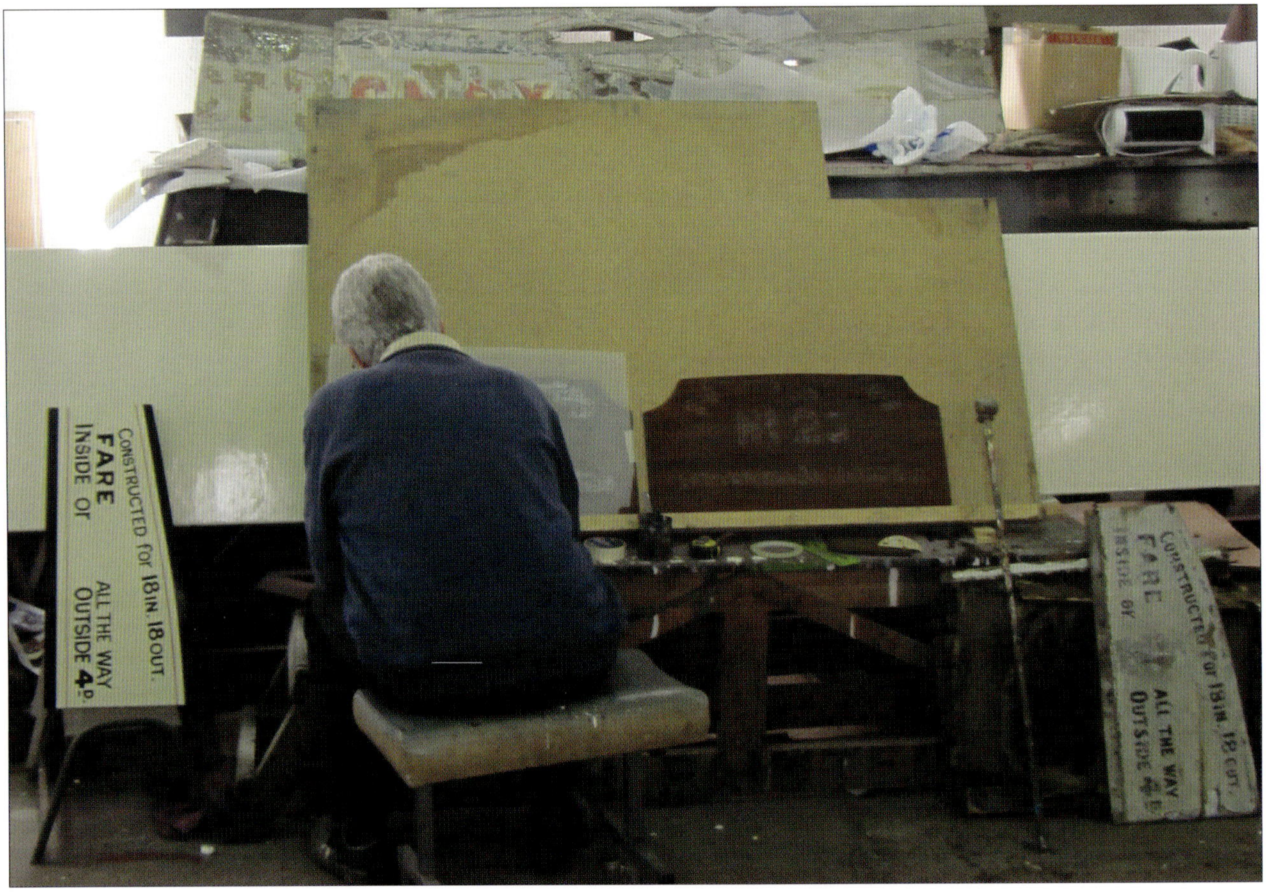

Above. Peter Mitchell at work on lettered boards for the tram. On extreme right is the original 'fare board' which was required to be displayed (even size of the letters was specified). Its completed replacement is at extreme left. One of the internal number boards is prepared.

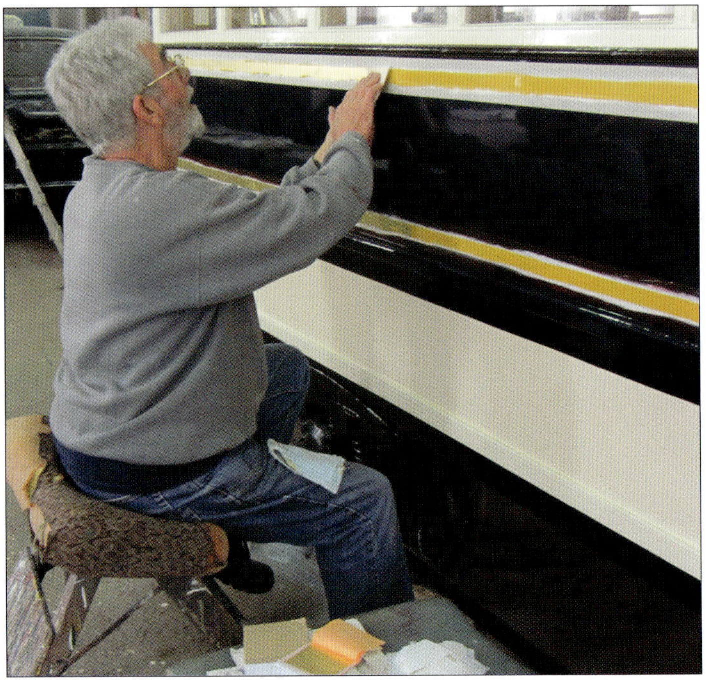

Right. Application of the lining, in gold leaf. Edinburgh's horse trams were lined out, not in yellow or gold coloured paint, but in gold leaf. After the build-up of the 'body' of the coach-painted surface, gold leaf is applied to set off the finished article.

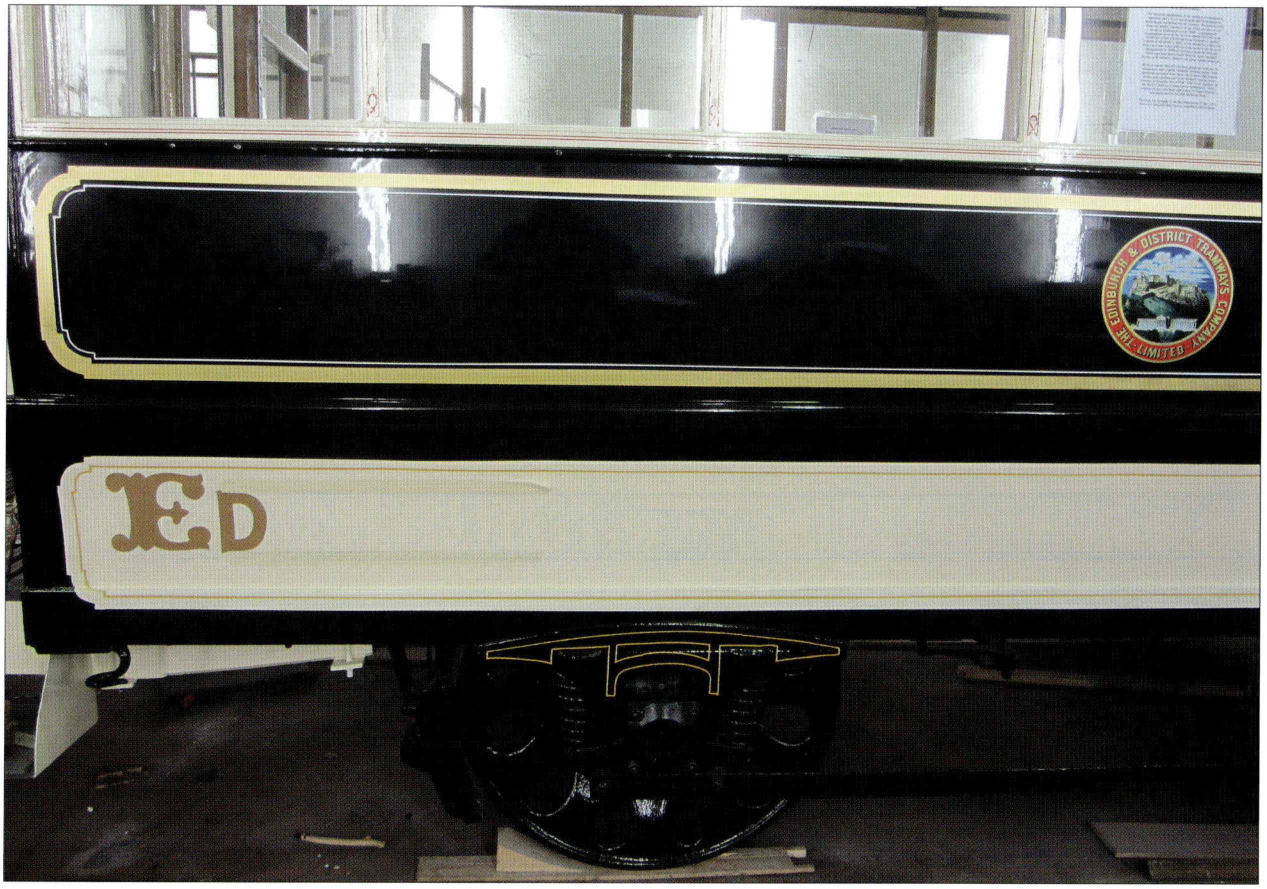

The high gloss finish is seen to good effect by the reflections of the paint shop lighting. After lining attention turned to lettering. As the tram was owned by two successive companies, and as precise details of both liveries are known, one side of the tram has the livery of the Street Tramways Company, the other side being detailed and lettered for the District Company.

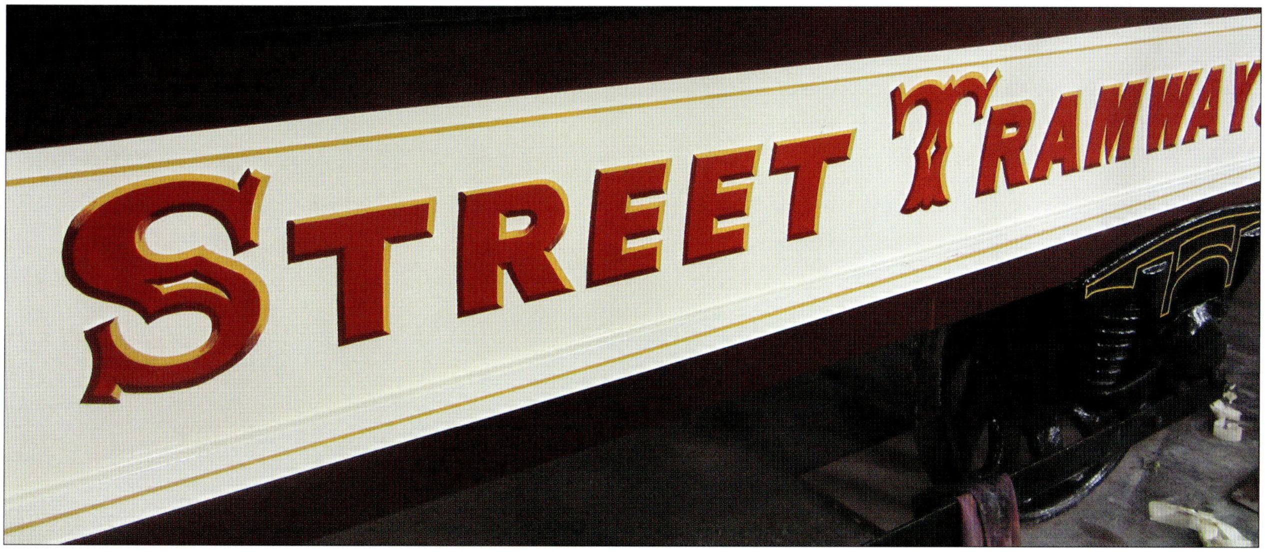

And this is the newly-completed Edinburgh Street Tramways livery in all its glory. The rocker panel lettering style and colour appears to have varied from tram to tram, possibly to complement the route colouring.

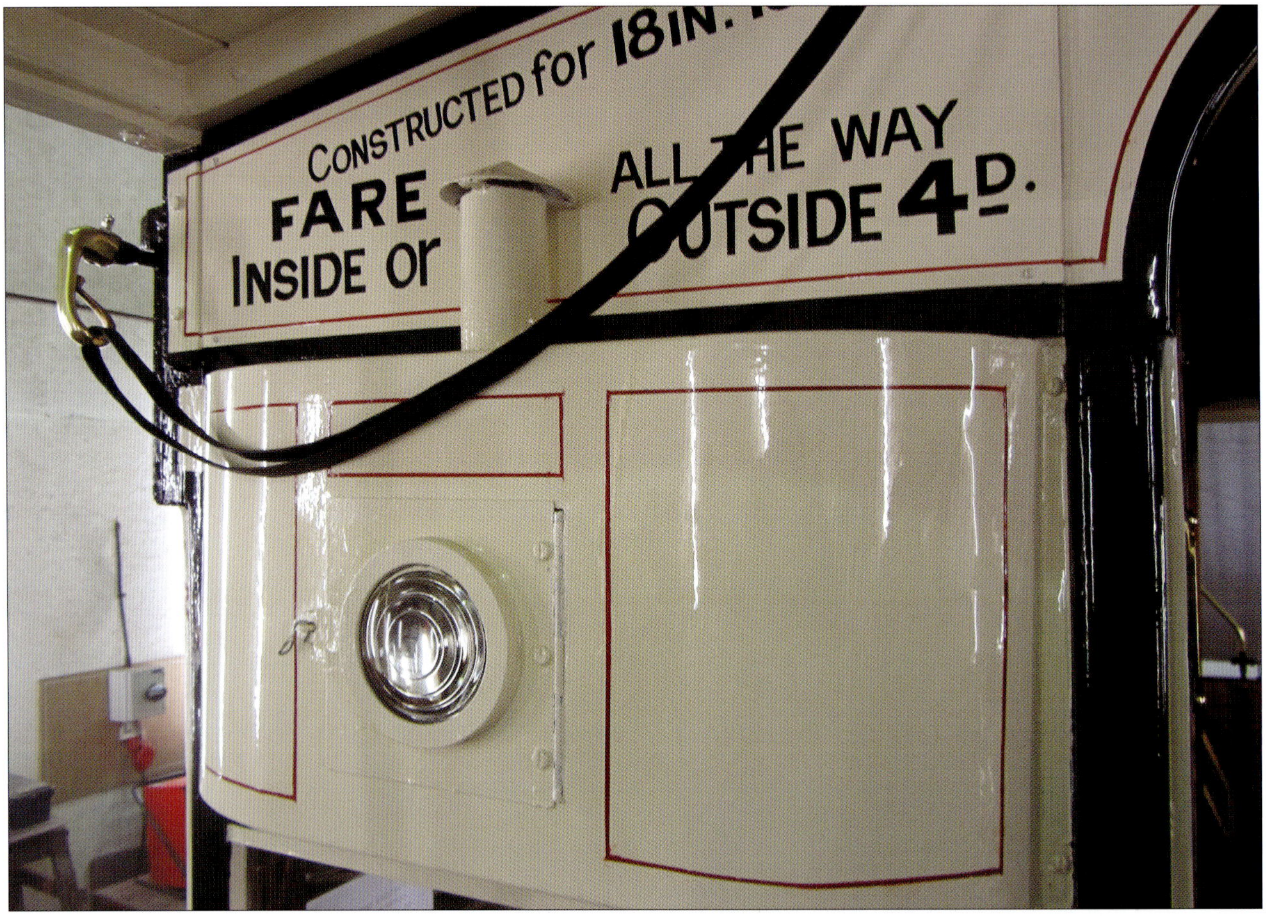

Above. Completed details of the fare board and the lamp housing. The leather strap is for the use of the conductor and is attached to the bell rod then to the bell at the opposite end of the car. Later versions of this design had this rod inside the tram, with handles which could be operated by a passenger wishing to leave the car.

Right. Passengers-eye view from the top of the stairs. The end of the top deck knifeboard seat can be seen, also the iron wearing plates on the stair treads and the flexible 'mat' over the canopy.

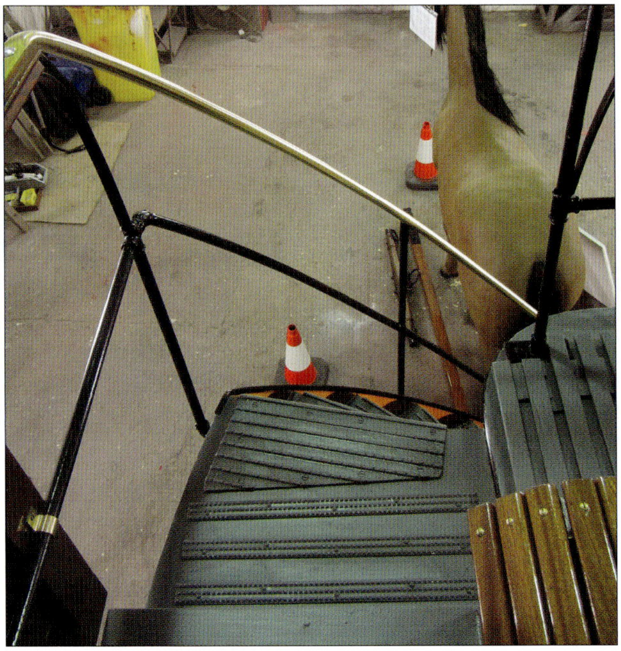

was a thin white line and a half-inch wide gold line. It was proved that this line was of gold leaf, and through the generosity of Ian Blair, the tram restoration was also able to use pure gold leaf. All lettering on the tram is an accurate representation of the operational condition. Fare information, passenger carrying capacity and secretary's name were all exposed and replicated. Fine red lining around windows and on corner pillars was copied from the original, of which examples have been preserved. The original panels showing lettering have also been preserved.

To prepare the main external panels, dashes and stair stringers, four applications of undercoat were made, each flatted down, finally with wet and dry paper; an initial coat of royal blue was applied, and then also flatted down. A second coat of royal blue was applied, and then lining added as described. Crest reproductions were prepared from originals in the collection of Gerald Hartley. Since the tram passed from the Street Tramways Company to the District Tramways Company, and as we had full detail of both liveries, it was decided that one side should be completed in the original livery, the other side in the second. Likewise both route descriptions have been shown, the first on the earlier livery, the second on the later. All lettered and lined panels were now treated with two coats of finest coach varnish.

It had been hoped to attract sponsorship from appropriate companies for the side advert boards (eight companies have been identified which had advertised on the trams in the nineteenth century, and which still trade; none expressed any interest). A decision was therefore taken that appropriate period advertisements be designed avoiding these eight. Adverts were thus painted for 'Nixey's Black Lead' and 'Neave's Food' – the latter having been carried by car 23, as seen in the 1897 photograph at the West End of Princes Street.

The re-fettled original brass-work was now replaced on the car, plus the internal wooden handrails. Leather straps were made to match an original pattern. These were screwed to the rail to hold them in place, the original screw holes being still evident. One of the final tasks was re-fitting the conductors' bells on the bulkheads, the activating rods for these running outside, above the windows. As on the original, leather straps were added to the brass end loops. Brass rods were fitted across the saloon end windows, using typical brass fixtures recovered from a Wemyss tram. The brake standards were re-fitted and the brake chains connected, these having been removed to facilitate painting and lining of the dash plates. A sand box was made to hang on the dash (with a non-authentic felt pad to prevent damage to the paintwork of the dash) and brass tube bent for stair handrails. This last was a tricky undertaking, with the handrail curving in three dimensions, plus twists at both top and bottom, but it was expertly undertaken by blacksmith Jock Moyes.

Final tasks were fitting the new brass commode handles plus the brackets for destination boards. Completion of varnishing was achieved on 17 August 2012. The following day the tram was on view to the public for the first time during the Bus Museum's open weekend – attracting much critical acclaim. Four weeks later it was moved to the Exhibition Hall. It is to be hoped that in the future the old car will not be merely a static exhibit, but that provision will be made for operation, either on a track within the bus museum grounds, or elsewhere.

Following an inspection the Transport Trust awarded the 2012 David Muirhead Award for the restoration at a ceremony on 10 June 2013. The accompanying certificate acknowledging this was presented by Prince Michael of Kent. Two plaques, one recording this award, and one acknowledging the generosity of Roger and Gill French, are displayed on the car.

Although this work records the restoration of Edinburgh horse tramcar 23, it would be remiss not to record that an Edinburgh horse bus was discovered some years ago which was restored by Edinburgh Corporation Transport Department in time to participate in the closing ceremony of the first generation electric tramway in the city, on 16 November 1956. This bus (number 83) may also have been built at Shrubhill, but is presently on extended loan to the British Commercial Vehicle Museum at Leyland, Lancashire.

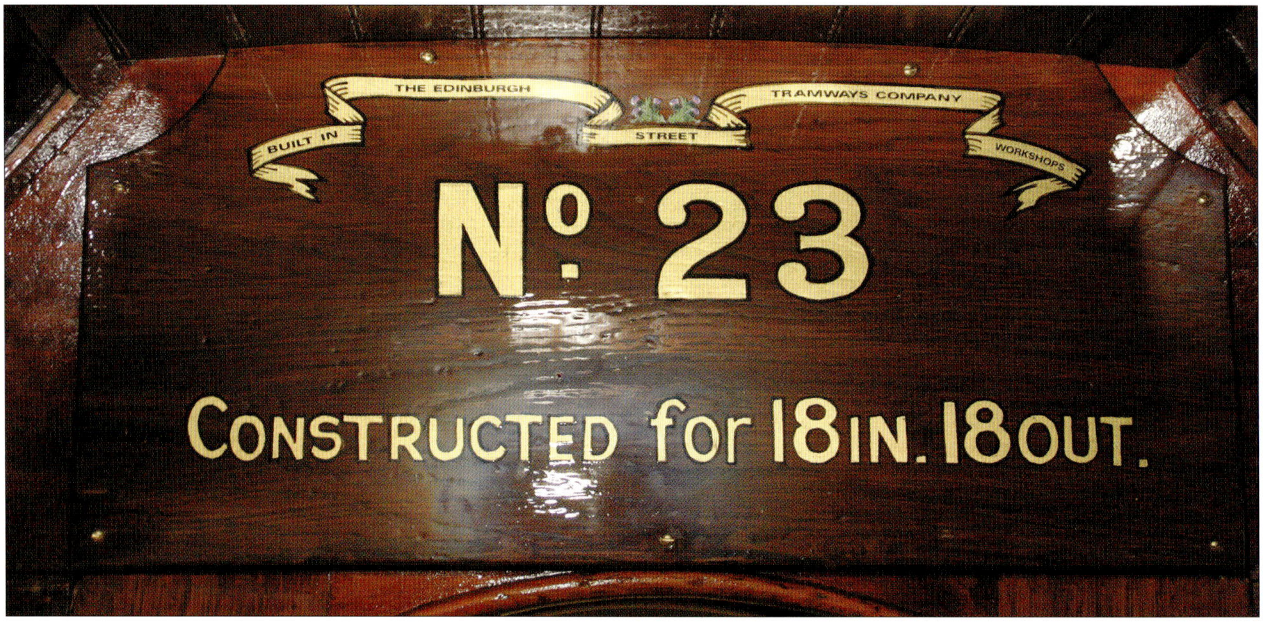

The new number board with the lettering which had been revealed by modern technology.

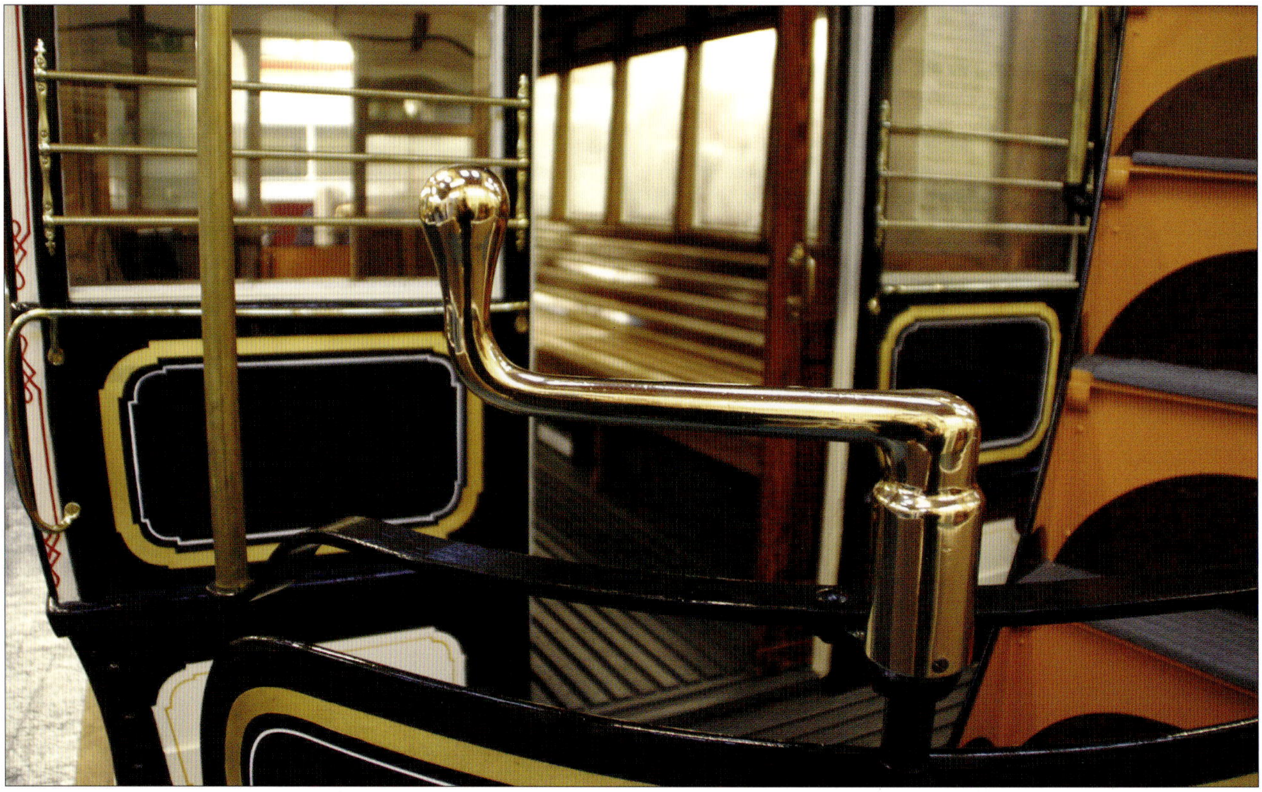
Platform detail of hand brake handle and stairs. On the stair risers, and on other vulnerable parts of the tram's bodywork, where there was potential for wear, sacrificial cover pieces of steel or timber were fitted to give protection. On the dash, where damage could be inflicted by the ends of the swingletrees, replaceable oval metal protective pads were fitted

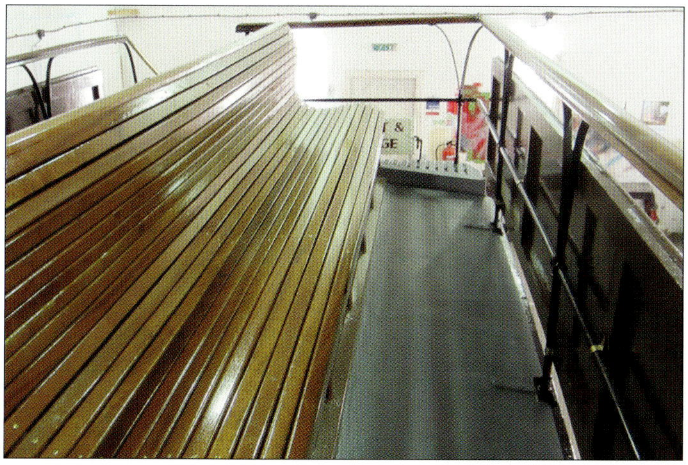

Left. View of the top deck arrangements. The 'knifeboard' seats are entirely new, to replicate the originals, but the tread boards are as found on the car, repaired. It is surprising that these showed no sign of ever having had wearing strips to protect them. While none of the side handrails remained, replicas were made and fitted based on photographs and drawings.

Below. The finished vehicle is removed from the Lathalmond paint shop, complete with its fibreglass horse. A second horse is still needed.

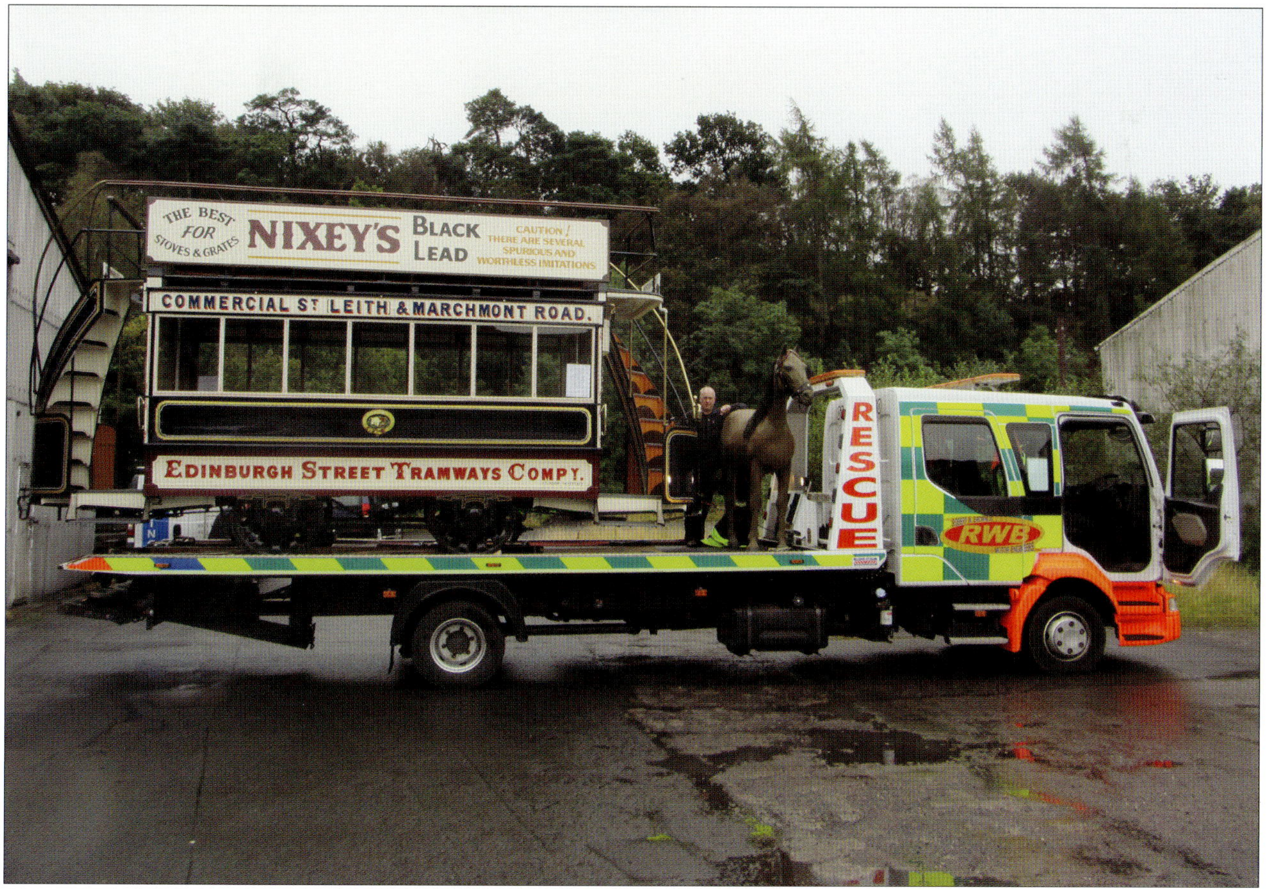

Restoration is now in progress of one of Edinburgh's cable tramcars. Number 226 also retired to the Borders and was retrieved for preservation in 1987. Built in 1903 it ran, converted for electric operation 1923–38. The intention now is to return it to its as built condition. With the several preserved motor buses, sufficient material now exists for a Transport Museum in the city. Glasgow has a magnificent example of the genre at Riverside – is it too much to hope that Edinburgh could follow suit?

With thanks to the following, without whose input completion would not have been achieved:

G and R French, Newtown St Boswells, for generous donation of their 'garden shed'
Stuart Rivers, Llandudno, Horse tram running gear
Andy Skirrat, Llandudno, Transport
Ace Vehicle Recovery, Methil and Dalgety Bay, Transport
Bernard Hunter, Edinburgh, Transport
Robert Purvis Ltd., Lochgelly, Transport and craneage
Keith Elgin Motors, Edinburgh, Metal work
Charles Laing & Sons, Edinburgh, Iron and brass casting
Z.Urbanska, Edinburgh, Leatherwork
Lindsay Henderson, Edinburgh, Shot blasting and priming
Berland of Edinburgh, Brass fettling sand finishing
Roemac Ltd. Lathalmond, Engineering, Steelwork, Light boxes
J Moyes, Fife County Gates, Blacksmith and brass-work
The 47 Group, Lathalmond, Regauging of wheels etc.
Douglas Scoular, Edinburgh, Skilled carpentry and coach-building
A C Yule, Edinburgh, Safety glass
Peter Mitchell, Lathalmond, Coachpainting and signwriting
David Simpson, Musselburgh, Painterwork and related advice
Andy Crockett, Lathalmond, Metal and woodworking
Jim Fowler, Ladybank, Wood turning
Mark Blackadder, Edinburgh, Design of internal advertisements
Cameron Manson, Dalkeith Country Estate, Loan of model horse and harness
Emma McGarvie, Humbie, Artist in glass, new quarter lights
Premier Signs, Glenrothes, Signage etc
Craftmaster Paints, Over, Cambridgeshire, Specialist paint, enamel and varnish
Douglas Corporation Horse Tramways, technical advice
Ipswich Transport Museum, Commode handle loan
Scottish Vintage Bus Museum, Valued assistance
Scottish Tramway and Transport Society, Commode handles
Trinity Factors, Edinburgh, Financial support
The Transport Trust, Financial support
Lothian Buses, Accommodation
Alan Simpson and Richard Stenlake, Proof reading

Plus volunteers; Ian Blair, Brian Bradford, Alan Brotchie, Andy Gilchrist, Paul Geissler, Neil Mackenzie, and Jussi Virtanen

And, last but definitely not least, the numerous individual donors whose generous financial support made this project possible.

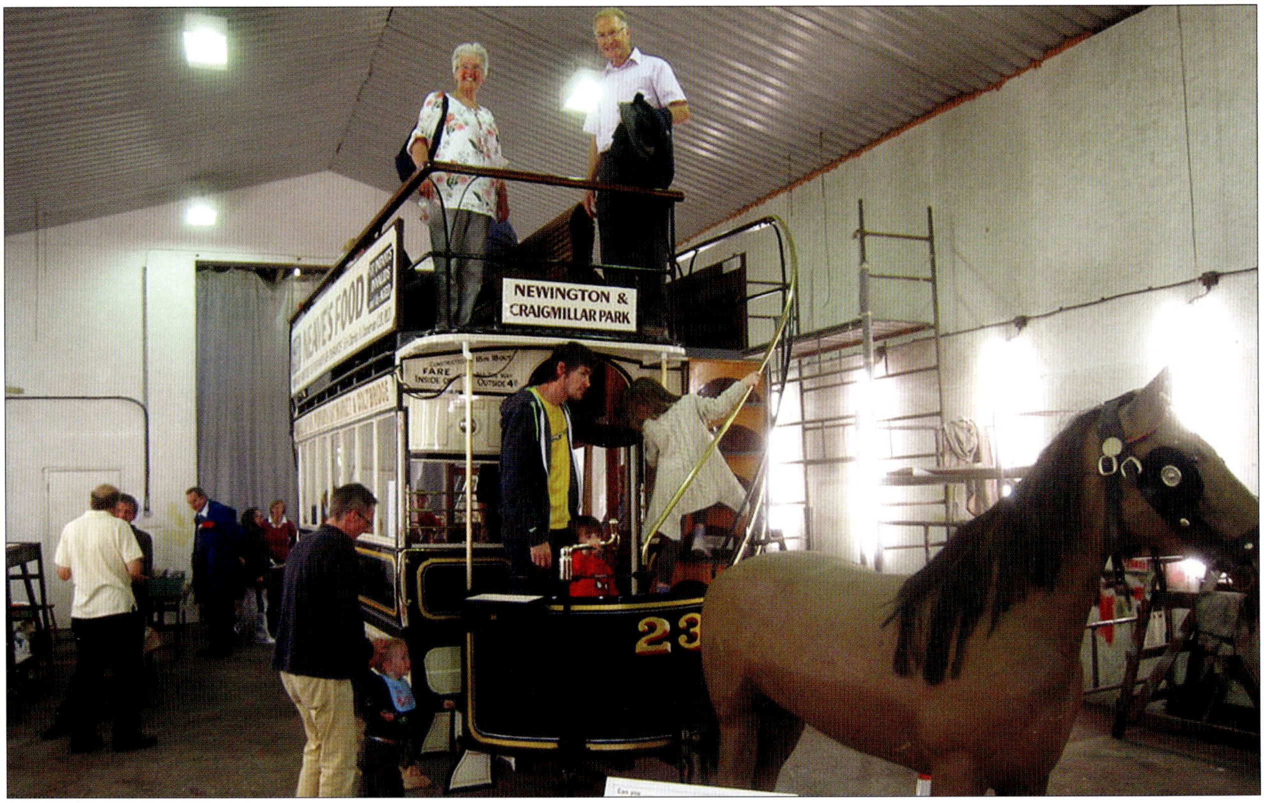

First public examination of the completed tram 18 August 2012, still in the paint shop at the Bus Museum and with some varnish barely dry. Mr and Mrs French, former owners of the tram are on the top deck. When they first enquired about the origins of their garden shed, they could never have conceived of this as the eventual outcome.

Notes

1 *The Scotsman*, 8 March 1869
2 *ibid* 11 July 1829
3 *Caledonian Mercury*, 20 July 1833
4 *The Scotsman*, 9 November 1833
5 *ibid*, 28 June 1834
6 *ibid*, 3 June 1837
7 *ibid*, 7 October 1837
8 *ibid*, 10 March 1838
9 *ibid*, 30 April 1842 and 26 July 1843
10 *ibid*, 31 May 1845
11 *ibid*, 21 April 1847
12 *Minutes of Edinburgh Magistrates*, 8 October 1858
13 *ibid*, 2 July 1866
14 *ibid*, 25 April 1857
15 *Liverpool Echo*
16 *Caledonian Mercury*, 31 October 1860
17 *The Scotsman*, 29 September 1860
18 *Magistrates Minutes*, 30 October 1860
19 *The Scotsman*, 17 November 1860
20 *City Paving Board Minutes*, 19 November 1860
21 *Caledonian Mercury*, 23 November 1860
22 *The Scotsman*, 2 March 1869
23 *Minutes of Edinburgh Magistrates*, 30 December 1869
24 *Minutes of the City Road Trust*, 19 October 1868
25 *The Scotsman*, 23 October 1868
26 Train, G F *My Life in Many States and in Foreign Lands*, 1902
27 *Sporvogne I Danmark, 1863–1972*
28 *The Scotsman*, 20 August 1869
29 *ibid*, 3 June 1870
30 *Minutes of Edinburgh Magistrates*, 13 October 1871
31 *The Scotsman*, 3 June 1870
32 *ibid*, 9 April 1872
33 *ibid*, 28 September 1869
34 *Aberdeen Journal*, 25 August 1869
35 *Glasgow Herald*, 26 October 1870
36 *The Scotsman*, 18 October 1870
37 *ibid*, 24 November 1870
38 *ibid*, 1 December 1870
39 *Report on Tramways*, 21 December 1870
40 *The Scotsman*, 30 December 1870
41 *London Daily News*, 23 May 1871
42 Slinn, Judy *A Radical Firm*, Cambridge 1977
43 *The Scotsman*, 24 September 1872 and 1 July 1882
44 *ibid*, 8 February 1871
45 *ibid*, 26 May 1871
46 *ibid*, 30 June 1871
47 *ibid*, 5 July 1871
48 *ibid*, 8 August 1871
49 *ibid*, 18 October 1871
50 *Glasgow Herald*, 26 October 1871
51 *The Scotsman*, 21 October 1871
52 *ibid*, 2 November 1871
53 *ibid*, 6 November 1871
54 *Edinburgh Courant*, 14 November 1871
55 *Minutes of Edinburgh Magistrates*, 28 March 1872
56 *The Scotsman*, 7 November 1872
57 *ibid*, 25 June 1872
58 Clark, D K, *Tramways, their construction and working*, 1894
59 *The Scotsman*, 23 January 1874
60 *The Scotsman*, 21 February 1874
61 *Magistrates Minutes*, 4 December 1874
62 *Edinburgh Courant*, 14 November 1874
63 *The Scotsman*, 26 July 1875
64 *The Scotsman*, 26 July 1875
65 *The Scotsman*, 1 February 1876
66 *Speed*, Summer 1935 edition
67 *The Scotsman*, 31 July 1875
68 *ibid*, 25 January 1876
69 *The Scotsman*, 1 February 1876
70 *Railway & Tramway Express*, February 1885, reprinted by the Omnibus Society
71 Clark, D K, *Tramways, their construction and working*. 1878 and 1894
72 Todd, L.J. *Remarks on Working Street Tramway Lines by Steam Power*, May 1874
73 *ibid*

74 *Magistrates Minutes*, various dates
75 *The Scotsman*, 1 February 1876
76 *ibid*, 1 August 1876
77 *Edinburgh Courant*, 11 September 1876
78 House of Commons Select Committee, from *The Scotsman*, 13 March 1877
79 *ibid*,
80 *Edinburgh Courant*, 19 April 1877
81 *The Scotsman*, 5 April 1877
82 *Edinburgh Courant*, 29 December 1877
83 *ibid*, 18 & 30 March 1878
84 *ibid*, 3 July 1880
85 *ibid*, 13 April 1881
86 *ibid*, various dates, February 1881
87 *ibid*, 23 & 25 April 1881
88 *Portobello Advertiser*, 7 October 1882
89 *The Scotsman*, 26 July 1882
90 Gladwin D, *A History of the British Steam Tram*, 2004
91 *Portobello Advertiser*, 28 October 1882
92 *The Scotsman*, 14 September 1876
93 *The Scotsman*, 24 February 1879
94 *Edinburgh Evening News*, 21 September 1880
95 *ibid*, 11 December 1879
96 *ibid*, 3 February 1880
97 *The Scotsman*, 1 February 1881
98 *ibid*, 21 September 1880
99 *Edinburgh Evening News*, 31 January 1881
100 *Portobello Advertiser*, 24 December 1881
101 *ibid*, 6 May 1882
102 *The Scotsman*, 1 July 1882
103 *Edinburgh Courant*, 28 May 1883
104 *ibid*, 9 December 1882
105 *ibid*, 6 March 1883
106 *Edinburgh Evening News*, 30 April 1883
107 *The Scotsman*, 7 May 1883
108 *The Scotsman*, 7 January 1884
109 *Edinburgh Evening News*, 30 October 1883
110 *Edinburgh Courant*, 22 November 1883
111 Board of Trade, *Annual return relating to street tramways ...* , various years, 1876–1899
112 Hunter, D L G *Edinburgh's Transport, Volume 1*, Edinburgh 1992
113 Horne, J B & Maund, T B, *Liverpool Transport, Volume 1*, London 1975
114 *Edinburgh Courant*, 8 October 1884
115 Turner, K *Directory of British Tramways*, Yeovil 1996
116 *Edinburgh Evening News*, 22 July 1885
117 *The Scotsman*, 17 August 1886
118 *Edinburgh Evening News*, 5 August & 29 October 1886
119 *ibid*, 1 to 22 November 1886
120 *ibid*, 28 June and 25 July 1889
121 Hunter, D L G, *op cit*
122 *The Scotsman*, 28 December 1889
123 *The Scotsman*, 15 and 17 June 1891
124 *The Scotsman*, 25 October 1892
125 *ibid*, 11 January 1893
126 *The Scotsman*, 25 January 1894
127 *ibid*, 10 January 1895
128 *Edinburgh Evening News*, 29 April 1896
129 *The Scotsman*, 18 June 1898
130 *The Scotsman*, 28 July 1898
131 *ibid*, 29 July 1899
132 *ibid*, 25 July 1900
133 *Edinburgh Evening News*, 15 September 1905
134 *ibid*, 14 November 1904.
135 *ibid*, 27 April 1905
136 *Edinburgh Evening News*, 5 April 1895
137 *The Scotsman*, 10 September 1896
138 *Edinburgh Evening News*, 1 March 1895
139 *The Scotsman*, 7 February 1895
140 *ibid*, 31 January 1898
141 *ibid*, 13 October 1899
142 *Edinburgh's Transport Vol 1*. D L G Hunter. Edinburgh 1992
143 *The Scotsman*, 11 February 1901
144 *ibid*, 14 January 1901
145 *ibid*, 14 January 1904
146 *The Scotsman*, 13 November 1871
147 *The Scotsman*, 21 October 1871
148 *Daily Record*, 21 October 1871
149 *North British Study Group Journal*
150 *The Scotsman*, 28 December 1871
151 *Edinburgh Evening News*, 31 July 1877
152 *The Scotsman*, 24 February 1872
153 *Edinburgh Evening Courant*, 24 February 1872
154 *ibid*, 27 August 1873
155 *The Scotsman*, 23 March 1872
156 *Patent Award* 213 of 1872
157 *Minutes of Edinburgh Magistrates*, 14 June 1872
158 *The Scotsman*, 5 July 1872
159 *Engineering*, 1 November 1872
160 *Edinburgh Evening Courant*, 6 August 1873
161 *Tramcar License Records*, Edinburgh City Archives.
162 *The Scotsman*, 29 July 1873
163 *Minutes of Edinburgh Magistrates*, various dates
164 *The Scotsman*, 24 April 1873
165 *Edinburgh Courant*, 23 January 1874
166 *The Scotsman*, 27 January 1874
167 *Edinburgh Evening News*, 31 January 1874
168 *The Scotsman*, 21 February 1874
169 *ibid*, 24 February 1874
170 Added for comparison, not in the Report
171 *Magistrates Minutes*, 28 March 1872
172 *The Scotsman*, 6 November 1874
173 *ibid*, 16 October 1873
174 *Edinburgh Courant*, 25 July 1874
175 *The Scotsman*, 1 August 1876
176 *Edinburgh Courant*, 1 August 1876
177 *ibid*, 19 May 1876

178 *ibid*, 1 August 1877
179 *ibid*, 22 December 1877
180 *ibid*, 17 May 1877
181 *ibid*, 26 July 1877
182 *ibid*, 22 December 1877
183 *ibid*, 27 November 1877
184 *ibid*, 13 December 1877
185 *ibid*, 22 December 1877
186 *Dundee Courier*, 7 & 8 August 1877
187 *Evening Telegraph*, 29 & 30 August 1877
188 *The Scotsman*, 25 January 1878
189 *Edinburgh Courant*, 1 February 1878
190 *Edinburgh Courant*, 22 May 1879
191 *The Scotsman*, 14 August 1879
192 *Edinburgh Courant*, 14 August 1879
193 *The Scotsman*, 26 July 1880 & 1881
194 *The Scotsman*, 25 January 1882
195 *The Scotsman*, 7 April 1882
196 *Evening News*, 7 April 1882
197 *ibid*, 5 July 1882
198 *The Scotsman*, 27 &28 April 1883
199 *Edinburgh Courant*, 4 July 1883
200 *The Scotsman*, 21 July 1883.
201 *Edinburgh Courant*, 31 July 1883
202 *The Scotsman*, 13 October 1884
203 *ibid*, 19 July 1884
204 *The Era* [London] 3 June 1882
205 *The Scotsman*, 18 and 19 July 1884
206 A Winstan Bond, *Modern Tramway*, May 1966
207 John Stevens, editor, *Pioneers of Electric Railroading*, 1991
208 *The Scotsman*, 24 April & 17 July 1886
209 *ibid*, 31 July 1886
210 *ibid*, 19 July 1890
211 *ibid*, 21 January, 1891
212 *ibid*, 26 July 1890
213 O'Connor, Dougill and Smeeton, in *Pioneers of Electric Railroading* (ed J R Stevens) 1991
214 *The Scotsman*, 6 February 1895, and *Magistrates Licensing Book*
215 *Edinburgh Evening News*, 9 October 1897
216 *Magistrate's Licensing Records*
217 *ibid*
218 *Aberdeen Journal*, 8 March 1899
219 *The Scotsman*, 1 February 1902
220 *Minutes of Leith Corporation*, 3 July 1906
221 *Railway & Tramway Express*, February 1885, reprinted by the Omnibus Society

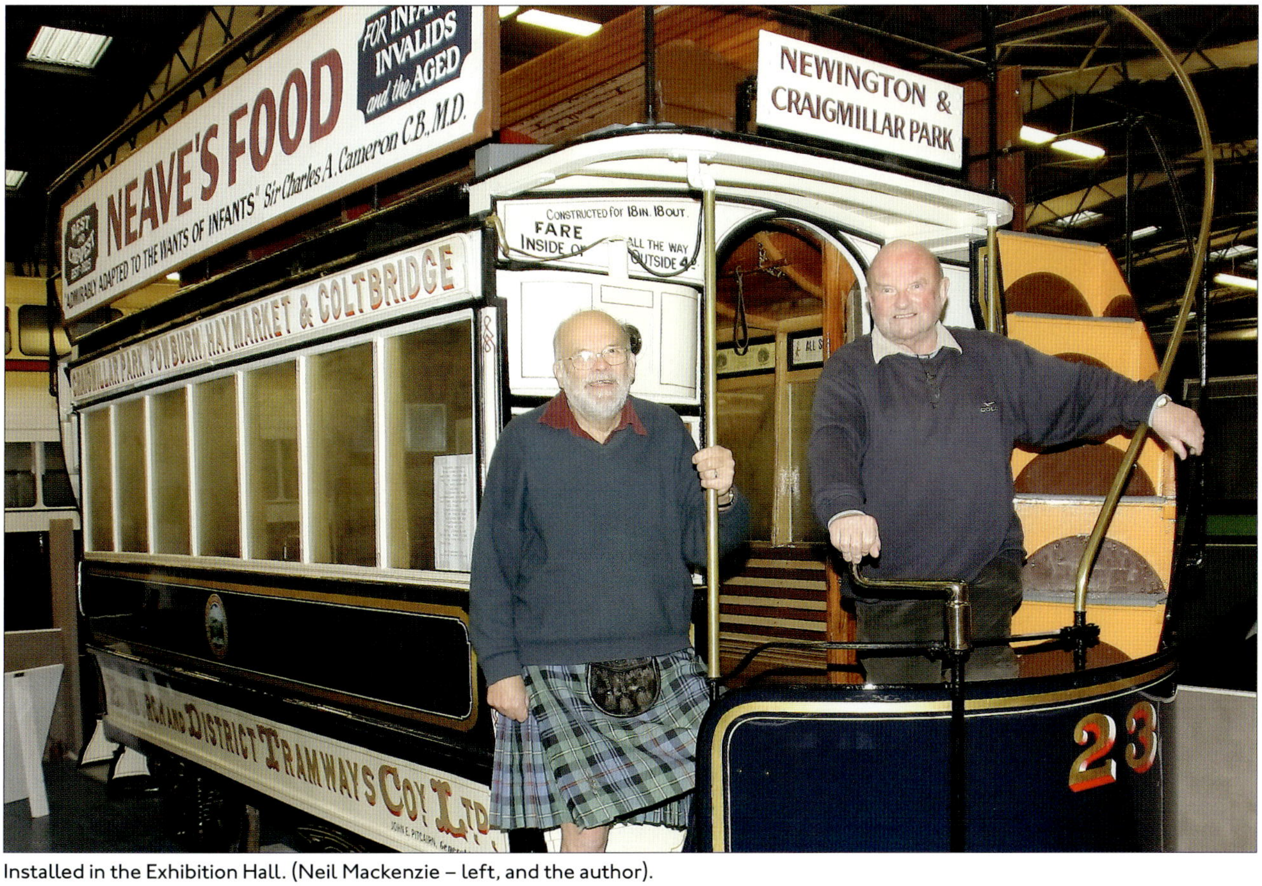

Installed in the Exhibition Hall. (Neil Mackenzie – left, and the author).

Index

(Page numbers in **bold** print indicate illustrations)

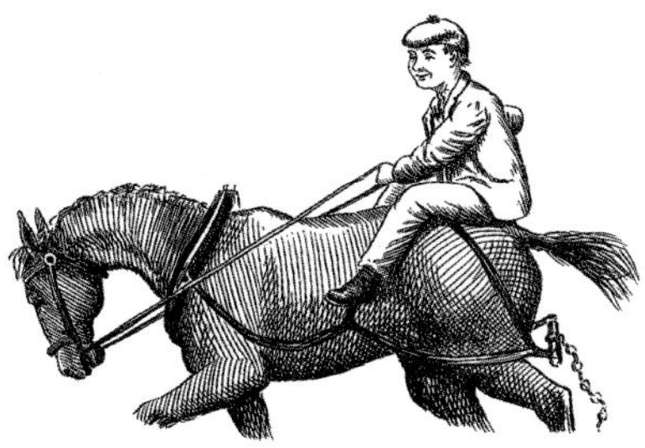

TRACE-BOYS—CIRCUS TIME.

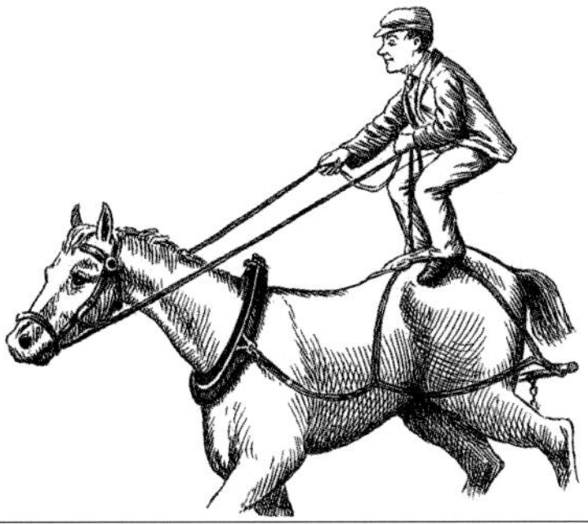

THE NEXT CHAPTER

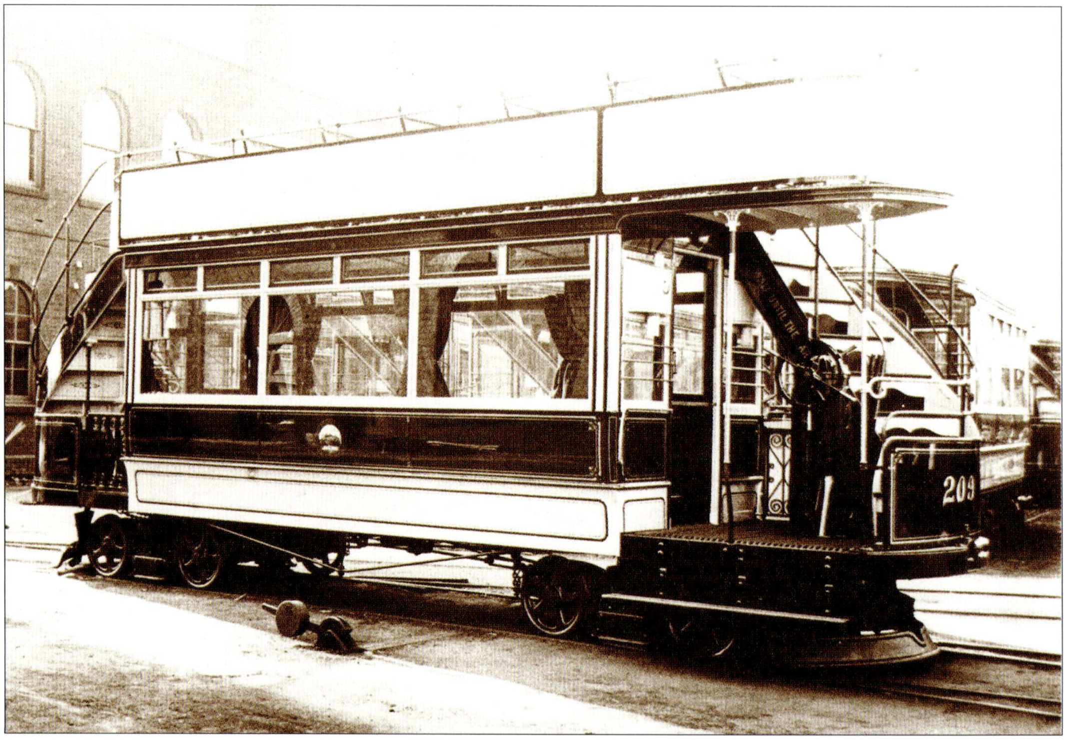

Car 209 seen here in 1903 in the yard of its manufacturer, in Preston, is of the same batch of twenty cars (209–228) as existing car 226 and represents the condition which it is intended to reproduce. A cable tram is the final missing piece from a physical record of Edinburgh's transport history.

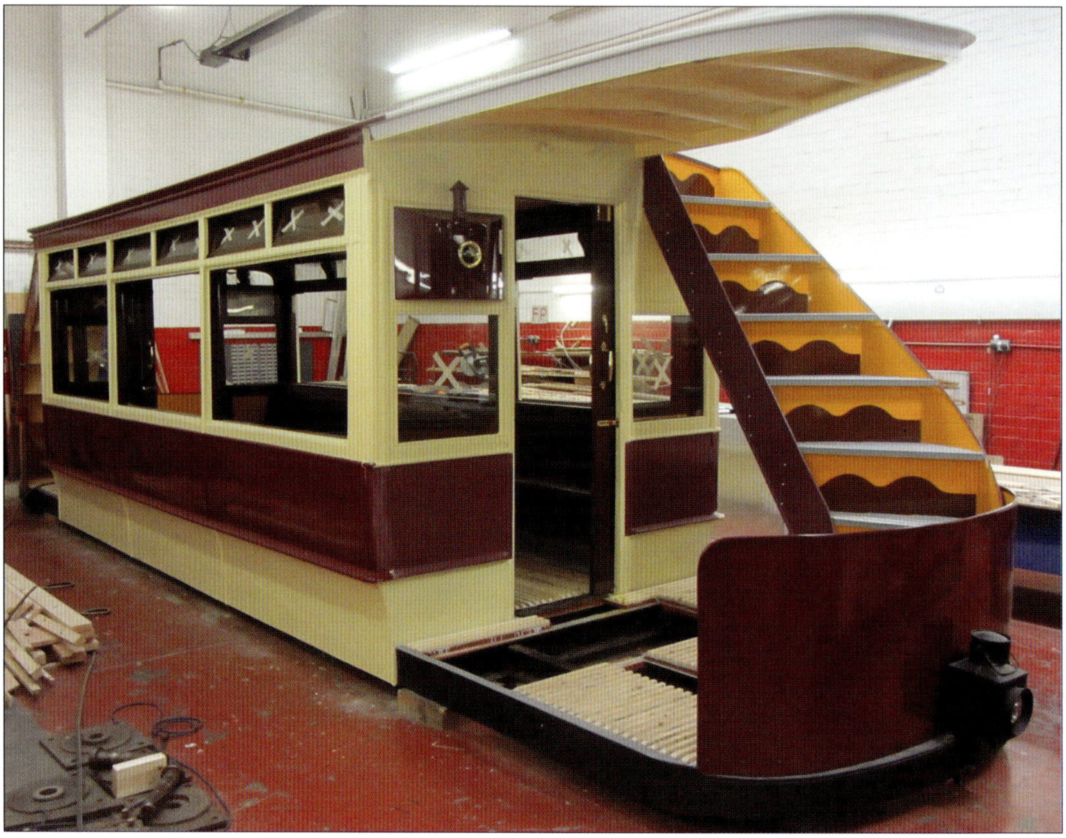

Car 226 has returned to the capital, and work is ongoing with its restoration. This records its state at the end of 2016. However, there is still a long way to go, so much patience is required ...